Southern Highlander & *His* Homeland

John C. Campbell

With a New Foreword by
RUPERT B. VANCE

& An Introduction by
HENRY D. SHAPIRO

The UNIVERSITY PRESS
of KENTUCKY

Publication of this volume was made possible in part
by a grant from the National Endowment for the Humanities.

Scholarly publisher for the Commonwealth,
serving Bellarmine University, Berea College, Centre
College of Kentucky, Eastern Kentucky University,
The Filson Historical Society, Georgetown College,
Kentucky Historical Society, Kentucky State University,
Morehead State University, Murray State University,
Northern Kentucky University, Transylvania University,
University of Kentucky, University of Louisville,
and Western Kentucky University.

Editorial and Sales Offices: The University Press of Kentucky
663 South Limestone Street, Lexington, Kentucky 40508-4008

08 07 06 05 04   5 4 3 2

ISBN 0-8131-9078-9 (paper)

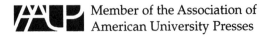

TABLE OF CONTENTS

LIST OF TABLES

A NEW FOREWORD

GOODLY PORTIONS of the reading public will be grateful that the University of Kentucky Press has been thoughtful enough to republish John C. Campbell's *The Southern Highlander and His Homeland*. Inevitable wear and tear and losses in circulation have depleted library stocks of this meaningful book. Now many interested in the area can possess their own copies of this classic, long out of print. Most grateful should be those librarians whose often sent tracers fail to bring back a lost book. "Temporarily lost," I seem to hear the library attendants murmur and I do speak from sad experience.

First published in 1921, this book has been in and out of the public eye for a long period. When the United States turned its resources in the direction of alleviating some of the problems of the Appalachians, students and administrators were delighted to find a benchmark study in Campbell's carefully written monograph. It is not often that the precise stage of a growing issue can be found so well marked off and so clearly presented.

The book, I happen to know, was immediately seized upon by the analysts of *The Southern Appalachian Region* (published by the University of Kentucky Press) as the one scientific project fit to serve as benchmark for their concerted undertaking. The contrast between the old and the new mountains proved most enlightening to these writers who already knew the book but now saw it in a new light. The same illumination is likely to strike those who read this volume for the first time.

They may hereby consider themselves warned. I wish to point out a difference between then and now which undoubtedly shows how far we have gone in approximately half a century. Note how much Mr. Campbell assumes religion and philanthropy will do for the region and how much we now assume will be done by the public government. And then before you put Mr. Campbell down as just another missionary—which he was—note how clearly he foresaw that all the church supported mountain academies would give way to public high schools. I must turn back and correct an impression which I do not want the last sentence to leave—a missionary, true; he did work in a home mission field—but just another missionary, never!

The truth is that John C. Campbell was, in the language of today, somebody special. Not a native of the area, Campbell hailed from Indiana. After graduation from Williams College and Andover Newton Theological School, he went South to head a mountain academy in the Alabama Highland in 1896.

He and his life and his book furnished a living contradiction to two old wives tales: (1) that no Yankee ever comes to understand the South and (2) that mountaineers never come to accept nor to appreciate an outsider. But for all his skill in interpersonal relations, Campbell never lost his critical faculty. Campbell was no yes man. Witness his comments on the effect of denominational competition and jealousy on the churches' efforts to serve the region. This too from a representative of the forces of religion. The Russell Sage Foundation chose well when they set Campbell his task.

Looking back to another day, another time, we must conclude that it was the great achievement of John C. Campbell [in his *Southern Highlander*] to stand above the battle. It was a time and an arena of controversy: the mountaineer should help himself; he was shiftless, else he would not be in the plight he was. He had been exploited and abused; if anything, he was better than other people. Science and rational planning would not work in the Appalachians; the mountain people must be saved by religion or not at all. Only a new kind of socialism would work in the South; the only program that could prevail must make use of the mountaineers' individualism, not trample it down. So the controversy ran.

In the face of these disagreements, Campbell produced a clear cool survey, one of the first objective studies of an area of misunderstanding and clashing attitudes. His accounts of mountain individualism, family life, health, schools, churches, religious rivalry, are unsurpassed and they convey the ring of truth. The personal memories which one finds never impede the survey; they give it impact and relevance.

Finally, let it be remembered that Campbell wrote before the general opening up of the region by state programs, improved highways, and public education. This was a period when many felt that unless home missions, private church academies, and outside philanthropy were adequate to save the mountain people from stagnation and isolation they could not be saved. Many doubted, in fact, that the true mountain people would be or could be moved. Campbell never minimized difficulties and he never relinquished hope nor released his grasp. One cannot read his work again without wondering what Campbell's reaction would be to what is going on today. Let us simply play it safe and say his feelings would be mixed. They were in his day, too. There stood no man of the single track mind. He was a meliorist and a pragmatist—not a dogmatist—possibly a zealot, but not a fanatic.

RUPERT B. VANCE

PREFACE

TO those who read this study of "The Southern Highlander and his Homeland," whether or not they knew its writer, some explanation is due. The following pages are the outcome of twenty-five years of life and experience in the mountain country of the South. Mr. Campbell became interested in the Southern Highlands while he was a student at Andover Theological Seminary between 1892 and 1895, and from the time of his graduation, when as a teacher he went into a remote section of the mountains, until the time of his death, when he was Secretary of the Southern Highland Division of the Russell Sage Foundation, he was almost continuously engaged in the service of the Highland people.

The first part of his life in the Highlands Mr. Campbell spent in three different schools—as principal of an institute in Alabama, as principal of an academy in Tennessee, and as president of Piedmont College in northern Georgia. When his health failed, largely as a result of the strain involved in raising an endowment, he took an enforced vacation of a year, and then, under the auspices of the Russell Sage Foundation, entered upon a study of the whole Highland country. Preliminary to this study he held conferences with many leaders and officials in Lowland and Highland South, as well as with numerous other people interested in bettering rural conditions throughout the country in order that the knowledge and experience he had gained in mountain work might be checked and amplified by the knowledge and experience of others. The cordial assistance given him at this time not only broadened his understanding of the problem he was about to investigate but undoubtedly played its part in the gradual growth of his conviction that co-operation was both necessary and feasible in this field.

Thus equipped he started out into the Highlands. Much of his journeying, which was more or less continuous for the following year or two, was necessarily by horseback or wagon, with many nights spent in the homes along the way. His great love for the people, whom he felt in a peculiar sense to be his own, his thorough understanding of them, and his simple and spontaneous friendliness won him a welcome everywhere. Many a time have I seen him before the hearth-fire of some little cabin, as much at home in the group there gathered as in the most polished assembly and far more happy. Many a night have I known him to lie sleepless trying to devise means whereby the hard conditions of mountain life might be eased, or help brought to some crippled or suffering child. He never left a home without feeling that the parting was one between old friends, a feeling which usually seemed to be shared by his hosts.

In the course of his journeys through different parts of the Highlands he visited seventy or more typical church and independent schools. Often a school was used as a center from which to study the surrounding mountain region. In this way he became personally acquainted with the problems faced by each school as well as with a large number of those who were striving to meet these problems. The connection thus established with schools, workers, and communities was not lost in succeeding years, but formed the basis of the very wide influence which he was able to exert in shaping policies and in bringing about a better understanding between workers and officials of the same board, and between workers and officials of different boards and agencies. Nor did his study cease with the confidential report which he gave to the Russell Sage Foundation of his findings, nor with the establishment of the Southern Highland Division which was the natural outcome. From time to time he visited not only places known through former journeys but new schools and communities; and in addition he maintained a wide correspondence with others, so that his knowledge and influence grew continually.

During the last six years of his life his efforts were directed mainly to bringing to those living or at work in the Highlands the help of every agency and movement that had in it any promise for the Highland country. His office in Asheville became a bureau of information and a center freely sought by all interested in mountain work—whether they were large givers, officials of boards, or workers facing day by day conditions in the field. No cause was too small, no individual too insignificant to enlist his sympathy. It was indeed to the lonely men and women in remote settlements that his heart was particularly drawn, for he knew through his own experience the many discouragements which they must meet. To cheer them, to send them on their way with new hope and perhaps a wider conception of their opportunities, was a matter to him not of business routine but of personal concern. He was truly interested in every one.

More and more, however, as time went on, he laid his emphasis upon the working together of all kinds of people and agencies, Highland and Lowland, Northern and Southern, denominational and secular, public and private. He felt that if people were honest in their desire to help and could be induced to talk things over in a friendly fashion they would come to understand one another's point of view and a basis for working together would usually be found. To the realization of this end he brought his ripened experience, tact and inexhaustible patience, and the charm of a personality that radiated kindness and humor.

The measure of this kind of intimate effort can never be taken, but it found an outward manifestation in the Southern Mountain Workers' Conference, which owed its existence in large part to Mr. Campbell's initiative and which for seven years was fostered and directed by him.

Again and again he was urged to publish the results of his experience and studies, but as he says in the Foreword that follows, he refused to be "merely an investigator." He looked upon himself as "a co-worker with all agencies, foreign and native." At another time in explanation of his attitude he wrote: "Some who have been most helpful in the promotion of better understanding have yet not understood the desire of the Southern Highland Division to share in this endeavor. They have wanted an historical recital of denominational differences and overlappings, although within their own field and within specific schools they have seen the wisdom of not giving publicity to evidences of human frailties, selfishness, or perfidy, if such there be. Where they have criticized it has been because they have not recognized that the Southern Highland Division stands in a close official relationship to many agencies that have given it their confidence, which must not be violated any more than that given to a physician. Its effort is the same as that of a physician—to correct, not merely to diagnose and publish. Its work is constructive. The division is ready always to give confidential information confidentially to those who may be social physicians and who will hold to the social and professional code."

It should be added that Mr. Campbell understood thoroughly the difficulties in the way of writing of a people who, while forming a definite geographical and racial group, were by no means socially homogeneous. Many statements applicable to the remote rural folk who were the particular object of his study were not true of their urban and valley kinsfolk, yet to differentiate groups in discussing phases of life common to all was not easy. Moreover, it was impossible usually to secure data on a strictly group basis. That misunderstandings would arise, however carefully he defined his group or limited his discussion of them, he felt was inevitable, and deeply concerned as he was in the working together of all forces he questioned the advisability of publishing a book which might result in division rather than in union. Not until the last year of his life did he finally consent to edit, in the light of his many years of experience, his mass of notes and material for publication. I will not say that it was too late, for he was able to outline his book thoroughly and even to finish entirely certain portions; but health long impaired by a life of many hardships and much sorrow failed rapidly, and death came before the manuscript could be completed.

Writing of Mr. Campbell, Warren H. Wilson, Director of the Church and Country Life Work of the Presbyterian Church and a widely known student of rural life, says:

He was of a rare type of Christian, and rarer still as an inter-church worker. . . . He was a prophet of the spirit of the Church rather than a servant of its body. He never became antagonistic to any one, even the narrowest, though his work was such that he must have been a progressive in theology. He had the patience and gentleness which believed and loved men of all faiths and of all types. He left no one out of his care. He made himself the bishop of the mountain people all. With increasing knowledge he never diminished his breadth of affection . . .

He would take no action to offend any group or any leader of the mountain people.

* * * .* * * * * * * *

I hope that Mr. Campbell's researches may be published, for they are of value. No one else has the material which he possessed. He alone had seen with his eyes the whole mountain problem. By publication alone can his full service be made available. During his life his power was pent up within his own unselfish personality. Now it should be made a contribution for all men to possess. . . . Only through a book that shall initiate discussion, criticism and reply can such a man's life become the property of all men.

It is this book, completed from the notes and material which he left and from a knowledge of his general point of view and conclusions, that is now presented to the public. No one can be more conscious of its limitations and defects than the editor, whose office—great as was the happiness that attended it—was not always an easy one. It would have been far more difficult had it not been for the generous assistance furnished by Mr. Campbell's friends within and without the Highlands and for the tireless enthusiasm of Edith R. Canterbury, secretary to Mr. Campbell, who has given unsparingly of her time, effort, and knowledge of the mountains.

Special acknowledgments are due to Dr. L. C. Glenn, Professor of Geology, Vanderbilt University, for information supplied and interest extending through many years, and in addition for critical reading of parts of the manuscript dealing with the topography of the country and its resources; to Dr. Taliaferro Clark, Assistant Surgeon-General, United States Public Health Service, and to Dr. Paul Johnson, Department of Health Service, American Red Cross, for their very helpful suggestions in regard to the chapter on Health; to the Director of the Census and to the Director of the Geological Survey; and to many in Federal and State Departments, especially those of Health, Education, and Forestry, for their cordial co-operation in furnishing data.

The list of acknowledgments would be incomplete without some recognition of the indebtedness which Mr. Campbell felt and would wish to express not only to the persons already indicated, but to the many other federal officials who personally and through their publications gave him great assistance; to Southern officials in various departments of government whose uniform courtesy, under-standing—especially the understanding of his motives and pur-poses—and co-operation were of such help and encouragement to him throughout his field study and later work; to many in private life in the South, physicians, teachers, ministers, bishops, and executive officials of church boards in North and South; and to presidents of colleges, principals of schools, and scores of teachers in the church and independent schools visited, county superin-tendents of education, and others who constitute a host to whom only a general but none the less sincere expression of gratitude can be made.

The book, as planned, was intended to "define and clarify, and to point out opportunities and responsibilities." It has not been possible always to carry the plan to the full extent that was intended, nor even to follow exactly the outline suggested in Chapter I. There are too, doubtless, certain things to which Mr. Campbell would have given an interpretation somewhat different from that presented here; other things perhaps to which he would not have given expression; still others which would have been treated fully and must now be left with little or no mention. Sub-stantially, however, the book is as he planned it. It is hoped that the reader will view it in the spirit in which it was undertaken, and if he feels any lack of sympathetic understanding, any narrowness or prejudice, attribute the limitations to her whose privilege and responsibility it has been to make ready the manuscript for publi-cation.

OLIVE DAME CAMPBELL.

FOREWORD

TO MY FRIEND WHO MAY READ THIS BOOK

IN addressing this foreword to you I am not certain at the moment just whom I am addressing. You may be a high administrative official in a far-away northern or southern metropolis, endeavoring to the best of your ability to shape and direct the mission work under your charge for the Southern Highlander; or you may be the Southern Highlander himself, who like the rest of us does not at all relish the idea of being uplifted or missionary-ized. Possibly you are a mission worker from North or South who feels that your urban-minded bishop or superintendent does not comprehend your problems or fully sympathize with them, because he keeps to the Pullman routes of travel and frequents all too little the bridle path which leads to your dwelling. Perhaps you are just an eager American, interested in a wonderfully picturesque section of your own country, wanting to be told facts about it by someone who is supposed to know; or a member of some church, wondering if the work which is being done and to which you contribute is well conceived and well administered.

It would be an easy matter to fill these pages with figures, but should I do so I know, and you know, that you would not want to read this book. Besides, statistics, however carefully gathered, tell only partial truths, and conditions have changed so rapidly in certain sections of the mountains as to make it impossible to keep any data properly checked. Only such figures, therefore, have been included as appeared necessary for an understanding of the subject under discussion.

The things that I am telling are some of the things that seem to me worth telling. You know that you would not want me to relate in public print all that you have confessed to me, even though you might like to know what others have confided to me of themselves. The revelations that friends make to friends in moments of confidence at the hearthside are sacred. If what I have to say, then, does not entirely satisfy your desire for intimate knowledge, the severity of your criticism may be minimized somewhat by the admission I now make that I do not claim to have compassed the whole truth. I do assert, however, that what I say seems true to me at present writing and necessary to be known.

You will pardon, I am sure, the personal confessions in these pages. The matters of which I write are such as have passed for the most part through my own experience, and there is therefore much of self in the chapters. The writer of this book has been in an administrative office and knows something of your difficulties, my administrative friend. He has been at the other end of the line— a man under authority, a teacher in the mountain field under a church board; and what is more, may I say to you, my ministerial friend, that he knows something of your problems, for he too, though not an ordained minister, has been through a theological seminary. The study of church history and dogma is as fascinating to him as to you; the way honest men have thought on matters of such great import commands unbounded respect; the compromises that men have reached in order to find a basis for working together are also of deepest interest, and help one to understand somewhat the same processes now going on in the minds and hearts of other men who honestly think differently from one another on matters of polity and dogma. We admit, however, do we not, you and I, that deep knowledge of these subjects does not take the place of an under-standing of human nature; and—let us confess it—that a familiarity with the legitimate activities of youth and the ability to participate in them helps with the young, at least, to win to the larger things more readily than does ability to discourse learnedly on the dogmas to which we adhere.

A few of our church friends, though not many, I feel, may peruse the following pages in vain for certain things which they feel should have been included. One of my first struggles in the field—a struggle which I won and which I hope some of you in the field have also won—concerned my refusal to keep a finger constantly on the spiritual pulse of the community in order to make reports of how many rose for prayer and attended Sabbath school to be published in cold print and distributed widely in the solicitation of funds.

The mountaineer's relation to his Creator, and the way in which he shows that relation, are his own, as are yours and mine. Many of you who feel as I do have in all probability had to summon courage to face the charge of timidity because you declined to set forth such intimate details and other particulars that might have made interesting reading, attracted the attention of the unthinking in another environment, and perhaps brought in a bit more to the collection on Missionary Sunday.

The writer realizes that a recital of denominational differences and frictions, and the causes thereof, by one who is regarded as an impartial investigator might help some in setting forth to their constituency the necessity for certain phases of their own work; but he refuses to be merely an investigator—he has conceived his office to be that of a co-worker with all agencies, "foreign" and native. He has not been slow or remiss, as you, my administrative friend, will admit, in pointing out the weaknesses of your own work; but the enumeration of your shortcomings, as he has viewed them, he has made directly to you or to your accredited representatives—not to your denominational rivals or in a specific way to the general public. Dwelling to others upon the faults of one's friends does not make for co-operation.

The writer does not profess to be free from the predisposition that prompts most of us to give the benefit of a doubt to peoples and causes in which we are deeply interested. It is true, my Northern friends, that I may see your faults more clearly than I do those of our Southern friends, for by training I am one of you. If I seem lenient to those of the Southern Highlander or Lowlander, bear with me while I tell you the reason.

I first went to the Highlands of the South nearly a quarter of a century ago. To be honest, it was not that I felt a great mission to uplift anybody. The pioneer call was irresistible as it came in striking contrast to the call of the conventional. Perhaps, too, there was what I then felt to be the call of the blood, for my people in earlier times were Highlanders in those other Highlands; but underneath all was gratitude to the South for having taken within its hospitable doors, during a great epidemic in ante bellum days, a lad just from Scotland who had come to seek his fortune in this land of promise—a lad whose memory is very dear to me. If

xix

there was any thought of uplift it was not recognized as such, but regarded merely as a debt of gratitude to be paid by his son.

In our highest and best moments we all recognize ourselves as Americans, equally at home in any part of this land of ours. Every moment, however, is not our highest and best. We have been Northerners and Southerners, Easterners and Westerners, and Hyphenates. With the going of the hyphen must go sectional designations. As an American, born in the West, educated in the East, and by preference a resident of the South, the writer has felt what you sometimes have felt—the provincialisms of the different sections. He has almost wished at times, my Southern friend, that he might have first seen the light of day south of the Mason and Dixon line, for then you would have accepted him as one of you always, even though he lived the rest of his life north of that line. In your eyes, had that been the case, he would have been just a bit different person from what he seems because he was born north of that line and has lived half his life south of it, hospitably accepted as he has been by you.

It must, however, in all fairness be said that you, my Southern administrative friend, have sought from him such assistance as he was able to give, and in accepting it have evidenced the same broadmindedness as my Northern administrative friend. That you have not full control over many of your difficulties, often the same as those that confront him, you as well as he have admitted in confidence. Moreover you, just as cordially as he, have given to the writer the advice, help, and criticism which he has sought from you.

In our work in the Highlands, whether we be from a mission, independent, or public school, or whether we be a social worker, if we may use that much abused and much misunderstood term, and from whatever section we come, it should be remembered that if we deal on intimate terms with the Highlander or his children, a fine code of ethics—equal to that of a physician or nurse—should be observed. We need not go to his land unless we wish, nor to his home; but having gone, received his welcome and shared his hospitality, it behooves us, if we cannot maintain that courteous code, to leave.

However far the writer may fall short in the pages following of satisfying your desire for knowledge or even your curiosity, he has endeavored to set forth such things as will, he hopes, tend to bring about a better understanding. While for purposes of description we must use the terms Highland and Lowland, Northern and Southern, Eastern and Western, it is his hope that he has used them in such a way and with such a spirit as to hasten the time when we shall all be known by the simple designation, American.

If enough of importance be attached to any statement in these pages to make that statement appear an unjust reflection upon a particular section, we ask that pardon be granted. Our sole hope has been that if the thought and feeling of different sections be understood even in part through a fallible presentation of them, efforts for betterment might be undertaken with a sympathy so large as to sense the part each section is to have in the formation of the national character that is to be, when complete understanding shall exist, when the need of one shall be recognized as the rightful concern of all, and when there shall be no thought of dependence other than the mutual dependence of brothers.

A ministerial friend of mine once prepared a sermon especially for a certain sinner in his congregation and preached it at her with all the power that was his. When he came from the pulpit she was the first to take him by the hand and thank him for his sermon, which she said she enjoyed the more in that none of it applied to her.

The writer would say that when he speaks of conditions and work generally in the Highlands, he has in mind tendencies and groups rather than special instances and individuals. But if you, making a personal application, are conscious of being one of a group evidencing tendencies that should not exist, what he has written is meant for you. If, on the other hand, you belong in such a group and do not recognize the fact, his sense of failure will be mitigated somewhat by the thought that in other parts of the book you will perhaps have found something worth while.

Let us now come to the Highlands—a land of promise, a land of romance, and a land about which, perhaps, more things are known that are not true than of any part of our country.

INTRODUCTION

JOHN C. CAMPBELL was one of those men so right for his time as to seem almost the creation of the ideas and events which he influenced. As an educator connected with denominationally sponsored schools in the Southern mountains and as secretary of the Southern Highland Division of the Russell Sage Foundation, he made private perceptions the basis for his identification of public issues and, in the process, articulated for his generation a new conception of the relationship of Appalachia and America. At the same time his work was the culmination of more than fifty years of interest in the "strange land and peculiar people" of the mountain South by "foreigners" from the North, the creation of the institutional and intellectual context in which he worked and to which he was heir. His distress at the traditional parochialism of uplift activity and his efforts to facilitate cooperation among competing agencies at work in the mountain field were at one with the larger movement toward federation so characteristic of American philanthropy in the early twentieth century. His use of the objective techniques of the social survey in assessing the problems and the possibilities of mountain life was at one with the movement toward the use of the new social sciences as tools for social betterment. His identification of the problems of Appalachia as qualitatively no different from those of rural regions more generally and his search for solutions which would preserve the integrity of mountain life reflected the "country life movement" which saw rural and urban life not as the limits of a continuum of historical development but as equivalent modes of social and economic organization. His acceptance of the ambiguity of Appalachia's place within a nation apparently unified and homogeneous in all other respects and of the validity of the separate but nonetheless American culture which had developed within the mountain South was a manifestation of the emerging spirit of regionalism and pluralism which would soon transform America's conception of herself and permit, at least for a time, the acceptance of diversity as the quintessence of Americanism. One may argue whether another might have heard the call of history in his place, had he not. The fact is, he did. John C. Campbell changed our ideas about the relationship of Appalachia and America and changed the history of both in the process.

John Campbell was born in La Porte, Indiana, on September 14, 1867, the son of Anna Kipp and Gavin Campbell. He attended Phillips Academy, Andover, Massachusetts, and Williams College, from which he graduated in 1892. After completing the three years of study for the bachelor of divinity degree at Andover Theological Seminary, Campbell accepted an appointment as principal of a mountain academy in Alabama under the auspices of the Congregational American Missionary Association, thus beginning an involvement with the problems of mountain life which was to continue with the briefest of interruptions until his death in 1919.

Campbell spent the winter of 1898-1899 as a teacher in the public schools of Stevens Point, Wisconsin, but returned to educational work in the mountains the next autumn as principal of an academy in Tennessee. In 1901 he was appointed superintendent of secondary education at Piedmont College, Demorest, Georgia, which he subsequently served as dean and then as president. The death in 1905 of his wife, the former Grace H. Buckingham, whom he had married after his graduation from Andover Seminary, and the exertions of a fundraising campaign for the college in 1906 led Campbell to seek some relief from his duties. Early in 1907 he announced his resignation as president of Piedmont College, married Miss Olive A. Dame of Medford, Massachusetts, and set out with his new bride on a European vacation. By the winter of 1907-1908 the Campbells were back in Demorest, where he received an invitation from Mrs. John Glenn to attend the annual meeting of the National Conference of Charities and Corrections, to be held that spring in Richmond.

Appropriate to the unusual southern meeting place of the conference, the sessions of 1908 were generally directed at an assessment of the problems of philanthropic work in the South.

Indeed the Richmond location had been chosen in order to make attendance by workers in the southern field possible and to permit them to exchange ideas among themselves and with the representatives of sponsoring agencies with headquarters in the North. As chairman of the section on Needy Families and their Neighborhoods, which was to consider the peculiar character of Southern mountain life and the chaotic state of uplift work in Appalachia, Mrs. Glenn was particularly desirous of bringing workers in the mountain area to Richmond for the discussions which were to be given focus by Bruce R. Payne's address, "Waste in Mountain Settlement Work." John Campbell accepted Mrs. Glenn's invitation and must have found much satisfaction with Payne's statement of the problems of benevolent work in the mountains—a lack of coordination which led to competition between agencies and unnecessary duplication of effort; a lack of communication among the workers in the field, even those affiliated with the same sponsoring agency; and a general ignorance of those needs "peculiar to mountain peoples in isolated communities" which led necessarily to the failure of programs developed originally to meet the needs of the urban poor. Not only had these been his own observations, Campbell told Mrs. Glenn after the meeting, but he had in fact long been interested in conducting just such a preliminary survey of mountain conditions and of the state of mountain uplift work that Payne had advocated as a necessary first step in improving the effectiveness of the work. "It was my purpose, had I been able to carry out the plan myself, to prepare maps, routes, and gather data during the summer, perhaps to spend a few weeks at the Amherst Agricultural Summer School where they are making a very wise beginning in the study of rural conditions. With this preliminary work done, I had intended to start in with a conveyance in the mountains of Virginia and work southward visiting schools, and during the brief winter rainy season to settle down in some center such as Asheville, in whose environs are many schools that can be easily reached. Then when the spring opened, to continue the journey and during the early summer to visit the conferences and religious gatherings that are held. . . . It has seemed to me that the time has come for an impartial but sympathetic study to find out what needs are common to these isolated sections, and what needs are peculiar to each, in the hope that when the diagnosis is made a remedy may be found."

As wife of the director of the newly established Russell Sage Foundation, Mrs. Glenn was in a position to assist Campbell in carrying out this proposed survey, as he must himself have known well. At her request, he prepared a brief statement of what he hoped to accomplish by such a tour of the mountains for consideration by Mr. Glenn and the trustees of the foundation, and an estimate of expenses; by early June, the Campbell survey had been approved as one of the activities of the foundation, and the work of assessing the characteristics of mountain life was begun. The foundation's appropriation for expenses was renewed annually after 1908 (Campbell and his wife served without salary at this time). In late 1912, the work of the survey and Campbell's related activities in the Southern mountains were given a more formal existence by the creation of a Southern Highland Division with a permanent budget. In January 1913 a base of operations was established at Asheville.

From then until his death, John Campbell and the Southern Highland Division of the Russell Sage Foundation were one and the same. He was himself the central repository of data concerning conditions in the mountains to which workers in the field might turn. He was the disinterested outsider, sympathetic to the needs of the mountaineers and familiar with the personnel and programs of the several benevolent agencies active in the region, who could facilitate the cooperation of diverse organizations to improve the quality of mountain life. He was the impartial observer who might judge with impunity the appropriateness of particular solutions to the problems of the area, and of particular conceptions of the relationship of Appalachia and America, in light of the new ideas and new techniques which were transforming American philanthropy in the early twentieth century. The foundation provided support and encouragement, but it was the force of Campbell's personality which made the operations of the division a success, and when he died the Southern Highland Division simply ceased to be.

Throughout its existence, the Southern Highland Division functioned in the three areas which Campbell had initially designated as critical to the conduct of effective benevolent work in the Southern mountains, and hence to the betterment of mountain conditions: the dissemination of accurate information concerning the region so as to dispel the notion of charmingly hopeless degeneracy which dominated all popular, and most professional, literature on Appalachia; the facilitation of communication among workers in the field, and of cooperation among agencies; the redirection of mountain work from the "americanization" programs of the denominational home missionary boards towards new approaches which looked to the creation of a viable mountain culture and the redefinition of Appalachia as an alternative version of, rather than as the opposite of, America. Although these were inevitably combined in the day to day operations of the division and in the activities of its secretary, it was the last of the three which most engaged Campbell's attention and concern, for it was upon this that the future of the mountain region depended.

The "discovery" of Appalachia had come about in that search for the "interesting" in American life which competition among the new monthly magazines had precipitated during the immediate post-Civil War years. Emerging in the mid-seventies as the local color movement, this quest for good copy yielded a substantial volume of literature describing life in the "little corners" ostensibly typical of America during the antebellum "seedtime" of the new nation which was to emerge. Alone among the fields for fiction staked out and mined by the local color writers, however, Appalachia was at once of the past and of the present. In the Southern mountains, as Charles Dudley Warner and others noted with distress when they traveled the region in search of literary material, the primitive conditions of pioneer days persisted, while the influx of summer visitors to the developing resort areas of the mountain South, like Asheville, North Carolina, seemed only to heighten the contrast between Appalachia and America. Not until the early twentieth century —as a result of the efforts of John Campbell primarily—were the peculiar conditions of the region identified as the result of poverty and the normal isolation of rural life. For Americans of the eighties and nineties, mountain life appeared as an earlier phase of American development preserved, like a mammoth in ice, by some accident of nature, while the mountaineers themselves seemed to be "our contemporary ancestors."

By the end of the nineteenth century, those very qualities which had made Appalachia seem picturesque and interesting began to be viewed instead as social problems demanding analysis and solution. The past was past; its persistence into the present was in itself disturbing, and from the point of view of the modern America undesirable. Explanation was called for. Was the backwardness of Appalachia the result of the mountain environment, which cut the region off from participation in those transformations which had affected the rest of the nation? Or was it rather the result of some genetic incapacity for progress beyond the most rudimentary stage of civilization on the part of the mountaineers? The continued identification of Appalachia with America's pioneer past was made by many because it signified for them the inherent nobility of mountain poverty, and hence of the remediable quality of mountaineer "degeneracy," but in fact did much to impede the development of truly productive attitudes toward the problems of mountain life. Not only did this identification provide a conceptual scheme in terms of which the relationship of Appalachia and America could be understood, and hence accepted, as natural and by implication proper, but it served to crystallize the emerging idea of Appalachia as a discrete region, in but not of America, unavailable *as such* to the melioration of organized benevolence. Only by a program of rapid modernization through the introduction of the essential institutions of modern America, the schoolhouse and the factory, could the pastness of the Appalachian present be altered and the region as a whole integrated into an otherwise homogeneous nation.

At the same time, however, a peculiar tension was created, as the undesirable characteristics of mountain life were balanced against the desirable characteristics of natural simplicity, independence of spirit, health, and patriotism held to be Appalachia's exclusive inheritance from the pioneer past she had once shared with the rest of the nation. By the early years of the twentieth century, Appalachia had come to seem at once the opposite of America and the quintessence of America, while the mountaineers became at once a "submerged tenth," desperately in need of uplift, and a "saving remnant," reserved by a gracious providence for the regeneration of the nation's spirit and the rejuvenation of her blood. The result of this dichotomy was the striking irony which dominated uplift work in the mountains during these years and which resulted in the confusion that John Campbell hoped to ease; for though their own work, directed at the modernization of life in the Southern mountains was effectively americanizing, and hence destroying Appalachia, it was the representatives of the denominational home mission boards and of the secular agencies at work in the mountain field who were most insistent on the need to preserve the integrity of Appalachian life, and loudest in their opposition to the suggestions of Southern industrialists that the problem could best be solved by moving the mountaineers from unarable land to the mill-towns and mining-camps of the new industrial South.

It was this irony inherent in the practice of benevolent work in Appalachia (that it destroyed what it pretended to value) against which John Campbell directed his most strenuous and systematic efforts and which not incidentally brought into focus for him the ambiguity of Appalachia's situation in America. As early as 1908 he had indicated to Mr. and Mrs. Glenn his doubts about the appropriateness of conventional uplift techniques in the hyperrural situation which prevailed in the mountain region, although his primary concern at that time was with the lack of coordination in mountain work. By the end of his four year survey of mountain conditions, however, he had become convinced that what was needed was some adaptation of the Danish folk-school or a people's college "which combines the cultural—the mountaineers' want—with the cooperative spirit— the mountaineers' need" while it "gives training, largely developed through the cooperative spirit engendered, for bettering economic conditions. The mountain field will forever remain a 'mission field' unless its people are trained to manage their own institutions and to have money enough to maintain them."

With the assistance and encouragement of the staff of the Russell Sage Foundation and of the U. S. Bureau of Education, John Campbell began a campaign to reeducate the leaders of educational work in the mountains concerning the failure of the traditional curriculum-oriented schools to meet the challenge of mountain conditions and to emphasize the need for innovation in the total conception of the "foreign" school in the region. Especially as the state school systems developed the capacity to support education in the mountain counties, Campbell saw it as the obligation of the church and independent schools "to find through experiment, and to inspire by example, a new type of school which will serve the country. This truly rural school will meet more effectively the economic needs of the Highlanders, will point out the possibilities of a richer, fuller life in the country, and will impart the spirit of altruism and training necessary to make the possibilities real."

John Campbell's advocacy of educational experiment based upon the experiences of Grundtvig and Kold in Denmark and Sir Horace Plunkett in Ireland was of enormous consequence, for it drew him increasingly to conceive of Appalachia as a kind of folk society manqué rather than as an incomplete version of the larger American society which surrounded it. The rhetoric of a natural discrepancy between Appalachia and America, which had previously functioned in a mythic way as explanation by naming, Campbell now took literally as a guide to the reality of the present. The conventional description of Appalachia as a land defined by geography rather than by history became the basis for social analysis and social action, as he sought to identify those areas within the mountains where similarity of problems and resources and modes of social and economic organization would provide the context in which natural community might develop. He had maps drawn in which topography was featured more prominently than political boundaries. He had statistics tabulated on a regional rather than on a state basis exclusively. He encouraged the establishment of a Synod of Appalachia within the (northern) Presbyterian Church in order to bring the mountain congregations of that denomination together in a single, self-governing unit and to force the denomination's national boards to confront the peculiar problems of mountain life. He was instrumental in organizing the annual Knoxville Conference of Southern Mountain Workers, which sought to cut across traditional "field" boundaries and to facilitate cooperation among uplift agencies on a regional basis.

The very fact of the persistence of a traditional culture in Appalachia, which had seemed so strange to American eyes in the late nineteenth century and so great an obstacle to the necessary and inevitable modernization of life in the mountain region, now appeared to Campbell as the essential foundation upon which a revitalized folk society might be built. The Danish folk school adapted to mountain conditions would then be the vehicle not only for the development of social service techniques appropriate to the needs of rural regions but for the restoration to the mountaineers of that indigenous culture which they had previously been asked to discard—a possibility to which his wife's discovery of a vital folksong tradition in the mountains (later exploited by the English collectors Cecil J. Sharp and Maud Karpeles) lent credence. For Campbell the conventional remark of the local color writers concerning the appropriateness of the log cabin to its mountain setting thus became a symbol of the Appalachian community which might, while at peace with itself and with its environment, be linked to the outside America by ties of blood and language and patriotism but spiritually and economically independent in its mountain fastness.

John Campbell did not live to complete his work in the mountains, nor certainly to see his vision fulfilled. Yet his ideas concerning the possible future of Appalachia in America, as expressed in the brief essays published during his lifetime and in this posthumous volume, but more particularly through his personal contact with the leaders of benevolent work in the Southern mountains, were to dominate America's conception of the region for two decades after his death, and to generate a series of new programs directed at the creation of a viable mountain culture. Folk schools, agricultural cooperatives, handicrafts guilds, the frontier nursing service, the good roads movement in the mountains, and most important a sense of pride in the unique characteristics of mountain life was his legacy to Appalachia; a sense of the legitimacy of the American culture of Appalachia, and of the possibility of improving standards of health, education, and welfare without in the process destroying the culture or violating the sensibilities of those who were to be helped, in the mountains or anywhere else, was his legacy to America. If from the vantage point of our current "rediscovery" of Appalachia his vision seems neither new nor in itself particularly viable, it is only because it has already become an integral part of our conception of that "strange land and peculiar people," whose plight, because we have come to understand it so well, we have almost forgotten.

HENRY D. SHAPIRO

New times demand new measures and new men:
The world advances, and in time outgrows
The laws that in our fathers' day were best;
And, doubtless, after us, some purer scheme
Will be shaped out by wiser men than we,
Made wiser by the steady growth of truth.

  * * * * * * * *

Truth is eternal, but her effluence,
With endless change, is fitted to the hour;
Her mirror is turned forward to reflect
The promise of the future, not the past.

        —JAMES RUSSELL LOWELL.

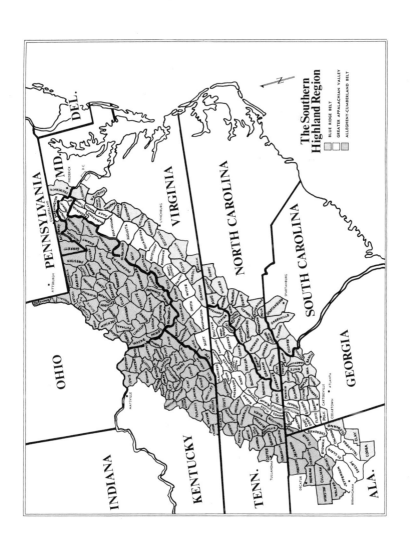

The Southern Highland Region

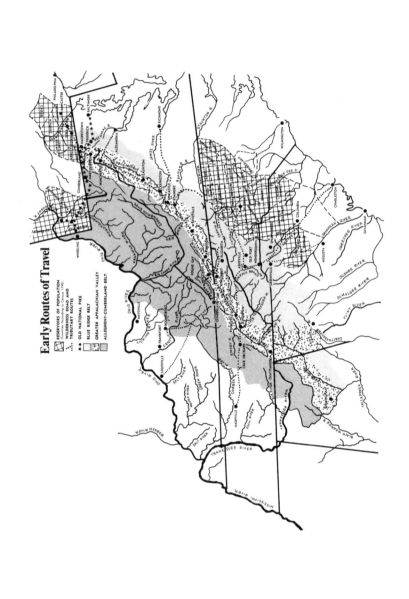

Early Routes of Travel

RESERVOIRS OF POPULATION
(Counties According to Census 1790)
WILDERNESS ROAD AND
TRIBUTARY ROUTES
OLD NATIONAL PIKE
BLUE RIDGE BELT
GREATER APPALACHIAN VALLEY
ALLEGHENY-CUMBERLAND BELT

CHAPTER I

MORE OR LESS PERSONAL

NEARLY twenty-five years ago the writer entered the Southern Highlands as a teacher. The spot where his education began was a little mountain hamlet many miles from a railroad. Rival towns defeated at baseball were wont to refer to us as a "wide place in the Big Road," as the public highway was called, but it was wounded pride that led to such disparagement. Our breadth was caused by the crossing of two roads, not by the widening of one. Clustered about the cross-roads were the four buildings which constituted our business section. Naturally the post-office was an edifice of importance, for there we called daily for the letter someone might chance to write us, and we never could be sure when the package of seed from our congressman might arrive.

But of first importance, and dearest to the hearts of all, were our three emporia that competed with each other in a leisurely way in the sale of coffee, coal oil, sidemeat, sugar, flour, calico, snuff, tobacco, and a few other necessities.

Our complacency in matters of mere getting and spending was occasioned by our deep interest in subjects of real importance—politics and religion. The prominent place accorded our marts of trade, in fact the reason of their being, was that they were, after all, council lodges, or fora, if you please, where vital topics were discussed in daily sessions by the Solons of the countryside. Including the post-office, each building commanded an angle of the cross-roads, and the four together the cardinal points of the compass. The breezes that tempered the summer's heat must of necessity pass through one of them, and our sages adjourned from council chamber to council chamber under the influence of sun, shade, and breeze—and in winter, of firewood supply—to secure a maximum of comfort with a minimum of exertion. Such was the visible

1

center of our municipal life, which ministered both to our bodily and intellectual need.

The chance traveler over the Big Road would know little of the teeming life hidden away in the nearby coves and clearings. Children abounded; in fact they were the chief asset of the community, if community it could be called; and on the opening day of school the Professor, as he now came to be known, faced a group of one hundred and eighty-five students, ranging in age from five to twenty-five.

When the enrolment was complete, he was dismayed to find that he was called upon to instruct not only Polly Ann, Victoria, and Australia; but Noah, Isaac, Joseph, and Jesse, Daniel, Malachi, and Elisha; John Wesley and his little brother Luther; Virgil, Homer, and Pliny; Cyrus, Alexander, and Napoleon; Columbus; and our own George Washington and Grover Cleveland. "Whence these names?" was the instinctive query.

George Washington was not the only one who could fell a tree. Little Joseph, too, swung a lusty axe, and Pliny did not "ride the saw," but did his full share with his big brother Homer in cutting up the logs for firewood. Surrounded by great ones performing their tasks greatly, the Professor would not fail in performance of his duties. Therefore until he could effect an exchange of skill for courtesy by satisfying John Wesley's ambition to become a curve pitcher, the Professor would rise at 4:30 in the morning and saw and split enough wood to last the household during the day. From eight to four (save for the noon hour) he taught, and after school was over continued his education by making "mission" furniture from barrels and dry-goods boxes, and rustic furniture from gleanings in the forest to supplement the cook-stove, bed-springs, dining-room table, and the few chairs brought in from the county-seat.

By virtue of his position as principal of the school, he was also superintendent of the Union Sunday school, and teacher of the men's bible class. Although this was a Union Sunday school, harmony did not always prevail, for loyal theological allegiance was given to Methodist, Baptist, "Campbellite," Old School Presbyterian, Cumberland Presbyterian, Universalist, and Perfectionist beliefs. Occasionally a Primitive Baptist was in attendance, who had overcome his theoretical objection to Sabbath schools in his need of social diversion. It was often difficult, despite earnest effort, to steer the discussion between the Scylla of dogma and the Charybdis of polity and practice. Methods of baptism *would* come to the fore, and polemics between those of Calvinistic and those of Arminian persuasion could not always be avoided. The Perfectionist, theoretically unable to sin, found it easy to step from his pedestal in anger induced by apt Scriptural quotations, recalled for his benefit by others of the class; and the lone Universalist waged a losing battle against all his fellow-members, steadfastly united through belief in eternal punishment.

The death of the Universalist brought the first break in the ranks of the Sabbath school class, and relaxed, too, for the time being, the rigid hold of dogmas. The Missionary Baptist gave evidence of his kinship to the departed by making his rough casket. The Old School Presbyterian and the Campbellite combined their funds to send to the county-seat for black calico and nickel nails to adorn the pine box fashioned by Baptist hands. The Methodist loaned his new wagon for the hearse, and the Cumberland Presbyterian his mules for the cortège. The wives of other members united in making, or loaning, garments of mourning for the bereaved widow and daughters; and all lamented a brother and neighbor lost to class and community.

This touch of nature which made us all kin did not, however, keep us akin, for despite fervent hopes the day of burying denominational hatchets had not yet dawned. A militant evangelist from an aggressive denomination, feeling called to give overemphasis to isolated Scriptural texts, made great inroads into the ranks of the local churches; and two itinerant Mormon elders almost convinced the Perfectionist that his perfection might be of an absolutely perfect brand were he to unite with them.

In spite of the number of denominations represented in the community, and the fact that there were two church houses and the school house, all open to preachers, preaching services were held but once a month. The Professor, to supply the need, was urged to add to his duties by holding services appropriate for Sunday on every Sunday night. He accepted, and being young, ventured one evening to avail himself of the opportunity offered to reconcile

3

theological differences and animosities by quoting what he regarded as unquestionable authority from the Scriptures, the words of the Great Teacher addressed to the Woman of Samaria when she put to Him a question pertaining to religious form rather than to spirit.[1] The echoes of the closing hymn had scarcely died away when he was confronted by a group whose spokesman, white with anger, demanded whether he had ever been to college and studied Greek. The angry disputant could not read English, but he none the less felt able to inform the Professor with much emphasis that certain ceremonies referred to in the address must be performed in definitely prescribed ways because the " 'riginal Greek" meant but one thing, and by no possible exegesis could be construed to mean anything else.

The questions that presented themselves thus early were how denominational differences might be minimized, at least to the extent of co-operation in the large things upon which all denominations agree; and, furthermore, how the head of a denominational school in the mountains could promote these larger things without appearing, by reason of his very connection with such a school, to be in the community for the purpose of advancing the interests of that denomination. For a number of years the latter question was merely academic because of the liberal policy pursued by the board under whose auspices the particular school in which he taught was conducted. Fortunately for him, the officials of the board did not regard it as essential that he should be a minister, or even that he be affiliated with the denomination maintaining this academy. His position in the community was that of a teacher incidentally helping out in the Sunday evening services, and not that of a preacher, a denominational champion, incidentally teaching.

In the view of his neighbors and his class it did not, therefore, fall to him to police the convictions of the community; and it was not resented when he and some other members of the class did not acquiesce fully in the views of the extreme Predestinarians as to the unavoidableness of the death of our classmate. In our judgment he might have been helped by calling the doctor from the county-seat, when the local doctor was too drunk to operate and

[1] John IV, 21 to 24.

4

give him the one chance for life that an operation afforded. Nor did we believe that it had been decreed from before the foundations of the earth that Minty, who hobbled daily the weary three miles to school, must limp through life because the same doctor when called had been too drunk to set her broken leg. To sisters in travail good women ministered as best they could, but joy in many a home was turned to mourning because there was no one who knew how to help in the right way. Powerless in these times of sorrow and need, the Professor wondered often whence help would come, and whether he had not erred in judgment in not following out the half-formed resolve of college days to study medicine.

As the complexity and oversupply of things theological tended to divide the elders, especially when it was felt, justly or unjustly, that undue importance in leadership was being given to one denomination, so the lack of any social organization whatsoever for the young people acted to keep them apart. The organization of the ball-nine helped out the boys as boys, and was the most potent factor in the community in winning them from very questionable practices; but there were few opportunities for boys and girls to come together socially. Practically the only opportunity for this, or for girls to meet with other girls, was at funerals, prayer meeting, Sabbath school, and occasional preachings.

Only the uninitiated, or the wilfully blind optimist, could ascribe the great gatherings at funerals or the occasional church meetings to instinctive religious aspirations; they were an evidence not alone of religious aspiration, but of social hunger, in old and young alike, using these avenues for its satisfaction. The taboo put by various denominations upon many amusements relegated them to the few homes in the community where such amusements were often associated with pastimes justly tabooed.

In his endeavor to be a clear-eyed optimist, the Professor had to admit, to himself at least, that the crowding to the fount of learning was not due merely to a desire to slake a thirst for knowledge. One hesitates to question the foundation upon which so much of delightful romance relating to the mountain youth's eagerness for knowledge is builded, but speaking for this one school it must be said that attendance was due, in large part, to a desire to satisfy

5

the social instinct. Not all of our boys were Abraham Lincolns, burning with zeal for learning; nor were all the girls impelled to seek an education by a desire to marry missionaries to China.

Our school was a very good school of its kind, and we were justly proud of it. We had more and better grades than some of the county-seats adjoining; we had better textbooks and a better library; and the teaching, such as it was, was not bad. How proud we would have been then could we have foreseen that a number of our boys would go to state universities, one to Yale; that some would become ministers and lawyers of promise; and that through our graduates our influence would be felt not alone in the cities of the South but to some extent in life elsewhere.

The complacency with which we viewed our work for several years was destined to receive a severe jolt. It was at the noon hour, after a busy morning, that one of the girls came to the desk. She was a little older than the average of her class, and had shown some hesitancy about entering school at all. On looking up the Professor noticed that she had been weeping, and in reply to his inquiry she said:

"I've come to tell you good-bye, for I'm aimin' to quit school."

"But why, Myrtle?"

"What's the use of educating me? I'm only a girl, and they's eight young ones at home. You know where we live."

"But you will be a more helpful girl with an education, and you will have a much wider influence through your own home, later."

"That ain't fer me," she said; and in answer to a surprised look, for she was winsome, "Don't you see what's happening? The best boys, the only kind I would want to marry, don't stay here when they finish school. There's nothing ahead fer me but to stay home and let my men-folks support me, or to marry someone I don't want now I been to school. I'm wanting things I can't have. I'd better be left in my ignorance."

The Professor does not remember all he said in reply, but he knows it was inadequate. Myrtle did remain in school. For a time he almost regretted her decision, for her presence was a protest and a reminder of bitter failure. Another stage in his education had been reached through the knowledge that the school upon which he had prided himself had failed.

It is to the people of this little community that the mind of the writer reverts again and again. They taught him more than he ever taught them. If anything of enlightenment is shed upon the problems of the Highlands in the following pages, it is due in large part to the trains of thought set in motion by them, long ago. After a quarter of a century, when perplexing questions arise as to how people may be brought to work together, there comes to him the picture of Brother C., the Baptist preacher, rising from his seat at the closing exercises of the school; and he hears him say again:

"We've had a right good session, and are proud of our school; and now, this being the last meeting of the year, and the Professor going to his home-folks for a visit, after the benediction let's all give him the right hand of fellowship, while we sing 'God be with you till we meet again.' "

Before him in memory pass Baptist, Methodist, Campbellite, Cumberland Presbyterian, Old School Presbyterian, Perfectionist, and sinner—especially numerous—forgetting all about their differences in their loyal pride in their school, the common community interest.

Justification for this personal recital is not that the experiences depicted are unique, but because they are the common experiences of many teachers in the mountain country. The problems and perplexities that confronted one teacher in this one little community are, after all, questions that confront all rural workers not alone in the Southern Highlands but in almost every part of our land. They are, in substance, how to obtain sympathetic understanding of the people and their background, unanimity of spirit rather than discord by reason of the forms that embody it, better public health and sanitation, a kind of school that does not divorce the so-called cultural from the necessary economic life of the neighborhood, and practical co-operation toward all these ends.

CHAPTER II

THE SOUTHERN HIGHLANDS AND THE SOUTHERN HIGHLANDER DEFINED

RECENTLY, while indulging in the somewhat melancholy pleasure of sorting letters and manuscripts yellowing with age, the writer uncovered an address delivered by him during his first year of acquaintance with the mountain people and mountain country. The address, while not so very bad, yet gave evidence of that comprehensive knowledge which frequently characterizes a limited acquaintance with the subject under discussion. Since that time he has heard many discourses upon mountain questions, builded in the same way, and of similar material. All were permeated with the kindliest feeling for the mountaineer, and were colorful with descriptions of local, exceptional, or picturesque conditions, but few told who the mountaineers were, or where they lived. This lack of information was supplied, generally, by a sweeping gesture toward the South, accompanying the statement, "In the mountains of our fair Southland lives a people of purest Anglo-Saxon blood, upon whose cabin walls hang the rifles with which their illustrious ancestors at King's Mountain turned the tide of the Revolution."

Few discourses on mountain questions are complete without this reference. The audiences to whom such addresses are given, unless nurtured on Fiske's misinterpreted and misapplied theory that the mountain people are descendants of mean and indentured whites of colonial days,[1] would feel cheated without it. They look for it as expectantly as the Bostonian does for the closing phrase in the Governor's Thanksgiving Proclamation, "God Save the Commonwealth of Massachusetts."

---

[1] See Appendix B.

8

If the speaker has French blood, there is certain to be some allu-
sion to the Huguenots and the Revocation of the Edict of Nantes;
if German, a strong reference to the Palatinate element in this
early stream of migration; and if there is a drop of Scotch-Irish
blood in his veins, not the least doubt is left in the minds of the
audience as to who the mountain people are—they are the worthy
scions of this worthy stock, and all, of course, Presbyterians by
heritage.

The writer longs for the certitude of knowledge with which he
spoke twenty-five years ago. But fortunately his education was
not allowed to end there. The mountain hamlet where he lived,
learned, and tried to teach, lay on an old route of travel. Occasionally there would straggle through the cross-roads a train of canvas-covered wagons, and at times he had privilege of converse with
the hopeful adventurer in search of the Eldorado lying always just
beyond. Now and again the stillness of the night would bring the
echo of some locomotive threading its way through the mountain
defiles, or was it the faint whistle of a packet on the Tennessee?
Such experiences served to intensify his desire to know more of
the early pioneers of our Highlands, of their routes of travel, their
successors, and the land in which they dwell.

Associated in memory with these experiences are others of college days in the Berkshire Hills of far-away Massachusetts. Of
these, one stands out vividly. On a "mountain day" expedition to
the top of Greylock, the return trail had been lost in a gathering
storm. Forced to seek shelter, we finally made our way to the door
of a log cabin, such a cabin as one may see today nestling near the
foot of Graybeard or Grandfather in the Carolina Blue Ridge.
Given a cordial welcome by the young mother within, we sought to
establish friendly relations with the little daughter cuddled, in fear
of the storm and in shyness of strangers, in her mother's arms. The
fire lighted up the room furnished with a simplicity one might
duplicate in many a mountain cabin of the South. With the passing of the storm came a halloo from the stalwart young husband, as
he returned from the clearing with axe gleaming over his shoulder.
We lingered at the bend to wave them good-bye as they watched
us down the trail—mother, babe now in father's arms, with the
rainbow over all.

The beauty of the picture lives fresh in the writer's memory, but in later years there has come to him more than the memory of its beauty. To the haunting, half-asked question of the connection between this family group and the straggling train through the mountain hamlet, between the cabin on the slope of the Berkshires and the cabins in the Southern Highlands, an answer has at last been given. What he saw in the Berkshires, and what one still sees occasionally in the Green Mountains and White Mountains, the Catskills and the Adirondacks, are, as it were, re-enacted scenes of the great drama of settlement once lived from New England to Georgia along the frontier line moving ever toward the West. Physiographic and other natural causes will explain why in our Southern Highlands these scenes persist along lingering segments of that frontier line; and why they are found only at isolated points in the Highlands of the North.

Although we must limit ourselves to a discussion of the Southern Highlands, it is well to keep in mind that Southern and Northern Highlands together constitute a whole, a great upland realm extending twelve hundred miles or more from northeast to southwest. Distinctive social customs and standards of living, so interesting to many, are strange only when one forgets that these were common to the daily life of our pioneer fathers North and South alike, but a few decades ago as history is measured. Some, still young though growing gray, whose childhood days were of the West, will recall a share in this life and in these customs.

THE SOUTHERN HIGHLANDS

But where are, and what are the Southern Highlands, and who are the Southern Highlanders? For purposes of discussion, the writer has isolated a part of the great Appalachian province which extends from New York to central Alabama, and has called it the Southern Highlands. Within the boundaries of this territory are included the four western counties of Maryland; the Blue Ridge, Valley, and Allegheny Ridge counties of Virginia; all of West Virginia; eastern Tennessee; eastern Kentucky; western North Carolina; the four northwestern counties of South Carolina; northern Georgia; and northeastern Alabama. Our mountain region, of approximately 112,000 square miles, embraces an area nearly as large as the combined areas of New York and New England, and almost equal to that of England, Scotland, Ireland, and Wales.[1]

The boundary which we have regarded as dividing the Southern Highlands from their northern extension is the famous Mason and Dixon line. More specifically, this boundary line begins at the northeast corner of Frederick County, Maryland, and extends west to the southwest corner of Pennsylvania, thence north along the western boundary of Pennsylvania to the point where the Ohio leaves the state just west of Pittsburgh. For purposes of convenience the southern, or more properly the southwestern boundary, may be considered as a base line running diagonally northwest to southeast, passing through the neighborhood of Birmingham, Alabama, and terminating in the southeast corner of Coosa and the northwest corner of Winston Counties. An approximate eastern boundary for this extended territory is formed by connecting the northern and southern boundaries by a curved line passing in a southwesterly direction slightly to the east of Frederick, Maryland, through Lynchburg, Virginia, a little to the east of Asheville, North Carolina, through Spartanburg, South Carolina, and to the north of Atlanta, Georgia. This line is roughly paralleled by the western boundary which, beginning at Pittsburgh, continues down the Ohio to Kentucky, coinciding with the northwestern boundary of West Virginia, and follows the river nearly to Maysville, Kentucky—the Limestone of pioneer days, where river immigrants disembarked for their cross-country journey.[2] From this point it passes southwest through Tullahoma, Tennessee, and Decatur, Alabama.

The lines by which the Southern Highlands are defined are not chosen arbitrarily. They correspond for the most part with boundaries of natural divisions; on the east with the face of the Blue Ridge, which defines the western margin of the Piedmont Plateau, on the south with the upper limits of the Coastal Plain, and on the west with the western escarpment of the Allegheny-Cumberland

---

[1] A word of explanation is necessary to those who in earlier years have sought from the writer data for addresses and publications. To the counties previously enumerated by him he has added the four western counties of Maryland, and also Winston and Walker Counties of Alabama. The area and population of the region included under the name of Southern Highlands are therefore slightly larger than previously accounted.

[2] More accurately, it is a little east of Maysville, at the point where the western line of Lewis County touches the Ohio.

Plateau. The northern line, in part purely political, was in its beginnings a surveyor's line to determine a boundary dispute of long standing, growing out of the claims of Penn and Lord Baltimore.

The name Southern Highlands has been chosen for several reasons. Southern Appalachians is a term sometimes used, but inasmuch as this term is limited by geographers to that part of the Appalachian mountain system lying south of the New River Divide in southern Virginia, some other name for the whole territory under consideration is necessary. The designation Southern Mountains has also been used. But because so often descriptions of depressed social conditions, which are true only of limited areas, have been given without qualification as existing throughout the Southern mountains, this term has come to carry with it the implication that such conditions prevail generally throughout the region.

The traveler who follows the trails of this far country, fords its rushing streams, and forces his way through thickets of rhododendron and laurel to rest upon some beech-shaded bank of moss, and who toward sunset checks his horse upon the ridge to trace the thread of smoke which signals welcome, may yet be at a loss for a name to describe the land; but when at dawn he wakes with mist rising from every cove and valley, and echoes still sounding of half-remembered traditions, folk-lore and folk-songs, recited or sung before the fire by "granny" or "grandpap," he knows there is but one name that will do it justice—the Southern Highlands.

It is a land of mountains, valleys, and plateaus. Each of the three parallel belts which lying lengthwise, northeast to southwest, form the Highlands, is characterized by the predominance of one of the physical features just indicated. The outstanding feature of the easternmost belt is the Blue Ridge Mountain Range, and we call this belt therefore the Blue Ridge Belt, though it is often referred to technically as the Appalachian Mountain Belt. The western is known as the Allegheny-Cumberland or Appalachian Plateau. Between these truly upland belts extends the Greater Appalachian Valley, better known in its several parts as the Valley of Virginia, the Valley of East Tennessee, and the Coosa River Valley of Georgia and Alabama.

The use of the term Valley, as applied to the great central zone of depression, is likely to mislead. It is more truly a valley-ridge section, with its true valley feature prominent on its eastern side and with ridges toward the west. The floor of the Valley reaches in southern Virginia an altitude of from 2,600 to 2,700 feet above the sea, descending toward the north to an altitude of 500 feet at Harper's Ferry, West Virginia, and southward to 500 feet or less in Alabama. The whole Southern Highland region is therefore an upland region, with a great central depression, and not merely two separate mountain areas with a dividing valley.

More than one-half of the entire territory is included within the Allegheny-Cumberland Belt, a little more than one-fourth in the Blue Ridge Belt, and something less than one-fourth in the Greater Appalachian Valley.[1]

Blue Ridge Belt

In Maryland and Virginia the Blue Ridge Belt is narrow, varying in width from ten to sixteen miles, until near the headwaters of the Roanoke it begins to expand into a lofty plateau. This plateau, lying for the most part in North Carolina, reaches a maximum width of seventy miles, and a maximum height in Mount Mitchell of 6,711 feet. Passing southward into Georgia, it becomes irregular and indefinite until it is lost in the Piedmont Plateau. In general outline it may be compared to a narrow lance-shaped leaf whose stem is the single Blue Ridge Range of Virginia, and whose tip rests in the region of Cartersville, Georgia. After an interval of nearly one hundred miles, there is in Alabama a recurrence of the belt for fifty miles in the Talladega Mountains.

The Blue Ridge Range proper, from its point of expansion in Virginia, continues southward under that name as the eastern border of the plateau. It carries the main divide between waters flowing into the Atlantic and into the Gulf, and rises from an average altitude of over 3,000 feet to a height of almost 6,000 feet in Grandfather Mountain, North Carolina.

Its eastern slopes are very precipitous, and the Yadkin, Catawba, Broad, and other streams that rise here and make their way to the Atlantic, dash down to the Piedmont Plateau below in a series of high cascades and deep gorges. To the west the descent is more gradual. Westward flowing streams at first for some distance pass

[1] For full data on area of belts, see Table 16 of Appendix E.

through broad high valleys. Deepening their channels as they go, the rivers—chief among which are the New, Watauga, Nolichucky, French Broad, Big Pigeon, Little Tennessee, Hiwassee, and Ocoee—cut through the mountains bounding the northwest edge of the plateau in deep narrow gorges, and escape to the Greater Valley and eventually to the Mississippi and Gulf.

This northwest mountain boundary of the plateau has been and still is known locally and popularly as the Great Smokies, from the largest of the segments into which it has been divided by the river gorges, but the general name Unaka is now applied to the whole range as well as to two of its five principal segments. From northeast to southwest, these chief segments are called respectively the Iron, Unaka, Bald, Great Smoky, and Unaka Mountains.

The Unaka Range, although it does not bear the divide, is higher than the Blue Ridge and more rugged on both its eastern and western slopes. In point of fact these are younger mountains which rose so gradually on the western edge of the more ancient plateau as to permit the rivers to keep their early westward direction. While it is difficult to give an average height, owing to the broken character of the range, its general altitude is probably about 5,000 feet. Two of its peaks, Guyot and Clingman's Dome, are but a few feet lower than Mount Mitchell, and numerous others are above 6,000 feet.

The whole plateau section lying between the Blue Ridge and Unakas is cut by ridges and cross-ridges which have no uniform direction, but form for the most part the divides between the main stream basins, and are connected more or less closely with the enclosing ranges to the east and west. The main ridges are the Yellow, Black, Newfound, Balsam, Pisgah, Cowee, Nantahala, Cheoah, and Tusquitee Mountains, of which the Black (wherein lies Mount Mitchell), the Balsam, and Pisgah Ranges are the highest.

In general, the mountains of the Blue Ridge Belt are heavily wooded to the top, and the whole region is one of extreme beauty.

Allegheny-Cumberland Belt

Bordering the Greater Appalachian Valley on the northwest, and facing it in bold escarpment, is the Allegheny-Cumberland Belt.

Throughout its extent it is a plateau belt, although to parts of it in both northern and southern Appalachians the name mountains is applied. In the northern Appalachians, the Catskill Mountains of New York and the Allegheny Mountains of Pennsylvania are really misnomers, arising from the fact that the edge of this great plateau wall appears to the traveler approaching from the seaboard as another mountain range. In the southern Appalachians, the Cumberland Mountains of Kentucky and Tennessee are, in popular usage, coming to be known as the Cumberland Plateau, a much more descriptive term.

The plateau character of the belt is much more prominently marked in Tennessee and Alabama than farther north, but throughout its course it may be viewed as a great wall facing the Greater Appalachian Valley and sloping gradually to the northwest toward the Interior Lowlands.

The eastern escarpment of the Allegheny-Cumberland Plateau Belt, or the Allegheny Front as it is here called, enters the northern limits of our field between Cumberland and Frostburg, Maryland. Along the Virginia-West Virginia boundary it rises to commanding heights. It declines farther south, but in the Big Black Mountains of Virginia and Kentucky again attains to a height of 4,000 feet. In Tennessee the plateau is much lower in altitude. At Cumberland Gap, made so famous in early settlement and later civil strife, its altitude is from 3,000 to 3,200 feet, while the height of the Gap itself is but 1,649 feet.

In Alabama the eastern part of the plateau is deeply cut by long narrow valleys, separated by isolated plateaus. The easternmost of these plateaus is Lookout Mountain, the eastern face of which marks the boundary between the Greater Valley and the Allegheny-Cumberland Belt in this state. To the west beyond Lookout and Wills Valley lies Sand Mountain, and still beyond, the deeply dissected remnants of the Cumberland Plateau proper, sloping gently to the southward until they merge into the Gulf Coastal Plain.

The western bounds of the Allegheny-Cumberland Belt are the western boundary of West Virginia, the broken "knob country" of eastern Kentucky into which the western escarpment of the Cumberland Plateau is here worn, and the irregular but more

15

clearly defined line of this escarpment in Tennessee and in part of Alabama.[1]

While less imposing, the wild and rugged ridges of the Allegheny Front are hardly less beautiful than the loftier wooded peaks and slopes of the Blue Ridge, which forms the front of the eastern belt.

Greater Appalachian Valley

Between these higher belts, the Blue Ridge on the east and the Allegheny-Cumberland on the west, extends the Greater Valley—itself an upland region—which has played so important a part in the settlement of the Southern Highlands and in the history of our country.

Toward the north the valley character of this great, much fluted valley zone is more marked on its eastern side. In Maryland the distinctively valley portion is an extension of the Cumberland Valley of Pennsylvania. In Virginia it is really a series of valleys, taking their names from their rivers—the Shenandoah, the James, the Roanoke, the Kanawha or New, and the Holston or Tennessee. In general configuration, however, the Valley is continuous. It is often referred to as the Shenandoah, from its most famous part, but is better known in its entirety as the Valley of Virginia.

On the western side of the Greater Valley is a series of ridges known collectively as the Allegheny Ridges, lying between the Allegheny Front which forms the eastern escarpment of our plateau belt, and the true valley section of the eastern part of the Greater Valley. To the southward, especially in Tennessee, the ridge portion of the Valley becomes less prominent and the valley character of the belt more marked, although in Tennessee there are still prominent ridges or mountains in the Greater Valley.

In Georgia and Alabama the Valley broadens and descends in altitude, the valley ridges and enclosing mountain walls gradually lose their character, and the whole belt becomes indistinguishable from the rolling plateau and coastal plain to the southward.

The gentle beauty of much of the Greater Valley, especially on its eastern side, with its green fields and dark cedars, forms a marked

[1] The Piedmont Plateau region, lying to the southeast of the Blue Ridge Belt, and the Western Piedmont region, or Interior Lowlands, lying to the northwest of the Allegheny-Cumberland Plateau, are not included in the Southern Highlands as defined in this study.

contrast to the ridges that border it, some of which assume true mountain proportions. This belt is the seat of many flourishing cities and is traversed by a number of railroads; yet parts of it are very inaccessible, and almost as isolated as the remote sections of the higher belts to east and west.[1]

Though our study is limited to the territory just described, we would repeat that the Southern Highlands should not be disassociated in thought from their northern extension. The Allegheny-Cumberland Belt is continued in the so-called Allegheny Mountains of Pennsylvania and in the Catskills of New York. The Greater Appalachian Valley finds extension to the northeast in the Cumberland and Lebanon Valleys of Pennsylvania, and the Paulinskill and Wallkill Valleys of New Jersey and New York. Though the mountain character of the Blue Ridge Belt loses itself in the modest altitude of South Mountain in Pennsylvania, the belt itself is traceable in the highlands of New Jersey and New York, and its ancient remnants, greatly changed by geologic forces, may be followed to the northeast in the Berkshire Hills and Green Mountains of Massachusetts and Vermont, and on into Canada.

In considering our Highland region, or the entire Appalachian province of which it is a part, it is difficult to resist the lure of the geologist who invites us to witness its first narrow crest emerging from the primordial sea, and to hearken to the roar of the ocean upon its eastern shore, and on the west to the wash of the waves of a once great inland sea. Portions of this empire are indeed exceedingly ancient, and the eastern belt especially includes some of the oldest lands of the continent—a fact which invests the region with peculiar appeal to the imagination, as well as with importance to the student of geology. Equally difficult to resist is the temptation to wander in the fascinating by-paths of its more recent history, and to dwell upon the geographic influences exerted by this great barrier which has been so potent in shaping the political, social, and economic life of both North and South.

Those who would understand a people must know the land in which they dwell, and a careful study of the topography of the Southern Highlands will repay the painstaking student. A study

[1] A more detailed description of the physiography of the several states will be found in Appendix A.

of elevations, depressions, and slopes is a dry task in and of itself, but if the narrow winding valley and broad fertile plain, the isolated mesa and expansive plateau, the steep slope and towering peak be translated into terms of life, the study becomes of absorbing interest as the forces are revealed which have influenced some groups to face the future, and others to linger in the past.

THE SOUTHERN HIGHLANDER

To circumscribe territory and give it a name is one thing; to call people by a name not of their choosing is quite another. Obviously, if the term Southern Highlands be allowed for the land, native-born residents of the region are Southern Highlanders. Yet within the Highland area are many native-born inhabitants of urban or valley residence who do not regard themselves as mountain people. The writer has two friends, one living in the Greater Appalachian Valley and one in a prosperous mountain city, and both devoted to the interests of their own people, who refer in conversation to "those mountain folks," although at other times jocosely alluding to themselves as "mountain whites." This opprobrious term, coined as a term of distinction by well-meaning advocates of the mountaineer, is resented by all who dwell in the Highlands, by whatever name they may be designated.

If all that had been accomplished by illustrious men of the mountains, and that now ennobles the history of their several states, had been recorded to the glory of a single Appalachian commonwealth, the matter of nomenclature might be easier. Perhaps, then, residents of the "State of Appalachia" would have been proud to call themselves "Appalachians," "Southern Mountaineers," or "Southern Highlanders." They might even have taken the "typical" mountain cabin, now the cause of so much contention, as their state crest, with encircling wreath of mountain laurel, and underneath have inscribed a Latin motto expressive of their loyalty and pride. The mountain areas of certain states are, to be sure, so large and so influential as to kindle a worthy regional pride, and to win respectful consideration both within and without the state. But the name by which such an area is known indicates merely that the district to which it is applied lies in the eastern or

18

western part of the state. It does not convey the impression that the people who live there are Highland people.

Without at all raising the question as to whether some other division of the mountain region would have been better than the existing one, the fact remains that the Highlands were not welded into one commonwealth, nor are they generally regarded as a continuous tract. They lie within nine Southern states, and too often are called, disparagingly by some and apologetically by others, the "back-yards" of the Southern states. It is not easy to assign a reason for the feeling which has found expression in this phrase, and which makes it difficult to define the Southern Highlander. There are, however, a number of causes which indirectly have contributed to it.

Prominent among these is the relation borne by the mountain region to the states within which it is included. The Highlands as a whole make up about one-third of the total areas of these nine states.[1] Their population is nearly a third of the total population. Their influence is less easily determined. Highlands and Lowlands in each state act upon each other reciprocally, their influence varying with the size and population of the Highland area in proportion to the state area, and somewhat, too, with its topography. In certain states regional differences between the two sections have caused a difference in political alignment. Though some of the mountain areas are admittedly the garden-spots of their states when climate and scenery are considered, and others are contributing largely from their natural resources to the state wealth, the

[1] The proportion noted above by no means represents the average proportion of the mountain area in each state to its respective state area. West Virginia, for example, is a mountain state in its entirety, while the mountain section of South Carolina, the smallest state mountain area with the exception of Maryland, is about one-eleventh of the entire state area. In Virginia the mountain area is about one-half, in Tennessee three-sevenths, in Kentucky one-third, in Alabama one-fourth, in Maryland one-fourth, in North Carolina one-fifth, and in Georgia one-seventh of the total state area.

It may be questioned whether the state of West Virginia should be regarded in its entirety as a mountain state. It is to be remembered, however, that the characteristics which differentiated it from the "Old Dominion" and which led to its separation from it, were the outgrowth of its topography. The Valley of Virginia, although kept distinct for a while from the eastern part of the state by the narrow barrier of the Blue Ridge, was finally assimilated. The western part of Virginia, because of its mountain character, remained unassimilated, and as a result the state of West Virginia, formed from it, differs from the mother state in its political, social, and economic life. (See Appendix A.)

fruits of political power have naturally been most in evidence in the constituencies that have the most votes. There are still echoes of old political struggles for full representation of "east" or "west"—whichever of these localities may indicate the mountain portion of the state—even where one party dominates both sections. These political influences are easily exaggerated, but they are to be considered in a summary of causes affecting mountain life.

Another influence tending to diminish the natural pride in his section felt by the mountain dweller, has been exerted unconsciously by travelers from urban centers in the South, or from Northern states where urban life has been a prevailing influence. By accounts of the simplicity of life in the Highlands, picturesque without qualification, they have unwittingly aroused the antagonism of the people living there by causing them to feel that they have been caricatured. It were well for those from states dominated by urban influences, abounding in wealth and unhandicapped by great regional diversities, to reflect that even within their own borders are large rural areas not different from the mountains in the absence of many of the so-called advantages of city life. The folk dwelling within our Highland country are naturally hospitable, and there is a sense of injury that grows into resentment when former guests in their homes, who need not have come unless they had wished, make sweeping statements that do them and their people gross injustice.

There is another great source of irritation. In earlier days, when public funds were less available for education in the mountains, both Northern and Southern church boards established mission schools in communities not adequately supplied with public schools. Despite all the high endeavor that the word "missions" conveys to us individually, no one of us cares to be regarded, even by implication, as a worthy object of betterment, uplift, or missionary effort.

It has come about, therefore, that the term "Southern Mountaineers" has been made to suggest a peculiar people, with peculiar needs. The South as a whole has shown the natural reaction toward any seeming suggestion of peculiarity on the part of any of its people, though at times it would appear to admit the same implication by its use of the term "Hill-Billy." It is as if two brothers reserved to themselves the right to call each other what they would and when they would, but united in resistance against an outsider who offered affront to a member of the family.

The South holds no monopoly of this sensitiveness. A former classmate of the writer, who twenty years ago described conditions as he viewed them in a northern highland area, aroused the ire of the whole region, urban as well as rural, though writing of only a limited part. Even today, though remedial measures bear witness to the truth of some of his statements, his name is uttered occasionally in country life conferences with a degree of feeling too heated to be mistaken for affection.

Perhaps enough has been said to suggest our difficulty in telling who the Southern Highlanders really are. The reader will, however, allow the use of the term in these pages to cover the population within the region described. We cannot conceal our hope of its ultimate adoption. The people living within the boundaries of the Southern Highlands have too much that is worthy of conservation, both in the past and in the present, to allow themselves to ignore their solidarity or to apologize for it.

CHAPTER III

PIONEER ROUTES OF TRAVEL AND EARLY SETTLEMENTS

THE broad expanse of level country that stretches westward from the South-Atlantic seaboard reaches in the Carolinas a width of one hundred to one hundred and fifty miles. As one moves up the leisurely watercourses the land becomes more rolling, a hill country begins to appear, and the rivers issuing from it descend in steep cascades and rapids to the plain below.

One has, according to the geographers, crossed the Coastal Plain, which first appears south of New York harbor as a narrow strip bordering the sea, and extends southward in an ever-widening zone. The cascades mark that famous "fall line" where rivers fall from the Piedmont Plateau to the low-lying lands of the coast. Here in early days were established the first trading posts, and here later grew flourishing cities.

Further separating the Coastal Plain from the Carolina Piedmont extends a broad strip of piney barrens. Beyond these barrens, as one continues westward, the Plateau becomes more rugged, the rivers divide and fork into innumerable branches and rivulets which cut their way through a stiff red soil. The forests change in character, the air grows cooler, until at length against the horizon there lifts a misty blue line. Nearer, it resolves itself into a lofty range of peaks, still hung with blue haze, and fronting the southeast with precipitous rocky cliffs.

Here at last is the Blue Ridge. At its foot the early hunter, eager to add to his string of pelts, paused, fearful of hidden foes beyond the ridges. Here, too, the cattle-driver, following in his steps, stopped to raise his rough shelter in the wilderness. And here, still later, the pioneer settler, gazing up at the formidable barrier, halted his pack-horse or wagon and built his cabin by the side of a rushing stream.

The traveler today, weary from his long train ride, looks out at the railway winding serpent-like up the face of the mountain and no longer wonders why westward expansion from the South Atlantic seacoast was so slow. He wonders rather that the first advance to the Far West was begun across this mountain country at a time when the settlers of New York State had scarce ventured beyond the Valleys of the Hudson and the Mohawk, and when Maine and Vermont formed one frontier of a New England which was just beginning to cross the Berkshire barrier.

History has concerned itself but little with our Southern Highlands, except in incidental fashion as it has dealt with movements, early and later, across the mountain barrier to the west, and with settlements within the mountains, notably in the Valley of Virginia and in the Holston region, which marked or contributed to these western movements. From these movements and settlements, however, came the early population of the Highlands, and a brief review of them and their sources is an integral part of any study of the region.

For an explanation of the first large movement into the mountain country, we must turn from the South to Pennsylvania. Hither, between 1720 and 1770 approximately, came many thousand Germans from the Palatinate, Ulster Scotch or Scotch-Irish[1] from the north of Ireland, and immigrants from other countries. It is not necessary here to enter into the causes, political, religious, and economic, that led to their migrations. They were on the whole a sturdy, virile people, fitted by nature and experience to meet the hardships of pioneer life.

There were few good Atlantic ports in the South; New England did not welcome the strangers;[2] and although many went to New York, by far the greatest number were directed to the great central

[1] "From the year 1720 to 1776 this people came on the average of 12,000 a year, or 600,000 people before the Revolution."—Scotch-Irish Society of America, Vol. III, p. 132. Proceedings of the 1st–8th Congress, 1889–1896. Cincinnati, R. Clarke & Co., 8 vols.

Kuhns estimates that the grand total of German immigration was probably 110,000.—Kuhns, Arthur: The German and Swiss Settlements of Colonial Pennsylvania, New York, 1901.

[2] "The explanation of the antipathy excited by the Scotch-Irish immigration lies not in the character of the arrivals, but in the character of the economic system of the community."—Ford, Henry Jones: The Scotch-Irish in America, Ch. VII, p. 224. Princeton University Press, 1915.

port of Philadelphia.[1] The lands lying near the coast of Pennsylvania were by this time comparatively well settled, and it seems to be due largely to this fact and to the abundance of cheap territory farther west, that the newcomers pressed on to the frontier. The movement was, however, undoubtedly encouraged by the colonial authorities, as thereby a barrier was established between the seaboard settlements and the Indians.

The Blue Ridge, it will be recalled, which was so formidable an obstacle to early westward expansion from the southern coast, is lost for an interval in Pennsylvania, and a natural entrance is thus afforded into the part of the Greater Appalachian Valley which lies in that state. Following along the lower courses of the Delaware and Susquehanna, and ascending their tributaries, the early immigrants pre-empted the better lands and entered the Greater Valley. They formed, in Pennsylvania, a great reservoir of population, fed by transatlantic immigration passing through the port of Philadelphia.

That this reservoir, overflowing, should send its first great stream into the Southern Highlands was determined by natural causes. Extending to the southward, the Greater Appalachian Valley with its fertile limestone soil lay like a great pathway walled between highlands to east and west. Pushing on along this pathway through Maryland and what is now West Virginia, the pioneer entered the Valley of Virginia, out of which flow the waters of the Shenandoah to join those of the Potomac. Continuing southward up the Valley, he was moving up to the headwaters of the Shenandoah.

An examination of the river systems will aid in an understanding of his further movements. Interlocking with the headwaters of the Shenandoah are those of the James, and just beyond lie those of the Roanoke—rivers which both flow diagonally southeast across the Valley, out through the Blue Ridge to the Piedmont Plateau, and thence to the Atlantic. Still beyond, to the southwest, and seeming to terminate the Valley, ridges over 3,000 feet in height separate the waters of the Roanoke from those of the New River flowing northwest to the Ohio.

---

[1] "Emigrants usually landed either at Lewes or at Newcastle in Delaware, or in Philadelphia."—Hanna, Charles A.: The Scotch-Irish, Vol. II, p. 60. G. P. Putnam's Sons, 1902.

The southward movement of migration did not at first swell over this divide and continue across New River down the Greater Valley into Tennessee, but as though it were a veritable stream, it was deflected through the Blue Ridge to the southeast, to pour over the lower lying lands of the Carolina Piedmont. It is to be kept in mind that this movement from Pennsylvania to the Carolina Piedmont commonly involved two or three generations of pioneers, each new generation moving on a journey farther into the wilderness. So rapid was the movement, however, that the Virginia Valley, which in 1730 had few inhabitants, by 1750 was well populated; and Mathew Rowan, who in 1746 estimated that in Anson, Orange, and Rowan Counties, which at that time composed the entire section between Virginia and South Carolina, "there was not then one hundred fighting men," in 1753 wrote, "there is now at least 3,000, for the most part Irish Protestants and Germans, and dayley increasing."[1] In 1765 alone, over a thousand immigrant wagons are reported by Governor Tryon to have passed through Salisbury, North Carolina.

The "Great Road from the Yadkin River through Virginia to Philadelphia, distant 435 miles," as indicated on Jeffrey's map,[2] or, to follow it from north to south, from Philadelphia to the Yadkin, ran through Lancaster and York, Pennsylvania, to Winchester, Virginia, up the Shenandoah Valley, across the upper waters of the James to the Roanoke River, thence down the Roanoke through the Blue Ridge southward, crossing the Dan River, and still farther southward to the headwaters of the Yadkin in what is now Forsyth County, North Carolina.

To the southeast of the Blue Ridge barrier, therefore, grew a second reservoir of population, fed not only from the north but from the south by later and lesser streams of transatlantic migration through the ports of Charleston and Wilmington.

There had been early a seepage of settlers into western and southwestern Pennsylvania from the great reservoir in the Valley of Pennsylvania. In 1750 those who had established themselves on the upper waters of the Monongahela had to be warned back by the

[1] North Carolina Colonial Records, Vol. V, pp. 17–18. Mathew Rowan was President and Commander-in-Chief of the Province of North Carolina, 1753–1754.
[2] A map printed many times, first about 1760 and last about 1790.

colonial authorities, as their presence was a provocation to the Indians, always hostile in this region. After the establishment of Fort Pitt in 1759, and the laying out of Pittsburgh in 1765, the western movement to this region began again, to be largely augmented, in the southwestern counties especially, by streams of settlers from Maryland and Virginia. Thus by the time of the Revolution, to the northwest of our territory was formed a third reservoir of population perhaps best visualized in Pittsburgh, which was to influence greatly the settlement of Kentucky and that part of Virginia now known as West Virginia.

While these three reservoirs were forming, two to the north and one to the southeast of the mountain country, the Highlands south of Virginia remained an almost unbroken wilderness. In the region lying west of the Blue Ridge and extending to the Tennessee and Ohio Rivers, even Indian settlements of any size seem to have been infrequent. The country was claimed for the most part by the Cherokee Nation, but it was used as a hunting-ground by other tribes as well. The war-path of both northern and southern Indians ran the entire length of the Greater Valley, branching through Cumberland Gap into Kentucky to the Ohio, and formed the main artery for an intricate network of trails which crossed and recrossed the mountain country.

Into this wilderness hunters and traders had early penetrated. Imagination pictures for us these first daring men who threaded the narrow forest trails and matched their skill against Indian cunning; but few are the records of these woodsmen, forerunners of the pioneer settlers.

It is impossible to trace with any definiteness the early white settlements in this Indian territory. On Mitchell's map, published in 1755, a number are indicated, "Walker's"[1] in the neighborhood of Cumberland Gap being shown as the most western point of English occupation in 1750. A trail is also indicated across the

---

[1] "Dr. Thomas Walker, who lived at Castle Hill, Albemarle County, Virginia, penetrated these wilds in 1750. He went by Staunton and up the Valley, crossing the Alleghany on the watershed at the present site of Blackberry, crossed New River at Horseshoe, went down the river to the mouth of Walker's Creek, and up the creek along the face of Walker's Mountain to the headwaters of the Clinch River. Passing down the Clinch he made his way to the Gap to which he gave the name of Cumberland."—Speed, Thomas: The Wilderness Road, p. 14. Louisville, Ky., John P. Morton & Co., 1886.

divide in southwestern Virginia, and the region about the head-waters of the Holston is marked "Settled."[1] While it is probable that this outpost was destroyed, as were most of those in Indian territory indicated by Mitchell, there appear to have been permanent settlers in the Holston region before 1760.

From the early part of the eighteenth century a series of treaties had been made with the Indians, whereby their boundaries were pushed farther and farther west. The new lines established, however, did not prevent the encroachments of the white men, who continued to raise their cabins beyond the limits defined by the latest treaty, while a fast growing number of traders and hunters penetrated deeper into the wilderness. Suspicious and alarmed, the Indians were further aroused by the instigations of the French, to whose colonial aspirations the westward advance of the English was a constant menace. The Treaty of Paris in 1763 put an end to French pretensions east of the Mississippi; and King George, to placate the Indians, decreed by royal proclamation that there should be no white settlement beyond the sources of streams flowing into the Atlantic. That this decree was impossible to enforce was apparent from the first, and it was generally disregarded.[2] Not only had lands already been granted and purchases made in good faith to the west of this boundary, but new settlers were not to be restrained from entering in ever increasing numbers the forbidden territory.

Out from among the shadowy figures of this period, whose deeds and even whose names were lost in the dark forest, emerges about this time a youth destined to descend to succeeding generations as the great pioneer of American history. Daniel Boone was born near Reading, Pennsylvania, in 1734, but in 1750 his family left for North Carolina, following the old route up the Valley of Virginia, across the Blue Ridge near the dividing line between Vir-

---

[1] This settlement may perhaps be that made by the Inglis and Draper families somewhere about 1750 near the present Blackberry, Virginia, which was raided in 1755 by the Shawnee Indians. Blackberry, however, lies at the headwaters of the Roanoke, and the Roanoke and Holston systems are clearly distinguished on Mitchell's map despite its poor perspective.

[2] An attempt was made to adjust matters by a number of new treaties, of which that at Stanwix, New York, in 1768, with the Iroquois, and of Lochaber, South Carolina, with the Cherokees, in 1770, were the most important. By these various treaties most of West Virginia, Kentucky, and much of North Carolina and eastern Tennessee were ceded to the English.

ginia and North Carolina, and on to the forks of the Yadkin in the Carolina Piedmont. A mighty hunter even in those days of mighty hunters, young Boone was fired by the tales of a returned trader[1] to make a trip of exploration into Kentucky—the first of a number of expeditions which were to result in the laying out of the Wilderness Road and the opening of that western land beyond the mountains.[2] There is a tradition, questioned by some, that in the spring of 1769 Boone and James Robertson stood on a mountain path and looked down upon the beautiful Valley of the Watauga. It was in this region in this same year that William Bean, from Virginia, settled in what is now known as the Valley of East Tennessee, but was then supposed to be Virginia, later found to belong to North Carolina, and for a while was embraced within the territory known as the state of Franklin. This was the first permanent settlement of which we have authentic record within the present state of Tennessee.

At first this settlement seems to have been but an extension of that mentioned previously as existing before 1760 in Virginia at the headwaters of the Holston, but it was soon increased by accessions of other settlers. In 1771 came James Robertson with sixteen families from North Carolina; and in 1772 followed Sevier, later to be the first governor of the state of Tennessee. Within a few years of Bean's coming there were a number of hunters, herders, and small farmers with their families in the valleys of the Watauga, Nolichucky, Holston, and Clinch. Just how many came directly from Virginia, and how many from North Carolina, and when they came, is impossible to say, but after the defeat of the Regulators[3] in the Battle of Alamance, 1771, their numbers were largely increased by migrations from the Piedmont counties of North

---

[1] Probably John Finley, or Findlay, a Scotch-Irish trader with whom Boone is supposed to have first made acquaintance during Braddock's campaign. Finley had been through Ouasioto, or Cumberland Gap about 1752, and recounted to Boone in glowing terms his memories of the immense herds of buffaloes he had seen in Kentucky, the abundance of bears, deer, and elk, the great salt licks where they gathered, and the innumerable flocks of wild turkeys, geese, and ducks. See Henderson, Archibald: The Conquest of the Old Southwest, Ch. X. New York, Century, 1920.

[2] See Appendix C.

[3] A body of associates in western Carolina, formed to preserve order on the frontier, and to resist the collection of excessive and fraudulent taxes. For fuller information see Ch. VI, p. 91.

Carolina. In 1772 these scattered settlements were formed into an association known as the Watauga Association.[1]

Writing of this association in his Winning of the West, Theodore Roosevelt says:

> It is this fact of the early independence and self-government of the settlers along the headwaters of the Tennessee, that gives to their history its peculiar importance. They were the first men of American birth to establish a free and independent community on the continent. Even before this date there had been straggling settlements of Pennsylvanians and Virginians along the headwaters of the Ohio; but these settlements remained mere parts of the colonies behind them, and neither grew into a separate community, nor played a distinctive part in the growth of the west.[2]

The next few years witnessed a great influx of hunters and explorers into Kentucky, despite the continued and fierce opposition of the Indians. Boone, in 1773, leading a party of six families which included the first white women and children to enter Kentucky, endeavored to make a settlement, but was attacked and forced to turn back. His eldest son and five others of the party were killed.

[1] There was great disappointment among the settlers in the Watauga region when it was found that they were on North Carolina instead of Virginia soil. Under Virginia they could have expected some protection from the Indians, but the government of North Carolina east of the mountains was too unsettled to afford help to any settlers to the west. The formation of the Watauga Association secured for six years not only a peaceful administration of local affairs, but a certain measure of preparedness against Indian attack. When the association came to an end through the creation by North Carolina of Washington County, now Tennessee, the general system of government continued to work successfully for some years longer. When, however, North Carolina ceded her lands lying "west of the mountains and extending to the Mississippi" to the Federal Government, giving the Government two years in which to accept, not only was great doubt felt in the Holston region as to the Government accepting the territory, but the settlers felt that while the matter was pending they would be left unprotected. North Carolina, also, had not acceded to demands which the association felt to be just. The Wataugans therefore set up an independent state which they called Franklin, adopted a constitution, and carried on their own negotiations with the Indians. So scarce was money in this new state that the following according to Haywood (History of Tennessee, p. 150) were recognized as currency: "Good flax linen ten hundred, at three shillings and six pence per yard; good clean beaver skins, six shillings each; raccoon and fox skins, at one shilling and three pence; deer skins, six shillings; bacon at six pence per lb; tallow at six pence; good whiskey at two shillings and six pence a gallon." Lack of recognition by the Federal Government, internal dissension, and poverty, led, in two years, to collapse.

[2] Roosevelt: Winning of the West, Vol. I, p. 231.

The defeat of the Indians north of the Ohio, at the close, in 1774, of Lord Dunmore's War, secured the outposts a brief respite from Indian attack, and with the cession of lands in Kentucky opened the way for the establishment of permanent transmontane settlements. In 1775 Boone was employed by "a number of North Carolina gentlemen"[1] to lay out the Wilderness Road, which offered a direct route from the Watauga Settlement to Cumberland Gap, and thence to the fertile limestone lands of Kentucky. In that same year were laid the foundations of Boonesborough and Harrodsburg.

A review of the population of the Southern Highlands on the eve of the Revolution shows the Valley of Virginia northeast of the divide well populated; scattered clearings follow the valleys on the upper courses of the Greenbrier and Kanawha Rivers in what is now West Virginia, and mark the vicinity of Fort Henry, later the city of Wheeling; and in the Valley in southwestern Virginia and northeastern Tennessee are planted a sturdy group of federated settlements coming to be known as the Holston Settlements. Beyond the Highlands to the west, and separated even from Watauga by over two hundred miles of wilderness, are the feeble beginnings of the state of Kentucky. They all marked, as it were, the first rivulets from the reservoirs banked to northwest and southeast, which after the Revolution were to overflow through the Highlands to that great western country as yet scarcely discovered.

The years of the Revolution were strenuous ones on the frontier. The Indians, whose services were enlisted by the British, continued to harass the whole border, and the settlers, shut away by long miles of ridges, could expect little help from east of the mountains where all were engaged in the struggle for independence. On them alone, therefore, fell the defense of the montane and transmontane settlements.

One is tempted to dwell upon the many thrilling tales, half-legendary, that have come down to us of these pioneer leaders—

---

[1] These gentlemen were Colonel Richard Henderson and eight others, who, by a treaty with the Cherokees in 1775, had obtained title to all the land lying between the Kentucky and Cumberland Rivers, some seventeen million acres. The "Proprietors of the Colony of Transylvania," as they called themselves, were not allowed by the Virginia legislature to hold this immense territory, but Henderson, in consideration of his services, was granted 200,000 acres on the Ohio.

Sevier, Robertson, Clark, Shelby, Campbell, and many others whose names are inseparably associated with the history of this period—but it is perhaps enough to say that under their able guidance not only was the foothold already obtained in the west strengthened during the war, but new steps were taken forward into the wilderness. Slowly settlement crept down the valleys of the Nolichucky,[1] Holston, and Clinch; and in 1779 Robertson set out from Watauga for the Cumberland country to make the beginnings of what is now Nashville. Nor must we leave this period without turning to view again those stalwart frontier fighters, who in 1780, the darkest year for American independence, went out by forest trail and gap to dislodge the British from King's Mountain and stem the tide of war.[2] "Rearguard of the Revolution," they have been called, and America owes to them the opening and possession of the great West.

Movement through the mountains had continued even during the Revolution, but at its close the western settlements drew to themselves from all our reservoirs of population; they drew even

[1] "In 1778–9 Jonesboro, the oldest town in Tennessee, and county-seat of Washington County, was laid out, and court-house and jail erected."—Rule, William: History of Knoxville. Chicago, Lewis Publishing Co., 1900.

[2] Major Ferguson, dispatched by Cornwallis into the western part of North Carolina to "subdue the back counties," sent word to the Watauga settlers that if "they did not desist from their opposition to the British Arms, he would cross the mountains, hang their leaders, and lay waste the country with fire and sword." In characteristic fashion the frontiersmen determined to attack Ferguson at once, before he could move upon them. At Sycamore Shoals of the Watauga River they gathered, over 1,200 men, including some 400 from the Virginia frontier. A draft was taken to provide a guard for the home settlements. Then, after a powerful sermon by the famous Presbyterian pastor, Dr. Doak, in which he exhorted them to "go forth with the sword of the Lord and of Gideon," they set out to cross the mountains. All were armed with the usual rifle, tomahawk, and hunting-knife, and wore sprigs of evergreen in their coon-skin caps; nearly all were well mounted. Ferguson, forewarned of their approach, discreetly retired from Gilbert Town in Rutherford County, and entrenched himself just over the border in South Carolina, on King's Mountain, from which he stoutly asserted that neither "God Almighty nor all the rebels outside hell, could dislodge him." The frontiersmen, under William Campbell, John Sevier, and Isaac Shelby, after thirty hours in the saddle, drenched by rain, and with inferior numbers, proceeded at once to storm the stronghold. They fought with a combination of tactical skill and Indian cunning, taking advantage of every bit of cover. The battle lasted for some hours, during which, the old chronicler tells us "the whole mountain was covered with smoke and seemed to thunder"; but at last Ferguson was killed and his men who were left alive surrendered. Not more than a month later part of this same band of frontiersmen fought the Indians at Boyd's Creek, Kentucky, more than three hundred miles away across the mountains.

from the territory north of Pennsylvania, sweeping in their stream some from the frontiers of New York and New England.

The great northwest territory of Ohio, Indiana, Illinois, and Michigan, which in the next century was to be the goal of desire, had not at this time been clearly defined by treaty boundaries and was occupied by hostile tribes. Northern routes, moreover, were dangerous of travel, and not made safe until the British, by Jay's Treaty in 1795, gave over the Lake Forts.

For many years, therefore, the tide of migration to the west flowed along the southern routes. The Kentucky country was widely known for its fertility. It was also accessible, and its government was early organized and stable. To this pioneer land of promise, then, migration flowed in a swollen stream after the Revolution.

A study of this great westward migration shows it moving along two main lines or routes—one the famous so-called Wilderness Road, a large part of whose course lay within our Southern Highlands, and the other the Ohio River, which forms part of the northwest boundary of the mountain region.

The Wilderness Road was the first route to the west to be extensively used. To reach it from the north, emigrants followed the old route up the Valley of Virginia; but instead of turning southeast to the Piedmont, they crossed the divide in southwestern Virginia to Fort Chissell. This rude block-house and outpost in the wilderness, built in 1758 by Colonel Bird as a menace to the Cherokee Indians, was situated near the site of the present Wytheville, on the headwaters of the New or Kanawha River, which flows northwest across the Valley through West Virginia to the Ohio. Here the traveler reached the borders of the "great Wilderness," that dark and mysterious forest which stretched over valley and mountain almost two hundred miles to the Cumberlands, whose cliffs, in the words of Boone, were "so wild and horrid that it is impossible to view them without terror." Thence it was about one hundred and fifty miles to the young transmontane settlements. So dense was this forest wilderness that travelers are said to have moved in a leafy gloom, lightened only where a great tree had fallen and let in the sky.

Interlocking with the headwaters of the New River, those of the

32

Holston flow south until, joining the Clinch, whose sources lie not far to the west of its own, they form the Tennessee. The course of the traveler followed down the Holston Valley to the region of the Holston settlements, the first outposts in the wilderness, and later, receiving stations through which passed the great migrations to the Far West. Here was a block-house, and here travelers rested in comparative safety before facing the dangers of the next step in the wilderness.

It might be supposed that the tide would have continued to the junction of the Clinch and Holston,[1] and so on down the Tennessee.[2] Later travelers wishing to reach the Cumberland settlements about Nashville did indeed proceed this way as far as Fort Campbell, situated on the site of the present Kingston, Tennessee. They then struck up the plateau through Crab Orchard, and across and down to Nashville, or on to southwestern Kentucky. After 1783 this route was marked by a well-defined wagon road. Knoxville was not founded and named until 1791, although a fort was there in 1786 "on the extreme border-land of the Indian country."

But the greatest number of travelers turned northward from the Holston settlements, across the Holston River, into Virginia through Moccasin Gap, across the Clinch, over a spur of Powell's Mountain, and down Powell's Valley to Cumberland Gap.[3] This great portal to the west, once probably a river gap, was situated at the point where the boundaries of Virginia, Tennessee, and Kentucky come together, and to it converged many trails. An important contributing route from North Carolina was joined at the French Broad by one from South Carolina, probably just about where the railroad line runs today, and this in turn was joined by another route which led from Augusta, Georgia. From Cumber-

---

[1] By Act of the Tennessee legislature, April 6, 1887, the Tennessee River now begins at the junction of the North Fork of the Holston with the Holston at Kingsport, Tennessee. In early descriptions, however, the river was known as the Holston to the point where it united with the Clinch at Kingston.

[2] This route was pursued, 1779–1780, by most of Robertson's party, who took boats down the Tennessee, and up the Ohio and Cumberland—a perilous route on account of the hostility of the Chickamaugas. Generally, however, prior to 1783, early travelers came into western Tennessee and Kentucky by the Wilderness Road, through Cumberland Gap as far as Rockcastle Hills, then turned south and followed a trace which led to the Bluffs on Cumberland River, afterward Nashville. This was the course taken by Robertson himself in 1779.

[3] See Appendix C.

land Gap the Wilderness Road passed northwest to the Bluegrass region of Kentucky.[1]

Records are few of the great concourse which for many years passed to the west over this rough trail. Usually the travelers formed companies to lessen the danger of Indian attack, and axe and rifle were always ready. Until 1795 the road was but a trace, to be traveled only on foot or horseback. In the years before the road was open to wagons, 75,000 persons at least are estimated to have passed over it.

> Through privations incredible and perils thick, thousands of men, women, and children came in successive caravans, forming continuous streams of human beings, horses, cattle, and other domestic animals, all moving onward along a lonely and house-less path to a wild and cheerless land. Cast your eyes back on that long procession of missionaries in the cause of civilization; behold the men on foot with their trusty guns on their shoulders, driving stock and leading pack-horses; and the women, some walking with pails on their heads, others riding with children in their laps, and other children swung in baskets on horses fastened to the tails of others going before; see them encamped at night expecting to be massacred by Indians; behold them in the month of December, in that ever memorable season of unprecedented cold called the "hard winter," traveling two or three miles a day, frequently in danger of being frozen or killed by the falling of horses on the icy and almost impassable trace, and subsisting on stinted allowances of stale bread and meat; but now lastly look at them at the destined fort, perhaps on the eve of merry Christmas, when met by the hearty welcome of friends who had come before, and cheered by fresh buffalo meat and parched corn, they rejoice at their deliverance, and resolve to be contented with their lot.[2]

The Ohio River route had its great portal at Pittsburgh, situated where the Allegheny and Monongahela unite to form the Ohio. Along the Allegheny came immigrants from Philadelphia;

[1] There are two important branches of the road in Kentucky; one laid out by Boone followed a buffalo trace to Rockcastle River, and thence up Roundstone Creek, through Boone's Gap in Big Hill, through the present county of Madison, down Otter Creek to its mouth at Kentucky River. About one mile below the mouth of Otter Creek, Boone established his fort and called it Boonesborough.

The other branch, laid out by Logan in 1775, left Boone's at Rockcastle River and bore west through Crab Orchard to the falls of the Ohio. This became known especially as "the road leading through the great wilderness."—Speed, Thomas: The Wilderness Road, pp. 26-27. Louisville, Ky., John P. Morton and Co., 1886.

[2] Chief Justice Robertson, in an address quoted ibid., p. 41.

while those from Maryland and Virginia followed the Monongahela. The latter often, however, cut across to Wheeling, ninety miles below Pittsburgh, and took boat there or followed down the Greenbrier to the Kanawha and thence to the Ohio. In any case they were carried in "keel-boats and Kentucky flat-boats and Indian pirogues," generally in flotillas down the Ohio to Limestone, Kentucky, at the site of the present Maysville, and there disembarking, continued across the country by well-marked roads. Returning travelers almost always came overland to avoid the pull against the current.

This route, at first less used because of the greater danger of Indian attack and the difficulty, too, and expense of securing boats, became during the last decade of the century so important as to deflect most of the northern migration from its old channel through the Highlands. "Its complete downfall," says Bruce, speaking of the Wilderness Road, "may be said to have been accomplished with the building of the celebrated national turnpike, the Cumberland Road, which led from Baltimore through Cumberland, Maryland, where unhappy Braddock had marshalled his troops, to Wheeling, in West Virginia, being ultimately extended into Ohio."[1] This new road, which greatly shortened and improved the old Monongahela route to the Ohio, was, during the second quarter of the nineteenth century, one of the great highways between east and west. A description given by Colonel Searight, of its aspect during the height of its use, forms an interesting contrast to the account quoted above of the stream of settlers passing through Cumberland Gap:

> As many as twenty four-horse coaches have been counted in a line at one time on the road, and large broad-wheeled wagons, covered with white canvas stretched over bows, laden with merchandise and drawn by six Conestoga horses, were visible all day long at every point, and many times until late in the evening, besides innumerable caravans of horses, mules, cattle, hogs, and sheep. It looked more like the leading avenue of a great city than a road through rural districts.[2]

All of these routes, it must be remembered, while undoubtedly affecting the growth of population in the Southern Highlands, were

[1] Bruce, H. A. B.: Daniel Boone and the Wilderness Road, p. 298. New York, The Macmillan Company, 1910.

[2] Searight, Thomas B.: The Old Pike, p. 16. Uniontown, Pa., 1894.

not directed primarily to the mountains, but through them to the west. Some settlements which have been indicated, already existed within the limits of our territory, and these continued to grow and expand, but not by leaps and bounds as was the case in Kentucky.[1] Indeed, many who for awhile shared the fortunes of the mountain settlers joined the westward tide, and, like Robertson of Watauga, moved on to found new cities beyond the ridges.

Early settlements within the Southern Highlands were either in parts of the Greater Appalachian Valley, or in the larger river valleys of the upland belts to the east and west of it, on or near what were to become important routes of travel. The relation of these valleys to each other, and to the river systems, suggests the course of further settlement within the mountain country.

South of the New River Divide in Virginia the drainage of the Southern Highlands is into the Ohio and the Gulf, save for the steep eastern slopes of the Blue Ridge, down which plunge streams which are to find their way into rivers flowing across the Piedmont Plateau and Coastal Plain into the Atlantic. Thus to the population massed in the Carolina Piedmont, about the headwaters of the Yadkin, the Catawba, and other eastward flowing streams, and separated by wide piney barrens from the coastal settlements, were offered natural routes of travel up to the sources of these rivers, high in the Blue Ridge Front, and thence to the nearby headwaters of the Nolichucky, French Broad, and other waters which flow northwest down into the major streams of the Greater Valley. The main routes leading from the Valley across the Allegheny-Cumberland Plateau to the west have already been described.

It is not to be understood that the pioneer always followed closely the bed of a river, though the use of water, as defined by a mountain pupil today, "to make a road," was well recognized in frontier times. On the contrary, the Indian and buffalo trails

---

[1] The population in the forks of the Holston in 1790 is variously estimated from "thousands" to 40,000.

Roosevelt (Winning of the West, Vol. III, p. 276) says: "When peace was declared with Great Britain, the backwoodsmen had spread westward in groups almost to the Mississippi, and they had increased in numbers to some 25,000 souls, of whom a few hundred dwelt in the bend of the Cumberland while the rest were about equally divided between Kentucky and Holston. These figures are simply estimates, but they are based on careful study and comparison, and though they must be some hundreds, and maybe some thousands out of the way, are quite near enough for practical purposes."

36

which he commonly used kept often to the high ground, even to the top of the ridges, their general course controlled by the direction of the ranges, location of gaps, and courses of streams.

An inference, however, as to the early importance of rivers, creeks, and branches as routes of travel, may be gathered from a recital of directions actually given to the writer a year ago when he was about to take a ninety-mile ride from one mountain school to another and thence to a county-seat. These directions, it should be explained, were not furnished by one person, the morning informant generally closing his instructions with the advice to "stop by and ask . . . , at the mouth of . . . , and he will tell you how to go."

"Go up the Trace Branch of the right fork of Troublesome; down Betty's Troublesome to Carr; down Carr to the mouth of Defeated; up to the head of Defeated; over a mountain; down Bull's Creek to the North Fork of the River; down the River for a mile to the mouth of Leatherwood; up Leatherwood four miles to Stony Fork; up Stony Fork to the head; cross the mountain; follow down the least branch on yon side of the mountain to Line Fork; up Line Fork to the headwaters of Greasy; down Greasy to the 'college.'

"From the 'college' go down Greasy six miles to the mouth of Rockhouse; go up Rockhouse and take the right fork over the mountain; across Wolf and Coon to the headwaters of Cutshin; down Cutshin, fording three times; up Flacky, across a right rough little hill to the head of Owl's Nest; down Owl's Nest to Middle Fork, and up Middle Fork a piece to a deep ford; ford the River, and you are at the place you are aiming at."[1]

---

[1] Notes on directions:

Trace Branch. There are a number of "trace" branches or forks in the mountains of Kentucky. They are the branches or forks of streams which the trail or trace follows.

Defeated. According to tradition, some hunters were defeated here by Indians, and several killed.

Leatherwood. So-called from a kind of tree formerly prevalent along its course. As described by our host, "hit were a tree what sprangles out at the top, kindly like a rosy bush."

Greasy. According to our host, called Licking Branch when Kentucky was part of Virginia; then Laurel, from one of its tributaries; later, a hunter killed a bear upon a flat rock, threw the entrails into the creek which became greasy in appearance; asked where the bear was killed, he replied, "Up there on Greasy," and the name stuck.

Rockhouse. So called from the rocky banks being worn away by the action of the stream, with tops overhanging like a roof.

Cutshin. One tradition holds that it was named from an accident to a wood-

Clearness of understanding as to progress of settlement will be facilitated if the Highland country be pictured as consisting of two parts: first, the Valley section, which includes the Greater Appalachian Valley and the larger river valleys of the two belts that border it; and secondly, the more rugged portions of the mountain country composed of the ridges and mountains which separate the larger valleys. There are, of course, within the ridge and mountain sections lesser valleys, and the rivulets and branches which find their way down the mountain slopes are tributaries of the larger streams of the major valleys, and also trails or "traces" from minor valley to minor valley, and from minor to greater valley. There is often, too, bordering these lesser streams, much fertile and tillable land, so that settlement has been pushed at times to the springs which feed them.

Viewing the Southern Highlands as a whole, the accessible valleys were first settled. The passage of military expeditions and western settlers over the mountain trails, from the Carolinas into Tennessee, early advertised the fertility of the broader valleys and led toward the close of the eighteenth century to the rise of such mountain communities as Morganton and Asheville,[1] North Carolina. The country along the main routes of travel would naturally be soonest developed, although this was by no means always true. As late as 1790 there was a stretch of one hundred miles on the Wilderness Road with no sign of habitation, and Michaux,[2] in 1796, traveling a much used trace in North Carolina, reports many miles along the road desolate and unpopulated.

The cessions, at different periods, of lands held by the Indians were determining factors in settlement. The Highlands were not open to white occupation by one treaty but by a series of treaties. Consequently some mountain areas were available earlier than some valley areas, though it was true that with each cession the valleys were settled earlier than the ridges.

The last treaty of the Colonial Period that affected the High-

cutter, who here cut his shin. Another, to the effect that here in winter the stream freezes so hard as to cut the shins of mules and horses which break through the ice.

[1] Tradition has it that the earliest settler of Buncombe County came in by way of Old Fort to the headwaters of the Swannanoa River, and down its valley, a route now followed by the Salisbury and Asheville Branch of the Southern Railway.

[2] Michaux, Vol. III, in Reuben G. Thwaites' Early Western Travels.

lands was that of July 20, 1777, when a tract of 6,064 square miles, largely of mountain land within western North Carolina and eastern Tennessee abutting it, was given over by the Cherokees. Including this cession there was thus open to entry by 1777, all of our territory in Maryland, Virginia, West Virginia, Kentucky, almost all of the limited upland section of South Carolina, and about one-fourth of western North Carolina and east Tennessee—in all, an area of approximately 68,000 of the 112,000 square miles of the Southern Highlands.

The first Indian treaty made after the establishment of the Federal Government was that of November 28, 1785, when the boundaries of the Cherokee Nation were defined. These boundaries, however, did not enlarge the amount of land available within the Southern Highlands, save for an area of 550 square miles along the French Broad River in North Carolina, lying just west of the land ceded on July 20, 1777. By successive treaties more of the Highlands was opened to occupation, but it was not until 1805 that Indian claims to the Cumberland Plateau section of Tennessee were extinguished; and not until 1835–1838, when the Cherokees gave over all of their land east of the Mississippi and were finally removed to their reservation beyond it, that the larger part of our territory in northern Georgia and northeastern Alabama and the last mountain lands in western North Carolina and southeastern Tennessee were legally free for entry. Even then a few Cherokees, still unresigned to banishment from the land of their ancestors, refused exile and hid themselves in the wilderness. A small reservation was later set aside for them in western North Carolina, where their descendants still live.

It is not to be supposed, however, that there were no cabins raised on Indian soil prior to the drawing of treaties. Early descriptions of lands, metes, and bounds, were inaccurate, and unintentional transgression often took place. There was also wilful transgression in the appropriation of lands, and individual squatters would occupy tracts apparently with the hope that later treaties with the Indians would legalize their holdings. Speaking generally, however, there were few settlements in the mountain-ridge section until the last decade of the century and none in large numbers until after 1800.

39

The Watauga Settlement in 1769 served as an advance guard to that of the mountain-ridge section. While in general it may be said that the broad central valleys of the Holston, Watauga, and Nolichucky offered sufficient opportunity for the expansion of population for some years, yet, from the time of William Bean's entrance into this mountain region, the valleys of the neighboring ranges began to receive a scattering immigration. Almost contemporaneously, home seekers made their appearance in western North Carolina, which is geographically a part of the same mountain area. These sections were settled partly from the Watauga district of Tennessee, and partly from the North and South Carolina Piedmont frontier.

In eastern Kentucky it is probable that the first settlers entered the border counties somewhat after 1790, and that its mountains as a whole did not receive any great influx of population until after 1800. This was largely due to the fact that in Kentucky the Wilderness Road passed for most of its course to the west of the mountains, and that on account of the Cumberland barrier to the east there were few gateways into the eastern part of Kentucky.

Imlay, whose travels were first published in 1792, referring undoubtedly to the mountainous areas within West Virginia, western Virginia, and eastern Kentucky, says:

> The country that separates the back counties of Virginia from Kentucky is the greater part of it mountainous, and through which to its champaign lands is nearly 250 miles, the whole of that tract of wilderness, extending from Holston nearly north, crossing the Great Sandy River, the Great and Little Kanhaways, quite into the fine lands in the district belonging to Pennsylvania, exclusive of some small tracts in the upper counties of Virginia upon the Ohio, all of which are occupied, is altogether broken into high, rugged, and barren hills, the bottoms excepted, and, in all probability will not be inhabited for centuries to come, by reason of the immense tracts of good lands lying west of the Ohio and Mississippi.[1]

adding:

> that tract of country lying southeasterly from Holston and extending to Cumberland; Powell's Valley, Nolichucky, French Broad, and Clinch excepted, is little better.

[1] Imlay, Gilbert: A Topographic Description of the Western Territory of North America, p. 239. New York, Samuel Campbell, 1793.

This later reference, we may infer, is to the mountainous mass, or at least to a portion of it, which in its entirety includes the mountainous section of eastern Tennessee, western North Carolina, and part of northern Georgia.

It is probable that much of the settlement of the mountain-ridge section was due to the natural increase of families, the rapid succession of generations pushing their clearings farther and farther up creeks and minor valleys away from the land already under cultivation by older members of their families. There was, too, more or less movement back to the mountains by families who had passed through to the west, and who then, for various causes, turned back and took up land in the mountain-ridge section.

This rougher country of itself had certain definite assets which invited immigration. Among these, the discovery of salt springs in Kentucky and West Virginia was a strong inducement to settlement. These "licks," so called from the fact that the spring basins incrusted with salt were the resort of buffalo, elk, deer, and other wild game, had long been familiar to the Indians, who had manufactured salt in early times. The lack of this commodity was keenly felt by the first settlers, and even now there are in the mountains those who tell of the long annual journey to the east, made by their great-grandparents in search of salt.[1]

The rapid growth of population in the region of a salt spring may be illustrated by the early history of Clay County, Kentucky.

[1] The importance of the discovery of salt in the development of the United States is thus described by Turner:

"The early settlers were tied to the coast by the need of salt, without which they could not preserve their meats or live in comfort. Writing in 1752, Bishop Spangenburg says of a colony for which he was seeking lands in North Carolina: 'They will require salt & other necessaries which they can neither manufacture nor raise. Either they must go to Charleston, which is 300 miles distant . . . Or else they must go down to Boling's Point in Va. on a branch of the James & is also 300 miles from here . . . Or else they must go down the Roanoke—I know not how many miles—where salt is brought up from the Cape Fear.' This may serve as a typical illustration. An annual pilgrimage to the coast for salt thus became essential. Taking flocks or furs and ginseng root, the early settlers sent their pack trains after seeding time each year to the coast. This proved to be an important educational influence, since it was almost the only way in which the pioneer learned what was going on in the East. But when discovery was made of the salt springs of the Kanawha, and the Holston, and Kentucky, and central New York, the West began to be freed from dependence on the coast. It was in part the effect of finding these salt springs that enabled settlement to cross the mountains."—Turner, Frederick Jackson: The Frontier in American History, Report of the American Historical Association, 1893.

The first settler of whom there is record in this section, one James Collins, is said to have discovered a salt spring in 1800 while following a buffalo trace, and to have made the first salt ever made in that country. In the court house at Manchester, Clay County, Kentucky, there is on record the sale to James White, of Washington County, Virginia—a quartermaster of General Cox of Tennessee—the salt mines of Ballenger, occupied by outlaw[1] and patented under a grant to Jacob Meyers—4,000 acres. This was in 1804. Two years later the population had so increased as to lead to the organization of the county. As late as 1846, Clay County had fifteen furnaces producing 200,000 bushels of salt annually. So great indeed was the attraction of the salt works as to lead to a back settlement of this section from central Kentucky, and tradition presents the picture of wealthy landlords from the Bluegrass living on baronial mountain estates in almost feudal fashion, surrounded by slaves and retainers.

The discovery of gold in northern Georgia in 1828 brought into that part of the mountains hundreds of people in search of treasure. It will be recalled that this section, then known as Cherokee County, was, together with northern Alabama and parts of North Carolina and southeastern Tennessee, held by the Cherokees until 1838. The inrush of gold seekers into Indian territory, with the drinking, gaming, and brawling that accompanied it, provoked from Governor Gilmer of Georgia the following letter, dated May 6, 1830, and addressed to John McPherson Berrien, then Attorney-General of the United States:

> I am in doubt as to what ought to be done with the gold diggers. They with their various attendants, foragers, and suppliers, make up between six and ten thousand persons. They occupy the country between the Chestatee and Etowah Rivers, near the mountains, gold being found in the greatest quantity deposited in the small streams, which flow into these rivers.[2]

In spite of the Governor's proclamation prohibiting gold mining in north Georgia, these "paper bullets" as he described them, "had little influence over a people who could not read," and miners man-

[1] Occupied by squatters until they had obtained title by adverse possession.
[2] Quoted in A Preliminary Report on a Part of the Gold Deposits of Georgia, by W. S. Yeates, S. W. McCallie, and F. P. King, Bulletin No. 4 A, Geological Survey of Georgia. Atlanta, Ga., 1896.

aged to continue operations. The first deposit of gold from Georgia, made in 1830, amounted to $212,000; and so important were these fields that a branch of the United States Mint established at Dahlonega, Lumpkin County, in 1838, was maintained for some years. While many of the gold seekers left the country after the first rush was over, some remained to become permanent residents.[1]

Other causes which brought settlers to the mountains were war bounties to soldiers, often taking the form of grants of land, and the opening up of Indian boundaries. In addition, the mountain country was rich in game and timber, and had a cool climate and an abundance of pure water.

For many years, even as late as the middle of the nineteenth century, immigrants in large numbers continued to travel along the mountain trails and passes. The conditions causing these migrations were religious, social, and economic. The struggle of the non-conformists, especially the Baptists,[2] against the Established Church in Virginia; social conditions of the Tidewater; and in particular the Revolution, which freed the western territory from restraint, and thus offered new opportunities to men impoverished by long war, were all factors in the early movements.

By 1800 the great migration from north to west had been deflected almost entirely from the Wilderness Road to the Ohio River route, or was moving overland toward the great northwestern territory of Ohio, Indiana, Illinois, Missouri, and Michigan, then open to settlement and accessible by northern routes. Emigration from Virginia and the Carolinas, especially from the Tidewater sections, however, continued for many years to flow through the mountains both by the old channels and by routes not before available because of danger from Indian attack. Thus in Ken-

---

[1] "Gold was looked for in all these Cherokee counties, and so the lots were only 40 acres in size. When gold was not found, and there was no indication of it, the lands were very cheap; from $10.00 to $20.00 was the price of a single lot, and many a man bought a small farm for the price of an Indian pony. The cheapness of the lands led to rapid and thick settlement. The country was soon filled up with enterprising young people, and numbers who became substantial farmers on large farms began life in one of these Cherokee Counties on forty acres of poor land."—Smith, George Gillman: The Story of Georgia and the Georgia People, 1732 to 1860, pp. 423–424.

[2] See Chapter VIII, p. 158 ff.

tucky, while numbers used the great routes of early days, emigrants later were also able to pass directly from Virginia into Kentucky through gaps in the wall of the Cumberlands and by trails along the Kanawha,[1] Big Sandy, and other rivers. Many now living in the eastern part of the state claim that their ancestors came in through one of the various eastern gaps,[2] and it has often been said that the Kentucky mountains were populated almost entirely by Virginia. This is undoubtedly an overstatement, for the evidence of names, pension lists, and Kentucky traditions as well, point to a large percentage of settlers from North Carolina; yet in connection with the claim just mentioned, it will serve to indicate the later lines of movement through the mountains.

The history of the migrations of one of these Kentucky families, as given by the original pioneer's great-great-grandson, whose grandmother remembered the journey and told him of it, may be suggestive, the more in that it is probably the history of much of

[1] "The main New-Kanawha Trail with which they (the more northern transmontane trails) connected, and its branches, were regarded in Virginia simply as portage paths to the head of navigation on the Kanawha River, whence the Ohio might be gained. . . . It was not until after 1783, when Indian attacks had become less frequent, . . . that serious attention was given to the betterment of the main trail and a Kentucky extension, as a 'short cut' between east and west. . . . Imlay's map, published 1793, gives the 'New Road to Virginia,' extending from Lexington by way of the junction of the two forks of the Big Sandy at Balclutta, now Louisa, to the falls of the Kanawha, where it connects with the main road, which extends along the Kanawha and Greenbrier Rivers to Winchester, situated on the road leading to Richmond, Alexandria, and other cities. Indian attacks rendered this route unsafe until after the close of the period."—Verhoeff, Mary: The Kentucky Mountains, Transportation and Commerce, 1793 to 1911, Ch. III, p. 90 ff. Filson Club Publication No. 26.

[2] "The first County Judge was Nat Collins, son of Jim Collins, and a very strong preacher, who came here in 1806 from North Carolina and was making his way for the Bluegrass section. There were eight men and women and Preacher Collins led the bunch. They had come by the way of Cumberland Gap and did not know how to get across the Stone Mountain into the Bluegrass region. There was no Cumberland Gap tunnel then or any railroads, only a wild wilderness. The bunch came up Powell's River to where Wise, Va., is now, and struck out through the Pound Gap and on to the head of Kentucky River and down the river to where Whitesburg is now located. There was not a family living in Letcher County then, as Daniel Boone had left his camp at the mouth of Boone's Fork and went to the fort at Boonesborough, so they passed through where Whitesburg now is and up Sandlick Creek and over a hill on to Camp Branch. It was just before Christmas and they all went up a small drean under a cliff and laid out. The next morning the snow was six feet deep, and they were all covered with snow. The snow lasted about three months, so they lay up all winter, and the men would kill deer and wild turkey, and they all had a very good time camping out."—History of Corporal Fess Whitaker, Life in the Kentucky Mountains, Mexico, and Texas, p. 107. Louisville, Ky., Standard Printing Co., 1918.

the settlement in the mountain section of Kentucky.[1] In 1825 one Ambrose Amburgey came over from the Clinch River, Virginia, into what is now Knott County, Kentucky. The country was exceedingly rough, but he found a couple, James and Priscilla Davis, living near the mouth of Defeated Branch. From them he bought, for $600, the rights to over 10,000 acres of lands along Carr Creek, a narrow but fertile and lovely valley. He then went back to Virginia, gathered up his wife and two children, his parents, and brothers-in-law, together with their families and their slaves— in all a goodly company. The next year they started for Kentucky, going through the Pound Gap into Letcher County. There they "tented" and made their crop through the summer. In the autumn they moved on to Carr. Amburgey settled the several families along various parts of his purchase. The children were many, ten or fifteen in each household, and in a generation or so there were literally hundreds of the family in that region. Now, in this and neighboring counties, there are thousands of their descendants.

That some settlers came unintentionally into the mountains of Kentucky, through the purchase of land which they had supposed

[1] The old surveys and land patents of eastern Kentucky, dating 1815–1825, were made along either side of the big rivers and creeks; that is to say, they covered the larger valleys. In the beginning when land was plentiful, little importance was attached to the smaller valleys or to the ridge slopes. It is possible that the settlers did not claim these, or it may be that they did not consider it necessary to designate them especially. Later, however, as families increased greatly, the value of land bordering the small streams and on the sides of the mountains became apparent. Many of the original owners moved their patents back, and back again, of their first boundaries, but in the course of time it became commonly accepted that a man holding a patent covering the valley or bottom land where he lived, owned on either side in a straight line to the top of the ridge, even if this was not so entered on his survey. Blazing, or otherwise marking such boundaries, was held sufficient evidence of ownership.

The indefiniteness of such claims gave rise not only to great confusion but to the practice of "wild-catting," which was at its height from 1860–1870. "Wild-catters" were men who, through familiarity with the country, or through agents or surveyors who were familiar with it, knew the deficiencies of the various land patents. In order to get a title to such territory as had not been legally registered, they would throw a blanket claim over a designated area, usually from the top of a ridge down either side in lots of several thousand acres. In this way they secured a claim to thousands of acres of unpatented ridge lands and irregular tracts of unpatented territory along the smaller branches. For some years much litigation and bitter feeling were engendered by these "wild-cat" claims. Ultimately, little was gained by the practice, as it could be proved in court, generally, that the mountain citizens were using, or tending toward the use of these lands for legitimate purposes, whereas the "wild-catters" had left them undeveloped.

lay in the far-famed limestone region, is also true. William Savage, writing in 1819, mentions the case of an Englishman from Yorkshire who bought 30,000 acres in Kentucky,[1] and who upon his arrival found that:

> His land was barren, situated on rocky mountains, far removed from any settlers; no roads, no river in the vicinity; and totally unfit for cultivation or settling. . . . He consoled himself when he found that his land abounded with coal, . . . but this consolation was not of long continuance; his friend, who knew the customs and manners of the people better than himself, assured him that the low price of land enhanced the price of labor, for any man could purchase a few acres by working a few months, and everyone preferred living upon his own property, however poorly, to being a servant; so that it was difficult to procure laborers to work even above ground; and he would find it impossible, while land continued so plentiful, to find men who would work in the bowels of the earth. Nay, that if it were possible to raise coal, to transport it to Lexington and pitch it in the market-place; then to send the bell-man round the town to inform the inhabitants there was coal to distribute gratis to those who would fetch it, that it would still remain on his hands, as the inhabitants would not burn it, preferring wood.
>
> Thus his visionary expectations vanished; his property wasted; he became dissatisfied; the tax collector each year sold a part of the land for non-payment of the land tax; and this enthusiast in the purchase of land in America died a disappointed man; and his son, anxious to return to England, sold the remainder of his father's purchase, amounting to *many* acres, to a person in America, who knew the lots, for $50.00!
>
> I do not mention the name of this individual who was ruined by his speculation, but it is not the less a fact. It was sufficiently well-known to many in England; and is a matter of notoriety in Kentucky.

From 1830 to 1850, the westward migration from the Southern states received a new impetus. The decline in prices of cotton and tobacco in the South, together with the exhaustion of the soil, sent many thousands, including not only the poorer small farmers but planters caught by the general financial depression, to the northwest and southwest. In this new tide which passed along the old

[1] Savage, William: Observations on Emigration to the United States of America, illustrated by original Facts, pp. 26–28. London, 1819.

46

mountain trails,[1] might be seen "every conceivable sort of conveyance, from a handsome family carriage to the humblest sort of ox-cart."

"The Southerner packed up his household goods," says Pooley, "faced the west, and travelled by the most convenient road." An illustration of this characteristic is given in the answer made by a North Carolina man who, travelling westward with all his earthly possessions, was asked where he was going. "No where in pertick'lar," he answered. "Me and my wife thought we'd hunt a place to settle. We've no money, nor no plunder—nothin' but just ourselves and this nag—we thought we'd try our luck in a new country." (From Chicago *Weekly American*, June 20, 1835.)[2]

Pooley estimates, moreover, that:

Before 1850, Virginia had lost by emigration 26 percent of her native-born free inhabitants. South Carolina had lost 36 percent, and North Carolina 31 percent. Further examination of statistics will, however, show that the movement was probably almost entirely within the limits of the planting states themselves. From 1831 to 1840, Georgia gained nearly 34 percent in population; Alabama 91 percent; and Arkansas 275 percent. In the next decade, while the percentages of increase were lower, the actual gain in population in these states was little less than in the preceding decade; and if Texas, which appears for the first time in the Census reports, be included, the increase was nearly 200,000 in excess of that of the preceding decade.[3]

Contemporary with and succeeding these later migrations, the mountain trails were also used for transporting merchandise and for moving large droves of stock—horses, cattle, and hogs—from

---

[1] "The roads up the Virginia valleys converged at the Cumberland Gap, although some movers preferred to travel towards the Potomac River striking the old National Road there. Still others followed along the road leading through Charlottesville, Lewisburg and Charlestown to Guyandotte on the Ohio. From the Carolinas they followed the Yadkin through Wilkesville, thence northward through Ward's Gap (Virginia) across the valley to the Great Kanawha; or turning southwest from Wilkesville some went through the State Gap (North Carolina) and found their way to one of the Ohio River towns by way of the Cumberland Gap. The roads of South Carolina followed the rivers, and converging at the Saluda Gap in the Blue Ridge, passed through Asheville (North Carolina), through the Smoky Mountains and the Cumberland Gap to Kentucky. As a general rule where there was any tendency to follow a beaten line of travel it was towards some point on the Ohio between Cincinnati and Louisville."—Pooley, William Vipond: The Settlement of Illinois from 1830 to 1850, p. 356. Madison, Wis., May, 1908.

[2] Ibid., p. 353.   [3] Ibid., p. 334.

the west to the east. Four or five thousand hogs were driven at a time from Ohio eastward, and the droves passed often through Tennessee, Virginia, and the Carolinas, where the forest mast supplied abundant food. Through Cumberland Gap, mules and horses were driven to the Tennessee Valley, and so southward to supply southern plantations. In 1828 the value of livestock passing through Cumberland Gap was estimated at $1,167,000; while in 1824 at Saluda Gap, the main gap for trails connecting the coasts of South Carolina and Georgia with transmontane regions, the value of horses, cattle, and hogs, brought from the west to supply the south is held to have amounted to more than a million dollars.[1] The chief center for distribution of merchandise into the back regions of the Carolinas and Alabama was Knoxville.

In view, then, of all the various movements through the mountains, and of the fact that the accessible valley regions were early occupied, it seems reasonable to suppose that some, journeying through the mountains in the later migrations, passed by many routes and trails into the less accessible valleys of the mountain-ridge section. That there should be men of inferior stamina and ability among them would seem inevitable; but it can by no means be claimed that as a whole the later settlers were inferior. This period, throughout the United States, has been designated as one of movement. All classes were in motion, and at a time when isolation was a characteristic of frontier life it was not easy for a pioneer to foresee that choice of a home in what has now become a remote part of our mountain-ridge section, would result as the years went on in the separation of the life of his descendants from that of the greater part of the state.

The poorness of mountain roads was probably not as much a deterrent to travel before 1850 as later. All travel was difficult. In Kentucky, until 1830, there was little difference except in grade and the likelihood of washouts between the mountain thoroughfares and those of the Bluegrass region. The rapidly increasing population and wealth of the Bluegrass, however, as well as perhaps the availability of good highway material, soon led to the establishment of macadam turnpikes in that part of the state. It

[1] Turner, Frederick Jackson: The Rise of the New West, 1819–1829, in The American Nation, a History, Vol. XIV, p. 100 ff. New York, Harper Brothers, 1906.

was during this period, from 1830 to 1850, that the mountain country, left to provide for itself in the matter of roads, began to be shut off from the life of the remainder of the state.[1]

What was true of Kentucky was probably true in greater or less degree of the other states in which the Highlands are situated. Road building in the more prosperous, thickly settled portions led to distinctions between Lowlands and Highlands and between valley areas and mountain-ridge sections; and with the gradual subsidence of the streams of migration from east to west and the separation of the new frontier in the northwest and southwest from the old frontier by a belt of a more advanced stage of development, the mountains, especially the mountain-ridge areas, became more and more isolated.

After the middle of the nineteenth century no large migrations passed into or through the Southern Highlands. Such movement as there was affected for the most part the valley areas or the sections where industrial development was taking place. Individuals of course made their way from one section to another, but the composition of the population remained on the whole the same.

An intensive study, county by county, would be necessary to determine accurately the date of settlement of different areas. We have been concerned with the broader questions of early and late settlement mainly as a basis of discussion as to the probable nationality of the ancestors of those now living in the Southern Highlands, and to provide a background for an understanding of some of the aspects of life in the mountains today.

[1] Verhoeff, Mary: The Kentucky Mountains, Transportation and Commerce, 1750–1911, Ch. IV. Filson Club Publication No. 26.

CHAPTER IV

ANCESTRY

THE given names of pupils mentioned in the first chapter serve as evidence of different things to different people. Until definite assurance is forthcoming that they were the real names of pupils in school, some may believe that they bear evidence only of vivid imagination on the part of the writer. For him history is repeating itself as he recalls little red-headed Alexander, striving daily to conquer his primary world with rocks, clubs, fists, or pocket-knife; or as he sees again little Joseph as he was wont to watch him trudging to school in a vivid polka-dot waist of many colors, which his fond parent had gleaned from some mission barrel.

The frequent use of the names of religious reformers and of Biblical characters as given names in sections of the mountains will serve as cumulative evidence to those who hold that the great number of religious names signed to early petitions was proof of the non-conformist character of mountain population.

Homer and Virgil (there were two such in our school) and Pliny will be of special interest to certain friends who found copies of Greek and Latin classics in mountain cabins. The possessors of the texts, it is said, were unable to read or write, but the books bore the signatures of ancestors whose descendants held them as precious heirlooms. Milton, Byron, and Shelley, of our list, will add weight to the contention that such names are evidence of descent from ancestors familiar with the classics.

While it is permissible to draw such inferences, the unexpected name is more likely due to the pressing necessity of parents in a populous neighborhood to find an appellation distinguishing—not necessarily distinguished, but if so all the better—by which to designate the new little one. This necessity would be apparent to anyone who had seen the dilemma of our postmaster with envelope in hand "backed" with the words "Jim Green." So numerous were Jim Greens in the district that when a rare letter came to one of them, the postmaster had three guesses as to whether it was intended for "Black Jim," "Pink Jim," short for Pinckney, or "no-account Jim" Green, who might perhaps better have been called "Red Jim" Green had his ruddiness been more pronounced than his "no-accountness." Possibly the appropriateness of "Heliotrope" would have been seen had our knowledge of Greek words extended beyond "baptizo." "No-account" was thus dubbed from his confirmed habit of letting his women-folks tote water and chop wood on chilly mornings, while he turned ever toward the sun at the village store, about which were congregated other sun-worshiping Solons for their daily session to settle weighty affairs of Church and State.

Early release from this necessity of finding distinguishing names was not given to many. All understood, therefore, the relief in Brother Culpepper's tones, as he christened the child of his old age "Finis."

Conjectures have been many as to the ancestry of the Southern Highlanders. Some would make their progenitors Scottish chieftains, transplanted to the Highlands of the South, unchanged, save that here they preferred the rifle to the broadsword, the hunting-knife to the dirk, the buckskin and homespun to the brighter hued tartan. Others find in them the offspring of English redemptioners and indentured servants,[1] swept beyond the mountain ridges by the swollen tides of immigration flowing through the valleys and left to subside in the hollows and grow stagnant. In just resentment to this claim, other theories more sane have been put forth, but often with such extravagance as to make those not of "illustrious Scotch-Irish descent" or "purest Anglo-Saxon lineage" shrivel before the effulgence emanating from such stock.

Inquiries of the Highlanders themselves as to family history and racial stock rarely bring a more definite answer than that grandparents or great-grandparents came from North Carolina or Virginia, occasionally from Pennsylvania, and that they "reckon" their folks were "English," "Scotch," or "Irish"—any of which designations may mean Scotch-Irish—or "Dutch," which may and usually does mean German.

[1] See Appendix B.

51

Some years ago the writer found himself at the noon hour in a remote river valley in the mountains of Kentucky. Hallooing, as is the custom, at the gate of a cabin which had been pointed out as "Bill Campbell's," he was answered by a fine-looking gray-haired woman of sixty.

"What might your name be?" came the question; and on his giving answer, there followed the hearty welcome,

" 'Light, brother, I reckon we're kin."

We were soon joined at the hearth by her husband. In the conversation that followed it was learned that there were forty or more families of Campbells in that particular bend of the river, none having less than six and some as many as twelve children. Because of the prevalence of the name, the district was known as Campbell's District. There were several hundred in the county, and as many more in the adjoining county.

The ancestors of those whom the cabin sheltered had left North Carolina nearly a hundred years before. The father of our host, still living in the neighborhood, was but a lad of nine at the time. There was a family tradition that one of the maternal ancestors, the great-great-grandmother, had come from Scotland and had lived to see five generations of descendants.

Great interest was manifested in the guest's given name, the name of his father, brother, and kinsmen, and he wrote them down upon request in order that they might be used as occasion arose. Doubtless some student of genealogy, coming some day upon these future Gavins, Archibalds, and Colins, will cite them as evidence of pure Scotch ancestry, confirmed by the tradition of the maternal grandmother. The tradition, however, failed to give satisfactory evidence as to just who these Campbells were, whether connected with the Highland Campbells of the lower Piedmont, with the Scotch-Irish Campbells of the upper Piedmont of North Carolina, or whether they might not even have been of Lowland Scotch blood. Some belonged undoubtedly to the large clan of Campbells in east Tennessee and southwest Virginia, among whom is a tradition of direct migration from the north of Ireland.

If one turns to history for the source of Highland descent he is again on uncertain ground. We have seen that the population of the Highlands was derived in the main from a series of migrations which came to a close about 1850, and that the migrations preceding 1800 differed in origin from those of the succeeding fifty years. To ascertain, however, the proportionate elements of the various races in the movements of these two periods is less easy, and there is the further question as to whether the people now living in the mountains are to any extent descendants of the earlier settlers, or have come, in great degree, from the later movements.

The sources of the early migrations through the Highlands were, it will be recalled, the three reservoirs lying one in central, one in western Pennsylvania, and the third in the Carolina Piedmont. Turning to these in the order of their formation for data which will be of service in determining the racial elements in the streams which proceeded from them, we are confronted at the outset with obstacles. While it has been generally claimed by historians that the dominant race along the whole early frontier was the Scotch-Irish, not only is there dispute as to the relative proportions of Scotch-Irish and Germans in the central Pennsylvania reservoir, but the significance of the term Scotch-Irish is questioned.[1]

It has been contended that the so-called Scotch-Irish were not in fact a people distinct in blood, but were so designated merely to distinguish their geographical location; and that those thus distinguished ought properly, on the basis of racial stock, to be classed as Lowland Scotch and north of England folk. The question of the racial classification of the Scotch-Irish, Ulster Scotch, or Presbyterian Irish, is of great interest but cannot be discussed here in detail.[2] That there was a people from the north of Ireland strongly influencing pioneer westward movements, is indisputable; and tradition and historical evidence point to their presence in large numbers on the frontiers of Pennsylvania during the second and third quarters of the eighteenth century. When, however, we

[1] Lodge classifies the Scotch-Irish as a distinct race stock. In reply to criticism he said: "I classified the Irish and the Scotch-Irish as two distinct race stocks, and I believe the distinction to be a sound one historically and scientifically. . . . The Scotch-Irish from the north of Ireland, Protestant in religion, and chiefly Scotch and English in blood and name, came to this country in large numbers in the 18th century; while the people of pure Irish stock came scarcely at all during the colonial period, and did not emigrate here largely until the present century was well advanced."—Lodge, Henry Cabot: The Distribution of Ability in the United States, *Century* Magazine, Sept., 1891.

[2] See note by Commons, Appendix D.

endeavor to get an estimate of their numbers, we are met with further difficulties.

While enumerations more or less accurate were made of the population of some of the colonies during the colonial period, no thorough enumerations were attempted either in the colonial or continental periods in Pennsylvania or the Carolinas. An estimate of the entire population of the United States, generally considered by historians too high,[1] was made by the Continental Congress in 1776 as a basis for apportioning war expenses, but it was not until 1790 that a census was undertaken. To determine the racial elements of this population, or more accurately, to determine what may be termed "nationality strain," the compilers of A Century of Population Growth[2] have endeavored to classify the names of heads of families as they appear upon the existing schedules of the census of 1790, on the basis of name studies. The headings under which the groups were entered were English and Welsh, Scotch, Irish, Dutch, French, German, Hebrew, and "all others."[3] There was no attempt to classify the Scotch-Irish.

Those who hold that the Scotch-Irish were a distinct racial stock will see a very evident flaw in this classification; and all will see difficulties besetting one who seeks to determine how many of the original settlers of the mountains came from England or were of pure English descent, and how many were from the north of Ireland; however, they may be classed ethnologically. Not only are many names found in the mountains common to both countries— such as Moore, Collins, Mitchell, Gillespie, and Morrow—but others, not of Irish orgin—White, Rice, Reed, Carr, Allen, Berry, Henry, and Morris—have been common in Ireland for generations.

---

[1] See Appendix D.

[2] A Century of Population Growth, from the First Census of the United States to the Twelfth, 1790–1900. Washington, Government, 1909.

[3] Thus, when in our central Pennsylvania reservoir we seek to determine the proportions of Scotch-Irish and Germans, through the returns of the census of 1790, we can only compare the German population with that of the English, Welsh, Scotch, and Irish combined. Or, similarly, when we seek to determine for the same date the racial elements in what was then known as the Morgan District of North Carolina—the district including the then counties of Burke, Lincoln, Rutherford, and Wilkes, from which a large part of the present mountain counties of western North Carolina were formed—out of a total of 30,687 inhabitants we find that 24,405 are listed as English and Welsh; 3,560 Scotch; 730 Irish; 47 Dutch; 31 French; 1,884 Germans; and 30 "all others."

These latter were without doubt classed usually by the census bureau of 1790 as English, as they were obviously of Anglo-Saxon heritage; yet when they are given in the last years of the eighteenth century as names of emigrants from sections strongly Scotch-Irish, so-called, or when they are borne at the present day by people who lay claim to Scotch-Irish descent, the quandary of the investigator is obvious. The name, with the added evidence of family tradition, is in one instance Scotch-Irish; yet without that evidence the conclusion is not warranted that all other families of that name are Scotch-Irish.

Roosevelt, in the Winning of the West, pays a high tribute to the Presbyterian Irish as the "vanguard of the army of fighting settlers, who with axe and rifle won their way from the Alleghenies to the Rio Grande and the Pacific."[1] He holds that they were a mixed people, descended from Scotch ancestors, originally from both Highlands and Lowlands, from among Scotch Saxons and Scotch Celts, with a few French Huguenots among them and quite a number of true old Milesian Irish extraction. "Of course," he adds, "generations before they ever came to America, the McAfees, McClungs, Campbells, McCoshes, etc., had become indistinguishable from the Todds, Armstrongs, Elliotts, and the like."[2] The corruption of Scotch and Welsh names, MacGregor to Gudger or Greear, Stephenson to Stinnert, Applewhaite to Applegate, and the translation and Anglicization of foreign names, Coontz to Coots, Gehrheart to Gayheart, Beber to Beaver, Rees to Rice, Ammon to Hammond, Schwartz to Black, Zimmerman to Carpenter, DeLisle to Dials, Cartier to Carter, are additional and potent sources of confusion. Bishop, for example, may be Scotch-Irish, English, or German.

In the absence of definite numerical data as to elements of population, we must rely upon tradition and historical evidence, and upon the conclusions of historians. Faust, historian of the Germans, and Hanna, historian of the Scotch-Irish, have made careful computations of the numbers of their respective peoples.[3] According to their estimates, the numbers of Scotch-Irish and Ger-

[1] Roosevelt, Theodore: The Winning of the West, Vol. I, p. 134. New York, G. P. Putman's Sons, 1900. [2] Ibid., Vol. I, p. 135, note 2.
[3] Faust, Albert Bernhardt: The German Element in the United States. Also Hanna, Charles A.: The Scotch-Irish. For fuller reference see Appendix D.

55

mans in Pennsylvania were approximately the same. Each race formed about one-third of the population of Pennsylvania.

By an examination of six frontier colonies of Pennsylvania, in which lay our central reservoir—Berks, Lancaster, York, Dauphin, Cumberland, and Franklin—we find that in all but Berks the combined English, Welsh, Scotch, and Irish in 1790 far outnumbered the Germans. In York they were one-fifth more numerous, while in Franklin and Cumberland Counties, from which the tide that had been moving westward first turned to the south, they outnumbered the Germans from three to seven times. It would seem, therefore, in the absence of any census classification of peoples from the north of Ireland, and with the probability that many from that country were classed by the census as English, together with the strong tradition as to the large numbers of Scotch-Irish in this region, we are probably justified in holding that in our central Pennsylvania reservoir the north of Ireland folk exceeded the Germans. This assumption is strengthened by a comparison of the numbers of Germans and Scotch-Irish in the Valley of Virginia.

This region, the earliest settled within the Southern Highlands,[1] received the first overflow from Pennsylvania. Tidewater Virginia was in large part English, and while from early times pioneers did find their way up the rivers to the Piedmont region, and later across the Blue Ridge, the movement from the coast did not assume large proportions until the nineteenth century. There was a small English colony in Clark County, and undoubtedly many scattered English, Huguenots, and some of other nationalities among the Valley people. As a whole, however, the population of the Valley was overwhelmingly Scotch-Irish and German, the Germans predominating in the lower or northern part, and the Scotch-Irish in the southern or upper part. That the bulk of these two races in Virginia, as in Pennsylvania, was on the frontier, and that the Valley population was for many years distinct from that of the eastern part of the state, is generally agreed by historians. Therefore when Hanna claims that there were 75,000 Scotch-Irish in the state of Virginia in 1775, and Faust for the same date claims 25,000

[1] Most historians, even Hanna (Vol. II, p. 45) say that the earliest permanent settlements in the Valley (probably about 1726 in Jefferson County) were by German immigrants.

Germans, it would seem to indicate, if these estimates are approximately correct, a predominance of Scotch-Irish in the Valley.

"The· development of the frontiers of Virginia was not dependent on the tidewater gentry, and their inferior servitors," writes Justin Winsor, "but rather upon the virile folk, particularly the Scotch-Irish, who had brought the Valley of Virginia into subjection, and were now adding to their strength by an immigration from Maryland, Pennsylvania, and north Virginia. These, crossing the divide by Braddock's road, were pushing down the Monongahela, and so on to the Ohio country. They carried with them all that excitable and determined character which goes with a keen-minded adherence to original sin, total depravity, predestination, and election, and saw no use in an Indian but to be a target for their bullets."[1]

That the Scotch-Irish were in the ascendancy in the second Pennsylvania reservoir about Pittsburgh, to which reference is made in the quotation above, seems to be more generally accepted. For estimates here as to the numerical proportions of Scotch-Irish and Germans we can use only the same method of deduction as was used in the case of the central reservoir, which contributed so largely to its formation. In the four counties of Westmoreland, Fayette, Washington, and Allegheny, which in 1790 covered much of the western part of the state, the English, Welsh, Scotch, and Irish combined outnumbered the Germans twenty-one to six. Furthermore, it may be noted that here as in the central reservoir, the proportion of English, Welsh, Scotch, and Irish is largest in the counties farthest on the frontier.

It will be recalled that the third reservoir, that in the Piedmont of the Carolinas, was fed from a number of sources, the main stream flowing from Pennsylvania through the Valley of Virginia, while lesser streams issued from the ports of Charleston and Wilmington. The ethnic strains in these various tides were the same, save that in the southern currents there was a greater representation, relatively, of Highland Scotch[2] and French Huguenots. The pre-

[1] Winsor, Justin: The Westward Movement, p. 12. Boston, Houghton, Mifflin and Co., 1897.

[2] There were large settlements of the Highland Scotch in the lower Piedmont of North Carolina. One of these was in Cumberland County, of which the county-seat, Fayetteville, was formerly called Campbelltown. To this settlement came Flora MacDonald, about whose name cluster so many romantic tales. Wheeler gives an interesting account of her assistance to the "Pretender," Charles Edward,

ponderant races early on this frontier then, were, as might be expected, Scotch-Irish and German, and if tradition and historical estimates[1] may be trusted, here, too, the Scotch-Irish were in the ascendancy. There is likelihood, however, that there was a greater admixture of races in this than in the other reservoirs. In addition to the French Huguenot and Scotch Highlander elements, the reservoir probably contained proportionately more English, who had worked their way from the Virginia Tidewater through the Virginia Piedmont and lowland North Carolina to the Carolina Piedmont. Hunters, traders, and cattle raisers had begun this movement in early times, and even before the middle of the eighteenth century there were scattered settlers among the Carolina foothills, drawn by the fine pastures, clear streams, and cooler climate. Such stragglers from the coast contributed their quota to the race amalgam, but they were swallowed up in the greater streams just described, which began to flood the Piedmont region about 1750. Here, as in Pennsylvania and Virginia, the frontier settlements were for some time distinct from the older eastern settlements in race, religion, and democratic tendencies.

"Thus it happened," writes Frederick Jackson Turner in The Old West, "that from about 1730 to 1760 a generation of settlers poured along this mountain trough into the southern uplands, or Piedmont, creating a new continuous social and economic area,

after the Battle of Culloden, aiding him, disguised as her waiting-maid, to escape through many dangers to France, of her subsequent arrest by George the Second, and her acquittal because of her youth, kindness of heart, and ready wit; of her marriage to her kinsman Allan MacDonald, and their emigration to America in 1775.

It will be recalled that the Highlanders were pardoned after the Battle of Culloden upon the condition that they take the oath of allegiance, and emigrate. Generally they felt so strictly bound by this oath that they became Tories. The chief of the MacDonald clan in America accepted a commission under the British, and marshalled the loyal Highlanders of North Carolina under the Scottish pibroch to unite with the English bugles. They suffered hard defeat at the hands of the rebels, and Allan MacDonald was imprisoned for a time. After the Revolution, "broken down in hopes, with property plundered, and lands confiscated, he and Flora returned to Scotland. Flora is said to have remarked, 'I have hazarded my life for the house of Stuart and for the house of Hanover, and I do not see that I am the great gainer by either.' Her shroud was made of the sheets in which Charles Edward had slept at Kingsburg (her home in Scotland) which with woman's romantic temper she had preserved in all her wanderings for this express purpose."— Wheeler, John H.: Historical Sketches of North Carolina, 1584–1851, pp. 126–128. Philadelphia, Lippincott, Grambo, and Co., 1851.

[1] There were, according to Hanna, 110,000 Scotch-Irish in the Carolinas at the opening of the Revolution; and according to Faust, 23,000 Germans.

which cut across the artificial colonial boundary lines, disarranged the regular extension of local government from the coast westward, and built up a new Pennsylvania in contrast with the old Quaker colonies, and a new South in contrast with the tidewater South.

* * * * * * * *

"Among this moving mass, as it passed along the Valley into the Piedmont, in the middle of the eighteenth century, were Daniel Boone, John Sevier, James Robertson, and the ancestors of John C. Calhoun, Abraham Lincoln, Jefferson Davis, Stonewall Jackson, James K. Polk, Sam Houston, and Davy Crockett; while the father of Andrew Jackson came to the Carolina Piedmont at the same time from the coast. Recalling that Thomas Jefferson's home was in this frontier, at the edge of the Blue Ridge, we perceive that these names represent the militant expansive movement in American life. They foretell the settlement across the Alleghenies in Kentucky and Tennessee; the Louisiana Purchase, and Lewis and Clark's transcontinental exploration; the conquest of the Gulf Plains in the War of 1812–15; the annexation of Texas; the acquisition of California and the Spanish Southwest. They represent, too, frontier democracy in its two aspects personified in Andrew Jackson and Abraham Lincoln. It was a democracy responsive to leadership, susceptible to waves of emotion, of a 'high religious voltage'—quick and direct in action."[1]

From the Carolina Piedmont a small stream had found its way to the west before the Revolution to meet another stream which had just begun to cross the New River Divide in southwestern Virginia. Joining in the Greater Appalachian Valley in northeastern Tennessee, these forerunners of the tide which ten years later was to sweep thousands through this region on their way to the lands beyond the mountains, formed the settlements which were bound together in the Watauga Association. That the Watauga colonists were largely Scotch-Irish has been generally accepted, and in view of the fact that the areas from which they came were so largely occupied by this race,[2] the belief seems justified. It is, however, interesting

---

[1] Turner, Frederick Jackson: "The Old West," in Proceedings of the State Historical Society of Wisconsin at its 56th Annual Meeting, 1908, pp. 212, 217. Madison, Wis., 1909.

[2] There is an admission on the part of Faust that the Scotch-Irish were in the ascendancy in the upper Valley of Virginia, although he says that there were more Germans on the southern slope of the valley than is generally supposed. He also states that the Scotch-Irish were farthest toward the frontier in the Carolina Piedmont, adding that the Germans were close upon their heels.

to note, in this connection, the variety in stock as shown in the leaders, most of them American born. For example, while Robertson was of Scotch-Irish parentage, Sevier,[1] who like him came from the Valley of Virginia through the North Carolina Piedmont to Tennessee, was of French Huguenot and English ancestry; and the Shelbys, from Maryland, were of Welsh extraction.[2] The original settler of the Watauga, William Bean, is said to have been English.

As if to offset this preponderance of other strains, a German claim has been advanced that the most famous of all figures on the frontier, Boone, was of German descent. His name, ending in " e" and so like the common German name Bohne, is offered as an argument; and as further evidence, are cited his birth in a Pennsylvania county where there were many Germans and his ability to speak German fluently. His biographers, however, say that he was of English and Welsh Quaker extraction.[3]

By the close of the Revolution the three reservoirs already overflowing were freed from restraint, and the streams which issued from them poured through the Southern Highlands and along their northern boundaries. That in these migrations, which covered

[1] "Sevier, or 'Nolichucky Jack' as he was called, was in thirty-five fights, and was always victorious. His tactics were simple. He moved with such celerity as to be always the herald of his own coming. Then he dashed on the Indians, overwhelming and dismaying them by the impetuosity of the charge. It was the rush of the tempest. All was over in a few minutes. Some of his expeditions into the Indian country rival the tales of romance. Roosevelt states that Sevier was the first and greatest of all the Indian fighters of the west."—Temple, Oliver Perry: John Sevier, Knoxville, Tenn., the ZI-PO Press, 1910.

[2] General Evan Shelby, a Welshman by birth, settled in Maryland about 1750, and afterwards became a leader in the Watauga Settlement. His son Isaac, born in Maryland, was the most famous member of that pioneer family. Isaac Shelby was successively in skirmishes with the Indians, surveyor in the "dark and bloody ground" of Kentucky, active in the Treaty of Long Island with the Indians, and Major and later Colonel in the Continental Army, where, at the head of several hundred mounted riflemen from the frontier, he won a number of noteworthy engagements with the British. After the Revolution he made his home in Kentucky, where he took an active part in the organization of the state and became its first Governor. Wheeler says, his was "the first pre-emption and settlement granted in Kentucky, and it is a remarkable fact that at his death he was the only person who occupied his original pre-emption."—Wheeler, John H.: Historical Sketches of North Carolina, 1584–1851, pp. 98–103.

[3] "His mother was the daughter of an unassuming Welsh-Quaker, John Morgan. His father, who bore the odd name of Squire, was an Englishman by birth, a native of the obscure Devonshire village of Bradninch."—Bruce, H. A. B.: Daniel Boone and the Wilderness Road, p. 2. New York, The Macmillan Company, 1910.

approximately a period of twenty years, from 1780 to 1800, the Scotch-Irish would predominate, would naturally be inferred; as well as that they would be more numerous in the settlements made at this time in the Highlands.

Referring to a list of 4,000 or more names attached to petitions addressed by early inhabitants of Kentucky to the General Assembly of Virginia, James R. Robertson makes this interesting statement:

> The list of names is important for two main reasons; first, it throws light on the racial composition of the early population of Kentucky, and second, it is of use for the student of genealogy.
> The earlier petitions show a decided preponderance of Scotch and Scotch-Irish names with a large number of English and a few German, Dutch, and French. The number of English names increases in the later petitions. The large number of religious names indicates the non-conformist character of much of the population.
> While the list will not give much detail to aid the genealogist, it fixes the existence of a certain name in a locality at an early period and thus gives a clue that may be followed further.[1]

While it is not likely that many of these Kentucky petitioners were living at that time in the mountain section of the state, it is to be noted that they had come of necessity by routes leading them through the mountains, or by the Ohio River, and from one of the reservoirs described. The large increase of English names in the later petitions is an indication, we believe, of what was taking place toward the end of this period in the streams of migration flowing to and from these reservoirs—a much larger admixture of English. "There was possibly," says Winsor cautiously, writing of conditions in 1790, "a preponderance of English blood in all these diversified currents, but the Scotch-Irish and the Germans were numerous enough to give a strengthening fiber in this mingling of ethnic strains."[2]

The question, therefore, which in final analysis confronts the investigator, is not as to which of the two elements, Scotch-Irish or

[1] Robertson, James Rood: Petitions of the Early Inhabitants of Kentucky to the General Assembly of Virginia, 1769 to 1792, pp. 31–32. Filson Club Publication No. 27. Louisville, Ky., John P. Morton and Co.

[2] Winsor, Justin: The Westward Movement, p. 400. Boston, Houghton, Mifflin and Co., 1897.

German, was strongest in the mountain settlements made during the latter part of the eighteenth century, but as to what were the relative proportions of the Scotch-Irish and English in these settlements.

The growing prominence of the English on the frontier is increasingly marked in the next fifty years, during which migrations through the mountains came from less distinctively Scotch-Irish areas, and more from the lowland and English sections of the South. As has been seen, the settlement of the mountain-ridge section was contemporaneous with these later movements. That the stock which settled the mountain-ridge areas differed substantially from that which earlier settled the valley areas has not been proved. An intensive study, such as was suggested in the last chapter, would be necessary to determine not only the time of settlement of different areas but the composition of population within them. We have been able merely to indicate in a general way the races prominent in the movements of the two periods. It still remains for us to find whether the people living in the Highlands today are to any great extent descendants of early settlers, in order to arrive, if possible, at some conclusions as to race and stock.

To this end some years ago a careful study[1] was made of 1,200 or more mountain surnames with a view to ascertaining the length of residence in the mountains and the racial stock of those who bore them. Only names common in a neighborhood and held by old inhabitants to be representative were included. Of those selected 360 were of families living in Kentucky, 497 in North Carolina, 228 in Tennessee, and 182 in Georgia. The remainder, too inconsiderable a number to warrant the drawing of any conclusions as to early settlement or predominant stock, were from South Carolina and Alabama. These names were compared with names of heads of families quoted in the United States census of 1790;[2] with Revolutionary War pension lists (Act of 1832), in which all veterans drawing pensions were enrolled[3] and their residence at that time

[1] Part of a study on mountain settlement and ancestry made for the writer by Ruth Dame Coolidge.

[2] The census returns of 1790 for Virginia, Georgia (including Alabama and Mississippi), Kentucky, and Southwest Territory (Tennessee) have been lost. The Virginia returns, however, are replaced in some measure by lists of inhabitants at state enumerations made near the close of the Revolution.

[3] These included also a few veterans of the Indian Wars subsequent to the Revolution, and of the War of 1812.

given, as well as the state in which they had originally served; early lists of settlers, some with nationality indicated; and with numerous other sources,[1] such as state histories, journals of travelers, and records of churches and historical societies.

This study of names was supplemented whenever possible by actual historical evidence and by the tradition of the people themselves. As examples, may be cited the cases of two families—the Westmorelands of White County, Georgia, and the Benges, a family very numerous in Clay County, Kentucky. Tradition says that three Westmoreland brothers came from England to Virginia in the eighteenth century, one settling in Virginia, one in North Carolina, and the third in South Carolina. This is confirmed by the census of 1790, which places Westmorelands in 1782 in Mecklenburg County, Virginia, in 1790 in Stokes and Orange Counties, North Carolina (in a southwesterly direction from Mecklenburg), and in 1790 in Spartanburg County, South Carolina (almost precisely a continuation of the diagonal line from Mecklenburg through Stokes). Conjecture that the Georgia family came from this same stock, based on tradition and supported by sound data, is therefore reasonable.

The Benge family claim that they are of German extraction and descended from a David Benge of Revolutionary fame, who came into that region from North Carolina. The Revolutionary War pension lists of Kentucky show one John Benge to have been living in Clay County in 1832, having served with the North Carolina militia. There is no record of any of the name in North or South Carolina on the Revolutionary War pension lists of those states nor in the census of 1790, but the census does show Benges present in Albemarle County, Virginia, in 1790. It therefore seems probable that the family came to Kentucky from Virginia by way of North Carolina, and it is of course possible that through some confusion in first names, either in tradition or in the pension lists, John and David were the same person. It is also possible that one or both may have been Virginians who served with the North Carolina militia, as the pension lists in such cases do not indicate the state from which the veteran came. Still another possibility is that they came from Virginia, lived a short time in North Carolina, and

[1] See Bibliography.

then moved to Kentucky. Instances of such change of residence are by no means uncommon.[1]

Further details of this study cannot be discussed here. Only the tentative conclusions can be given. In general it may be said that of the 1,200 representative names selected of families now living in the mountains, many were recorded in the census of 1790 as having been present on what were then the frontiers of Virginia and the Carolinas. Out of the 360 names obtained from Kentucky,[2] 247 were so placed in 1790. Of the 497 North Carolina names, 290 were in the Piedmont and western part of the state in 1790, 190 of them in the identical counties in which they are found today. Of the 228 Tennessee names, 126, or more than one-half, were common in 1790 to the frontiers of Virginia, North Carolina, or South Carolina. Owing to the disappearance of the 1790 census returns for Georgia, it is impossible to identify any of the 182 names of families from that state.

The fact that many families of frontier settlement remained continuously in the mountains until the present day finds documentary proof in pension lists made after the counties were settled. For instance, the Kentucky pension lists of 1832 contain the names of 297 Revolutionary War veterans, 168 names of which are common today in the Kentucky mountains, a number in the same counties in which they were found in 1790. Of the names of 154 war veterans mentioned by the pension list of 1832 as living in the mountains of North Carolina, 110 are common there today. In Tennessee, evidence seems to indicate that the veterans settled largely in the Valley areas, as the names on pension rolls have persisted in the Valley more than in the mountain-ridge areas. In the upper part of the Valley of East Tennessee were found many of King's Mountain lineage, of whom the Shelbys, Seviers, and Beans traced descent from the famous pioneers of the Watauga

---

[1] In Michaux's passage across the barrens of western Kentucky he speaks of meeting one family which had made three removals since leaving Virginia, and was on the point of moving again.—Michaux, Vol. III in Thwaites' Early Western Travels.

[2] As immigration into the mountains of Kentucky did not begin, at least to any great extent until after 1800, the location of a Kentucky name on the Carolina or Virginia frontier in 1790 would tend to prove that settlers came originally from that state.

Settlement, and the Doaks from Dr. Samuel Doak,[1] who founded what is known as "the first institution of classical learning west of the Alleghenies."[2] Tradition, however, also places today many descendants of King's Mountain veterans in the mountain-ridge areas of Tennessee and North Carolina.

To reach conclusions in regard to the numerical superiority of nationalities based on a study of name lists, would necessitate not only a complete list of all the different mountain names but an estimate of the number of individuals bearing each name. We offer our findings, however, for what they are worth. We have grouped Scotch, Scotch-Irish, and Irish names together under the heading Scotch-Irish. Where an English name is common to both England and Ireland, it is assigned to England unless the family bearing it is definitely known to have come from Ireland.

Of the 497 names on our list from North Carolina, the English and Scotch-Irish appear to have formed each about one-third; of the 228 from Tennessee the same proportion held; of the 360 from Kentucky, the English constituted four-tenths, and the Scotch-Irish three-tenths. The Germans showed their greatest strength in North Carolina, where they formed one-fifth of the entire number. In Tennessee they constituted one-seventh, in Kentucky but one-twelfth. There were a small number of Welsh in each state, chiefly in Kentucky, a few French, and a few strays from other countries. In Georgia, of 182 names, English and Scotch-Irish formed each about 40 per cent, German 19 per cent, and the remainder were Welsh or unidentified.

Although the limits of this name study give no real basis for conclusions as to the preponderance in the Kentucky mountains of the English over the Scotch-Irish, yet the very slight superiority found does support the claims of some of those best acquainted with this region, who hold that it has a larger strain of English than of any other stock.

---

[1] As pastor of a Presbyterian congregation at Limestone, Washington County, he opened a school in 1785 which was incorporated in 1788 as Martin Academy, and in 1795 as Washington College. See note on page 164.

[2] "West of the Alleghenies" is a phrase used with such varying significance as to cause confusion. Here it is evidently intended to refer to the region south of Virginia and west of the Blue Ridge Belt.

In a further effort to discover whether the people in the mountains today were descendants of original settlers, names were secured of those to whom early land grants had been made, and these names compared with those of families now living in the same general section of the Highlands.

The lands in North Carolina that lie within the present counties of Buncombe, Madison, Henderson, Transylvania, and a part of Haywood, were thrown open to settlement through a treaty between the state of North Carolina and the Cherokee Indians concluded on July 20, 1777.[1] In 1796 a large grant (No. 251),[2] covering most of this territory, was made to David Allison.[3] Attached to the surveyor's plot and report of survey, upon which the state grant to Allison was based, was a list of lands already appropriated within the bounds of the plot at the time of the making of the survey—lands which had doubtless been taken up by settlers who had come in after the treaty of 1777. The list[4] contains 44 different names. Thirty-four of these are names of large families still living in the five counties previously mentioned as covering the territory opened for settlement by the treaty of 1777. Both family and local tradition attribute very early settlement of the region to the progenitors of those bearing these 34 names, and in the case of some large families such as the Alexanders, Davidsons, McDowells, and Pattons, the reputation of being descendants of the first settlers is commonly recognized.

---

[1] This treaty was made at Long Island on the Holston River, and has generally been designated as the Treaty of Holston. A later treaty is also referred to as the Treaty of Long Island. By this Treaty of Long Island, the lines separating lands of the Cherokee Nation from those open to settlement to the white men were defined.

[2] For this information, and for much other valuable information relating to early settlement and early land grants, the author is greatly indebted to Mr. Cameron F. McRae, Special Assistant to the Attorney-General, United States Department of Justice, Asheville, North Carolina; and to Mr. Judson S. Bohannan, Attorney, United States Department of Agriculture, Asheville, North Carolina.

[3] There are many Allisons now in the North Carolina mountains, but they are not descendants of this David Allison. He was an Englishman owning thousands of acres of land all over the state, but he died in the poor debtors' prison in Philadelphia.

[4] Many years ago the list of appropriated lands became detached from the plot and report of survey, and could not be found. A recent re-indexing of papers in the office of the secretary of state at Raleigh, North Carolina, brought this lost list to light, and it has been filed. Information relative to names contained in this list was thus made available for our purposes.

While the findings from land grants are confined largely to western North Carolina, our experience leads us to believe that similar results would follow a study of grants in areas of east Tennessee and sections of the Virginias and Kentucky.

The value of family traditions in casting light on lines of migration, method of settlement, and the stock and character of early settlers may be illustrated by a few examples. In Madison County, North Carolina, live a large family of Sheltons, of English blood, who claim that the first of the name came into that region from Yancey County, North Carolina, about 1790. Intermarried with them, as well as with a number of other families in this neighborhood, are those who claim direct descent from John Sevier, who it will be recalled was of French Huguenot and English ancestry, and closely identified with the Watauga Settlement which lay just to the northwest of this section in the Tennessee Valley. A large family of Tweeds, of Irish descent, whose ancestors came about 1826 from Charleston, South Carolina, hold that they were the sixth family to settle in this part of the county, the other families already living there at the time of their coming being Sheltons, Franklins, Rices, and Cutshalls—all common names still in this neighborhood. The two earliest recorded grants of land to Sheltons, on "Lorrel" Creek in this region, were to David and Lewis Shelton in 1815, while a grant was made to one William Rice in the same general neighborhood in 1799. The date of the Shelton grant does not confirm the family tradition that they settled in what is now Madison County in 1790, and were the first to do so, but it does not necessarily invalidate it, as many early settlers did not take out their grants until some time after occupation.

A direct tradition of migration from the Carolina Piedmont was given by an old woman in the Kentucky mountains, whose grandfather, she said, signed the "Declaration of Independence," later found to mean the Mecklenburg Declaration of 1775. Another Kentucky grandmother, who had no knowledge of the previous home of her family in America, knew that her grandmother came "from that far-away and absent land across the sea they call England." In the mountains of this state, also, a woman of about sixty, bearing a name well known in her section, gives this interesting account of the emigration from his native land of her first

American ancestor. It was the custom in England, she said, for school children to make, at Christmas time, a present to their teacher, of a hen, or goose, or duck. Her ancestor—how many times removed from the present generation she did not know—owned a goose and had asked his stepmother to let him take it to his teacher. Upon her refusing, he took it without her consent. For this, under the rigorous laws existent, he was convicted and had come to America. Although she had been criticized by her relatives for telling this story, she said she herself felt it to be no discredit to her people, showing as it did the independent spirit of the family, which claimed what belonged to it. Her immediate grandfather had moved from North Carolina to Tennessee, to the Nashville region, evidently in the early days of the settlement of that country, and later on into Kentucky. He was an educated man, and had had his sons educated, but did not believe in schooling for his daughters, so the girls had never received any book learning, or, as she expressed it, "were educated in everything except book learning." Her father, she went on to say, on coming into Kentucky, "took up a broad boundary of land at the mouth of the creek, hit were a sight to see," and she had been "born and raised in the wilderness, and never knowed anything."

This tradition is particularly interesting as showing the backward movement into the mountains mentioned in the previous chapter as taking place through the return of those who had passed through them earlier on their way to the West. It illustrates also the attitude toward the education of women which still exists in many places in the Highlands, as well as the natural result of having been "born and raised in the wilderness."

There is a theory of origin to which it may bear evidence. A reference has already been made to the much discussed question of whether the Highland people are to any extent descendants of those transported for alleged crimes, and indentured service.[1] That some of the mountain people are sprung from such stock is undoubtedly true. The freedom of the frontier at this period as at others made it a refuge for criminals and the oppressed, and its cheap lands attracted those who from poverty and debt as well as from natural ambition and the spirit of adventure, wished to improve their for-

[1] See Appendix B.

tunes. Those, however, who have pressed the theory, have failed to mitigate the severity of their verdict by calling to mind the high character of some of the indentured servants and the exiled political prisoners, or the harsh and brutal penalties exacted at the time in England for very minor offenses. In the present instance it could not be learned whether the ancestor in question had been sent to this country by the English authorities after conviction, by his own hard kinsmen, or whether he had come of his own initiative.

Another hint of an origin of this sort was found in a family whose early ancestor in America was said to have been an "English outlaw." One could not but speculate on the nature of his alleged crime, for among his many descendants were some of the most substantial and respected citizens of the neighborhood in which they lived. Another highly esteemed family also traced, by tradition, their descent from an ancestor who, eager to come to this country, had bound himself out to service for a number of years to pay for his passage. These three instances are the only clues, borne out by tradition, which have come to our personal notice as evidence of the indentured or redemptioner theory, but naturally evidence of this kind, if held by mountain families, would not in the very nature of things be spread broadcast.[1]

A side light has been thrown upon the question of the ancestry of the mountain people by Cecil J. Sharp, Director of the Stratford-on-Avon School of Folk Song and Dance and a recognized authority on these subjects. Mr. Sharp became interested in a collection of ballads made by Mrs. Campbell during her numerous journeys while the writer was making his field study. He spent many months in the mountains of North Carolina, Tennessee, the Virginias, and Kentucky collecting ballads and folk-songs from the people themselves. In response to an inquiry as to his views of the ancestry of the people, Mr. Sharp makes this reply:

> The racial origin of the inhabitants of the Southern Appalachians, so far as I know them, is an extremely intricate problem and one which I am quite sure is not going satisfactorily

[1] It is claimed by one mountaineer of eastern Kentucky that certain sections of this mountain area received poor and indentured white stock from Virginia through the eastern gaps, and that this circumstance has strongly influenced the character of life on at least one fork of the Kentucky River.

to be solved by speculative generalizations on the part of hap-
hazard travellers like myself. The elucidation of the problem
needs the assistance and careful investigation of ethnologists,
anthropologists, as well as the examination of land titles and
other legal documents concerning the settlement of the mountain regions. Nevertheless, for what they are worth, I will
gladly give you my impressions. My first observation, and, perhaps the one upon which I feel that I can speak with some
certainty, is that whatever may be the racial origin of the mountaineers, their predominant culture is overwhelmingly Anglo-
Saxon, or, perhaps, to be more accurate, Anglo-Celtic. That is
to say, whatever admixture of races there may be in the mountains, the Anglo-Celt has managed pretty completely to absorb
them, to take them into his own orbit without himself being
appreciably infected by them. I have formed this opinion from
several considerations; from observing the everyday manners,
habits, and customs, all of which are demonstrably Anglo-Saxon;
from an analysis of their traditional songs, ballads, dances, sing-
ing-games, etc.; and finally, in a general way, from their physical
characteristics. The strongest argument in favor of this view
is based on the character of the traditional songs and dances
which seem to me to be saturated with the Anglo-Celtic idiom to
the exclusion of every other. The one dance that I have seen
and collected is a very strong and concise piece of evidence,
because I think there is no doubt that it represents a stage in the
development of the English Country Dance of a very early date,
certainly prior to 1650; and the fact that the mountaineers
could not have left Great Britain for a century or more after that
date can only be accounted for upon the supposition that they
came from a part of England where the civilization was least
developed—probably the North of England, or the Border country between Scotland and England. The same deduction can
be made with regard to the language, which, I take it, is far
more archaic than the language of the South of England at the
time when these people must have emigrated,—but on this
aspect of the question I cannot speak with any authority. The
argument with regard to the dance I have developed more fully
in my introduction to the Fifth Country Dance Book[1] which will
be published in a week or two. It is possible, of course, that the
musical idiom of the songs in the mountains has become more
archaic and primitive in character since the original emigrants
arrived in this country, owing to the extreme isolation of the
country in which they have resided; and this is a point of view

[1] The Country Dance Book, Part V, by Cecil J. Sharp.   London, Novello & Co.
Ltd.;   New York, The H. W. Gray Co.

which Mr. Fox Strangways has suggested in his review of our book[1] in the London *Times*.[2]

All the other observations that I have to make are much more speculative. There is, of course, the evidence of the surnames of the mountaineers, for what it is worth, and even there the names that have come under my own observation are necessarily very few in number, too few really to justify one in forming any trustworthy theory. But so far as they go they seem to me to strengthen and bear out the theory of origin that I have already enunciated. The majority of the names of my friends in the mountains are English, or Scottish; the Irish names are very few, and the German names still fewer. But here again one stands on shifty ground, because the pronunciation of names is perpetually changing.

Perhaps Mr. Sharp's designation "Anglo-Celtic" may be a name under which can unite the contending forces that have arrayed themselves as supporters on the one hand of the claim to Scotch-Irish blood, and on the other to Anglo-Saxon lineage—meaning thereby pure English. Without doubt these two elements are the strongest in the mountain population, though the Highland people are not different from the Lowland Southerners in this respect. The Scotch-Irish strain is strongest in some mountain sections; the English in others; and in some communities may be surmised an influence of German ancestry.[3] Personally, however, we have been unable to trace distinguishing characteristics, whether in Lauder-milks—by tradition Pennsylvania Dutch, Westmorelands—English from Virginia, or Campbells—be they Highland, Lowland, or Scotch-Irish. The vast majority of the Highlanders are descendants of settlers who were native born, and who, by their common interests, hardships, and struggles, were blended into a homogeneous people—the type which has come to be called "American."

[1] English Folk Songs from the Southern Appalachians, collected by Olive Dame Campbell and Cecil J. Sharp, G. P. Putnam's Sons, 1917.

[2] London *Times*, Literary Supplement, January 17, 1918.

[3] Some have made much of the Indian element in the mountain population in certain areas, and the author has found a number of families who claim Indian blood. Undoubtedly there is some Indian admixture in the Highlands, as in much American pioneer stock; but it is doubtful whether it has been sufficient to cause marked characteristics.

CHAPTER V

THE PRESENT HIGHLAND POPULATION

IN any consideration of the people now living in the Southern
Highlands, certain questions as to their ethnic composition,
distribution, increase, and social groupings inevitably present
themselves. One is reminded often by friends of the Highlander
that he is the true American, and the type of American usually
seized upon as representative of all Highlanders is the early pioneer
type. The pioneer is, indeed, still to be recognized in many of his
mountain descendants—tall, lean, clear-eyed, self-reliant, never
taken by surprise, and of great endurance.

Recently on a midnight train a mountain youth answering to
this description and clad in his country's uniform, was returning
home from overseas service. His parents lived in the country at
some distance from the railroad. They were not expecting him so
soon, and he aimed to "slip up on them against sun-up." This
involved his tramping twenty to twenty-five miles over rough
mountain roads in the darkness, carrying his overcoat and heavy
leather suit-case. This is not an exceptional instance. Nearly
every mountain teacher has stories to tell of much longer distances
covered on foot in surprisingly short times by both boys and girls
going to spend week-ends with their home folks.

Popular fancy would not be satisfied if the home folks were pictured anywhere but before the hospitable hearth of the little log
cabin of pioneer days. No other dwelling can ever fit so well into
the wooded hills and coves of our mountain country. Built for
service rather than for appearance, there is yet real beauty in the
long lines of the roof. Comfort breathes in the smoke that curls
up from the squat chimney; and when spring plants its daffodils
beside the gray walls and the neighboring peach bloom hides the
dark-hued cedar, there is a charm about the mountain cabin that
few other homes in any region possess. More and more as time

goes on it will be recognized as a symbol of the pioneer life which shaped America, and which still lingers in its strength and in its simplicity in sections of our Southern Highlands.

All mountain homes are not cabins, however, nor are all High-landers of the compelling type described. That life within different areas would vary greatly will readily be inferred from previous chapters. Here the land lay in large unbroken areas of mountain and plateau, there in long fertile valleys or ranges flanked by the rolling country of the Piedmont; now it was disposed in extensive lofty uplands cut by valleys, and again in smaller tracts accessible to urban communities of the bordering hills or of the Valley. In one case the original stock would be little affected by influences from the outside; in another an easy outlet would be offered for native ambition and initiative, as well as a ready retreat for dis-satisfied elements of the Lowlands. At certain points because of strategic position cities would spring up, and at others the variety of the mountain country would account for a rural life of different degrees. Common ancestry would not, of course, insure equality of social standing nor the same measure of character among all settlers. Roosevelt's comment as to the composition of pioneer society held true of society in the mountains: "The influence of heredity was no more plainly perceptible than was the extent of individual variation. * * * * * All qualities, good and bad, are intensified and accentuated in the life of the wilderness."[1] The good became heroes; the bad, criminals.

Continued isolation would tend to further accentuate these dif-ferences, and accessibility to minimize them. The urban dwellers of the Southern Highlands are, as a rule, the more accessible, and on the basis of accessibility and inaccessibility some deductions may be drawn as to existing groups, for inaccessibility suggests not only the obstacles arising from topography and distance but the various and often more difficult obstacles to economic and social contact and intercourse engendered by isolation.

It is to be regretted that statistics on population, its size, com-position, and distribution, must be based on the census of 1910. Conditions are changing fast in many sections of the Highlands.

[1] Roosevelt, Theodore: The Winning of the West, Vol. I, p. 167. New York, G. P. Putnam's Sons, 1900.

Increases in the groups of non-native stock and in urban populations, especially in the Greater Appalachian Valley and in mining
areas of the Allegheny-Cumberland Belt, are to be expected in the
returns of 1920. The figures given in Table I, however, will serve

TABLE I.—POPULATION OF THE SOUTHERN HIGHLANDS AND DISTRI-
BUTION OF POPULATION BY NATIVITY AND RACE, BY BELTS. 1910

Belt	Total popula- tion	Per cent						
		White					Negro	Others
		Native born		Foreign born	Total white			
		Of native parents	Of foreign parents					
Blue Ridge	1,257,230	84.1	0.5	0.3	84.9		14.9	0.1
Greater Appa- lachian Valley	1,581,307	78.9	1.8	1.0	81.7		18.3	(a)
Allegheny-Cum- berland	2,491,574	87.8	3.4	2.8	94.0		5.9	(a)
Total	5,330,111	84.3	2.2	1.7	88.2		11.7	(a)

[a] Less than 0.05 per cent.

to indicate the size and composition of the present mountain population.

There was in the Highlands, according to the census of 1910, a
population of 5,330,111 persons. Of these, 4,493,727, or 84.3 per
cent, were native white of native parentage. The elements entering into the mountain population and their proportions in each of
the three mountain belts are shown in the table.[1]

How far the unbroken masses of the plateau region have acted to
preserve the native stock is shown by the fact that 87.8 per cent of
the population of the Allegheny-Cumberland Belt is native white
of native parents. The Blue Ridge Belt, owing probably to its more
broken character and the accessibility of some of its valleys, has a
lower percentage of native stock, while as might be expected the
lowest proportion of native white population is found in the Valley.

[1] Detailed statistics are presented in Appendix E showing the amount, density,
rate of increase, and composition of the population of each of the mountain belts,
and of the non-mountain population of the nine Highland states, by states.

To those who have heard the often repeated statement that there are no Negroes in the mountains, the percentage of Negroes in the Blue Ridge Belt and Greater Appalachian Valley may come as a surprise. In the connection, however, that the assertion is usually made, it is true. In many of the remoter counties, especially those where there are few large valleys, few mining or industrial developments, or few cities, there are very few Negroes. The Negro population is largely in the cities of the Highlands, in the Greater Valley, especially in its southern reaches, and in the larger accessible valleys of the Blue Ridge Belt.

The foreign born, who show their largest percentage in the Allegheny-Cumberland Belt, are for the most part congregated in the mining sections, being more numerous naturally in those centers longest developed. In such places they have intermarried somewhat with the native stock, but up to this time their influence upon mountain life has not been noticeable.

It will be seen in Table 2 that the population is distributed among the three belts rather closely in proportion to area. The population is a little less than proportional to area, however, in the Blue Ridge and Allegheny-Cumberland belts, and correspondingly more than proportional in the Greater Appalachian Valley. The latter has accordingly a considerably higher density of population than the other two belts.

TABLE 2.—DISTRIBUTION OF AREA AND POPULATION, AND DENSITY OF POPULATION IN THE THREE HIGHLAND BELTS. 1910

Belt	Per cent of total area	Per cent of total population	Population per square mile
Blue Ridge	27.1	23.6	41.6
Greater Appalachian Valley	22.8	29.7	62.1
Allegheny-Cumberland	50.1	46.7	44.5
Total	100.0	100.0	47.8

The figures for density given in Table 2 cannot serve adequately to give an idea of the concentration of population in certain sections. South Carolina in the Blue Ridge Belt has a population per square mile of 75.6, but this high density is accounted for by the

75

fact that the mountain region in this state occupies only part of the four counties listed as being in the Blue Ridge Belt. The remainder of their areas is taken up by a wide Piedmont Belt in which the cotton textile industry has grown rapidly. West Virginia, which likewise has grown fast by reason of its industrial development, has in that part of the state within the Allegheny-Cumberland Belt a density of 52.4 per square mile. The Valley section of Tennessee, wherein lie Knoxville and Chattanooga, and the Valley section of Alabama, in which Birmingham is located, reach a density of 72.9 and 80.7 respectively; while all of the three belts of Maryland, the Valley early settled and accessible, the one Blue Ridge county including a wide Piedmont area, and the Allegheny-Cumberland region with extensive lumbering and mining development, show high densities, 79.4, 108.1, and 73.2 respectively.

While the concentration of population indicated by these figures is due in large part to urban and industrial development, the Kentucky mountains with an area of 13,302 square miles, in which in 1910 there were only six incorporated places of 2,500 inhabitants and over, surprise one with a density of 43.7, which is higher than that of the entire state of Alabama and almost equal to that of the state of Georgia, although it has hitherto been a region very much shut in. Moreover, here as well as in other less extensive but remote areas of the mountains there is in some valleys and coves and along the watercourses, even to the headwaters of many of the smaller streams, a concentration of population much greater than the density of the general region in which it lies would lead one to suppose. There are, it is true, long stretches of comparatively thin-soiled, level, plateau land sparsely inhabited, and extensive areas of uninhabited land are found among the higher ranges; yet it is by no means true that areas of the mountains generally considered poorest agriculturally always have the lowest density of population.

Comparison of the population increases and densities within the mountains, state by state, and with the non-mountainous areas of these states, brings to light some interesting facts as to population in sections popularly regarded as lacking in natural advantages. The Kentucky mountains again surprise one with an increase of 18 per cent between 1900 and 1910, as compared with an increase in the extra-mountain area of Kentucky of 3.3 per cent. Not only have the Kentucky mountains outstripped the other portions of that state, but the rate of increase has been greater than that in the non-mountainous areas of all of these nine Southern states except Georgia, where the increase is only 1 per cent greater than that in the Kentucky mountains. Yet the rate of increase in the mountains of Kentucky during 1900–1910 was materially less than that for the previous decade.

The increases and the rates of increase in population in the decades 1890–1900 and 1900–1910 for the different belts and for the mountain region as a whole, as compared with those of the non-mountainous region of the states and the states in their entirety, are given in Table 3.

TABLE 3.—INCREASE IN POPULATION IN THE SOUTHERN HIGHLANDS AND IN THE SOUTHERN HIGHLAND STATES FROM 1890 TO 1900 AND FROM 1900 TO 1910

Region	Increase 1890–1900		Increase 1900–1910	
	Number	Per cent	Number	Per cent
Blue Ridge Belt	141,401	14.2	117,727	10.3
Greater Appalachian Valley	191,281	16.6	235,087	17.5
Allegheny-Cumberland Belt	411,072	25.4	462,485	22.8
Total mountain region	743,754	19.7	815,299	18.1
Non-mountain region	1,497,435	15.9	1,258,401	11.5
Total Highland states	2,241,189	17.0	2,073,700	13.4

It will be seen that while the Highland region shows a falling off in the rate of increase during the decade 1900–1910, there was, nevertheless, an actual gain in population between 1900 and 1910 of 815,299, as against 743,754 for 1890–1900. Moreover, the rate of increase for that decade in the entire mountain region is not only considerably above that of the non-mountain region of the same states as well as that of the states in their entirety, but in the Greater Appalachian Valley is actually higher than in the preceding decade. As a matter of fact the population is still increasing rapidly, although a shifting in its position and certain county losses, which have not arisen simply from a subdivision of counties, might give an impression to the contrary.

The study of gains and losses in different parts of the Highlands presents such startling contrasts in regions sometimes closely adjacent as to demand local explanation. Surveys would be necessary to determine the various conditions acting to produce decline in numbers. Some of these losses are in good agricultural sections and would seem to be due not merely to agricultural conditions but to social and industrial causes which have operated in other parts of the United States to decrease rural populations. From a study of groups of counties showing decreases it would appear that the buying up of large tracts of land by lumber and water-power companies and the pull of the cotton mills to the Piedmont section have been among the prominent factors.

The largest increase of population has been in the Allegheny-Cumberland Belt, due to the development of coal mining and the industries attendant upon it. The second largest increase is in the Valley Belt, where transportation facilities were established earliest, where most of the first cities grew, and where there are the largest areas of good land. In all the belts the urban group is increasing rapidly, and in the mountains as elsewhere the causes that hasten this tendency are the economic, educational, and social poverty of rural life.

The urban and rural groups of the Highlands offer, as previously suggested, on the basis of accessibility and inaccessibility, certain features by which the population may be classified. The obvious danger of such a basis for classification lies in inferences that may be drawn as to the ratio of poverty and need to accessibility or inaccessibility. Extremes of wealth and poverty are associated with urban quite as much as with rural conditions, and sometimes the greatest need is found not in the most remote parts of the Highlands, but near urban centers and in connection with comparatively accessible but poor soils on the edge of the mountains.

It is difficult, moreover, to give to those who have not traveled in the more inaccessible sections of the Highlands an idea of what one means by nearness or remoteness. Nearness cannot here be measured by an air line, and the way that intervenes between the Lowland or urban center from which a traveler may set out and the remote mountain community that he reaches, though short as reckoned in miles, often proves long and wearisome. Whether the journey be made long by the roughness of the road or lengthened by the generous mountain mile, measured as the mountain saying has it "by a coon-skin with the tail thrown in," as acquaintance with conditions grows the traveler comes to feel that such distances cannot be estimated rightly by linear measure. A standard of time is needed to indicate the interval between the two places, for they are separated not so much by miles as by years, decades, or generations.

Before entering upon any discussion of urban and rural groups it is necessary to define what is meant by these terms. The United States census of 1910 classifies as urban population residents in cities and other incorporated places of 2,500 inhabitants or more, although in computing mortality rates it limits the term urban to places having 10,000 or more inhabitants.

It has been questioned whether in matters that distinguish the relative advantages of urban and rural life, a number as small as 2,500 should be used as the urban minimum. Some even go so far as to class the dwellers in communities of less than 25,000 inhabitants as essentially rural people, on the theory that only where a community has reached that size are the important distinguishing differences between urban and rural life apparent.

It is interesting to find that in the entire extent of the nine Southern states whose mountain areas are under consideration, there are but 27 cities of more than 25,000 inhabitants. These nine states with a total area of 345,332 square miles and a total population of 17,521,672, have but two more places of over 25,000 inhabitants than has Massachusetts, with an area of 8,040 square miles and with a population of 3,366,416 inhabitants.

The extent to which the population of the Highland region is rural has been computed on each of these three bases, a minimum population for cities of 25,000, 10,000, and 2,500 respectively, and also on the basis of a smaller urban minimum of 1,000 population. The results are shown in Table 4, which also gives the number of cities in the Highlands on each basis of classification.[1]

From this table it appears that should we apply as the urban standard a population of 25,000 or more, in order to distinguish

[1] For more detailed data see Tables 20 to 25, Appendix E.

urban from rural dwellers, our entire urban population would be confined to six cities (Wheeling and Huntington in West Virginia, Knoxville and Chattanooga in Tennessee, Roanoke in Virginia, and Birmingham in Alabama) and would number 321,311.

TABLE 4.—URBAN AND RURAL POPULATION COMPUTED ON FOUR DIFFERENT BASES. 1910

Urban minimum, used as basis of classification	Number of cities	Urban population		Rural population	
		Number	Per cent	Number	Per cent
25,000	6	321,311	6.1	5,008,800	93.9
10,000	21	541,730	10.2	4,788,381	89.8
2,500	91	859,644	16.1	4,470,467	83.9
1,000	247	1,098,349	20.6	4,231,762	79.4

A better basis of classification is the minimum of 10,000 inhabitants, which is used by the Census Bureau in computing mortality rates. This minimum, however, which is attained by only 21 cities, including approximately 10 per cent of the entire Highland population, is also of doubtful value as applied to the mountains where even the smaller towns are distinguished in comparison with the country about them by features more or less characteristically urban.

On the basis of the city minimum of 2,500 inhabitants, which is more commonly used by the Census Bureau, approximately 16 per cent of the mountain population, or the aggregate population of 91 cities, is distinguished as urban, while approximately 84 per cent is rural. We make use of this division to approach a working classification of the mountain population.

The urban population of the Highlands as thus defined, or 859,644 people, may on the score of accessibility and characteristics generally associated with city life be considered as one group; but inasmuch as a county-seat or a county center of 1,000 inhabitants is a much more important place in so distinctively rural a section than is a similar place in regions more populous, we include with the urban what we call the near-urban folk, or those living in incorporated places of from 1,000 to 2,500 inhabitants. We may also include in this class some communities of smaller size situated in readily accessible fertile coves and valleys, and some industrial nuclei which are more or less difficult of access.

Our first group is then made up of urban and near-urban folk; and as there were according to the census of 1910, 1,098,349 people in the Highlands living in incorporated communities of 1,000 and over, we may approximate the number of this group as a million and a quarter. It is composed largely of those who have been able to compel their environment to minister in large part to their necessities, and who through co-operation might easily carry out measures for wholesome community life where it does not exist. We shall in the course of this study have little occasion to refer to this part of the mountain population,[1] whose characteristics and problems are on the whole not different from those of groups living in similar places in other parts of the United States and who need little assistance save as all groups need touch with the forces working for social advancement. Our attention is directed for the most part to those members of the rural population who for one cause or another are living under the extreme limitations of more distinctly rural life.

Having eliminated the group just described—those in places of 1,000 or more inhabitants, in industrial nuclei, and in the most accessible smaller places—there are yet 4,000,000, or more than three-quarters of the total population remaining in the rural group. This rural population, defined as consisting of those dwelling in communities of less than 1,000 inhabitants, in scattered hamlets and in isolated homes, may be divided, although not entirely on the basis of locality, into our second and third groups.

The second and largest group is made up of the more or less prosperous rural folk, on the whole perhaps not so fortunate as in early times when game and virgin soil gave abundance and even luxury as measured by pioneer standards. While members of this group are likely to live in comparatively accessible parts of the rural districts, near the mouths of creeks or rivers or along main mountain highways, yet in sections that seem to the traveler very remote and inaccessible are families which have always been, if one may trust report, what a mountain economist termed "corn-

---

[1] Rural mortality statistics in Chapters VI and X are based on an urban minimum of 10,000 inhabitants and therefore refer to a large portion of this first group.

sellers" as opposed to "corn-buyers." On the basis of their own-ings and their more generous manner of living, they belong clearly to the second class and must be so considered.

The third class is small as compared with the first and with the second. In it are those with small and usually poor holdings, in distant coves, at the heads of streams, and on the mountain and hillsides, tenants, and all who have found it impossible to adapt themselves to the changes taking place. In general the members of this group may be designated as the most inaccessible, but in-dividuals properly belonging to it are found scattered through areas and communities occupied by the other two. In such cases they are less likely, of course, to be owners of land, and more likely to be renters or common laborers eking out a precarious existence.

Because of the impossibility of giving separately the number in the second and third groups, of necessity they have been enu-merated together. To some it would seem wise to regard the two as but one group, considering what we call our third as the helpless portion of the second. The general status of our second group is, however, so high as to necessitate in fairness a separate classifi-cation.

To distinguish our second and third groups by a description of family status and living conditions is difficult. The range is wide and change is rapid. Views generally accepted are based upon observations of a decade or two ago. This is not to say that these views are not true within certain areas today, but conditions were more static earlier and are much more in flux today. While it is possible still to survey a community, or even a county, and to draw true pictures of the various groups within that particular area, one is less able than in the past to make such a survey and to say that what is found is typical of large areas. There must be more com-parison neighborhood by neighborhood and county by county.

Distinctions based, at least in part, upon differences in living conditions are more easily discerned by the traveler through the mountains. One who has enjoyed for a night the hospitality of a more prosperous family in the remote Highlands, carries away with him a pleasing picture of the comfort and simplicity of such moun-tain life.

Here, where the bottom land along the creek widens, he sees at the end of a day's hard ride a cluster of low gray buildings flanked by gnarled and untrimmed apple trees and backed by an imposing row of bee-gums. In the center is the home itself, a rambling log house grown to accommodate successive generations; or it may be a more pretentious new white frame house trimmed with the bright blue so dear to the mountain heart. About it are numerous smaller buildings generally of logs—loom-house, "plunder room," corn-crib well filled, and the roomy barn, too much open to the elements as judged by an eye accustomed to barns of other sections but well supplied with fodder for all the stock.

The traveler does not need to be told that here lives Uncle Big Jim Franklin who "keeps" people for the night. Hallooing at the gate, he asks the woman who comes to the door if she can accommodate his party of two, three, or four, as it may be, and at her assent he and his comrades slip wearily from the saddle, turn the animals over to a son of the house or to the hired man who comes from the region of the barn, and pass through the paling gate and up the step into the house.

The room they enter is plainly furnished—a bare floor, a few chairs, and two or three beds. On the walls hang large crayon portraits of father and mother, with their first-born in her arms, together with pictures of the older brother or the little sister who died (now twenty years ago) enlarged from some crude photograph or tintype taken by a traveling photographer. Often there is an organ, and the guests are eagerly urged to play.

"Washing up" is generally relegated to the porch, and fresh water is drawn from the well or brought from the spring for this purpose.

By this time the fire has been lighted in the big fireplace, and all gather about to "warm." Our host, it seems, is getting out some of his timber, and after a brief time he appears, followed at intervals by the sawmill hands who slip in unostentatiously to join the group about the hearth.

Desultory conversation as to season, crops, and timber is interrupted by the announcement of supper, and all file out to the long table set in a room near the kitchen. Places are taken without ceremony. The host sits at the head. One of the guests is generally asked to return thanks. The hostess and the women who are helping her wait upon the men and upon the guests. There is an abundance to eat—pork, usually fried, and if it be hog-killing time, the backbone is offered as a great delicacy; fried potatoes, cornbread, hot biscuits, honey, apple-butter and jellies of various sorts, canned peaches, sorghum, coffee, sweet milk and buttermilk, fried chicken, and fried eggs. The meal is not interrupted by much conversation, and there is no lingering afterward. Eating is a matter of business.

Adjournment to the fireplace is prompt, and the women, after eating their supper, betake themselves to the kitchen to clean up after the meal. This kitchen is an interesting place, holding as it sometimes does both the old and the new. Here is the modern cookstove, on which supper has been prepared, and where now water is heating for the dishes; and there the old fireplace, still used by some in the preparation of certain foods, glows with the cheering warmth of oak or hickory embers.

The menfolk have in the meanwhile become better acquainted, and the host is easily persuaded to tell of early days in the mountains and to give his views on political questions in which he is interested. In turn the guest is called upon to give an account of the outside world, and if his sojourn there has been within the last few years his views on the World War and a recital of its outstanding events are eagerly sought, for many sons of the mountains have crossed the "great waters," and the accounts that they have sent home have whetted the appetite of their families for more information as to submarines, airplanes, and tanks, and of the countries of the Allies. Surprising, often, is the accuracy of the observations made and the knowledge shown concerning the countries at war, and equally surprising are some of the deductions drawn. The right and wrong of the various questions raised is always measured by the Scriptures, or rather by the speaker's interpretation of the Scriptures. England, according to one host, who described the geography of Italy with great accuracy, was likely to be punished because she had made lords of some of her people, and the Scriptures plainly taught that there was to be but one Lord.

The evening closes with our host's giving his views as to how certain prophecies of the Old Testament are being fulfilled in the outcome of present-day events, as read by him in the Toledo *Blade* or some other paper to which he subscribes. It is all, of course, his own interpretation of the events about which he may have read; or if he be illiterate, of reports of events upon which he has "studied."

The guests have hardly closed their weary eyes, or so it seems to them, when they are called to arise. It is long before day. The surrounding hills are not yet visible. Making a hasty toilet they join the growing group at the fireplace, where they await sunrise and breakfast. This early rising is not a sign of pressing haste. The host has time after breakfast to take the visitors several miles into a rough boundary of virgin timber, where the yellow poplar, still uncut, rises straight and tall among the other trees.

One who in foreign lands has experienced the mental struggle as to whether to offer a gratuity to the lordly personage at the entrance of a palace, will know something of the struggle in the mind of the guest in parting with his host. The hospitality of the Highlander is proverbial, and last night's guest, now his personal friend, would not insult him by offer of payment. After a number of diplomatic approaches the offer is finally made. It may be rejected. In late years, however, so many have come into the mountains upon purely business matters, sometimes to the detriment of the mountain people, that the Highlander has become accustomed to strangers, and occasionally strangers are "taken in" in more senses than one. So the guest may plead the largeness of the party and finally secure a reluctant assent to payment. If, however, it is known that the traveler is in any way connected with school work or church work, the refusal to receive payment is still quite general.

Frequently at parting the host and hostess will bring a little something for the ladies to take away—a pocket full of apples, walnuts, or hickory nuts; and the guests ride on their journey with the hearty injunction to "come by soon again."

From this more prosperous type of mountain home the homes grade downward. Differences in the status of families at either end of the group are sometimes striking, but often such disparity as exists is not noticeable save in the size of the houses and the land holdings. One may remark a less bountiful table and the absence of milk, butter, and eggs, breads made of white flour, jellies, and preserves. He may note, too, if he is observing, less stock and a scantier farm equipment; but the life of this class is homogeneous, and the absence of some things noted in the homes of the more well-to-do is not of necessity an indication of greater poverty. It may be merely a sign of greater simplicity in the tastes of a family whose standing in the community equals that of the more prosperous household pictured above.

Almost all of this class are farmers. There are some, however, who do not engage actively in farming, but rent out their lands and give their personal attention to "merchandising"—keeping the country store. Usually the more prosperous store-keeper is also postmaster. Others supplement their farming by running mills, grist mills and sawmills, the latter generally of the portable kind easily moved to a neighborhood where some farmer wishes to cut a stand of timber. Where the character of the land allows, and where local ambition has led to the planting of other than the universal corn crop, the owner of a threshing machine increases his income by going about threshing the crop of his neighbors.

The second class has, of course, its professional group, of whom the doctors and lawyers are usually congregated in the county-seats. They generally maintain a touch with the soil, and many of the lawyers, when not engaged in their practice, operate farms personally or under their general direction. Some of the doctors also have farms under their supervision.

A number of the native ministers have partial support from various church boards and are supposed to secure the rest from their charges on the field; but many of them, though called to preach, make their own living from the farm. There are exceptions to this, but the mountain minister gains with the Highland people a certain prestige in that he earns his living from pursuits such as their own, and has a standing with large numbers because he is not a "factory made" preacher.

There are very few professional teachers. Teaching is generally a stepping-stone to something else—to law, to the ministry, or to politics, to which all mountaineers are greatly addicted.

The third group, while smaller, is more varied in character than the second. The stronger members are those who have in them the

86

potentialities of the second or the first class—the holders of small tracts of the poorer land and the young people just starting out for themselves, whose meager home equipment would mislead the casual observer as to their capacities. In this group, too, are the tenant farmers. These are not nearly so numerous as in the Lowlands. Perhaps it is not yet an overstatement to say that nearly two-thirds of the mountain farmers still own their own farms. But tenancy is growing as the more well-to-do feel the need of a fuller life for their children, or as the children themselves feel this need, and the family moves to the county-seat or out of the mountains and lets out the old homestead to "renters" or "croppers." Too often the desire in the children to leave their old surroundings is incited by the ostentatious dress and expenditure of those whom shrewd exploitation of mountain resources has made newly rich; by tourists, or even more unfortunately, by some of the teachers from the outside world who do not appreciate the simple beauty of many aspects of the Highlander's life. The influence of the schools themselves in this movement away from the country, because education is not adapted to rural life, has not been sufficiently recognized.

Other active causes of tenancy are the buying up of large tracts by mining and lumber companies. One cannot forget the pathetic stories of some, once freeholders of the second class, who had fallen into the third class and were unable to rise again. Tempted by the bait prepared for them by agents of lumber or mining companies, they sold their land and moved to the West, where "there warn't no tall timber, and nary spring of running water." Homesick for their mountains, they had returned to become tenants or squatters upon the land that was once theirs, graciously allowed to remain by those who had despoiled them, as payment for some service of profit to the despoiler. Perhaps they had been enticed to the cotton mill by that self-heralded forerunner of the millennium, the mill agent, and had come back shattered in health and less able than before to meet the increasingly hard conditions of life in their old environment.

Among the homes of the third group, as would be expected, may be found the "typical" one-room log cabin, and its successor the box-house, hastily constructed of rough lumber. Some homes, where equipment is reduced to a minimum and conveniences of all kinds are lacking, are yet carefully tended and dispense a clean and cordial, if somewhat limited, hospitality. Others, equally hospitable, are far from clean. One is at times forcibly reminded of the words of Bishop Asbury, traveling in 1803 the Wilderness Road. "The people, it must be confessed," he wrote, "are among the kindest souls in the world but kindness will not make a crowded log cabin, twelve feet by ten, agreeable."[1]

One hesitates to portray these homes which have been described with so free a pen in literature and "missionary" tracts, the more so because there is such great variety in them. The best, which shade imperceptibly into those of the second class, show evidences merely of a picturesque poverty.[2] The poorest are, in their sordid dirt, confusion, and lack of all comforts unrelieved save by the beauty of their surroundings. In some the fireplace is still the only means of cooking, and the food in quantity, variety, and preparation is much inferior to that found in even the more modest homes of the second class. Among the very poor, cooking dishes are at times almost entirely wanting,[3] the same utensil being used again

[1] Journal of Rev. Francis Asbury, Vol. III. New York, 1821.

[2] "One cabin which we visited near the foot of Pine Mountain, though of the better sort, may be taken as typical. Almost everything it contained was homemade, and only one iron-bound bucket showed the use of hardware. Both rooms contained two double beds. These were made of plain white wood, and were roped across from side to side through auger-holes to support the mattresses. The lower one of these was stuffed with corn-shucks, the upper one with feathers from the geese raised by the housewife. The sheets, blankets, and counterpanes had all been woven by her, as also the linsey-woolsey from which her own and her children's clothes were made. Gourds, hung on the walls, served as receptacles for salt, soda, and other kitchen supplies. The meat-barrel was a section of log, hollowed out with great nicety till the wood was not more than an inch thick. The flour-barrel was a large firkin, the parts held in place by hoops, fastened by an arrowhead at one end of the withe slipped into a slit in the other; the churn was made in the same way, and in neither was there nail or screw. The washtub was a trough hollowed out of a log. A large basket was woven of hickory slips by the mountaineer himself, and two smaller ones made of the cane of the broom corn and bound at the edges with coloured calico, were the handiwork of his wife. Only the iron stove with its few utensils, and some table knives, testified to any connection with the outside world. The old flint-lock gun and powder-horn hanging from a rafter gave the finishing touch of local color to this typical pioneer home. Daniel Boone's first cabin in the Kentucky wilderness could not have been more primitive."—Semple, Ellen Churchill: The Anglo-Saxons of the Kentucky Mountains: a Study in Anthropogeography. Vol. XLII, p. 10–11. Reprinted from Bulletin of the American Geographical Society, August, 1910.

[3] In one exceptionally poor cabin where there were father, mother, and nine children, the cooking outfit consisted of one pot, one bread pan, and one big spoon.

and again for numerous household purposes. The only furniture of which there is a generous supply is beds, three or even four being not uncommon in one room.

There is little privacy in such homes, but the stranger who may chance to spend the night in one of them will be surprised by the delicacy with which a semi-privacy is often insured in his sleeping room, shared, of necessity, with many of the family. It cannot be denied, however, that for those predisposed to criminality, these conditions and others growing out of them give opportunity for its indulgence.

The resentment that has been aroused in the mountains, and the misunderstandings that have been spread concerning the mountaineer in the Lowland South and throughout the North, have come generally from the exaggeration of the weaknesses and virtues of individuals in the third group, and from presenting as typical the picturesque, exceptional, or distressing conditions under which some of them live. The resentment, not unnaturally, is deepest in the hearts of those of the first and second groups when, through lack of qualification they are, by inference, pictured as living under such conditions.

The opening up of the country by railroads and industrial development is making rapid changes in many parts of the mountains. The wealth that has come accentuates social distinctions little noted in the days when the mountaineers subsisted chiefly by distinctively rural pursuits and lived as rural folk. The gap between the first and third groups has been widened, and while many of the second have shared in the increase of wealth that economic development brings, by opening to them near at hand a ready market for their surplus products, all of the group by no means share in the prosperity. The changes that one notes are the changes noted everywhere. Some pass into the first group; others fall into the third, through their inability to meet the demands of the new life arising from increase of population and the passing of pioneer conditions to which they had learned to adapt themselves well.

CHAPTER VI

INDIVIDUALISM IN VARIOUS ASPECTS

SPEAKERS who have sought to raise money in the North for mountain work have been wont to dwell upon the part played by the Highlander in the Civil War. They have told how the Highland South was thrust like a Northern wedge into the heart of the Confederacy; how Highland recruits in the Federal Army exceeded the number of those from many a Northern state, and how, like their famous ancestors at King's Mountain, these later mountain heroes went out and turned the tide of war. Such statements, admittedly true of the Highland country in large part, especially of its more northerly reaches, have not been accompanied by an explanation of the causes which led certain sections to support Northern arms. The impression, therefore, has grown that the Highlander is in reality a Northerner in a Southern environment. The impression is far from the real truth.

The Highlander is a Southerner not only in geographic situation but largely in sentiment as well, although the circumstances of his environment have sometimes aligned him with the North. He is, however, first of all a Highlander, and those without his favored land are "foreigners," be they from North or Lowland South.[1]

If the question were submitted to an impartial jury as to what is the chief trait of Highland people the world over, the answer would be independence. Should one ask the outstanding trait manifested by the pioneer, the reply would be independence. Inquire what is the characteristic trait of rural folk, particularly of the farming class, and independence will again be the answer. Put the query as to what is the prevailing trait of the American, and

[1] Commenting upon this use of the word "furriner" as applied to all people from without the mountains, Kephart, in Our Southern Highlanders, quotes the experience of a traveler who asked a native of the Cumberlands what he would call a "Dutchman or a Dago." "Them's the outlandish," was the answer, after a moment of deliberation.—Kephart, Horace: Our Southern Highlanders, p. 17. New York, The Outing Publishing Co., 1913.

the unanimous verdict is likely to be independence. We have, then, in the Southern Highlander, an American, a rural dweller of the agricultural class, and a mountaineer who is still more or less of a pioneer. His dominant trait is independence raised to the fourth power.

Heredity and environment have conspired to make him an extreme individualist. In his veins there still runs strong the blood of those indomitable forebears who dared to leave the limitations of the known and fare forth into the unknown spaces of a free land. Year by year they lived the solitary life of the pioneer, pushing on to south and west along the extreme border of the frontier; and generation by generation, facing alone the dangers and the hardships of the wilderness, they learned the ways of freedom. From among them in the Carolina foothills came, May 21, 1775, the first Declaration of Independence, whereby "we the citizens of Mecklenburg County" so ran the document, "abjure all political connection, contract, or association with that nation who have wantonly trampled on our rights and liberties," and "do hereby declare ourselves a free and independent people."

In the Piedmont of Carolina was born, too, the Regulation movement, which, though characterized by the colonial governor as "not wanting evidence of most extravagant licentiousness and criminal violences on the part of that wretched people,"[1] was withal the rising voice of democracy against the excesses of a privileged

[1] From a letter of Governor Martin of North Carolina, 1772.—Colonial Records IX, pp. 357–358.
"Bassett, who quotes this letter in his account of the Regulators of North Carolina, describes the war of the Regulators not as an attempted Revolution, but a popular uprising against corrupt and oppressive methods of administration employed by agents of the government, a government which, however, was in the hands of a privileged group who acknowledged no responsibility to the people. The movement was characterized by excesses and lack of organization, and was finally brought to an end by the defeat of the Regulators at Alamance, 1771. It was after this defeat that so many of the Regulators moved to the West. Morgan Edwards, who visited the regions of the Regulator trouble in 1772, is quoted as writing: 'It is said 1500 departed since the Battle of Alamance, and to my knowledge a great many more are only waiting to dispose of their plantations in order to follow them.' Bassett suggests that had the Regulator movement not been defeated, it might have run into a Revolution. As it was, it had no connection with the Revolutionary War. He adds that most of the Regulators were Tories, but it is assumed that he does not refer to the large numbers who moved West to the Watauga region, which evinced such marked loyalty to the American cause in the Revolution."—Bassett, J. S.: "The Regulators of North Carolina," in Report of the American Historical Association, 1894, pp. 210–212.

and corrupt official class, a voice which, silenced for the time and place, found later expression beyond the Blue Ridge in the formation of the Watauga Association, the first free and independent community on the continent made by men of American birth; in the struggle carried on in that far wilderness for the cause of American independence; and again in 1784 in the secession of the Association from the mother state[1] of North Carolina to form the new and independent state of Franklin.[2]

Not less the lovers of freedom were those frontiersmen who fought their way against hostile Indians across the Alleghenies to southwestern Pennsylvania, where lay, it will be recalled, in the counties of Westmoreland, Fayette, Washington, and Allegheny, the third reservoir of population from which the Highlands were supplied.

"They were, in fact, a warlike race," writes Brackenridge of these settlers; "besides their Indian Wars they had sent two regiments to aid in the cause of independence. The facility for obtaining land was no doubt a great inducement; but it is certain that the nucleus of these settlements was composed of an enterprising and intelligent population, and who, far from being a lawless people, as we have seen it the case in some of our new territories, held the law and constituted authorities in respect with an almost religious feeling."[3]

Yet in this very region, so strong was the spirit of independence among the people when they felt that their rights were invaded, was raised in 1794 the first revolt, the Whiskey Insurrection, against the newly organized government of America, a step barely averted in Virginia and western North Carolina[4] by the mediation of Washington and by extreme concessions.

[1] This was before North Carolina had ratified the new United States Constitution.

[2] See note, Chapter III, p. 29.

[3] Brackenridge adds further: "The number of very superior men brought on the stage by the western Insurrection cannot fail to excite surprise. The rapid increase of population toward the close of the Revolutionary War, somewhat alloyed the original character, by the accession of numbers among whom there was a proportion of desperate characters; and although the farmers were orderly and respectable, many of them possessing considerable landed wealth, yet there were others, little better than mere squatters, ready to engage in lawless enterprises at the instigation of a popular leader."—Brackenridge, H. M.: History of the Western Insurrection in Western Pennsylvania, Commonly Called the Whiskey Insurrection, 1794, p. 16. Pittsburgh, W. S. Haven, 1859.

[4] The Whiskey Insurrection was felt by Hamilton to be an important test of the strength of the new government. He thus wrote to Washington:

"Besides the state of things in the western part of North Carolina, which is

A century passed; cities grew within the greater mountain valleys. Railroads and highways joined the life of the urban Highlands to that of the rest of the country, but beyond the lines of travel within the ridges and smaller valleys the isolated existence of the pioneer persisted still, little trammeled by state or federal control. His independence became, indeed, intensified. Remote from ordered law and commerce, the Highlander learned by hard necessity to rely upon himself. In frontier fashion he responded to calls for aid in clearing land, in raising homes, and in other enterprises which demanded common effort. But labor of this sort was free and voluntary, controlled only by such public opinion as could be effective in a region rough and sparsely settled. Allegiance he gave to no one, unless he chose to give it. Each household in its hollow lived its own life. The man was the provider and protector. He actually was the law, not only in the management of affairs within the home, but in the relation of the home to the world without.

Circumstances forced him to depend upon his own action until he came to consider independent action not only a prerogative but a duty. "We are not easily aware," says Turner,[1] writing of the traits manifested on the frontier, "of the deep influence of this individualistic way of thinking upon our present conditions. It persists in the midst of a society that has passed away from the conditions that occasioned it." Moreover, in many sections of the mountains all conditions that produced it have not passed away. The temper of the Highlander is in fact the independent democratic temper of the frontiersman, caught between the ridges and hardened by isolation into an extreme individualism, while the frontier itself has passed on to the westward and vanished. In the mean-

known to you, a letter has just been received from the supervisor of South Carolina, mentioning that a spirit of discontent and opposition had been revived in two of the counties of that state bordering on North Carolina, in which it had been apparently suppressed. This shows the necessity of some immediate step of a general aspect, while things are preparing, if unhappily it should become necessary, to act with decision in the western counties of Pennsylvania, where the government for several obvious considerations, will be left in condition to do it. Decision successfully exerted in one place, will, it is presumed, be efficacious everywhere."—Works of Alexander Hamilton, edited by Henry Cabot Lodge. Vol. VI, p. 334, in Letter from Hamilton to Washington.

[1] Turner, Frederick Jackson: "The Significance of the Frontier in American History," in Report of the American Historical Association, 1893, pp. 199-227.

time a new age, one that calls for co-operative service and community spirit, peers over the mountain barrier and with puzzled and critical eye views this individualism not as a natural result of conditions which could not be controlled, but as evidence of a people strange and peculiar and somewhat dangerous withal.

A study of mountain individualism has its beginnings, as has been suggested, in certain aspects of pioneer history during the latter half of the eighteenth century. It is to this period that we must look first for the causes which were instrumental in shaping the relation the Highlander was to bear to the later life of the nation, and in particular for those causes which had their influence in the part so many Highlanders took in the Civil War.

It will be recalled that the early mountain population was recruited not from the slave-holding planters of the Lowlands but in the main from the poor but vigorous small farmer class of the Piedmont region, men who reared their houses and tilled their fields with their own hands. Later settlers of Lowland birth were, too, in many cases, small farmers who had been driven out by competition with slave labor. A few among them, it is true, held slaves where these were an economic asset. Sevier, we are told, farmed his rich lands on the south bank of the Nolichucky with slave labor, and there were some slaves early in the Valley of Virginia. Occasionally, here and there, prosperous families would bring slaves into strictly ridge and mountain areas, where their descendants may still sometimes be found.[1] Generally speaking, however, there were few Negroes in the Highlands in early times. Their number has gradually increased in the rich valley areas, particularly where there has been urban or industrial development, but they have never become a factor in rural mountain life. This is due somewhat to the climate, but largely to the fact that it has not been possible to utilize their labor advantageously in growing the usual crop, corn, in the narrow valleys and on the steep slopes of the more mountainous regions, and that through a large part of the Highlands cotton could not be raised. Even in recent times

---

[1] In one very remote Highland region there still exists a small community of this sort, living an independent and respected life. Social intercourse would seem not to be familiar between the two races, but feeling is kindly, and instances are known where colored and white preachers have officiated together at the same funeral meeting.

there have been very rural counties without a single Negro inhabitant, and where it was unpleasant if not unsafe for him to go. "A no-tail bear" he was dubbed by a terrified child who beheld him for the first time. The attitude of these counties cannot be considered as typical, for in parts of the mountains there is little race prejudice, while in other parts it is strong. The smallness of the Negro population in the Highlands and the causes which led to it, however, serve to indicate why, from an economic standpoint at least, large sections of the Highland South were in sympathy with the North on the Negro question.

There were other early causes which tended naturally to bring about a difference in political alignment between Highlands and Lowlands. For many years after the Piedmont region and the Valley of Virginia were well settled, control of governmental affairs continued to lie in the hands of the older Tidewater aristocracy. The struggle between the aristocratic planter of the Lowlands, with his slaves and large holdings, seeking to maintain the privileges which had been his from early times, and the new small hill farmer determined to secure fair representation in the councils of the state, continued from the eighteenth into the nineteenth century.[1]

The difference in interests between the two sections, due largely to political and economic reasons, was intensified by social distinctions. Not only did the gentleman planter of the Tidewater fear that, should control of government pass to the hill country, taxes for internal improvements which benefited him little would be levied upon that part of his wealth—slaves—which was practically non-existent in the uplands, but he dreaded the political control of those whom he considered his social and intellectual inferiors. The fact that the up-country people were, before the Revolution, predominantly Presbyterian, while the Tidewater aristocracy in whose hands lay most of the legislative power were largely of the Established Church, was an additional source of friction.

Adjustments in representation were not finally made until the

[1] "In Virginia, in 1825, for example, the western men complained that twenty counties in the upper country, with over two hundred and twenty thousand free white inhabitants, had no more weight in the government than twenty counties on Tidewater, containing only about fifty thousand; that the six smallest counties in the state, compared with the six largest, enjoyed nearly ten times as much political power."—Turner, Frederick Jackson: "The Rise of the New West, 1819–1829." In The American Nation: A History, pp. 51–52. Harper Bros., 1906.

first quarter of the nineteenth century,[1] and by that time the Piedmont region had become more closely identified with Lowland interests through the extension of slave labor and the cotton industry. In the meantime, however, many of the discontented Piedmont element had moved on into the mountain country, carrying with them an intense spirit of independence, a desire for self-government, and a feeling of antagonism toward the earlier settled Lowland regions.

That some of the Piedmont folk who passed on through the mountains and settled in the fertile level regions to the west should gradually become aligned with their former aristocratic rivals of the eastern coast, was determined naturally by the similarity of their economic interests. Equally natural was it, too, that large numbers of those who remained in the Highland region, isolated by ridges and rough roads, should retain their old traditions and prejudices. They held, withal, a deep though distant attachment to the Federal Government, for which they had fought in the Revolution, the War of 1812, and that with Mexico. The doctrine of States' Rights, separated from its slavery bias, was but an abstraction to them. With the outbreak of the Civil War, West Virginia, eastern Kentucky, and east Tennessee were found quite generally standing firm for the Union. The Highlands of North Carolina and Virginia showed a larger Confederate element, which was even larger in the southerly parts of the mountain country.[2]

In the little community toward the southern end of the mountains, where the writer taught his first school,[3] were many veterans, some from the Northern but more from the Southern armies. At his hearth sat often a man who had stood with the "Rock of Chickamauga," and another who had starved with Pemberton at Vicksburg and taken his tender farewell of Lee at Appomattox, and there was no bitterness or rancour between them.

In another community near the southern end of the Highlands, so many were the representatives of either side that a Blue and

[1] In West Virginia not until it became a separate state in 1863.

[2] It has been estimated by some that the proportion in the North Carolina mountains was about half and half.

[3] This region, however, was not generally settled until after the war. Many of those who came in at that time were from adjacent Highland sections, but there were also many from Lowland areas.

Gray Camp was organized. On the Southern Memorial Day, veterans in tattered uniforms of both colors marched to the school hall to listen to declamations on patriotism by the school boys for a gold medal which the camp itself had offered, while above them on the one side hung the picture of Lee beneath the Stars and Stripes, and on the other, framed in Southern garlands, the picture of Grant.

An amusing illustration of the different feeling existing in different sections is shown in local adaptations of two old English ballads, the one from northern Georgia and the other from Kentucky. That from Georgia, known as "Jack Fraser," recounts how the heroine, "dressed in men's array," is "landed in the wars of Germany" in the course of a search for her lover. According to a version frequently sung in the mountains she boldly declares:

> "It would not change my countenance
> To see ten thousand fall," [1]

The sympathies of the Georgia singer, however, led to the following rendering:

> "It has never dashed my countenance
> To see those Yankees fall.
> Oh—To see those Yankees fall."

The second ballad, on the other hand, collected in Kentucky and locally known as "Pretty Polly,"[2] causes the villain, addressed in a Child variant as a "mansworn man"[3] to receive the damaging characterization:

> "You are too bad a rebel"

It is probable that the Highland region as a whole, especially the Highlands of Kentucky and Tennessee, experienced some of the bitterest feeling of the Civil War. The roughness of the country led to a sort of border guerrilla warfare. Roving bands from both armies, and sometimes independent groups of "bushwhackers," wandered the hills, robbing and murdering. Many are the tales

---

[1] "Jack went a-sailing." See Campbell and Sharp: English Folk Songs from the Southern Appalachians, No. 55, p. 189. New York, G. P. Putnam's Sons, 1917.

[2] Ibid., No. 2, p. 3.

[3] Child, F. J.: English and Scottish Popular Ballads, No. 4 H, p. 6, "May Collin." Houghton, Mifflin, and Co., 1904.

still told of the suffering of those days, some with the picturesque quality seldom absent from any aspect of life in our Southern Highlands.

By the hearth-fire of a mountain home in the border country of Tennessee and North Carolina, a region even today rough and isolated, the writer heard from a woman of seventy how that section in wartime had been harried by "rebel" raiders. Women and children were imprisoned in a big log house, while the menfolk fled to the mountain tops for refuge. Night after night one of the women, escaping the guard when darkness fell, would steal to the mountainside with food and conceal it in the hollow trunk of a certain tree where the fugitives could find it. Our hostess, at that time but a young girl, slipped out one night with two or three companions to seek for the body of a kinsman who had been killed, so they had heard, by pursuers on the mountain. She drove a young mare hitched to a mountain sled, such a sled as may be seen today on almost any mountain farm. The body, which had been lying out for several days, was laid on the sled and they started down in silence through the steep black forest. At one place, where her companions crossed the stream by the foot-log, she was left to drive through the dark ford alone with the body. The moon struggling through the clouds shone full on the pale face of the dead man, and the young mare, nervous with the unusual conditions, started and tried to run. It was, the narrator said, the "most awful time" she had ever experienced.

It may be said in passing that this region has elected but one Democrat to office within the memory of the oldest inhabitant. A good-roads campaign is alleged to have been the occasion of the lapse from pure Republican principles. The voters wished the new road to be laid along a certain course, and they feared that personal interest would influence the Republican nominee to consider the improvement of his own farm.

That there were many Southern sympathizers in sections admittedly largely Union, it is hardly necessary to say. A friend of the writer, "born and raised" in West Virginia shortly after the Civil War, in a county which, he says, was practically Northern in spirit, tells how his father, a Kentucky mountain preacher who had left his native state because of the threatened outbreak of a local feud, brought up his whole family to be anti-Union and fiery Democrats. In his boyhood the Highlander actually believed, he says, that in the North a wounded Southern soldier would have been left to perish from neglect. Restless in the midst of Northern sentiment, at seventeen he slipped away and returned to his father's kindred. Kentucky was a revelation to him. The feud which his father sought to escape was at its height; the boy, who had never seen a murderer and but one man who had served a penitentiary term, was not only a witness to killings but himself shared in some actions of the "war." But while the immediate neighborhood of his father's old home was still Democratic and hated the "Yankees" as fiercely as the boy did, he found that the country all about was Republican, and it still remains so.

In a section not far removed from this, the writer recalls a house marked plainly with the inscription, "The Corner Stone of Democracy," to indicate to a Republican community the political sentiments of its owner. His must have been a valiant spirit, for so frequently was the declaration used by passing neighbors as a target, that "the corner stone" was at the time last seen, riddled with bullet-holes.

The political affiliations of the Highlanders make an interesting study. Largely a result of war and pre-war conditions, they still continue to be molded to a certain extent by environment. The Highlander is, in other words, an individualist in his politics. He cannot be depended upon to go with the "Solid South." Frequently, and in some states by large majorities, he votes the Republican ticket, and his stand upon various questions is opposed to that of his Lowland kinsman. The natural difference between Highland and Lowland interests may be illustrated by the recent defeat of a good-roads bill in one of the mountain states. The mountain portion of the state, after a strenuous publicity campaign, went almost universally in favor of the bill, which, however, was defeated by a Lowland majority. The reason for this action on the part of the Lowland voter is alleged to have been that the Lowland section already had many good roads and was about to build more, and that it was unwilling to have so much state aid diverted to the mountains, where roads were not only poor but road building very expensive. In addition, the expense would fall mainly upon automobile holders, and automobiles were far more numerous in Lowlands than Highlands, and likely to be for many years.

In no phase of mountain life, however, can one generalize from local conditions.[1] Counties have been sometimes gerrymandered, and in places senatorial districts have been so large as to permit the election of a nominee who represented a party majority over a considerable area rather than the dominant political sentiment of his own county.[2] Again, conditions may be the result of outright political trading.

The Highlander is a born trader. Indeed his faculty in this line seems little short of genius. Doubtless the scarcity in the past of actual currency in the mountains has contributed to his proficiency. It used to be the writer's wish that he could live to see a mountaineer trading horses with a Connecticut "Yankee." The match would be a close one, but the odds, he believes, would not lie with the Northern competitor.

If the reader would be convinced, let him go to a Highland horse-swapping. The riders spurring up and down the creek or Big Road present a stirring scene, and much may be learned of trade. A mountain neighbor, especially proficient in this branch of art, once sought to swap an ancient mule that was lame in one foot. The exchanges that he made were many, but nightfall found him ambling home on the same old animal with one dollar to boot.

With such incidents in mind we are not unprepared for the keen relish shown in parts of the Kentucky hills for the "Swapping Song," reminiscent not only of Mother Goose but of recent experiences:

[1] Fess Whitaker, in his electioneering for the office of jailer of Letcher County, says: "I told them in a very funny way that I had to peal to Jenkins very hard because she had votes at Dunham, Burdine, and Jenkins proper, and that I had none at home because I lived in the only Democratic precinct in the county and that I had five brothers, forty-three uncles, two hundred and seventy-one first cousins, and Jeff Ison, my father-in-law, and all were Democrats and I was the only Republican."—History of Corporal Fess Whitaker, Life in the Kentucky Mountains, Mexico, and Texas, pp. 79–80. Louisville, Ky., The Standard Printing Company, 1918.

[2] A few years ago, one mountain state senator represented ten large mountain counties with a population of about 150,000, as against some Lowland senators who represented two small counties with a comparatively small population.

" I swapped me a horse and got me a mare,
And then I rode from fair to fair.

> Tum a wing waw waddle,
> Tum a jack straw straddle,
> Tum a John paw faddle,
> Tum a long way home.

I swapped my mare and got me a cow,
And in that trade I just learned how.

I swapped my cow and got me a calf,
And in that trade I just lost half.

I swapped my calf and got me a mule,
And then I rode like a dog-gone fool.

I swapped my mule and got me a sheep,
And then I rode myself to sleep.

I swapped my sheep and got me a hen,
O what a pretty thing I had then.

I swapped my hen and got me a rat,
Looks like two little cats upon a hay-stack.

I swapped my rat and got me a mole,
And the dog-gone thing went straight to its hole."[1]

Contracts and all business transactions are regarded as trades. The foreigner in the mountains, struggling to light his stove with soggy chestnut wood which he ordered as hickory, is wont in moments of discouragement to call the Highlander dishonest. Dishonest he is sometimes, but more often his is the attitude of the trader. He gives you credit for knowing as much as he does, and if you "catch up with him" he thinks the more of your ability. If, on the other hand, you try to deceive him, you will find him a shrewd judge of human nature, whether it be urban or rural; and your characteristics, physical, mental, and moral, are likely to be unsparingly epitomized.

Politics naturally offer a wide field to his trading propensities, and trading is unfortunately many times interpreted as mere buy-

[1] "The Foolish Boy," in Campbell and Sharp: English Folk Songs from the Southern Appalachians, No. 115, p. 313. New York, G. P. Putnam's Sons, 1917.

ing and selling.[1] It has been claimed by some of Highland birth, whose familiarity with their courts through official position entitles their opinion to respect, that corruption in politics and elections, and such forms of crime as are connected therewith, have steadily increased in the mountains in recent years. In certain sections liquor has been brought in freely at election times and election day disgraced by drunkenness, rowdyism, and the more or less flagrant selling of votes. "Shameful," it was called by a Highlander, a native himself of a region remote from contact with the outside world; and he added that even in a case where a number of would-be politicians had pooled their money, they were known to have spent more in the pursuit of office than they could hope ever to secure in its performance.

It should not be inferred that conditions throughout the Highlands are worse than those elsewhere, but practices of this kind are peculiarly open to criticism in these rural areas, since the manner of the individual's life is more generally known than is the case in urban or near-urban regions. Conditions are, however, far worse than they should be in a region where native intelligence is high and where social problems are uncomplicated for the most part by the presence of other races. Strong causes may be found in the high rate of illiteracy which exists over large areas, and in the lack of social ideals—both closely related to isolation and independence.

As might be expected, interest centers in local rather than in national or even state politics. The election of a President is not a matter of deep concern to the Highlander, nor, in the past, has the course of his life been greatly affected by the proceedings of the legislature at the state capitol. Far more important to him is the election of county superintendent of schools, county attorney, or judge; and great interest is usually manifested as to the person of the circuit judge, for on his attitude, especially in very rural sections, depends somewhat the freedom with which certain classes of crime may flourish abroad.

The office of sheriff is perhaps the object of keenest competition

[1] "The mountain politician, however, is often a trickster, and knows all the by-paths of political chicanery and crookedness. He can buy votes on election day without the slightest moral reservation or remorse of conscience."—Combs, Josiah Henry: The Kentucky Highlanders from a Native Mountaineer's Viewpoint, p. 23. Lexington, Ky., J. L. Richardson and Company, 1913.

—"sheriffing," as its pursuit is sometimes called. The office is not an easy one, and great credit is due those men who, in the face of lax and sometimes hostile public opinion, have the courage to carry out the letter of the law. Such a sheriff the writer recently met; in person and in act he disproved the conception held by many that the Highlander's is a degenerate and dying stock. Above six feet in height, powerful in body, and fearless in purpose, he had, with the assistance of his deputies, captured forty-two stills during one year of his office, nine of them in one week, destroyed the tubs of some eight or ten more where the stills had been hidden, and had arrested or indicted about seventy-five moonshiners; and this in a country exceedingly rough and when some of the stillers were armed and desperate. He had with him, it is true, the general sentiment of a county tired of crime and anxious to be rid of liquor, which contributed so largely to it—an attitude far more common in the Highlands than is generally supposed.

The Highlander is, however, a clannish person, and he does not like either to inform on his kinfolk or to witness against them in court—obstacles to justice peculiarly effective in a country where most of the inhabitants are more or less closely connected by ties of blood. As an individualist he has, too, an instinctive sympathy with the person under arrest, unless that person has been guilty of an offense against himself. Evidence thought secure sometimes melts away in the publicity of the court room, and a verdict of "not guilty" may be secured when knowledge of the offender's guilt is quite general throughout the community.

In the performance of his duties as principal of a mountain school, the writer at one time became involuntarily involved in the attempted prosecution of a group of moonshiners. The news of the "Professor's" participation spread rapidly through the countryside, and he received many secret visits from men with whom he had had no previous acquaintance, who wished to inform him about the moonshine activities of certain of their neighbors. One in particular, an elderly man with long gray hair, who assumed an air of deepest mystery, asserted that his own cousin was, by his stilling activities, "breaking up the church and ruining the youth of the country." When the listener, impelled by curiosity, ventured to ask his visitor how he had come to inform upon a kinsman, a practice so uncommon in the Highlands, the reply came that the suspect was a bad man and was thought by the informant to have killed a sheep belonging to him. All information furnished in this manner was to be regarded by the recipient as strictly confidential and was, in point of fact, of little practical value. Much of the evidence was circumstantial, and hope of bringing the men to trial rested largely upon the judge, who had been a heavy drinker in youth but had reformed and could be relied upon to fight the liquor interests. It was learned later that three of the best-known moonshine suspects awaited the outcome of the hearing prepared for flight. One, at the top of a hill where he could overlook the court house, sat mounted on his mule, and when the signal came drove in his spurs and crossed the line to South Carolina. The second fled to North Carolina; the other to Wisconsin.

Of all phases of mountain life having root in individualism, those of moonshining and the feud are the ones most commonly attributed to the mountaineer and most widely advertised. Some of our readers, possibly, have wondered why it was that the moonshiner and feudist were not mentioned in the classes discussed in the previous chapter. Had public opinion among those who do not know the mountaineer been followed, they would, doubtless, have been listed with the professional groups of the second class. As a matter of fact they are not limited to any class. They may be found in all of our mountain classes, although they form a very small proportion of the whole.[1]

The moonshiner, as he is called without the mountains, or blockader, as he is more commonly known within them, is one who engages in the illicit distilling of spirituous liquors. Secrecy is necessary for this practice, and he is called moonshiner because it is supposed that he engages in his illicit traffic on moonlight nights when there is enough light to make work easy and enough darkness to make him secure. To dispose of the product of his still, he or his confederates must run the blockade thrown about the

[1] A Highlander who has occupied posts of responsibility in his county and state, thus expresses himself on this point in a personal letter to the writer: "I want to say that in all the feuds and in all the moonshining only a bare remnant of the population were engaged notwithstanding what any yellow journal, parson, or novel-writer may have said. I mean for 'yellow' to apply to all of them. A 'tinker's dozen' of mountain out-laws can get more notoriety from such people as these than all the out-laws in the entire country."

sale of liquor by government officials. He is, therefore, regarded as a blockade runner, or "blockader." While he may ply his trade with the assistance of but one or two associates, he is often a member of a ring made up of men of different groups, all of whom have more or less to do with the making or retailing of illicit liquors. There doubtless are in the mountains many of these whiskey rings, but one may travel long distances without seeing a sign of liquor, and should one unacquainted in a neighborhood and who has not the "open sesame" seek to procure it, difficulties would at once be apparent. In places, however, where public opinion is lax, liquor is retailed quite openly.

Any teacher in charge of a school in the Highlands is likely to come into contact with this moonshine problem sooner or later. At times it becomes to him a very potent source of trouble, especially when liquor is conveyed to boys who are under his charge. An occasion of this sort brought the writer at one time into open conflict with what proved to be a ring of blockaders. One group acted as manufacturers in the mountains; a second as middlemen in the neighborhood of the school; and a third as traders in the Lowland counties, swapping the moonshine for cattle and driving the cattle back into the hills. Several personal friends and school patrons were in the ring, and although later forced to pay the penalty they seemed to bear the school authorities no ill-will. They had matched their wits against ours and had lost—that was all. They admitted, moreover, that the president of the college and his colleagues would have been unworthy of their trust if they had not fought the ring, and that they themselves would not have cared to have their own children under less conscientious tutelage.

Later, when the practice was revived and it was necessary for the president to be away for several months on an endowment campaign, word was sent to him that he need not be anxious about his boys. The blockaders would see to it that no liquor was brought to town in his absence. They kept their promise while he was away, but soon after his return the familiar signal of three hoots of an owl, or three shots at regular intervals, broke the stillness of the night, and those who had been a-thirst during his absence were glad again. He was regarded not so much as an unfriendly opponent as a "foeman worthy of their steel," and the situation was again "up to him."

A steady and reliable student admitted in a moment of confidence when leaving school that he had made a portion of the money which had maintained him during the term by assisting distillers in his home neighborhood. His father did not know of it and would have been opposed to it, but he slipped out from home at night. "Hit hain't nary bit o' use, Perfessor," he went on, "to tell me hit does harm. Why! up in my country [a county notorious at that time for moonshining] a young feller don't think no more of asking a girl to take a drink of liquor than he does here to ask her to take a buggy-ride. I got two aunts, one eighty and one ninety, and both of them have drank liquor all their lives." Discounting what a student may tell a professor, especially upon parting, this statement illustrates the attitude held toward the use of liquor in certain neighborhoods.

Moonshining is due primarily to economic reasons. It is, too, an easy way to make money. It is condoned as a protest against a system of taxation which appears to give special privilege to few on the basis of a money standard merely. Yet in this country of paradoxes many mountain counties were dry before their states went dry, and furthermore, popular opinion in many other counties has long been against the manufacture and use of liquor. This is not altogether due to moral reasons. The absence of a rural constabulary, and the sad results arising from the practice of drinking and carrying guns, have served to reinforce moral causes and to create sentiment against liquor.

Changes have been so rapid in the mountains in this regard as in others as to make incidents based upon observations a few years ago somewhat untrustworthy, yet they will serve to show attitudes that still prevail. On a journey through a mountain county some time ago, the writer passed beside the Big Road a still operated under a federal license, although in that county local sentiment was against the use of liquor. Where there is such a conflict it is little wonder that moonshining is increased. The mountaineer argues, whether justly or unjustly, "So and so can get government sanction for distilling because he manages by hook or crook to get money for his license. If it is right, the poor man ought to have the same chance as the rich." In this case the charge was made that the holder of the license had bought it with money made by illicit stilling.

In a state, dry presumably throughout its territory, the law a few years ago was openly violated in its capital city. The moonshiner arrested for making and selling blockade liquor in the mountains and led to the federal court in the capitol to answer for his crime, would pass by saloons running in open defiance of the state law and serving liquor which might have been made, so far as the prisoner knew, in this dry state under a federal license. Is it to be wondered at that he should become confused and fail to see the justice of his arrest, or that when arrested and out on bail awaiting trial, he should continue to make moonshine to pay his lawyer and lay by something toward the support of his family in the event of his conviction, a situation not uncommon in the past? The justice of the Highlander's position is further strengthened in his mind by the thought that his corn, raised with hard labor and sold at small profit, will bring four to five times as much a bushel when distilled into whiskey. This is a strong argument with poor men having large families.

As has been suggested, moonshining is not new in the Highlands, nor was its practice unknown among the ancestors of the Highland people before they came to this country. Like the ballads it has survived, and has survived in the mountains longest because the conditions there have been suited to its survival.

Brackenridge has given an interesting review of the history of the Western Whiskey Insurrection in Pennsylvania, to which reference was made at the beginning of this chapter:

> The four western counties at the time of the Western Insurrection, or riots (Westmoreland, Fayette, Washington, and Allegheny) contained about 70,000 inhabitants, scattered over an extent of country nearly as great as that of Scotland, or Ireland. Except Pittsburgh, which contained about 1,200 souls, there were no towns except the few places appointed for holding the courts of justice in each county. There were scarcely any roads, the population had to find their way as they could through paths or woods, while the mountains formed a barrier which could only be passed on foot or horse-back. The only trade with the east was by packhorses; while the navigation of the Ohio was closed by Indian

wars, even if a market could have been found by descending its current.

The farmers, having no market for their produce, were from necessity compelled to reduce its bulk by converting their grain into whiskey; a horse could carry two kegs of eight gallons each, worth about fifty cents a gallon on this, and one dollar on the other side of the mountains, while he returned with a little iron and salt, worth at Pittsburgh, the former fifteen to twenty cents a pound, the latter five dollars per bushel. The still was therefore the necessary appendage of every farm, where the farmer was able to procure it;* if not, he was compelled to carry his grain to the more wealthy to be distilled. In fact some of these distilleries on a large scale were friendly to the excise laws, as it rendered the poorer farmers dependent on them.

Such excise laws had always been unpopular among the small farmers in Great Britain; they excited hatred, which they brought with them to this country, and which may be regarded as hereditary. Scarcely any of the causes of complaint which led to the Revolution had so strong a hold upon the people of Pennsylvania as the Stamp Act, an excise regarded as an oppressive tax on colonial industry. Every attempt of the colony or state to enforce the excise on home distilled spirits had failed; and so fully were the authorities convinced that they could not be enforced, that the last law on the subject, after remaining a dead letter on the statute book, was repealed just before the attempt to introduce it under the Federal financial system, by the Secretary of the Treasury, Alexander Hamilton. The inequality of the duty between the farmers on the west and on the east side of the mountains could not fail to strike the most common mind; for the rate per gallon on both sides was the same, yet the article on the west was worth but half of that on the other side. There were, moreover, circumstances necessarily attending the collection of the tax, revolting to the minds of a free people. Instead of a general assessment, a license system confined to a few dealers on a large scale, or an indirect tax on foreign imports, while in the hands of the importers or retailers; this tax created a numerous host of petty officers scattered over the country as spies on the industry of the people and practically authorized at almost any moment to inflict domiciliary visits on them, to make arbitrary seizures, and commit other vexatious acts; the tax was thus brought to bear on almost each individual cultivator of the soil.[1]

* "For these reasons we have found it absolutely necessary to

[1] Brackenridge, H. M.: History of the Western Insurrection in Western Pennsylvania, Commonly Called the Whiskey Insurrection, 1794, p. 16. Pittsburgh, W. S. Haven, 1859.

introduce a number of small distilleries into our settlements, and in every circle of twenty or thirty neighbors, one of these are generally erected, merely for the accommodation of such neighborhood, and without any commercial views whatever."—Petition of the Inhabitants of Westmoreland County, 1790. Pennsylvania Archives, XI, 671.

Kephart, in his volume on the Southern Highlander, brings the history of excise laws as they affected the mountains up to comparatively recent times.[1] The excise law of Hamilton was repealed in 1800, when Jefferson became President; re-enacted as a war measure in the War of 1812; repealed in 1817; and not re-enacted again until 1862, during the Civil War. Since then the activity of the moonshiners has varied with its profitableness. In late years state prohibitory laws have increased activity in certain quarters under the temptation afforded by whiskey at $18 to $40 per gallon. The high price, brought about by a limited supply, has added monetary stimulus to the natural protest and also led to very harmful adulterations.

An old acquaintance of the writer, yielding to the temptation, was wont to make one gallon of moonshine do service for two or three by diluting it with water and mixing it with lye or tobacco to give it a bite, and with Gold Dust washing powder for the bead.[2] As a result one of his patrons was found dead by the roadside one autumn morning. It had been the practice in the neighborhood to leave a jug in a brush heap with a cup. The patron, watched from some secure vantage point, would take what he wished and leave payment in the cup. In other places there would be a bell-tree, or a hollow trunk, which yielded its store when the bell was rung. In the case in point, circumstantial evidence was strong, but the difficul-

[1] Kephart, Horace: Our Southern Highlanders, Chapter VIII. New York, The Outing Publishing Company, 1913.

[2] "When it comes to concoctions used as a substitute for liquor by the inhabitants of many sections of the country where statutory prohibition prevails," says the Asheville *Gazette News* of January 6, 1916, "officials of the internal revenue bureau are not easily shocked. However, there was genuine amazement over a drink recipe figuring in a North Carolina moonshine case. It appears that two moonshiners got into a quarrel with the result that one went into court and exposed the business secrets of the other. Here is the recipe for the latest North Carolina 'temperance tipple' called 'white lightning': 'One bushel corn meal, 100 pounds of sugar, two boxes of lye, four plugs of tobacco, four pounds of poke root berries, two pounds of soda. Water to measure and distill.' This recipe is for fourteen and one-half gallons of the 'third rail' liquor."

ties in getting convincing proof were many. A verdict of homicide was rendered by the jury, but the evidence was of such nature as to lead soon to a pardon.

With the passage of the Prohibition Amendment to the Constitution, distilling in the mountains has become less a phase of individualism peculiar to the Highlands, and is taking on more and more the characteristic features of the problem all over the United States. This is especially true where the country has been recently opened up by railroads, highways, and industrial projects of different kinds. In one such county adjoining the one in which the sheriff cut up forty-two stills in a year, where coal mining is now extensively developed, officers cut up fifty stills in ten days.

In another section, not in the coal region but recently made accessible by a good road, automobiles from urban centers can in a night come almost to the distillers' door and escape with the booty in the darkness. As a result moonshining has greatly increased. It was claimed here that a bushel of corn, which under ordinary circumstances would bring but $1.50 to $2.00 a bushel in the market, could, by distilling and adulteration with water and extracts of lye and buckeye, be made to yield $53. A more recent claim is made of two gallons of whiskey produced from one bushel of corn and sold at $40 a gallon.

What the ultimate result of the prohibition amendment will be is as yet problematic, but it is likely to be wholesome if the moonshiner is brought to see that one law applies to all and is enforced against all. At present whiskey is being made very freely. " In ——— County alone," a Highland lawyer writes, " there were several hundred persons indicted at the last term of court for selling and making whiskey. This is true," he adds, " through the mountain section, as the people are engaging in it more now than ever. However, there are being steps taken to stop the making and sale of whiskey, which will bring about better conditions in the near future."

There has always been an intimate connection between whiskey and feuds. It was thus explained by a mountain friend and one-time feudist, who had given expression to the fear that the widespread renewal of drinking in his neighborhood, due to unmolested stills, would lead to a revival of the local feud, dormant for some years. As he put it, "The older folks are tired of fighting, but the young folks get to drinking this white lightning, and shootings and killings result. Then the older people are drawn in again, and the feud is on once more." The general "toting" of pistols, a part of their manhood creed, is a contributing cause. The attitude is that of a gentleman of old, ready at all times to defend his personal honor or the honor of his family by his own prowess. It would seem incongruous to see in court a lawyer whose pocket was bulging with an ill-concealed weapon, prosecuting a case in which the defendant was brought to trial for an offense resulting from his having carried concealed weapons. Such inconsistencies were not uncommon some years ago. The law was in advance of public opinion.

Miscarriages of law and justice have been perhaps the greatest cause of keeping up feuds, if not of originating them. "The greatest and most direct cause of the 'old feuds,'" says a Highland friend who had the courage in his youth to stop a feud by refusing to avenge the death of a near relative, "was the fact that the people who engaged in them lived in an isolated, out-of-the-way, law-forsaken mountain section, far removed from the courts, and when an offender was brought into court he was generally turned loose to run at large among the near relatives of him whom he had slain. These people having trusted their rights to the courts of justice (?) and finding their trust betrayed, and the offender, the slayer of their brother or son, insulting them with his very presence and most often with taunts, 'took the law into their own hands,' and killed. The killing of one naturally led to the killing of others, and each one killed brought other relatives and friends into the fray, and hence the feuds."

The situation was thus forcibly put by another mountain friend in reply to a criticism of the Highland feud: "You know folks are mostly related in this country. If I get into trouble, even if I am not to blame, there is no use of going to law if the judge is kin to the other side, or if the lawyer has succeeded in getting his own men on the jury. It doesn't make any difference what the evidence is, the case goes the way they want it to go. Then there is nothing for me to do but to accept, and let them throw off on me as a coward, if I stay in the country; to leave the country and give up all I own, and still be looked at as a coward; or to get my kinfolk and friends together and clean up the other crowd. What would *you* do?"

The original causes of many feuds were often very trivial, and sometimes lost in obscurity. These "wars" involved some of the best and some of the worst people in the mountains, and they were, therefore, at times unspeakably brutal, and at other times touched with chivalry and romance.

Romantic are the tales of the young daughter of a feudist chief, who rode alone by night the twenty rough miles from one county-seat to another to carry messages and give her kinfolk warnings. In a war raging in another county a chivalrous incident relieves some of the more revolting features of such strife. Two young men —we will call them Brown and English—prominent on opposite sides of a feud, had in addition to the feud animosity a personal quarrel, and were watching for a chance to shoot each other. Both, heavily armed, had on a certain day visited the county-seat but had not met. English left first in his wagon. Brown riding out later and suddenly rounding a turn of the road, saw English ahead, all unconscious of his nearness and with pockets bristling with firearms. Three courses presented themselves to him; he could easily shoot English in the back and escape without danger; he could turn and ride back to town, or he could pass English and run the risk of being shot himself. The first course would have been the natural one in such warfare, but it was repellent to him; the second was cowardly; therefore, without increasing his speed, he advanced as quietly as possible, with head straight to the front and pistols in their holsters. From the corner of his eye he saw his foeman start and thrust his hand to his pocket, then pause, pistol half drawn as the thought seemed to come to him that he had been completely in his enemy's power and ere now might himself have been shot. Still without turning his head or accelerating his pace, Brown rode on and out of sight, feeling, he afterward said, "a ball in his back at every step." From that time the two men preserved a silent truce with each other, while the war raged on between factions. Many years later when the feud had ceased they worked together harmoniously in civil office, but they never addressed each other except as duty made it imperative.

In only one feud, so far as is known to the writer, was there deliberate killing of women and children, and this was waged across state lines. There have been numerous cases where a noted feudist is said to have appeared in public in absolute safety, although foes on every side were lying in wait for him, because he was accompanied by his wife or children or had in his arms his young baby.

While feuds have existed in many parts of the mountain country, the most extensive and widely known have taken place in Kentucky. The name commonly applied to the feud in Kentucky is "war," and the principle upon which it was carried on was the principle of warfare—to do as much harm to the enemy as possible while incurring the least risk oneself.

The theory that the feudist's method of fighting his foe from ambush is a survival of frontier methods against the Indians, cannot be substantiated. Instances are not lacking in present days where Highlanders, opposed to each other, employed man to man the same code in fighting as their pioneer ancestors,[1] or the cowboy of a half century ago. However much the brutality of such early encounters may be deplored, there was a certain code of honor observed. They were, however, affairs of man to man, and as a rule not family, clique, nor clan matters fought under the principle of warfare. They were "magnificent, but not war." While men of lower grade in the Highlands undoubtedly did vent personal spites in cowardly ambush, yet if one keeps in mind the times when the great feuds were raging, the conditions of the courts, and the general attitude toward feuds as expressed in the word "war," one has a better vantage point for judgment.

[1] "To settle minor disputes and differences, whether for imaginary or real personal wrongs, there were occasional fisticuffs. Then, it sometimes occurred in affairs of this kind, that whole neighborhoods and communities took an interest. I have known county arrayed against county, and state against state, for the belt in championship, for manhood and skill in a hand-to-hand tussel between local bullies. When these contests took place, the custom was for the parties to go into the ring. The crowd of spectators demanded fairness and honor. If anyone was disposed to show foul play he was withheld or in the attempt promptly chastised by some bystander. Then, again, if either party in the fight resorted to any weapons whatever, other than his physical appendages, he was at once branded and denounced as a coward, and was avoided by his former associates. While this custom was brutal in its practice, there was a bold outcropping of character in it, for such affairs were conducted upon the most punctilious points of honor."—Arthur, John Preston: Western North Carolina, a History (from 1730–1913), p. 274. Raleigh, N. C., Edwards and Broughton, 1914.
Arthur quotes from Dr. C. D. Smith's Brief History of Macon County.

The feud leader was often a political chieftain. He may not have been so ostentatious as the city "boss," wont to don his silk tile and frock coat in attending the funeral of his henchman's baby, but his relations to his followers were much the same. He held a patriarchal attitude toward them, helping them in all times of need and expecting help in return. There were, too, at times, hired "gunmen" as in modern cities. One of the last of the great feuds to die out in the mountains was of this general character. Its end was hastened by the action of the daughter of the slain man, who went about herself collecting evidence against the murderers of her father and brought the case to trial.

It is, of course, possible that there may still be fitful outbreaks of old animosities in certain localities, but they are becoming increasingly improbable. Feuds have passed forever from large areas of the mountains.

The passing of the feud, however, does not mean that the Highlander has ceased to be an individualist in what he considers the administration of justice. The feeling still exists that a man has the right, if he so wishes, to take the law into his own hands, a conviction voiced in the declaration of one Highlander that he would not hesitate to "kill any man who needed killing." The implication of this remark is the stronger coming as it did from a man who, although he lived in a remote section, was progressive in thought, far-sighted, and of unusual beauty of character.

The popular impression that homicide is a common feature of mountain life has long prevailed. While complete and accurate statistics are impossible to obtain for many parts of the region, sufficient data for 1916 are available to throw light on the point. Table 5, including six of the nine mountain states—Kentucky, Maryland, North Carolina, South Carolina, Tennessee, and Virginia—has been compiled from federal and state reports, or, where these did not furnish data on a county basis, from material supplied through the courtesy of state officials.

It is to be noted that the homicide rates which are given in the table for the Highland regions are designated as rural rates, but as they are mortality rates, they are computed on the basis of an urban minimum of 10,000 inhabitants. They should not be taken, therefore, as applying only to the more strictly rural population, classes two and three as defined in Chapter V. In view, however, of the generally rural character of the Highlands, they are more indicative of conditions prevailing than are rates which include the larger cities. This is the more true in that the Negroes in the Highland region are congregated mainly in urban and industrial centers, and the Negro homicide rate is commonly high.

TABLE 5.—HOMICIDE RATES PER 100,000 POPULATION FOR THE MOUNTAIN AND NON-MOUNTAIN REGIONS OF SIX SOUTHERN HIGHLAND STATES. 1916

| State | Rural | | | | | | Urban and rural |
	Blue Ridge Belt	Greater Appalachian Valley	Allegheny-Cumberland Belt	Total mountain region	Non-mountain region	Total state	Total state
Kentucky	...	...	10.5	10.5	7.4	8.4	9.95
Maryland	4.7	3.7	...	2.3	6.4	5.6	7.0
North Carolina	8.5	...	...	8.5	7.7	7.8	8.4
South Carolina	6.3	...	...	6.3	12.8	12.0	13.3
Tennessee	8.2	8.5	10.3	8.9	12.6	11.0	19.0
Virginia	6.0	4.8	16.3	8.1	10.5	9.4	11.9
Total (6 states)	7.3	6.8	10.9	8.5	9.6	9.3	13.4

That the Negro homicide rate is disproportionately high and does raise the total rate not only in the urban centers of the Lowlands but in rural parts of both Highlands and Lowlands, may be gathered from Table 6, which shows white and colored rates for North Carolina, the only state where this comparison was possible. As there were no homicides recorded in 1916 for the city of Asheville, which alone in the Highlands of this state attained the minimum of 10,000 inhabitants, the urban homicide rate given for the North Carolina mountain region is zero.

Table 5 shows for the six states as a whole a higher homicide rate for mountain than for non-mountain regions. For North Carolina the lowland rate is almost as high as that for the mountain region, but as is shown in Table 6 this is due to the influence of the Negro rate, which is high in both uplands and lowlands. While the total rural rate for the mountain portion of the state is 8.5 per 100,000 compared with 7.7 for the lowlands, the white rural rate for the mountain region is 7.5 compared with 3.2 for the lowlands.

TABLE 6.—WHITE AND NEGRO HOMICIDE RATES PER 100,000 POPU-
LATION, FOR THE MOUNTAIN AND NON-MOUNTAIN REGIONS OF
NORTH CAROLINA. 1916

	Rural			Urban			Total State		
	White	Negro	Total	White	Negro	Total	White	Negro	Total
Mountain region	7.5	20.8	8.5	...	...	...	7.2	17.4	8.2
Non-mountain region	3.2	15.5[a]	7.7	11.7	28.7	18.1	3.9	16.7	8.5
Total state	4.2	15.8	7.8	10.2	26.3	16.1	4.7	16.7	8.4

[a] Exclusive of Yadkin County, where Negro population is not given.

Making, however, due allowance for the high homicide rate among the comparatively small Negro population in the Highlands, the rural rate of mountain homicides, 8.5 per 100,000, is yet a high one as compared with that, 5.2, for the entire rural registration area of the United States. It is higher than that of the rural part of any state outside the mountains within the United States registration area for deaths except California, 13.3, and Montana, 13.9, and is approached only by Colorado, 8.0. The rates for the rural regions of the remaining states of the registration area descend from 5.7 per 100,000 in Kansas to 0.8 in New Hampshire.

A study of homicide rates by belts and by counties in the Highland region of the six states for which data were secured is of interest. It is dangerous to draw conclusions from figures the exactness of which is limited by the many difficulties attending the collection of vital statistics in the Highlands,[1] and with which there are no data of a decade or more ago to serve as a basis of comparison. It is, however, worth noting that the rates within the Allegheny-Cumberland Belt are conspicuously higher than in the Valley and in the Blue Ridge section. This probably can be attributed to the greater industrial development of this belt which includes almost all of West Virginia. Rates were found to be especially high in those counties where mining operations are being

[1] For a fuller statement see Chapter X, p. 207.

carried on. For example, in 1916 the three largest coal producing counties of the Allegheny-Cumberland Belt of Virginia—Tazewell, Russell, and Wise—show homicide rates respectively of 15.4, 14.8, and 39.3 per 100,000, while across the state line in the recently developed fields of Kentucky, the largest coal producing counties—Pike, Bell, Perry, Harlan, and Letcher—show, respectively, rates of 18.7, 24.6, 30.4, 63.5, and 77.9 per 100,000. Examination of the number of mine employes in these counties reveals that where the miners form the largest per cent of the population the homicide rates are highest.[1]

The fact that the lower of the rates just given are in a number of instances equaled or surpassed by the homicide rates of other counties both in this belt and in the Blue Ridge and Greater Appalachian Valley Belts, compels caution in drawing conclusions. Some of the high rates in other than coal mining regions are in counties that have a comparatively large Negro population, and it is possible that this may account in part for the large number of such deaths. For any definite conclusion it would be necessary to know the local factors that enter into these rates both in mining and non-mining counties. One somewhat familiar, however, with conditions existing in and about new mining communities in the Highlands, need feel no hesitation in calling attention to the likelihood

[1] A report of the U. S. Geological Survey, Coal in 1917 (Part A. Production), furnishes the number of miners in certain counties and makes possible the following comparison between homicide rates and the per cent of miners in the population of these counties:

County	Mine employes		Homicides in 1916	
	Number	Per cent	Number	Per 100,000 population
Virginia				
Tazewell	1,573	6.1	4	15.4
Russell	1,678	6.2	4	14.8
Wise	5,291	12.2	17	39.3
Kentucky				
Pike	3,313	8.9	7	18.7
Bell	3,929	10.8	9	24.6
Perry	1,107	8.4	4	30.4
Harlan	2,086	18.9	7	63.5
Letcher	3,306	28.7	9	77.9

of violence when a people who are unprepared for industrial conditions and who hold still to some of the standards of a past age, are thrust into the congested life of a modern mining development. The increase of moonshining in such regions, previously mentioned, should also be considered as a contributing cause of other crimes.

The types of crime predominant among native rural Highlanders may in general be designated as those arising from a high degree of individualism. They are the crimes of a people hot-blooded and high-tempered, jealous of their rights,[1] and lacking all training in self-restraint—a people, in other words, intensely independent but not debased nor decadent.

A friend of the writer whose ancestors were among the earliest settlers of a Highland region which some years ago was torn by feudal strife, makes the following statement in answer to an inquiry as to crime among his people:

> I wish to say that I have been a lawyer here for fifteen years, and my father has practiced law here for fifty years, and my grandfather was a lawyer nearly a century ago, and I have talked to him about these crimes most generally found on our docket, as well as my father. Of course land suits predominate owing to the way in which this state formerly granted lands, and next to them the only suits of interest are murder suits. Recently since the State of ——, and the United States have gone dry, a great many illicit whiskey cases appear, and they now predominate. . . . From my experience as a lawyer there has rarely ever been a case of larceny, and there has been but one case of robbery in —— County during my recollection. The larceny cases are very few and far between, and assault occurs once in a while, but not very often. The greatest number of crimes now are murders, shooting and wounding, concealed deadly weapons, and discharging firearms on the public highway, illicit sale of liquor, and moonshining.

[1] "The prompt desire of the backwoodsman to avenge his own wrong; his momentary furious anger, speedily quelled and replaced by a dogged determination to be fair, but to exact full retribution; the acting entirely without regard to legal forms or legal officials, but yet in a spirit which spoke well for the doer's determination to uphold the essentials that make honest men law-abiding; together with the good faith of the whole proceeding, and the amusing ignorance that it would have been in the least unlawful to execute their own rather harsh sentence— all these were typical frontier traits."—Roosevelt, Theodore: The Winning of the West, Vol. I, p. 165. New York, G. P. Putnam's Sons, 1900.

From the other end of the Highlands another mountain lawyer writes:

> Our people are independent and are impatient of any restraint. They believe that they have a God-given right to live their own lives as they see fit, are very jealous of their personal freedom, and are usually ruggedly honest. This being the case, you will find that they are as a rule, only charged with crimes of impulse, such as assault and battery, homicides of the different degrees, etc., or crimes against prohibitory statutes which they think interfere with their personal freedom, such as "moonshining" and offenses of that nature. Seldom do you find them accused of crimes such as larceny, burglary, or what are known as social crimes.

Considering the Highlands as a whole, there appears to have been a decrease in crime during the past few years despite the high homicide rate and the increase in moonshining and political corruption cited previously. In many places the docket has grown noticeably lighter, especially where educational opportunities have been available for the people. High tribute has been paid by many prominent men of the mountains to the denominational and independent schools, which were placed many years ago in regions noted for their lawlessness. The influence of these schools, it is claimed, has had a direct connection with the reduction of crime in such neighborhoods. It is, indeed, to be feared that fiction will soon have to seek new fields for picturesque villainy. The Highlander is becoming, as has been wittily said, "less wicked, and, alas, less interesting."

One other aspect of individualism in the mountains should be mentioned—the relation of the Highlander to the Federal Government. Too often the word "federal" has suggested to him taxes and revenue officers. He has little money to pay the former, and while he may never have been remotely connected with illicit stilling, all his traditions and sympathies have been against the latter. He holds, however, a wholesome respect for the Federal Department of Justice, which has a disinterested and persistent way of gathering evidence and convicting a guilty man when once put upon his trail. This feeling was expressed lately by a sheriff who had failed to get a well-known moonshiner convicted before the county court. "He can pay his way out of the County Court," he said, "and perhaps out of the District Court. But we'll get him in the Federal Court."

Although his associations with federal activities have not always been entirely agreeable, the Highlander's loyalty to the government is unquestioned. A recent story which has figured in the columns of several magazines, pictures the mountain father as admonishing the soldier son on his departure for foreign shores to imagine the hostile Germans as revenue officers and "shoot to kill." We do not claim that the story is true, but it does illustrate the paradoxical attitude which is found sometimes in the Highlands.

The Highlands have always furnished a large and valuable quota to our Army and Navy, and its sons have made conspicuously brave soldiers. In the present war many mountain counties volunteered at once far in excess of their quota, and some even very remote counties contributed financially to war activities considerably above the amount apportioned them.

It is true that in parts of the mountains there was a somewhat general lack of understanding as to the causes of the war, the reason for our entrance into it, and particularly the operation of the draft. The feeling was often expressed that it was not our business to interfere, that the government did not have a right to make the boys go unless they so wished, and that they would never come back—a fear to which the "great waters," the submarine danger, and the general ignorance of conditions prevailing both here and on the other side lent unknown and terrifying probabilities.

Newspapers were not available for many, and by others could not be read where they could be secured. Unfounded reports grew by word of mouth.[1] Possibly there was, too, more or less anti-government propaganda, especially in connection with the food laws. For example, the report was circulated through the mountain section of several states that the government was going to seize all the goods canned above a certain amount, usually about two dozen cans.

Parents, anxious and alarmed, wrote to their boys in camp what

---

[1] Great suspicion was felt of strangers lest they should prove to be German spies. Three of the writer's friends, two of whom were in the mountains on government business, narrowly escaped jailing because of their supposed nefarious activities.

one Highland soldier called "pitiful letters." "If the government wants to stop fellows from deserting," he added, "they oughtn't to let the mothers write their boys that-a-way. It breaks their feelings. And they never ought to let the boys go home on furlough. They mean to come back, but their folks pester them to stay." Questioned, however, as to the attitude of the Highlanders as a whole toward deserters, he declared, "They haven't ary bit of use for them in this world!"

There is another factor which should be mentioned in connection with army service. The Highlander's individualism has been explained. His habit has been to do what he wants, when he wants, and only so long as he wants. Time is of no importance; tomorrow will do as well as today. Discipline is exceedingly hard for him to endure, and he is, moreover, a great lover of home, and very apt to be homesick when long out of the mountains. These characteristics are not generally understood by the outsider, who finds it irritating in the extreme to have his plans set at naught for no reason other than that the mountaineer who had promised to help him "just naturally got out of the notion."

Some of the Civil War leaders seem to have understood conditions better. We are told that during that period the mountain soldier who was seized with a sudden desire to see the home folks and disappeared for a few days without leave, was not treated with the harsh sentence of a deserter. He usually returned before long and was an effective if somewhat undisciplined fighter.

It is not the province of the civilian to suggest what methods should be used by army authorities to deal with cases such as these, but one might wish that the understanding spirit possessed at least by one officer had been more widely diffused. Sent with a small detachment into a very rough part of the Southern Highlands to apprehend deserters in hiding there, this officer, it is said, recognized at once the futility of attempting force to carry out his orders. He also understood the men with whom he had to deal. Taking with him, therefore, a number of guns of the newest pattern, he gave one day an open demonstration of what such weapons could do. The interest of the dwellers in the region round about was deep. The Highlander loves firearms and handles them with skill, but these had powers transcending his experience. A group soon gathered. The officer explained the guns, which led to further discussion of equipment, conditions in the camp and across the water, and reasons for the war. As a result a number of deserters, well armed to resist capture, were rounded up by the community, who advised them to return to camp and go on with their training.

Such tactics might not always have been successful, but it is possible that much trouble might have been avoided could the government have carried out an extensive and systematic educational campaign through which reasons for the war would have been made clear and had living conditions of the soldiers, camp activities, and similar information been explained with stereopticon slides as conclusive evidence.

One campaign of this nature, conducted under government auspices in a very inaccessible Highland region, demonstrated the possibilities of such a method. School houses where lectures were given were crowded, and great interest and enthusiasm were manifested. "You've been to a heap of trouble to talk to us," said one of the many who had listened attentively to a long explanation, "and I thank you. I never rightly understood these things before."

But while some of the conditions which have been indicated undoubtedly had their influence in causing evasions of the draft and desertions, which have been more or less widely advertised, it is the writer's belief that the number of such cases has been greatly exaggerated. Generally speaking, the response to the call of the government was one of which the whole mountain region may be justly proud, while the exploits of individual mountain soldiers have been given nation-wide publicity.

The Highlander is not without a humorous appreciation of his militant reputation and of his skill with firearms. "The next war that comes up," writes such a youth who served faithfully but without glory in the medical corps, " I intend to be a sniper. Then maybe I'll have a chance to do something, like Alvin York of Pall Mall, Tennessee. Do you know he is called 'The hero of the war'; not 'one of the heroes' but '*the* hero.'"

CHAPTER VII

THE RURAL HIGHLANDER AT HOME

THERE is nothing austere about the rural Highlands save the simplicity of life within them. There is a softness about the wooded heights and hollows, a beauty of melting curves, of lights and shadows, of tender distances wherein the hearth-smoke is a part and the cabin is at home. "Hit may be rough and rugged, but hit's a sweet home to us," and the Highlander who thus spoke from his heart expressed not only the feeling of his people but the homelike charm of these hills upon all who come to dwell among them.

Whether the long, forest-clad slopes be gray with winter; brilliant with the variant greens and flowering shrubs of spring; softened with the hazy serenity of summer; or rich with the russets, golds, and crimsons of autumn; the setting is one of exceeding beauty. Into it melts the wide-roofed cabin, at times to be distinguished only by the smoke ascending from the broad chimney, or the line of gaily colored quilts spread out to air and sun upon the palings. Nearer at hand the big wool-wheel on the porch is seen, and sometimes a loom with the housewife at work thudding out the yards of homespun, or the far-famed covers, quilts, and blankets. Hanks of wool of different colors are suspended from the rafters, with strings of beans, and "burney" peppers, and ears of drying seed corn. A saddle hangs from a wooden peg in the wall.

Through the wide-swung door the many beds with their bright quilts, the big fireplace where a fire smoulders even in summer, the little straight-backed chairs with their seats of woven hickory, all give a quaint and old-time atmosphere as charming as it is simple.

The yard is bare of grass, "swept smooth and pretty like the palm of your hand," but there is bloom for the summer through— a snow-ball and a rosy-bush, flowering quince and coral-berry. Daffodils are gay in spring, and lilies, dahlias, and sunflowers follow, while chrysanthemum blossoms make rich clusters of color until the "black killin' frost." Here a gnarled and ancient cedar, and there a thick-set tree of box, speak of the pioneer who chose this spot on which to rear his home a' century ago.

Close by is the branch, slipping through growth of "big" and "little" laurel and set with "holly-bush" and groups of towering "spruce-pine." Often the road lies in its bed—the only road, which must be "forded lengthwise" to the little homes which reach far up its course. Down it the man of the household finds his way to store or mill, to the neighboring hamlet and the county-seat; but the woman, especially if she lives up a smaller branch or away at the head of the hollow, is very much shut in. Home duties and the care of the children tie her closely, and the difficulties of travel during long seasons of the year serve still further to limit her to her immediate neighborhood. She has little to do with politics, and little to do with the management of church affairs save when occasion calls to prepare a bounteous repast for the visiting preacher and the many friends who come to hear him. Her place is the home, and in the home the relations of man and woman are Pauline.

From babyhood the boy is the favored lord of all he surveys. There is a dignity, a conscious superiority, in his youthful mien that says more clearly than spoken words that womankind are not his equals. Though by old mountain usage, now yielding in places to the new, he is not his own man till he is of age or marries and makes his own home, he enters early into the heritage of the past and holds himself the proud equal of any human creature. As a man, he recognizes from the first the man's prerogative to order and be obeyed, and right bravely does he stride in the long steps of his father and older brothers. With them he sits at table while mother and sisters stand to serve his wants, and from them he gathers much that were better unknown. He follows them to the field and learns to handle the plow and to crack the braided hickory lash over his yearling steer. He can swing an axe and wield a saw with the older men—valuable assets in the family economy—and always his ambition is to shoot the straightest in the countryside.

He has, however, neither training nor example in self-control. At times his father, equally undisciplined, "whups" him in a fit of furious temper; or the weary and exasperated mother puts into execution her frequent threat to "wear him out with a hickory," but for the most part he is free to follow his impulses whether they be for good or evil. The fact that he is one of many children gives him still greater latitude.

Nor do discipline and self-control come to him through play with his fellows. He has, in his isolation, small opportunity for neighborhood sports. Even the national game of baseball is little known in parts of the remote Highlands, and cannot be played in many cases because of the lack of a free space large enough for a diamond near well-settled regions. Such level spaces as exist are used generally for building sites, or for the bottom-land crop. Through the agency of some of the church and independent schools, basket-ball has been introduced and has met with favor, but it is not widespread enough as yet to be a factor in recreation.

In general it may be said that the common diversions open to the boy are those somewhat solitary in nature, such as hunting and fishing. He is from early years an inveterate hunter. In a southern part of the mountains a fall of snow used almost to break up school, every boy and every available gun being engaged in pursuit of game. So, too, in the spring season he is to be found haunting creek or mill pond for the horny-head, shiner, "pearch," or sucker; or miles away where high among the hills a mountain streamlet roars along its rocky bed, he seeks the trout in some black pool shadowed by rhododendron.

Yet while his forms of recreation are so often lonely ones, it must be borne in mind that there does exist in many neighborhoods, as in urban centers, a "gang" spirit. The boys "up the branch" or "down the creek" gather, especially on Sundays, for amusements which, if not vicious in themselves, are usually accompanied by more or less vicious features. It is such gangs that express their lawless independence and rural conservatism by "rocking" individuals and objects that meet with their disfavor, burning private and sometimes public property, robbing orchards, and similar offenses not peculiar to the mountain region. And gangs of this sort where there are private schools, are likely to manifest the old antagonism of town and country boys against school boys, resulting in petty but persistent annoyances to school authorities and sometimes consequences dangerous to teachers and pupils.

125

The Highland boy has, however, little knowledge of play as play. When he plays he plays to win. In contests of any kind he wishes passionately to be the victor, and if he finds defeat threatens him he is too inclined to give up or take what means he can to reach his end. He is, moreover, very sensitive and swift to take offense. Ridicule, or the suspicion that someone is "throwing off on" him, he cannot bear, and he is quicker with the knife, or, when he is older, with the pistol, than with the fists. Thus he incurs the reproach of being, in popular parlance, a "poor sport," one who does not know the art of "playing the game to a finish," regardless of what it costs. It must not be inferred from this statement that he is a coward, although from a true sportsman's standpoint there is an element of cowardice in his failure to meet defeat squarely and honestly. In feats of daring the mountain youth is brave to recklessness, and as has been indicated in a previous chapter, no man in the country makes a more valiant soldier. He needs, however, to learn the code of honest sportsmanship—the code of the "good loser"—which can best be taught through games which bring him into touch with his fellows in team-play and healthful competition.

Like other boys brought up in the open he is a keen observer, and his shrewd eyes are no more observant of woods and rivers than of the social order about him. He matures early; not into what might be called intellectual maturity, but a maturity resulting from being called upon at an early age to take care of himself and to do his part in meeting the needs of the family. Thrown much upon himself and upon those of the household, and lacking the contact with others enjoyed by the city child of the same social status, he is not forced to check up the opinions he has reached by reasoning from a certain premise with those of others who have reasoned from the same premise. Consequently he arrives at judgments quickly and tends to grow rigid in them; and if he remains in his native environment he swells the number already there who hold to the old and resist the new.

While he thus grows into the ways of mountain manhood his sisters are learning to tread the painful path of mountain womanhood. For them there are few of the child's irresponsible joys. The "least ones" of the large family are the "poppets" with which they play. Their playhouse is the home, in whose duties they must early take a share; nor are they freed from labor in the field but must help to plant, hoe, and harvest the crop; must share in the making of the family garden, and in addition do the many chores not held to be manly by their brothers.

These little girls with their shy and eager eyes are full of promise, but it has not been considered necessary in the past for them to be educated. Irregular attendance at the short terms of the country school was thought enough for woman. Conditions are changing rapidly in this respect. More and more, girls are demanding an opportunity to learn, but too often still, if one of the household is ill, if "mammy" is busy, or the baby needs tending, "sis" must stay at home. She is not an unwilling sufferer always, for she loves the freedom of home. The restraints of school, in particular of those private schools where girls are segregated, prove irksome at times, and not infrequently she runs away and leaves education to the menfolk, thus again inevitably sinking in their respect.

She, too, matures early into a vigorous blooming girlhood, whose aspirations are too often blunted and coarsened by the bald and unrelieved hardness of life. She is alternately suspicious, given to fits of fiery temper, emotional, and sullen—yet again of a delicate, a touching and gentle sweetness that has in it an unconscious pathos.

Though she may at first appear less responsive than the boy of her age, she is marvelously quick to appreciate the new and to adapt herself to changed conditions. Unfortunately this very adaptability, coupled with her emotional and independent spirit, is sometimes her undoing when she is thrust unprotected into the new distractions of urban and industrial centers.

Marriage is her goal. There is little comfort for the spinster, relegated to the hard tasks of life yet dependent for support upon her male and her married woman kindred, all of whom are agreed in thinking her a failure. "Then you be n't married," said the weary mountain mother of many children to a teacher from a distant church school, "and you don't look like you minded it nuther."

The prevailing view was expressed by a little chap of ten in one of the Sabbath school classes which the writer was called upon to teach, when visiting a mountain school. It being near the Fourth of July we drifted into a discussion of the meaning of that day. In reply to a question as to why we celebrated, came the answer, "We fit the British and we licked them."

"What did we fight them for?"

"Taxation without representation."

Thinking that this had been learned in a parrot-like way at school without knowing its meaning, the writer pressed the boy further and was somewhat surprised, although he ought after all his experience to have been immune to surprise, at the response,

"Paying taxes for things you don't have no vote for."

"Does anyone in this country do this now?"

"No."

"How about women?"

"They have an old man to vote for them."

"But suppose they haven't an old man?"

"Their brother."

"But suppose a woman pays taxes and hasn't any husband or brother, isn't that taxation without representation?"

There was a reluctant assent.

"Ought she not to vote then?"

A firm "No," followed by the all-convincing rejoinder, "A woman what ain't got sense enough to get her up an old man ain't got sense enough to vote."

Women are coming to occupy a larger place in the mountains, as without. How rapidly the change is coming about can little be inferred by those who know only the mountains of yesterday. But recently a young woman, graduate of one of the mountain schools, very nearly plucked the political plum of county superintendency of education from her male opponent, and this in a very remote mountain county. The new point of view is typified in the remark, made by a modern mountain mother: "I don't aim to learn my girls how to milk. If they know how, they'll have hit to do."

Apparently, however, judged even by the standard of the youthful male quoted above, mountain women might, at least in a negative fashion, be considered as qualified to vote, for most of them are married. In addition to this being the natural desire of most women, it is forced practically upon all because they have so few opportunities for economic independence.

The gathering of roots and herbs, and the sale of milk and butter in a very limited way, are almost the only means by which women can earn money in the mountains, and as these articles are often bartered at the country store for household commodities, they cannot be said to form a means of support under present conditions. Efforts are being made by some of the various agencies maintaining work in the Highlands to revive the making of linsey, coverlets, quilts, blankets, baskets, and similar "fireside industries." A ready market is found for all that can be secured, but the conditions under which they must be made, during intervals between household tasks and working the crop, make the output small and uncertain; nor is the movement yet one which promises an independent living to any large number of women. Neither is school teaching, under present conditions, a means of entire self-support. The only solution of life for the average girl who stays in the Highlands is marriage.

There is a certain primitive etiquette observed in the courting. Thinking of its conventions one is reminded irresistibly of a certain mountain ballad which would seem to indicate that the mountain girl is not without her humorous appreciation of the courting situation:

"A gentleman came to our house,
　　He would not tell his name.
I knew he came a-courtin'
　　Although he were ashamed.
　　　　O, although he were ashamed.

He drew his chair up by my side,
　　His fancy pleased me well.
I thought his spirit moved him
　　Some handsome tale to tell.
　　　　O, some handsome tale to tell.

And there he sat the livelong night,
　　And not a word did say,
With many a sigh and bitter groan,
　　He oft-times wished for day.
　　　　O, he oft-times wished for day!

The chickens they began to crow,
　　And daylight did appear,
'How-dye-do, good morning, sir,
　　I'm glad to see you here!'
　　　　O, I'm glad to see you here!

He was weary of the livelong night,
    He was weary of his life,
If this is what you call courting, boys,
    I'll never take a wife.
            O, I'll never take a wife!

Whenever he goes in company,
    The girls all laugh for sport,
They say, there goes a ding-dang fool,
    He don't know how to court!
            O, he don't know how to court!"

There comes to mind, too, that cheerful jingle of "Sourwood Mountain," so associated with the twang of the banjo by the evening hearth-fire, when the family is free to enjoy a brief interval of relaxation before the early bedtime.

"I've got a girl at the head of a hollow,
    Hay, didyum, didyum dum day,
She won't come, and I won't follow.
    Hay, didyum, didyum dum day.

Old man, old man, I want your daughter,
    Hay, didyum, didyum dum day,
To bake me bread and carry me water.
    Hay didyum, didyum dum day."

As a rule, however, courting is a serious matter and permits of no trifling. If a girl accepts the attentions of a young man she may not smile upon another. Many a fatal shooting has resulted from this very thing. One of the writer's first pupils was stabbed at a dance because he danced with a girl too often to suit the escort with whom she had come, the stabbing being undoubtedly precipitated by the fact that both young men had been drinking.

Dances in the mountains have been so often connected in the past with drinking, shooting, and evil of all kinds as to have gained the hearty disapprobation of most of the steady church-going population. Households which are accustomed to furnish such entertainment are not those, usually, which have a high reputation in the neighborhood. Yet in the democratic life of the remote Highlands distinctions are not strongly marked, and legitimate social events, such as singings and "workings" where a large crowd may be present, are attended by all who wish to come, regardless of difference in social or moral status. It is to be remembered, however, that these differences do exist and are recognized.

But while enough attends certain social gatherings in remote neighborhoods to warrant condemnation, too generally amusements of all kinds are preached against as sinful. Sentiment is generally against play and amusement, and the Church's condemnation when it does not make, helps to overcharge the atmosphere, so that the young people have not the benefits of social intercourse as have the young people in thickly settled communities.

Naturally the man is freer in this respect than the woman, but the fact that he has so little chance for legitimate amusement undoubtedly accounts for the license of much that is diversion in his eyes. He craves excitement and gets it in whatever form is available. To drink, to ride furiously, to "shoot up the town"—these, with "frolics" and "jamborees" are his way of breaking the monotony of a life barren of more innocent entertainment.

The girl may disapprove, but under the deadening influence of custom and the free mingling of all social groups, she is likely to view masculine failings with philosophic indifference. Too often she accepts the traditional attitude of man toward woman, evidenced in song and ballad of an earlier century. It is not perhaps by chance that some of the most numerous and favorite of the old songs which have survived in the mountains have to do with the faithlessness of men and the misfortunes of girls—such songs as:

> "Come all you young and handsome girls,
>   Take warning of a friend,
> And learn the ways of this wide world,
>   And on my word depend.
>
> I know the minds of girls are weak,
>   And the minds of boys are strong,
> And if you listen to their advice,
>   They will sure advise you wrong."[1]

[1] Campbell, Olive Dame, and Sharp, Cecil J.: English Folk Songs from the Southern Appalachians, p. 289, No. 103. New York, G. P. Putnam's Sons, 1917.

or:

> "I once did have a dear companion;
> Indeed, I thought his love my own,
> Until a black-eyed girl betrayed me,
> And then he cares no more for me.
>
> Just go and leave me if you wish to,
> It will never trouble me,
> For in your heart you love another,
> And in my grave I'd rather die.
>
> Last night while you were sweetly sleeping
> Dreaming of some sweet repose,
> While me a poor girl broken, broken hearted,
> Listen to the wind that blows.
>
> When I see your babe a-laughing
> It makes me think of your sweet face,
> But when I see your babe a-crying
> It makes me think of my disgrace."[1]

The question of illegitimacy is not absent from the mountains, but the social evil is not marked by enticement or seduction. It is more in the nature of animalism and may be traced in part to the lack of privacy in the home, early acquaintance with the sex relation, and a promiscuous hospitality. There is not, moreover, the same stigma put upon the "baseborn" child as in other sections. Many times he is known by his father's name or by the name of both father and mother, and the father feels some responsibility for him. The mother quite generally marries—an older man, often, or a "widder man" with children—and her husband provides for the child of her unmarried state as for his own. If she does not marry she lives, ordinarily, with her parents and her child is brought up as their other grandchildren, seemingly without discrimination. It has been by no means unknown for a father to bring up legitimate and illegitimate children together. Criminal practices to prevent the public knowledge of wrong, while not unknown, are not generally employed. These conditions change, however, when the unmarried mother enters the more complex life of the industrial centers or cotton mill towns, or when the country opens up.

There are not a few men and women in the Highlands living as

[1] Ibid., p. 204, No. 58.

husband and wife who have never been married by any legal form. It was not always convenient in earlier times to wait for a circuit rider to come around or to go to a civil officer; and when one's grandparents, or great-grandparents, and perhaps one's father and mother had thus lived in union regarded as honorable, standards were not rigid, and such marriages became a quick solution for error and transgression. While cases of this sort were held by several of the writer's mountain friends to be due to "pure wickedness," under all the circumstances of isolation, individualism, and illiteracy existing in remote sections of the Highlands irregular relationships have long been tolerated with something of indifference. Public opinion, however, is steadily growing against them throughout the mountain region. Boys and girls who have been away to school and seen life under different aspects not only demand, but set, new standards. It is through these new homes that the changes already begun will become established.

As a rule marriage comes early in the mountains. A girl is a spinster at eighteen, and on the "cull list" by twenty. The writer has had pupils leave school at twelve and thirteen to marry, although this is becoming less common every year. When it is known that the ceremony is to take place the occasion is a festive one, but it is very common for the young people to slip off without warning. Little is demanded in the way of preparation beyond the consent of the bride, the license, and the preacher. One father, keenly mindful of his early poverty, refused to allow his daughters to marry until each had forty quilts, a cow, a pig, two sheep, and a set of dishes. The home, however, is often begun with a less bountiful equipment.

To the sophisticated outsider, burdened with the care of an over-abundance of things of this world, there is a certain charm in the ease with which the young Highlander packs on his wagon his bed and bedding, his few chairs and utensils, his wife and baby, ties his cow to the tail-board, cracks his lash over his mule, and moves to another home.

The simplicity of such life, however, does not always make for ease for the housewife, who is often obliged to do her work without conveniences of any kind. It is a pretty domestic scene upon a bright summer day to see the mother and daughters doing the week's washing in a clear mountain spring or stream, the clothes spread out to dry on the green bushes in the sun. When, however, the weather is raw and cold and the housewife must walk some distance carrying heavy bundles of clothes, the picture has its reverse side. Equally laborious is it to draw all the water needed for washing from deep wells or to secure sufficient supply from those that are shallow. Even in sections where it would be comparatively easy to pipe water into the kitchen, at least for cooking purposes, the housewife is generally obliged to carry in from the spring or well all that is used, and because there is no sink must also carry it out; and when in the hot season the springs run dry and the shallow wells fail, she must sometimes go a long way for water. There are, to be sure, many homes now, especially in the more accessible places, where water has been piped into the house or yard. Sometimes it is made to flow through a hollowed mossy log, where milk pails may be immersed to the top and butter chilled to an icy firmness. But housework even under these conditions is far from easy, and in addition the housewife must help with the main crop, corn.

Criticism has often been directed against the custom of women's working in the fields. Within the writer's experience, however, they have many times expressed preference for outdoor over indoor work, and they take great pride and pleasure in the fenced-in garden plot—their peculiar province. Without wishing at all to minimize the hard lot of the rural housewife, here, as elsewhere, made harder by the absence of labor-saving devices, it should be said that a wrong impression is sometimes conveyed by overemphasis upon her outdoor labor. There are, of course, women whose husbands and fathers leave them to do the indoor and practically all of the outdoor work as well, while they respond to the call to preach or to politics. But the mere fact of outdoor labor does not necessarily indicate that women who engage in it do so unwillingly or regard it as a burden.

There comes to mind the pretty picture of a beautiful mountain girl, who graduated near the head of her class in one of the leading mountain schools. On her return home the family, as a pleasantry, had prepared for her the commencement present of a new hoe, tied with a white ribbon to be in accord with her diploma similarly decorated. The next day she was at work, hoe in hand, with her father, brothers, and sisters in the corn field, for it was the busy season and the crop must be worked.

There is a sociability in labor of this sort. Mrs. Murdoch, in a sympathetic study of mountain life, gives this description of the part the family takes in making the crop:

"The crop" in the mountains means corn, and to have one is an invariable and essential thing; the making of it is gone about quite in the spirit of a festival by whole families.

When the brown earth is warm and soft under foot, after the winter freezes, and the air is mellow with warmth and light and blossom sweetness, the women and children come teeming from their dark little homes in the valleys, like children let loose from school, to make a play of work on the hillsides and by the water courses.

The trees of the forest, for the most part, are still bare of foliage, save where an elm-tree shows a greening top among them; and the smoke from the burning brush-heaps in the clearings settles over their brown tops, a murky blue. The purple judas-trees bloom at the end of Lent with dogwood, and the white and red fringes of the sarvis berry and sugar maple make gay the fence-rows where the cardinals blithely call—"Sugar sweet!" "Sugar sweet!"

The grain is planted when the "oak-leaves are as big as squirrel paws" (and much resemble them), and corn-hoeing begins when the young plants are a few inches high and show plainly in green rows across the fields. The hoeing is more than all a family affair, and it is no unusual sight to see from six to eight members of a family each taking a row around a steep hillside, with the fastest hand leading, while the baby lies on a quilt under some convenient shade and the other small children play about. Small wonder that so much of the work is not well done, and the yield is too often small.

Making the crop is not all a spring festival, however. The whole must be gone over at least three times with the hoes, chopping out grass and weeds and hilling the earth up to the plants. It is delving hard work for women and children before the last plantings are "laid by" to grow without further cultivating in the intense heat of middle July.[1]

In the mountains the saying that "a woman's work is never done" is much truer generally than that "man works from sun to

[1] Murdoch, Louise S.: Almetta of Gabriel's Run, pp. 19–20. New York, The Meridian Press, 1917.

sun." That many mountain men do work hard the most severe of critics must admit, but even during periods of hardest labor they rarely appear hurried or pressed by the necessity of making a living, and there is always time in the long winter season to pick the banjo before the blazing hearth, or by the glowing stove of the country store to fathom the secrets of the universe and all the evidences thereof, as well as some less profound subjects. To this deliberate manner of life is due, possibly, the Highlander's air of detached leisure and calm restraint, which give little hint of his fiery and uncontrolled nature. There is, too, in his attitude something of the fatalism which comes from a long struggle with hard conditions and from a theology which admits neither of joy nor profit in the conduct of this existence. Yet, despite his seeming indifference, the Highlander is naturally emotional, responsive, and aspiring, as those who know him best will testify.

Until recent times a living which he has been accustomed to regard as adequate could be made by the man who worked four to five months during the year. He occupied himself during the other months with "following" whatever he wished. If what he wished did not include supplying the home with modern conveniences, it was not because he was neglectful by intent. It simply had not occurred to him that such appliances were necessary or even possible. Or, again, if he did not always help his wife, it may have been because certain work was women's work. This cannot be pressed too far, but as an illustration may be cited the milking of the cow. A mountain friend of the writer's earlier years was regarded as somewhat of a weakling because he milked the cow for his delicate wife. At about the same time a friend traveling in Scotland and entertained in a home where there were no servants, incurred the reproach of being a "sissy" because with American chivalry he preferred to black his own shoes rather than have the women of the house do it.

There are certain standards by which men and women are judged and in accordance with which their spheres of activity are measured. The writer's wife, traveling with him in a far part of the mountain country, received the doubtful compliment of being as good as a man because of her ability to keep up with the men of the party. The guide was especially impressed by her desire, one snowy winter day, to climb a mountain with the others.

"That little old woman of yours, Professor, is sure the stoutest woman ever I seed! Where's she from?"

At the answer of "Massachusetts," he evinced great interest.

"Why, I knowed a feller once in Tennessee, that went to that place, Massachusetts, ———", and then in all seriousness, placing his hand upon the shoulder of his companion, he added this further compliment, if he intended it as such, "Why, Professor, that feller told me that up thar in Massachusetts, nary woman ever sot her foot out of the house to do a lick of work. She don't milk the cow, she don't tote in the firewood, and she don't carry water from the spring, no matter how far away it is!"

Some overserious-minded reader may read into this more than is intended. Our guide was a fond husband and a loving father. So fond a husband was he that we had to climb to the top of the mountain for mountain birch, whose twigs are especially suitable for "tooth brushes" which he wished to take to his own little old woman who was, he said, "sure the dearest lover of snuff he ever did see," and so loving a father that the writer was compelled to cut short his excursion a day in order that his homesick guide might hasten back to his baby.

The relative positions of men and women must be taken into consideration in estimating many matters. The standard by which such positions are judged is not condoned by a statement of it; but if one seeks without injustice to interpret social actions, the standards on which they are based must be known. Furthermore, it must not be understood that there are universal standards throughout the mountains nor that they are peculiar to the region. It cannot be too often said that the mountains differ in different areas just as do rural sections elsewhere. The only false statements about them are the sweeping generalizations.

The married state of the women of the mountains is thus summed up by a native Kentucky Highlander in an interesting brochure:

The women of the mountains form an interesting study. It has been said they are sullen, grave, and of a retiring disposition. This is largely true, and is accounted for by the fact that their position in the social caste of the mountains is a hard one, and a deplorable one, for the most part. First, race suicide is no question for the sociologist to struggle with in the mountains of Kentucky. Whether or no it is better to rear up a small family and do it well, or to rear up a large family badly, is no concern for the mountaineer. Most families in the mountains are large, some of them very large, ranging from a dozen to eighteen or twenty under one roof. It is not difficult, then, to conceive of the multitudinous cares that must befall the lot of these women, which condition prevents much mingling and social intercourse with the world.[1]

The mountains do not hear the plaint of the childless. There is no need for its women to seek out substitutes upon which to shower pent-up maternal affection. "Seems like a body ought to have at least twelve," was the deprecatory reply of a mother of ten children when asked as to the size of her family. Doubtless she did not express the sentiment of all her sisters, but among the women there is something of the Israelitish woman's attitude of old toward child-bearing.

There is always a welcome for the new little son or daughter, while the affection of the older members of the family for the "least one" is beautiful and touching. Big brothers and sisters will quickly stop what they are doing to nurse the fretful baby, who royally takes precedence of all other interests.

One of the vivid recollections of the writer's experience is that of a scene on a Christmas morn in a school far away in the mountains. Here were scores of children who came from homes of poverty. Most of them were poor in the most common possessions of childhood elsewhere. Christmas was the one day when they might expect gifts because of the large generosity of the school's friends. A little daughter had been born to one of the faculty a few weeks before and made her first public appearance on Christmas morning. As the doors were opened to the room lighted with holiday cheer, and the bulging stockings hung by the fireplace caught the expectant eyes of the children, their faces lighted with anticipation; at the sight of the cradle, however, they turned and crowded about it to welcome the little stranger—forgetful for the time of ball, trumpet, drum, and doll.

[1] Combs, Josiah Henry: The Kentucky Highlanders from a Native Mountaineer's Viewpoint, p. 19. Lexington, Ky., J. L. Richardson and Company, 1913.

Several times within a somewhat extended experience as a teacher in the mountains has the writer been asked to grant a reduction in tuition because of the size of the family. The last request of the kind came from one who had not learned the intricacies and excesses of rebating. The petitioner, having a strong desire to educate his many children, and also having strong within him the mountaineer's proclivity for driving a good bargain, was moved to ask for a rebate if he should send his children by the dozen. He had twelve or thirteen of his own and had adopted six of his brother's upon the death of his brother and his brother's wife from the after effects of measles.

It is small wonder that the mother fades early. Little care is given her in childbirth, for doctors and nurses have always been almost non-existent in the very remote sections, ill-trained or beyond the financial reach of the poor man, and midwives where obtainable are usually ignorant and superstitious. While this statement must like others be modified in certain sections in view of the changes taking place, yet the neglect of women at this period, in the past and in the present as well, is, if not a cause of death the cause of lifelong suffering on the part of so many mountain women as to be a matter of comment by physicians.

Conditions are aggravated by the fact that the mother rarely ceases to work until it is practically time for the birth of her child, and begins again as soon afterward as she can get about. This getting about is often a matter of pride with her. It is by no means unknown for a woman to get up and do the household chores, even the milking and churning, within three or four days after her child is born. Before she has time to regain her strength, with the many calls upon her, there is a new little one in her arms.

If she leaves home the children must go with her. Those who have tried to address a mountain audience against the wailing of a number of restless infants will appreciate this fact. The writer has known one woman to walk seven miles to a meeting, carrying her three-year-old child because "hit wanted to come"; and another to bring her fifteen-months boy three miles in her arms, with her four older children clinging to her skirts.

That many women through the hard and sometimes almost brutal rudeness of their lives should become coarsened and sordid would be natural, yet it is true that suffering has often refined the Highland woman and given her a broad human sympathy not to be expected from the narrowness of her environment.

There is something magnificent in many of the older women with their stern theology—part mysticism, part fatalism—and their deep understanding of life. Patience, endurance, and resignation are written in the close-set mouth and in the wrinkles about the eyes; but the eyes themselves are kindly, full of interest, not unrelieved by a twinkling appreciation of pleasant things. "Granny" —and one may be a grandmother young in the mountains—if she has survived the labor and tribulation of her younger days, has gained a freedom and a place of irresponsible authority in the home hardly rivaled by the men of the family. Her grown sons pay to her an attention which they do not always accord their wives; and her husband, while he remains still undisputed master of the home, defers to her opinion to a degree unknown in her younger days. Her daughters and her grandchildren she frankly rules. Though superstitious she has a fund of common sense, and she is a shrewd judge of character. In sickness she is the first to be consulted, for she is generally something of an herb doctor, and her advice is sought by the young people of half the countryside in all things from a love affair to putting a new web in the loom.

It is not surprising if she is something of a pessimist on the subject of marriage. "Don't you *never* get married," is advice that is more than likely to pass her lips.[1]

Usually she has been a good weaver in her time, and likes to tell how, when young, she could weave five yards of linsey or three of coverlid a day. She would "love" to mix a "blue pot" now, but indigo is scarce and hardly as good as it used to be. She "hates awful bad" to have her dyes fade. She knits her socks her own

---

[1] "Well," said Orlena, "I ain't never been in no country but this one to larn any defferent ways f'm what we foller here, but I've studied on hit a heap myself; more in particular sence my own childern growed up and married. An I sensed hit that ef a young gal can make out to keep straight, and has a good home, she'd better stay by hit, an' let talkin' and marryin' be; anyhow until she's old and has larned enough to spend her opinions and have some 'tention paid 'em. The boys is all men from the time they can stan' up in a chair by the table and glaum theirselves with a spoon; an' when a young girl marries a man she ain't axed to spend her opinions on many subjects!" Murdoch, Louise S.: Almetta of Gabriel's Run, p. 73. New York, The Meridian Press, 1917.

way and does not care to learn new-fangled heels and toes demanded by Red Cross standards. Why should she change? Have not the socks she has knitted from girlhood supplied the needs of more than a generation of children and grandchildren? Yet she contributed many a pair of army socks, and many a sweater as well, and enjoyed immensely the social aspect of the Red Cross meetings held near her community.

Now at last she has leisure to enjoy herself as never before. If vigorous she likes to fish on the bank of the neighboring creek, and she is no mean fisherman, as her catch will prove. She is partial to company and to strange tales of new lands and new places—wants to see them too. One meets her sometimes going a-visiting, not mounted in the shameful new fashion which is creeping in even among her children, but sedately side-saddle, her full skirt and striped apron ruffled about her feet, a red kerchief around her neck, her hands encased in woolen mits. She has perhaps a clay pipe tucked deep down in her pocket, with a twist of home-cured tobacco raised on her own hillside. Under the big sunbonnet or gay handkerchief or "fascinator" her brown and weather-beaten face peers sharply but serenely out on a world which she has no longer reason to fear.

Old age has indeed its compensations both for men and women, more worth-while here in the mountains, perhaps, than in many places more urban and sophisticated. It has at least the respect of the younger generation and the dignity of labor achieved.

Rural life in the Highlands has its limitations, but its picturesqueness has invested with a romantic charm even its more unlovely features. The log cabin of the pioneer and the natural beauty of the country have combined to form a setting in which the simplest actions are imbued with a dreamlike glamour. The crossing of the foot-log above the ford, the washing of wool in the stream, carding, spinning, and weaving, the boiling of clothes in a black pot swung from a tripod, the salting of sheep from a gourd are, as it were, the shifting scenes of a homely drama set on the stage of an agelong gone. The mother who churns her milk and cooks her evening meal by the light of a fat-pine stick is unconscious that she moves in the heightened lights and shadows of a background of the past. So the father, seeking help for his sick wife in the night, rides by the flare of a burning torch and does not know how his lonely beacon touches the blackness with a deeper mystery.

One who has watched the family at fodder-pulling in the late summer, high up on the mountainside, and has heard floating down from that sunny space to the shadowed valley where he is standing the echoes of some old hymn or song, feels himself apart in an enchanted land. The sled or sledge, which alone can be used in fields so high and rough, adds to the illusive unreality of the scene, as, drawn by steer or mule, it descends the steep trail from the corn field.

The very rocks, ruts, and mud which render travel even on the Big Road a weary process have served to keep the canvas-topped wagon with its team or teams of mules not only a practical conveyance but a picture of pioneer days which fires the imagination and stirs the heart. Equally picturesque are the horsemen spurring their way to court or town.

It is afoot or horseback that corn is taken to the mill. The mountain mill with its mossy flume dripping in summer and fringed with icicles in winter season, never fails to make its picturesque appeal, whether the wheel be over or under shot; and then there is always the straggling file of boys and men, with a sack of corn across the shoulder, lingering along the way; or a mother perhaps seated atop the sack with which the mule is loaded, her baby in her arms and another child at her back.

There is romance, too, in the streams. The traveler may miss the lakes of other regions, but the Highlands in spring are a glittering network of rushing waters which gush from every hill and hollow. Summer is a more sober season, and autumn, especially in the western belt of the mountains, finds waters low in their stony beds. Few of the creeks or even the rivers will carry at any season a boat of deeper draught than a flat-bottomed punt, yet so swiftly do they rise that in a few hours or even minutes a small branch may become a raging torrent, which raises the shallow ford beyond imagining and holds in check all travel. With the rains come too the "tides" on creek and river, which set the stranded logs along the banks tossing and whirling down the current.

Few sights in the mountains are more inspiring than the moving out of the big rafts as, manned by stalwart mountain hands, they run the mad swirl of the upper waters and sweep on to calmer reaches far below in the Lowlands.

Log-rollings and house-raisings are not so general as in earlier days, but he who would build a log dwelling still relies on the help of a working. A home is after all but a simple undertaking when friends and neighbors help to set two logs as skids, roll up the others into place, and top the whole with wall-plates, beams, and rafters. The long hand-split shingles and the outside chimney that just clears the ridgepole may be left for another day, while the crowd that is gathered, conscience free, enjoys the mighty dinner which the women have been preparing.

More common today is the corn-husking; and the crushing of sorghum cane, and boiling down, are processes as delightfully picturesque as they are familiar. Here, while the fire glows and the great vat sends up a mist of yellow steam, are sometimes seen the intricate circles of the country dance, weaving and swinging in graceful winding figures through the trampled stubble of the darkening field. And when, the stir-off ended, the young folks adjourn to the nearby house, the shuffling of many feet on the rough floor and the voice of the caller[1] are borne far into the evening air. The dust rises in clouds and the dancers' faces are flushed with heat and weariness, for it is no mean muscular exertion to "run a set."

The "real old-time fiddler" should have a word for himself, for he is an institution in the Highlands, and the cheerful scrape of his bow sets the feet involuntarily a-moving. He seldom assumes the posture of the modern virtuoso, but lays his instrument across his arm or knee and so fiddles away—a sociable measure with none of the piercing sweetness generally associated with the violin. A "fiddler contest," in which all the local celebrities compete for an offered prize, is a feature of many a county fair; and he who can beat a measure with a reed on the upper portion of the strings, while the player undisturbed continues his tune, is the object of wondering admiration.

The dulcimer, which has been so great an object of interest to musicians, is probably related to the zither and came very possibly into the mountains with the early Germans. It is rare, and with one exception the writer has never met it outside the mountains of

[1] The one who calls the figures.

Kentucky. It is, however, a quaint and delightful little instrument, and with its slender waist and heart-shaped holes as picturesque as fancy could desire. The music is monotonous but sweet, and makes a pleasant undertone to the talk of the evening group.

Strangely enough, the banjo touches at times a deeper note than the violin, perhaps from association. It is more generally played throughout the Highlands, and breathes the life of many a lonely hearth far in the hills. Usually, however, it is off with all the gaiety of the mountain frolic on "Turkey in the Straw," "Possum up a Gum Stump," "Sugar in the Gourd," or "Sourwood Mountain."

"Gentlemen!" so spoke the famous and eccentric Judge Patten who used to live in eastern Kentucky, "Whenever you see a great big overgrown buck sitting at the mouth of some holler, or at the forks of some road, with a big slouch hat on, a blue collar, a celluloid, artificial rose on his coat lapel, and a banjo strung across his breast, and a-pickin' of 'Sourwood Mountain,' fine that man, gentlemen, fine him! For if he hasn't already done something, he's a-goin' to!"[1]

There is, too, in the language, a quaintness and a strength which set it apart from the English commonly used outside this romantic section. Not that the speech of the Highlanders as a whole differs from that of their Lowland neighbors, nor are many expressions that are pointed out as peculiar to the mountains different from those heard occasionally in the Lowland South or in parts of rural New England, but they are used oftener here. One may, in a conversation of a few minutes, hear expressions from Chaucer, Spenser, or Shakespeare; or, in lieu of these, be struck by the vividness or strength of the modern phrase chosen. Should ancient and modern phrase both fail to satisfy his need the Highlander, never at a loss, invents a new one, often more graphic than that employed in more conventional circles.

"Nary" and "ary," the sport of dialect writers, may not show their kinship at once with "ne'er a" and "e'er a," through "never a" and "ever a" of obsolete English; though "textes" and "nestes" and similar plurals bring to memory the Pilgrims to Canterbury. "I aim to" is much stronger than "I intend to," and so Othello found it. "Antic," in the expression "he is a natural antic,"

[1] Combs, Josiah Henry: The Kentucky Highlanders from a Native Mountaineer's Viewpoint, p. 23. Lexington, Ky., J. L. Richardson Company, 1913.

has the same meaning in the mountains as in the phrase "veriest antic" in the "Taming of the Shrew"; and one is "afeared" in the mountains, as in the "Merry Wives of Windsor." "Holp us as Thou hast holped our fathers" is no less a fervent prayer in the little mountain church-house, because the preacher has chosen to use the archaic form familiar to him in the Scriptures. The hunter seeks out the place where the wild turkeys "use," as Beaumont and Fletcher would have said; and a good Shakespearian "sallet" is made of the young leaves of the pokeberry bush, or of the mountain cress. The wood in the fireplace may not burn well because it is both "sobby" and "doty"—"sobby" meaning soggy, sappy, or soaked, and "doty," decayed.

A man wishing to hold a meeting in the mountains has it "norated"—that is, the announcement of it spread by report. The injunction to "surround the hole at the ford" is easily understood in its archaic sense of "go around"; and if we recall provincial English, we understand the mother who apologizes for the smeared condition of the baby's face when she says it is "all gormed up." "Right clever folks" means not necessarily adept, ingenious folk, but is a colloquial description of obliging and well-disposed people. To be told that one person is "ill as a hornet," and that another is "feisty," suggests on the one hand the irritated hornet, ready to fight, and on the other the little meddlesome dog, or feist, snapping at one's heels. Graphic was the description of him who told us of his adventures with a "big old rattlesnake, quiled up and singing the prettiest ye ever heerd," until he "mashed his head to a poultice." A hunter, who sought to trace the footsteps of a lost friend, saw the "dentures" in the moss, by which he found him.

A young man "talking to" a young woman in the Highlands is not giving her a scolding, as he might be understood elsewhere to be doing, were he so rash. He is paying attentions to her, and the young woman may be "ashamed" without having anything to be ashamed of—she is merely bashful. Granny has the sanction of the dictionary when she says that hers was a "singing and a dancing generation," meaning thereby that her family was given to song and dance; but when she "splunges" the kettle in water, she has the sanction of the Highlands, which, after all, is perhaps sanction enough.

The use of the past participle without auxiliary is common, as well as of strong or provincial past tenses; for example: "he shuck the tree"; "he drug the hog to the pen."

Emphasis is further secured by a free use of the double, and even triple negative; and such expressions as "hain't never seed nary" are not uncommon. Redundancies such as "church-house" "stair-steps," and "tooth-dentist" are frequent.

A favorite method of securing a descriptive word is to make a present participle an adjective superlative in degree; thus: "He is the talkingest man"; "he is the chair-flingingest boy"; "they are the money-makingest people"; "she is the knittingest woman."

Here one may be "devilled with the phthisic" all his life, and may see a "pig in a poke" without having to "study on it." There is a flavor of the Elizabethan Age in the description of the girl whose eyes "would puddle" when she was reproached, however slightly. Asking the morning wayfarer as to weather prospects, one is surprised to hear him call the mackerel sky "clabbered" until its appropriateness flashes upon him.

"People what delights to keep cattle" brings to mind the joys of pastoral life as depicted by Horace.

To hear a grateful invalid say, "Hit war just like stopping running water when the Doctor war away," carries one, in the beauty of its significance, beyond the time when "hit" was used as the neuter pronoun, to the prophecies of Isaiah, wherein a man is likened to "an hiding place from the wind, and a covert from the tempest; as rivers of water in a dry place, as the shadow of a great rock in a weary land."

The preservation of ballads and folk-songs sung in England one hundred to two hundred years ago, has been quite general in the remoter parts of the Highlands from Kentucky to Georgia. Brought by the ancestors of the Highlanders across the sea, these echoes of an earlier day have been carried down by oral transmission from the cabin on the frontier to the hearth of the mountain home today. Many have been greatly changed[1] during their

---

[1] "In this democratic region, where lords and ladies are unknown, 'Lady Margaret' sinks into 'Liddy' or 'Lydia Margaret,' and her 'bower-room' becomes her 'dowel-room.' Lord Orland, warned by his 'tinny foot-page,' inquires, 'Is any of my casten walls fell down?' The unknown 'ivory' comb becomes the 'high-row' comb, and the 'parrot-bird' is told that his 'cage shall be decked of the yeller

sojourn among the hills, but others are remarkably close to versions published in Child's collection of English and Scottish ballads, and to variants gathered in recent years in England and Scotland. The melodies to which these are set have not only a simple and touching beauty, but are peculiarly expressive of the temperament and environment of the people. The isolation of the Highlands has preserved these songs, and it is not surprising that they are fast disappearing with the opening up of the country. This is true also, in a measure, of the old religious songs, as the more modern and oftentimes inferior hymns become popularized.

Those who have watched the long procession of a mountain funeral, winding slowly to the hill-top, where cemeteries are almost always placed, and have heard the singing as it goes, will never forget the beauty and impressiveness of some of the old burial hymns.

Oh - - come, come with me   to the old church yard

I   well know the way   thro' the   soft   green   sward

beaten gold, and hung on the ivory.' Lord Randall is no longer 'fain to lie down, but 'sick to the heart and *fainting* to lie down,' and as a parting gift, bequeaths to his father his 'wagon and oxen.'

"Where no one rings a door-bell or 'tirls a pin,' but calls his greeting in frontier fashion from the road, 'Lord Thomas' indifferently 'tingles,' 'jangles,' 'dingles.' 'knocks at,' and 'darts out at' the 'ring' or 'wire.' 'Lord,' or 'Love Henry,' as he is called, boasts to his old sweetheart of the girl that he left, not at Clydes Water, but in Tennessee or Arkansas, and

'As they was leaning over the fence
Taking kisses all so sweet,
She had in her hand a keen penny knife
And she perched him sharp and deep.'
—Cf. Child, No. 68 C.

"Here the singer, who has been rocking her chair gently before the open fire, pauses to remark: 'Just like a jealous woman!' It is the truth of the song to elemental human nature that makes it real to her, and it is none the less real because it deals with a social life, with localities, objects, and terms widely remote from anything with which she is familiar."—Campbell, Olive Dame: "Songs and Ballads of the Southern Mountains," *Survey*, January 2, 1915.

or:

When I can read my ti-tle clear: To man-sions in the skies, I'll bid fare-well to ev-ry care, and wipe my weep-ing eyes.

CHORUS.

Been a long time trav-ling here be-low; Been a long time trav-ling a-way from my home, Been a long time trav-ling here be-low, To lay this bod-y down.

There is something indescribably pathetic about most of these graveyards, with the little cluster of mounds roughly fenced from the forest. Often the graves are protected from wandering and rooting animals by low latticed houses painted blue and white. Beyond this there are few signs of care, and the "soft green sward" of the hymn is entirely lacking on the barren top of the wind-swept hill. Many times, however, the "banch" of the mountain where they lie commands a sweep of valley, ridge, and peak, stretching on and on in swales and billows till they seem to melt in the blue of the Beyond.

A funeral preaching brings a great concourse to these sad little heights. Writers and speakers have made much of deferred funeral preachings, seemingly finding something very strange and striking in them. They are, after all, only memorial services delayed, of necessity, until the preacher could be present at a propitious season,

148

usually in the fall when there is enough of food and fodder to supply both the people and stock. Cases have been known where a preaching did not take place until seventy-five years after the death of the subject of the discourse, but it is customary to have it as soon as conditions make it convenient, which for different reasons may not be for several years. Arrangements are generally made some time in advance in order that there may be a large gathering. Naturally the day is not one of deep grief to many of those present. They have come in sober wise as the occasion befitted, but something too in the manner of a holiday, when neighbor may visit with neighbor seldom seen and learn the news of the intervening years. Usually there are several preachers, each of whom may speak for two or three hours at a time, being succeeded when he is at length exhausted. A good deal of informality is manifested about listening to the whole of all of the discourses, but there is a courteous hearing given to each man although the audience may vary from time to time. At noon a general rest is taken, and sometimes the opportunity is utilized for a baptizing.

The long delays that precede such memorial services and the largeness of the gatherings lead to situations which have dramatic and what would seem to be at times embarrassing aspects. Thus, the funeral preaching for a man who has been shot may be attended by the near relatives of the murderer, who listen to an account of the quarrel, the shooting, and the succeeding days of suffering, from which no detail is omitted; while the memorial sermon for a wife long dead is heard by the new wife, who weeps with her husband and meekly accepts the bidding of the preacher to be kind to her "poor little stepchildren."

Underlying this custom, however, is a real significance and use. In fact many things that have been pointed out as indicative of a "peculiar people" are, on better acquaintance, perceived to be only wise or necessary adaptations of means to ends in an exceedingly rural section. The picturesque has obscured the natural.

There is a romantic appeal, too, in some of the darker aspects of mountain life. It is this appeal, undoubtedly, and not a desire to misrepresent, that has led the journalist and writer of fiction to fasten upon the mountain people as a whole the reputation of being feudists and moonshiners. Instinctively they see in the lonely hollow the proper setting for the illicit still, then in imagination the smoke of the still itself rising among the misty tree-tops. The woman calling to her husband on the hillside is warning him of the approach of strangers. The far glint of mica is the sun on his gun-barrel. The remote mill seemingly smothered in a narrow green gorge or set by a lonely rush of waters is a moonshine mill, and the innocent horseman with his sack of corn is the blockader in pursuit of his trade. And there is just enough approach to fact in this picture to fasten it in the mind.

The traveler who meets suddenly five tall dark men galloping through the rain, their horses steaming in the wet, and learns that they are in truth United States marshals, summoned because it was not safe for the sheriff to face the animosity of this region, thrills involuntarily; nor is he likely soon to forget his impression nor the stories that cluster about the incident. And what more fitting close to a day that gives so dramatic an experience than to plunge at night with his companions into the deep black ford, to find on yon side the river the sheriff's son, forsooth, who had heard the splashing of the feet of many horses in the ford and had come to learn the cause. It is of small moment that the marshals return the next day without adventure. From the traveler's point of view local color is complete. He is not, perhaps, to be blamed if he gets a perspective warped by one experience. Nor is it the fault of the Highlander, but rather his misfortune, that the setting of his life and many of its natural aspects lend themselves inevitably to a dramatic interpretation.

In time, and the time in some places is at hand, the isolation of the Highlands will be overcome by railroads and good thoroughfares and their wild beauty disfigured by commercial exploitation, while the Highlander himself, his individualism and his picturesqueness gone, will become no better, no worse, but quite as uninteresting as other men.

He who stands where once the Tallulah River in northern Georgia leaped, a foaming torrent of waterfalls and rapids through a gray gorge whose steep sides were set with moss and bloom, cannot but regret the passing of that beauty. He knows that the electricity generated by that immense volume of water passes a hundred miles or more to cities which have never seen its source, but something has gone from out the land—not only of beauty, but of strength.

It is the part of those, both native and foreign, who have the interest of the Highland country at heart, to see that all that is strong and fair in that life is not drained away to other regions. It should be a reservoir clean and beautiful in itself, ministering to its own needs yet the source from which the exhausted pools of urban life may find renewal and refreshment.

CHAPTER VIII

THE GROWTH OF DENOMINATIONALISM IN
THE HIGHLANDS

IF ANY phase of mountain life calls for sympathetic understanding it is the spiritual phase, in comparison with which all else is of minor importance. To those who do not grasp the thought that in certain sections of the mountains a somewhat border and frontier stage of society still prevails, some of the Highlander's acts may seem impossible for one possessed of any spirituality. To those, on the other hand, who realize in how great degree his standards are the result of his environment and of his inheritance from his pioneer ancestors, understanding is not so difficult, nor will they doubt the genuineness of his religious convictions, although certain questions in connection with the religious life of the Highlands are still the subject of much speculation.

If the early settlers of the mountains were Scotch-Irish, how does it happen that the mountain people of today are not strongly Presbyterian, is the query most often put. Granting, in the beginning, that Presbyterianism is not the dominant faith of the Highlands, we must turn for an understanding of this fact back again to the latter part of the eighteenth century, and there, in the conditions of the mountain wilderness, as they were affected by the religious movements of the period, will be found an explanation of much that would otherwise seem puzzling in the religious expression of the mountains today.

Among the early settlers on the western frontier there existed a strong religious element, the dominant faith being without doubt that held by most of the Scotch-Irish—Presbyterianism. The Germans, too, were largely non-conformists, although divided among a number of sects of which the most important were the German Reformed, the Lutherans, and Moravians. That some of these sects remained as separate congregations for years in the wilderness is indicated by the diaries of early missionaries, as well as by the history of certain local churches which have existed continuously from the time of their establishment up to the present day. Many congregations, however, became in time affiliated with the Presbyterians, which denomination for some years was almost the only one to maintain established ministers on the frontier. Especially was this true, says Faust,[1] of the German Reformed churches, whose doctrines, held probably by most of the Palatinates, were very close to those of the Presbyterians. Of a list given by Bernheim[2] of fifteen German churches (nine Lutheran and six Reformed) in interior South Carolina in 1788, seven of the nine Lutherans were still in being in 1872, while all of the others had ceased to exist. This was due in large part to the fact that the congregations, having no ministers of their own, joined other denominations.

How few ministers of any denomination there were in the mountain region about the middle of the eighteenth century may be inferred from the accounts of early missionaries to which reference has just been made. Particularly interesting are the diaries of the Moravian missionaries,[3] Schnell, Gottschalk, and Spangenburg, who made numerous visits to the frontier. Schnell, who appears to have been in the West as early as 1743, says of his visit to the people on the South Branch of the Potomac, July 17, 1747: "After the sermon the people complained about their poor condition, that they had no minister, while in Pennsylvania there were so many. They asked me to stay with them. Then they brought me about six children, whom I should baptize, but I had to refuse." (The Moravians did not baptize children.)

"July 20: At noon we stopped with an Englishman. He complained that for two years he had heard no sermon, although he had been compelled every year to pay for the county minister."

In 1749 on his return from New River, Schnell visited the Scotch-Irish settlements near Fincastle, and volunteers the comment: "A

[1] Faust, Albert Bernhardt: The German Element in the United States, Vol. I, p. 123, and Vol. II, p. 419. Boston, Houghton, Mifflin, and Co., 1909.

[2] Bernheim, G. D.: History of the German Settlements, and of the Lutheran Church in North and South Carolina, p. 300 ff. Philadelphia, the Lutheran Bookstore, 1872.

[3] "Moravian Diaries of Travels through Virginia," edited by W. J. Hinke and C. E. Kemper. *Virginia Historical Magazine*, Vols. XI and XII, 1903 and 1904.

kind of white people are found here who live like savages. Hunting is their chief occupation."

Bishop Spangenburg, who visited the settlements in the extreme southern part of Pendleton County, West Virginia, in 1748, preached the first sermons ever preached there, while in 1775, Rev. Hugh McAden, a young Presbyterian missionary, traveled through a section of northwestern South Carolina never visited before by a clergyman. On November 2d he preached to a people "many of whom I was told," he writes, "had never heard a sermon in all their lives before, and yet several of them had families." One old man, he adds, "had never seen a shirt, been in a fair, heard a sermon, or seen a minister."[1]

There was at this time no settled Presbyterian pastor in North Carolina, and but three, all Irish born, were reported in western Virginia in 1748—one in Albemarle County and two in Augusta, west of the mountains. The people, however, were frequently organized into congregations even though the majority had to rely upon one of their number to read lessons or sermons, or upon the occasional missionary.

Hanna, in his history of the Scotch-Irish, gives long lists of early Presbyterian congregations in America. As nearly as can be determined, 138 of these were mountain congregations, organized between 1737 and 1799 and spread over a territory extending "in length from the New River on the northeast to the frontiers on the Tennessee River on the southwest, at present about 200 miles; and from the Blue or eastern Ridge of the Appalachian Mountains to the Cumberland Mountains, about 140 miles in breadth."[2]

It will be recalled that jurisdiction over a large part of this region was claimed for some time by the colony of Virginia in which the Church of England was established by law. Under the Toleration Act (passed by the English Parliament in 1689),[3] Dissenters were permitted to worship in their own way provided they took oaths of

---

[1] Ford, Henry Jones: The Scotch-Irish in America, p. 403. Princeton University Press, 1915.

[2] Hanna, Charles A.: The Scotch-Irish in America, Vol. II, pp. 108–118. G. P Putnam's Sons, 1902.

[3] The construction put upon this act was more liberal in England than in Virginia. In Virginia the licensing of ministers and registering of meeting-houses were in the hands of the General Court, a body composed of the conservative and aristocratic officials of the colony, while in England these functions lay with local courts.

allegiance and supremacy, declared against transubstantiation, had meeting-houses legally registered, and ministers duly licensed under certain restrictions. The Scotch-Irish settlers on the western frontier were furthermore given to understand by Governor Gooch of Virginia, when an appeal was made to him by the Synod of Pennsylvania in 1739, that no interference would be made with their religious observances provided that they "conform themselves to the rules provided by the Act of Toleration in England, by taking the oaths enjoined thereby, and registering the place of their meeting, and behave themselves peaceably." In fact persecution would have defeated the policy which had been pursued, of encouraging the migration of Dissenters to the frontier, as a protection to the colony against the incursions of Indians and French. The inaccessibility of the mountain country was in itself an additional guarantee of freedom of faith.

While conditions thus tended to confirm the mountain population in their independent views, so largely Presbyterian at that time, they also gave freedom in some degree from the dominance of the Established Church, certain features of which were very oppressive to Dissenters in Tidewater Virginia who were more closely in touch with centers of church and government control.

The law of the colony called for the establishment of a parish whenever a new county was formed. Control of local affairs[1] was largely in the hands of the vestry. This body, which after 1662[2] was made self-perpetuating, was formed by the election of twelve substantial landholders, who in taking the oath of office bound

---

[1] Administration of justice and various other county concerns were attended to by the County Court, an appointive body.

[2] "The intolerance of the Cavalier element in England, more political than religious, was reflected in Virginia by the Assembly of 1662."
"The legislation of this year fixed the character of the church up to the Revolution. The vestries were given all power in parochial matters, and, at the same time, were made irresponsible. A vestry once elected by the people of the parish might fill its own vacancies, and so continue to rule for many years without being called to account. Vestries fixed the amount of the assessment for the minister's salary, church expenses, poor relief, and the individual apportionment. They transacted the parochial business and presented the minister. As a consequence, a few leading gentlemen in each neighborhood administered religious matters to suit themselves, and the great mass of parishioners could make no protest. In many cases, however, the vestries doubtless acted in accordance with public sentiment, especially in keeping ministers' salaries as low as possible."—Eckenrode, H. J.: Separation of Church and State in Virginia, Special Report of the Department of Archives and History, pp. 12, 13. Richmond, Va., 1910.

themselves to conform to the doctrine and discipline of the Church of England.

McIlwaine in his very interesting account of The Struggle of Protestant Dissenters for Religious Toleration in Virginia,[1] speaking of the formation of the vestries of Frederick and Augusta Counties, 1744–1746, at a time when these counties covered the whole of the mountain country of Virginia, says:

> At first sight it would seem that it would be hard to find in counties whose population consisted almost entirely of Dissenters twelve representative men qualified to take the oaths. But such was not the case. The leading men of the section, knowing that each parish, as soon as it had been once established, was in itself practically independent, overcame what scruples they may have had in the premises, and carried out this provision of the law.

and he quotes Peyton as saying, in his History of Augusta County, that:

> The first vestry of Augusta Parish was doubtless largely composed of Dissenters, men who, so far as religion was concerned, were politically Episcopalians and doctrinally Presbyterians, but willing to submit outwardly to the powers in being, while they held themselves free to have their own private opinions.[2]

While, therefore, Dissenters in general were technically disqualified for holding office, and at the same time taxed for support of the Establishment, the Dissenters west of the mountains from the beginning practically controlled local affairs. One of the disabilities most keenly felt by them was that their ministers were unable to perform marriages legally valid—a prohibition working real hardship in a region where ministers of the Established Church were almost non-existent.

---

[1] McIlwaine, Henry R.: The Struggle of Protestant Dissenters for Religious Toleration in Virginia, Johns Hopkins University Studies in Historical and Political Science, 12th Series, No. IV, Ch. IV. April, 1894.

[2] Further referring to Peyton's History, McIlwaine adds:
"In the regulation of church services, a spirit of compromise was displayed. The minister was a regularly ordained Episcopalian, but Dissenters sometimes occupied his pulpit. Gown and surplice were not used by the minister, and the congregation received the sacrament standing. But this offshoot of the Established Church did not flourish. The congregation dwindled away when, owing to the increase of Presbyterian ministers in that section, the people had an opportunity of worshipping in a manner more in accordance with their preferences." Ibid., Ch. IV.

Thus it came about, that although western Virginia could be relied upon to support radical democratic measures, and did in fact have a decisive influence[1] in later efforts to bring about separation of Church and State, the initial steps in securing religious toleration were taken, and the brunt of the conflict for complete religious independence was borne by the Dissenters east of the mountains—by the Presbyterians first, and later in marked degree by the Baptists.

The story of the struggle for religious freedom in Virginia is a familiar one, but inasmuch as it helps to cast a light upon the religious affiliations and conditions in the Southern Highland region today, a brief review of it must be given here.

The early Presbyterians east of the Blue Ridge seem to have met with little opposition as long as they concerned themselves with their own affairs in an orderly fashion, even when they failed to secure licenses for ministers and for meeting places as demanded in the Act of Toleration. When, however, attacks began to be made upon the Established Church and the ranks of Dissent to be augmented from Lowland counties in which the Established Church was strongest, repressive measures were taken by the Colonial Council—measures which were as much an effort to check encroachments upon social and political privileges as a defense of the Anglican Church. The struggle was not marked by any great persecution, the means adopted being usually fines and refusals to grant licenses.

The object sought by the Presbyterians at this time seems not to have been separation of Church and State, although protests were made against the payment of parochial dues. Efforts were mainly directed toward securing the liberal construction of the Toleration Act enjoyed in England but not accepted by the Virginia Court, and in attaining this the denomination gained a substantial and influential place in the life of the colony.

The loyal defense afforded by the frontier Presbyterians in the

---

[1] "It was due largely to the solid western vote in 1784 in union with some of the Piedmont and Southern Virginia representatives, that a bill for a general state assessment in support of religion, failed to pass. Practically, the separation of Church and State in the west was completed in 1782, with the dissolving of some of the last vestries."—Eckenrode, H. J.: The Separation of Church and State in Virginia, p. 98.

French and Indian War had much to do with the increased leniency shown them by the Colonial Council at the close of the war; but the spread of their numbers, and of democratic ideas in general, was also responsible for the growth of their influence.

The part played in the spread of Dissenting doctrines by the condition of the Established Church was great. It would seem now that the "profligacy" of the Anglican clergy, so often advanced as a cause of the decline of the Established Church, has been much exaggerated. Greater cause lay in the inability of the State Church, characterized in that age by a cold formalism, and dominated by a political and social aristocracy, to hold its own against the fervid enthusiasm of Presbyterian, Baptist, and Methodist preachers under the influence of the Great Awakening.

> The awakening of popular emotion in the ordered life of old Virginia was startling in its manifestations because this was the first occasion. The poorer people, hitherto unreached by the establishment, were stirred to the core by the wandering Baptist preachers, who walked the highways and byroads, preaching in season and out and reproducing the apostolic age. The phenomena of the movement were such as mark all great revivals— hysteria, contortions, raptures, and even coma. The contrast between the overpowering sermons of the evangelists and the short prosy moral discourses of the Anglican ministers was great, and between the points of view of the two schools even greater, so that in time, as a result of the evangelical triumph, the "new light" religion came to be considered the only valid form of Christianity, and the unworthiness of the old parsons grew into a sort of legend.[1]

The success gained by the Presbyterians opened the way to the larger liberty which was to follow, but it remained for the Baptists to take the next step by refusing to abide by the Toleration Act and by demanding complete religious liberty. There would seem to have been as early as 1714 a group of General Baptists[2] in southeastern Virginia, and a number of Regular Baptist churches were by the middle of the century situated in the Virginia Valley and in the Piedmont at the base of the Blue Ridge. The total membership

[1] Ibid., p. 36.
[2] Arminian in doctrine; that is, emphasizing the belief that salvation is for all as against the Calvinistic view which emphasizes the doctrine of election.

of this latter group in 1770 is said to have been but little over 600. The great Baptist movement had its inception with the Separate Baptists. This sect, which owed its beginnings to Shubal Stearns, a Boston preacher who in 1751 established a church in Guilford County, North Carolina, spread rapidly through North Carolina into Virginia, even into the most populous parts of the colony where the hold of the Established Church was strongest.

The rapid growth of the Separate Baptists was due to several causes, but the fundamental democracy of their appeal, the right of every man, no matter how poor and unlettered he might be, to think for himself in matters of religion and to lead others, was at the base of the response found in the common folk of the country. At first, to be sure, the intensely emotional and highly dramatic and even grotesque methods of the Separate preachers seem to have aroused ridicule and even fear. In his account of the Baptists in Virginia, Thom states:

> Colonel Samuel Harriss, Rev. John Koones, and others were beaten with clubs and cuffed and kicked and hauled about by the hair; mobs ducked some preachers till they were nearly drowned; a live snake and a hornet's nest were, upon different occasions, thrown into the meetings to break them up; and drunken ruffians insulted the preachers.[1]

As the people, however, came to realize that the Baptists in reality were fighting their battles, violence practically ceased.

The close connection of the Colonial Government, the Established Church, and the aristocracy of the Tidewater, makes it impossible to treat the movement as solely religious. It was more than that—it was a protest against religious, social, and political privilege—and because education was so closely associated with the privileged classes, somewhat, too, against education.

As soon as it began to be evident that the growth of the Baptists threatened not alone the authority of the Established Church but of the privileged classes as well, a bitter persecution was begun against them by the aristocracy of the Tidewater. Ministers were flogged, starved. and imprisoned, but the Baptists throve on persecution.

---

[1] Thom, William Taylor: The Struggle for Religious Freedom in Virginia: The Baptists, Johns Hopkins University Studies, Series XVIII, 1900.

"Persecution," says Hawks,[1] "made friends for its victims; and the men who were not permitted to speak in public, found willing auditors in the sympathizing crowds who gathered around the prisons to hear them preach from the grated windows. It is not improbable that this very opposition imparted strength in another mode, inasmuch as it at least furnished the Baptists with a common ground on which to make resistance; and such common ground was in a great degree wanting in their creed; for not to speak of their great division into Regulars and Separates, some 'held to predestination, others to universal provision; some adhered to a confession of faith, others would have none but the Bible; some practised laying on of hands, others did not;' and, in fact, the only particular in which there seems to have been unanimity, was in the favorite exclusive opinion of the sect, that none but adult believers are fit subjects of baptism, and that immersion is the only effectual and authorized mode of administering that sacrament."

As a result of this agitation, where in 1770 there were something over 1,000 Baptists, in 1774 there were over 5,000, and according to estimates of Benedict they had the sympathy of one out of every ten free white inhabitants of Virginia.[2] The greatest accessions came from the early settled rich Tidewater counties, and as was natural, the first converts were usually from the poorer classes. Gradually, however, as the movement gathered strength, the more well-to-do and intelligent began to join the Church.[3] On the frontier there was little or no persecution.

[1] Hawks, Francis L.: A Narrative of Events Connected with the Rise and Progress of the Protestant Episcopal Church in Virginia, p. 121. New York, Harper Bros., 1836.

[2] Thom, William Taylor: The Struggle for Religious Freedom in Virginia: The Baptists.

[3] It is interesting to note the reasons Howell, the Baptist historian, advances to account for the failure of the Baptist Church in Virginia to hold its ground during the last part of the eighteenth century, at a time when the Methodists were flourishing. In brief, these were that the Baptists:
1. Abhorred proselyting, and refused to employ education as an auxiliary to denominational advancement. Incurred reproach of being enemies to education.
2. Failed to perceive true relation between religion and the use of money as means of advancement, whence
    (a) any enterprise among Baptists which required the use of money beyond the building of meeting-houses or support of the poor of the Church, was for many years almost impossible.
    (b) failure to adequately support their pastors.
3. Rich and aristocratic converts boasted of sacrifices they had made—sacrifices of society, friendships, and the refinements of social life.
4. Carelessness in defending the honor of the Church. It was charged that, as

Mount Mitchell
The Highest Point East of the Rocky Mountains

The Tennessee River at Chattanooga, where it Turns to the West from the Valley through the Cumberland Plateau

Steep Forest-Covered Slope of Hawksbill Mountain, seen across the Gorge of Linville River from the Cliffs of Linville Mountain, North Carolina

"The traveler who follows the trails of this far country."

"The modern is close to the pioneer."

Craggy Mountain—in the Blue Ridge

Allegheny-Cumberland Belt
The Deeply Dissected Type of Topography where it has Lost all Semblance to a
Plateau

"A picture of pioneer days."

A Train of Canvas-Covered Wagons

When a Tide makes Fording Impossible

Fording the Headwaters of the Nolichucky

"The only road, which must be forded lengthwise"

"To the little homes."

Box-House

"The more pretentious new white frame-house."

"Raising a house"—Rolling a Log up Over the Skids into Position

Crowd Gathered at the House-Raising Above

"Low, latticed houses, painted blue and white."

"There is something indescribably pathetic about most of the graveyards."

Augusta Church, Fort Defiance, Virginia. Built in 1749 (Presbyterian)

Timber Ridge Church, Timber Ridge, Virginia. Main body built in 1757 (Presbyterian)

Mountain Church and School House

Old School House, also used as Church House

Log Rolling

Making Rail Fence
"Enterprises which demanded common effort."

Making Long Hand-Split Shingles

Small Sawmill

In the Pasture

Salting Sheep from a Gourd

Shearing Sheep

Washing Wool in the Branch

Spreading Wool to Dry on Roof of Shed

Dyeing and Drying Wool

Picking Over Wool

Carding Wool

"From babyhood the boy is the favored lord of all he surveys."

A Family of Nine Girls

Carrying Straw to Fill her Bed-Tick

A Mother, her baby in her Arms and another Child at her Back

Bringing Baskets to the School

"He who can beat a measure with a reed on the upper portion of the strings."

"The dulcimer is a quaint and delightful little instrument."

"Bees are kept very commonly, sections of the gum-tree serving as hives."

"Beans are dried in the pod."   Winter Supply of Shucky Beans

Getting the Yellow Poplar out of Pine Mountain, Kentucky

"Waiting for a tide."

"The moving out of the big rafts."

Coal Bank

Small Coal Mine

Plowing a Hillside Farm

Family Planting

Bacon from the School Farm

"A certain kind of industrial work."

Laurel Thicket in the Highlands

"The remote mill, by a lonely rush of waters."

"Where once the Tallulah River leaped—a foaming torrent of waterfalls and rapids through a gray gorge."

"No other dwelling can ever fit so well into the wooded hills and coves of our mountain country."

The rapid growth and organization of the denomination, its aggressive policy, and its favor with the common people gave the petitions which from 1770 began to pour in upon the Colonial Assembly increasing weight. In these the special object varied, but as a whole the end in view was the same—the complete freeing of religion from state control. While Regular and Separates did not join until 1787, they made common cause of their religious and political disabilities.

It is to be kept in mind that other dissenting bodies, especially Quakers and Presbyterians, took part in this general movement. The Presbyterians, who by the time of the Revolution had become comparatively well established and respected, did indeed abide by the Toleration Act, but they were far from satisfied with the limitations of their position. At the outbreak of the war they stood prominently for the cause of independence, seeing in the defeat of the Mother Country not only their political enfranchisement but the overthrow of the "persecuting ecclesiastical arm of the English Government."[1] And after the Revolution, by petition and protest, they consistently opposed all religious discriminations. The Methodists undoubtedly contributed to the spread of popular doctrines, but as a Church they remained in the Establishment until about a year before the passage of the Act for Religious Freedom.

Complete separation of Church and State was not secured until this Act was passed in 1785. "At the end of the struggle," says Thom, "the Baptists had been largely instrumental in putting Virginia in the lead of the civilized nations in the assertion of the absolute freedom of religious faith from civil control. This was a great achievement, a thing new in the history of the world. And it is a record of which any denomination and any people may be proud, this record of the plain everyday people of our land."[2]

a class, Baptists were disreputably ignorant; that they refused to be enlightened; that their ministers were generally rough fanatics; that they were penurious and narrow-minded; that they had no regard for the moral training of the children.

5. Failure to plant churches in cities as opposed to rural districts.
6. Mistaken as to extent in which unassisted truth will take care of itself.
7. Carelessness in regard to the qualifications of their ministers. Refused to demand any specified amount of literary and scientific culture.
8. Failed to supply people with suitable books for their instruction.

[1] Roosevelt, Theodore: The Winning of the West, Vol. II, p. 113.

[2] Thom, William Taylor: The Struggle for Religious Freedom in Virginia: The Baptists, pp. 93-94.

We have dwelt thus at length upon religious movements in Virginia because of their effect upon the mountain country as a whole. It should, however, be added that the Carolinas, too, were under the Establishment during most of the Colonial Period, and that some of the features noted in connection with the state religion in Virginia as being oppressive to the Dissenters were also operative here. It seems to be true indeed that religious grievances as well as political had their part in bringing about the Battle of Alamance. From early times, however, Dissenters formed a strong and influential part of the population of these colonies, and the Established Church was never as strong here as it was in Virginia. Moreover, the somewhat unstable government of North Carolina exercised, as has been previously observed in connection with the Watauga Association, little authority over the settlers in the western wilderness. A practical separation of Church and State in North Carolina was effected in 1776, although the final formal steps were not taken until 1835.

For the great exodus of Baptists to the West after the Revolution there are probably several explanations. They belonged largely to the plain people upon whom the hardships of the Revolution had fallen with especial severity and to whom the possibilities of the new lands offered great inducements. Probably, too, some of the many Baptists among the Revolutionary soldiers received lands in the West as war bounties. Moreover, while all religious distinctions were legally abolished in Virginia in 1785, for some years the Baptists suffered much prejudice and a certain social ostracism, which probably led many to seek in the freer air of the frontier a refuge from the exclusiveness of other denominations. There is a tradition that during the time of persecution a number escaped to Harlan County, Kentucky, and it is claimed that soon after 1765 there were Baptists in east Tennessee, who organized two churches before they were driven out by the Indians in 1774. No particulars, however, have been preserved. In 1780 a considerable number of the denomination with eight or ten ministers removed from Virginia and North Carolina to the Holston region where by 1802 there were thirty-six churches reported, with a membership of

2,500. Semple[1] estimates that between 1791 and 1810 fully one-fourth of the Baptists of Virginia emigrated to Kentucky. Accounts have been passed down to us of their traveling in congregations,[2] their pastors holding services wherever the pause for rest was long enough. Many went with the great trend of migration through the mountains, but many others turned aside into the mountain ridge areas which were settled about this time.

How rapid, as a result of this great migration, was the spread of Baptist doctrines among those not previously of this faith, there is no way to determine, but conditions in the wilderness were peculiarly favorable to their growth. Ministers, as we have seen, had always been few upon the frontier. The Presbyterians, notably distinguished even in early times for their efforts to supply pastors and missionaries to their people, had been entirely unable to minister adequately to their scattered and moving congregations. Among the Valley settlements they succeeded in maintaining a strong influence,[3] and it was due to them that the first institutions of learning in the mountains—Liberty Hall in the Virginia Valley, and Washington, Tusculum, and Greeneville Colleges in the Tennessee Valley—were established.[4] Through much of the mountain wilderness, however, the children of the Presbyterians were obliged to grow up without either the offices of a minister of their faith or the educational opportunities, both religious and secular, so generally dependent upon him.

It is probable that the insistence of the Presbyterians upon an

[1] Semple, Robert B.: History of the Rise and Progress of the Baptists in Virginia, Richmond, 1810.

[2] Dr. R. F. Campbell, who has made a study of Presbyterianism in North Carolina, says that "this was also true of the early Presbyterians, in western North Carolina, who often came in in considerable bodies, bringing their pastor with them."

[3] "There was also a strong Lutheran element in the Valley. In 1813, two Lutheran ministers organized 13 congregations consisting of 1175 members in Washington County, Virginia, in Tennessee, and in parts of the present West Virginia."—Bernheim: History of the German Settlements, p. 381.

[4] The following list indicates schools founded by the Scotch-Irish Presbyterians within the mountain country or in the regions bordering it to east and west:

Hampden-Sidney, Virginia, 1774, Rev. Samuel Stanhope Smith, President.

Liberty Hall, first in Mt. Pleasant, Spottsylvania County, and later in Timber Ridge, Rockbridge County, Virginia, 1776. Changed in 1796 to Washington Academy, from which developed Washington and Lee University.

Liberty Hall, near Charlotte, North Carolina, 1768, founded by Joseph Alex-

educated ministry[1] and the practice followed of placing ministers in urban centers, had much to do with the decrease of Presbyterianism in the mountains and the growth of those sects whose educational requirements for the ministry were less exacting. The conditions of the frontier, too, giving emphasis as they did to individualism, perhaps led to a sentiment for direct management in church affairs, and in consequence the church connection of the mountaineer passed from the representative form of polity to the more direct democratic form of government.

It is not hard to believe that the early Baptist preachers, filled with a zeal which was rendered the more intense by their recent persecution, denouncing privilege, and proclaiming the power of the Spirit to act through the most ignorant and uneducated, exercised an immediate and powerful influence on the stern and unlettered Calvinists of the frontier.

ander; later became Queen's College, and from it developed the University of North Carolina.

Alamance, Guilford County, North Carolina, 1761. School founded by Rev. David Caldwell.

Martin Academy, Washington County, Tennessee, 1788. Rev. Samuel W. Doak, founder; later became Washington College.

Union Academy, near Knoxville, Tennessee, 1802, founded by Dr. Isaac Anderson; later became Maryville College.

Tusculum College, Bethel, Tennessee, 1818, Rev. W. Samuel Doak, founder.

Greeneville College, Tennessee, 1794, Rev. Hezekiah Balch, Founder.

In 1868 Greeneville and Tusculum were united, but kept the two names until 1912, when the name was changed to Tusculum College.

Transylvania University, Danville, Kentucky, 1783, founded by Rev. David Rice; moved to Lexington, 1788.

Kentucky Academy, Pisgah, Kentucky, 1794; amalgamated in 1798 with the institution at Lexington as Transylvania University.

Blount College, Knoxville, Tennessee, 1794, founded by Rev. Samuel Garrick; later became the University of Tennessee.

Center College, Danville, Kentucky, 1824.

[1] "In Ulster it was the regular thing for a candidate for the ministry to go to Scotland to get a classical education as the foundation of his theological studies. This insistence upon scholarship as a ministerial qualification was sharpened by sectarian tendencies in favor of substituting zeal for knowledge, and private inspiration for historical evidence.

"An educated ministry accompanied the Scotch-Irish settlements in America. It was a comparatively brief and easy matter for a student to go and come between Ulster and Scotland, by the short sea-ferry; but if there was to be in America a native born educated ministry, institutions of learning had to be set up. Log College, established by Tennent in Bucks County, Pennsylvania, in 1728, was one of a number of institutions which were progenitors of Princeton and various others." —Ford, Henry Jones: The Scotch-Irish in America, pp. 415, 416. New Jersey, The Princeton University Press, 1915.

"By the time Kentucky was settled," writes Roosevelt, "the Baptists had begun to make headway on the frontier, at the expense of the Presbyterians. The rough democracy of the border welcomed a sect which was itself essentially democratic. To many of the backwoodsmen's prejudices,—notably their sullen and narrow hostility towards all rank, whether or not based on merit and learning, the Baptists' creed appealed strongly. Where their preachers obtained a foothold, it was made a matter of reproach to the Presbyterian clergymen that they had been educated in early life for the ministry as for a profession. The love of liberty, and the defiant assertion of equality, so universal in the backwoods, and so excellent in themselves, sometimes took very warped and twisted forms, notably when they betrayed the backwoodsmen into the belief that the true democratic spirit forbade any exclusive and special training for the professions that produce soldiers, statesmen, or ministers."[1]

Newman writes: "The early Baptists of Kentucky were as a rule thoroughly imbued with prejudice against educated and salaried ministers. The experience of early Virginia Baptists in being taxed for the support of irreligious and vicious clergymen, whose only recommendation was that they had received a university education, led them to look with suspicion upon the highly educated, and to prefer a ministry from the ranks of the people earning a support by following secular pursuits. These sentiments became intensified in Kentucky, where for a long time educational facilities were almost wanting."[2]

The great revival at the beginning of the nineteenth century, which stirred Presbyterians, Methodists, and Baptists alike, also greatly increased the Baptist membership. In Kentucky it is said to have been doubled. It is interesting, too, to learn that while the growth of Arminian views was greatly increased by this revival, in the South the trend was back to extreme Calvinistic doctrines— doctrines which, as we shall see, still persist strongly in many Southern mountain areas.

The rapid growth of the Methodists in the mountains did not begin until after the Revolution.[3] There were Methodists in south-

[1] Roosevelt, Theodore: The Winning of the West, Vol. II, pp. 113–114.

[2] Newman, A. H.: History of the Baptist Churches in the United States, pp. 303–305. New York, The Christian Literature Co., 1894.

[3] At the time Asbury came to America, in 1771, there were only about 600 Methodist laymen and 10 Methodist preachers in the colonies, while the first Methodist preachers did not come into Virginia and North Carolina until 1772. In 1773 the numbers of the Society were computed as follows: New York 180, Philadelphia

western Virginia in 1773 or 1774, and possibly a church was organized at that time in Pulaski County. By 1776 there were many
in Piedmont North Carolina, and seven years later it is estimated
that there were in the Holston region about "sixty sheep scattered
over a large section of wilderness country." Even in 1787, through
part of the Holston settlements, meetings were held "all in private
dwelling houses, none in churches or schoolhouses, and there were
no stewards, no leaders, no exhorters, and only one local preacher."
In 1803 the Holston District, which included the circuits of Holston, Nolichucky, French Broad, New River, Clinch, and Powell's
Valley, contained 2,933 Methodists, of whom 205 were colored.

The circuit system, established early in America by Bishop Asbury, gave great impetus to the movement, which the visits of
Asbury himself confirmed.

"Elected a general superintendent in 1784," writes Tipple,
"for 30 years and more he traveled annually the largest Episcopal See any Bishop of any church in America ever had under his
continuous and, for most of the time, sole jurisdiction."
"He was the great itinerant of early Methodism. From Maine
to Georgia, to Kentucky and Ohio, and back to New York again,
year after year he swung around his immense circuit, a man
without a home. Once when entering the prairies of Ohio a
stranger met him and abruptly inquired, 'Where are you from?'
Asbury replied, 'From Boston, New York, Philadelphia, Baltimore, or almost any place you please.' This was literally true."[1]

In 1781 we see him on the South Branch of the Potomac, where
he found many "prayerless" and "wicked whiskey drinkers." In
the Dutch settlement on Patterson's Creek the people loved his
preaching and he reciprocated their affection, for he writes: "I
love these people; they are kind in their way." From 1800 to 1813
he made annual visits, usually in the autumn, throughout the eastern part of the United States and as far west[2] as Tennessee and

180, New Jersey 200, Maryland 500, and Virginia 100, or in all, a total of 1160.
—Price, R. N.: Holston Methodism; from its Origin to the Present Time, Vol. I,
p. 8. Nashville, Tenn., Smith & Lamar, 1904.

[1] Introduction to the Heart of Asbury's Journal, p. 9. Edited by Ezra Squier
Tipple, New York, Eaton and Mains, 1904.

[2] Evidently his work was done with the cordial sympathy of the Presbyterian
minister on French Broad, North Carolina, for in 1800 he mentions that "we had
about 80 hearers; among them was Mr. Newton, a Presbyterian minister, who made
the concluding prayer"; and again in 1807, Sabbath 18, "I spent a night under the

Kentucky—regions served very poorly by ministers of any denomination. The roughness of the country and the innumerable hardships of travel are vividly set forth in his journal. "What a road have we passed," he says, after crossing the Wilderness Road on October 14, 1803; "certainly the worst on the continent, even in the best weather," and on October 28, 1803, he exclaims with a somewhat unmissionary fervor, "Once more have I escaped from filth, fleas, rattlesnakes, hills, mountains, rocks, and rivers. Farewell, Western world, for a while!" Of the people themselves he speaks with appreciation, that he has been "well and generously entertained," that they are "kind and loving." "We lodged with James Patton; how rich, how plain, how humble, and how kind!" At other times, however, he criticizes severely their way of living, especially the making and drinking of whiskey; "there were too many subjects of the two great potentates of this western world— whiskey, brandy—my mind was greatly distressed"; and yet again, "I am of opinion it is as hard, or harder, for the people of the west to gain religion as any other. When I consider where they came from, where they are, and how they are, and how they are called to go farther, their being unsettled, with so many objects to take their attention, with the health and good air they enjoy, and when I reflect that not one in a hundred came here to get religion, but rather to get plenty of good land, I think it will be well if some or many do not eventually lose their souls."

Doubtless the long weary miles and the hard conditions of travel in general, lent to that day's writing a somewhat pessimistic note, yet there was much in the pioneer's way of life to discourage the missionary. Numerous are the accounts that have come down to us of the rudeness of the frontier—the drinking, brawling, and fighting. Cuming, who made a trip through the West in 1809, makes this rather sweeping generalization: "It may not be improper to mention that the backwoodsmen are very similar in their habits and manners to the aborigines, only perhaps more prodigal and

roof of my very dear brother in Christ, George Newton, a Presbyterian minister, an Israelite indeed." Dec. 2, 1810. "We dined with Mr. Newton. He is almost a Methodist."

Oct. 2, 1802, in southwest Virginia, he says: "I applied to Mr. William Hodge and to Mr. William McGee, Presbyterian ministers, to supply my lack of public service, which they did with great fervency and fidelity." Ibid.

more careless of life. . . . They have frequent meetings for the purpose of gambling, fighting, and drinking. They make bets to the amount of all they possess. They fight for the most trifling provocation, or even sometimes without any, but merely to try each other's prowess, which they are fond of vaunting of."[1]

Historians, however, while recognizing the flagrant evils, very generally bear witness to the sturdy blood which dominated this early frontier. If the first mountain settlers were "relentless, revengeful, and suspicious," they were also on the whole "upright, resolute, and fearless, loyal to their friends, and devoted to their country."

In any estimate of their characteristics, the standards of the frontier must be taken into account. Speaking of William Campbell, one of the leaders of the Holston Settlements, Roosevelt says:

> He was a true type of the Roundheads of the frontier, the earnest, eager men who pushed the border ever farther westward across the continent. He followed Indians and tories with relentless and undying hatred; for the long list of backwoods virtues did not include pity for either public or private foes. * * * He hunted them down with a furious zest, and did his work with merciless thoroughness, firm in the belief that he thus best served the Lord and the nation.[2]

It must be remembered, too, that men from the Watauga Settlement, notable in its early days for law and order, and which sent out its soldiers to King's Mountain under the minister's exhortation to "fight with the sword of the Lord and of Gideon," were sharers in outrages and cruelties which blotted that fair victory and the succeeding days.

It is in the light of such conditions and those growing out of them that we must view that part of the great revival to which reference has been made, which, beginning in east Tennessee, extended over Virginia, especially the western part, and over Kentucky during the early years of the nineteenth century; through it all the mountain churches increased their membership, but dating from it

---

[1] Cuming, Fortesque: "Sketches of a Tour to the Western Country, through the states of Ohio and Kentucky; a Voyage down the Ohio and Mississippi Rivers, and a Trip through the Mississippi Territory and part of West Florida, commenced at Philadelphia in the winter of 1807, and concluded in 1809," Vol. IV in Thwaites' Early Western Travels, p. 137. Cleveland, Ohio, Arthur H. Clark, 1904.

[2] Roosevelt, Theodore: The Winning of the West, Vol. III, p. 106.

the growth of the Methodist and Baptist Churches especially was very rapid, until now they have outstripped the original Church of the mountains in almost all areas.

Table 7 shows, on the basis of information obtained in advance from the 1916 religious census,[1] the relative standing of the denominations now represented in the Highlands as compared with their standing in 1906.[2] It is perhaps unnecessary to emphasize the difficulties in the way of obtaining exact religious data in remote mountain regions where the method generally followed in securing such statistics is, because of the roughness of the country, the slowness of travel, and the lack of organization in many of the churches, peculiarly inadequate. The absence of census data in 1906 for Moravians and Latter Day Saints is probably due to these causes, and undoubtedly the figures as presented do not truly represent the strength of the sects which are most numerous in the less accessible regions. With such limitations in mind, however, one may gain from the figures a general idea of the church affiliations of the Highland people.

Of the entire number of people in the Highlands, 1,948,779, or a little over one-third, were recorded as church members in 1916, and of this one-third, 90 per cent were Protestants. The remainder were included largely in the Roman Catholic Church which, with other non-Protestant bodies, is found almost exclusively in industrial and urban centers. It may be stated almost without qualification that the rural Highlander is a Protestant.

No other denomination approaches in numbers either Methodists or Baptists, although in certain state areas other sects show considerable strength. The relative strength in the different areas in

[1] These data were obtained through the courtesy of the Director of the Bureau of the Census. The method of enumeration as described by him indicates some of the obstacles encountered. The statistics for churches were collected mainly by correspondence with the local church organizations. Lists of organizations were obtained from year-books, etc., of denominations or from denominational officials, home missionary superintendents, etc. In many instances it was impossible to get any returns from individual church organizations. In the case of some loosely organized denominations, special agents were appointed whose official position or personal familiarity with conditions enabled them to supplement correspondence or to conduct the entire work of collecting statistics. In one such instance one special agent covering the entire mountain region and also New England, Louisiana, and Texas, reported many difficulties owing to lack of co-operation on the part of the Church, and the slow and uncertain means of travel and communication.

[2] U. S. Census: Religious Bodies, 1906, Washington, Government, 1910.

TABLE 7.—MEMBERSHIP OF RELIGIOUS BODIES IN THE SOUTHERN
HIGHLANDS.   1906 AND 1916

	1906	1916
Baptist		
Southern Baptist Convention	⎫	493,637
National Baptist Convention (colored)	⎬ 567,601 ⎰	177,258
Northern Baptist Convention	⎭	62,451
Primitive Baptist	22,256	20,671
United Baptist	9,393	16,750
Free-Will Baptist	2,649	4,180
Duck River Baptist	4,096	3,929
Primitive Baptist (colored)	5,200	708
Free Baptist	2,693	414
Total Baptist	613,888	779,998
Methodist		
Methodist Episcopal South	255,813	334,976
Methodist Episcopal	147,676	188,756
Methodist Protestant	23,458	25,701
Congregational Methodist	2,508	1,939
Methodist bodies (colored)	42,880	58,165
Total Methodist	472,335	609,537
Presbyterian		
Presbyterian Church in United States	51,127	68,408
Presbyterian Church in United States of America	19,654	32,876
Cumberland Presbyterian	17,742	9,802
Cumberland Presbyterian (colored)	2,778	2,651
United Presbyterian	1,026	1,776
Total Presbyterian	92,327	115,513
Disciples of Christ	68,087	81,577
United Brethren in Christ	32,164	42,287
Lutheran		
General Synod	14,705	18,793
United Synod in the South	13,747	16,003
Synodical Conference	587	2,283
Joint Synod of Ohio	1,540	2,147
General Council	1,176	1,347
Total Lutheran	31,755	40,573
Churches of Christ	13,053	33,356
Protestant Episcopal	21,267	28,445
Dunkers		
Conservative	14,303	21,008
Progressive	1,921	3,032
Total Dunkers	16,224	24,040
Reformed Church in United States	8,648	11,134

TABLE 7.—MEMBERSHIP OF RELIGIOUS BODIES IN THE SOUTHERN HIGHLANDS. 1906 AND 1916—(*Continued*)

	1906	1916
Latter-Day Saints		
Latter-Day Saints	..	4,914
Latter-Day Saints Reorganized	..	974
Total Latter-Day Saints	..	5,888
Advent Christian	1,476	4,389
Congregational	3,498	4,270
Churches of God in North America	705	2,122
Friends (Orthodox)	869	1,971
German Evangelical Synod of North America	120	1,187
United Evangelical	541	853
Moravian	..	717
Christian (Christian connection)	3,655	682
Non-sectarian Churches of Bible Faith	1,316	399
Total Protestant bodies listed	1,381,928	1,788,938
Roman Catholic	83,596	107,212
Greek Orthodox	955	1,700
Jewish	1,032	3,105
All other bodies[a]	34,177	47,824
Grand total	1,501,688	1,948,779

[a] Of the 34,177 listed under all other bodies in 1906, 32,365 were Protestant and 1,812 non-Protestant. Separate figures were not available for 1916 when the table was constructed.

1916 for the nine most important Protestant denominations and for Catholics is shown in Table 26 of Appendix E. In general it may be said that the Presbyterians, Lutherans, Episcopalians, and the Dunkers show their greatest numbers in the Valley, although they are all exceeded here by the Baptists and Methodists. In the Allegheny-Cumberland Belt the Methodists, Disciples of Christ, and United Brethren are strongest—the Methodists here even exceeding the Baptists.

The Baptists show their largest numbers in the Blue Ridge Belt; but so numerous are they in the Valley that they outnumber both the Methodists and all other denominations combined. They also predominate in the Allegheny-Cumberland Belt in eastern Tennessee, eastern Kentucky, and Alabama. In addition to the impractica-bility of enumerating all of this denomination in remote areas, it is probable that large numbers not listed as church members are sym-pathetically at least affiliated with this Church.

The relative proportion borne by Baptists, Methodists, Presby-terians, and all other religious bodies to the entire number of church members listed in the mountain regions of the several states is shown in Table 8.

TABLE 8.—PERCENTAGE OF TOTAL CHURCH MEMBERSHIP IN THE SOUTHERN HIGHLANDS FOR THE THREE LEADING PROTESTANT DENOMINATIONS. 1916

State	Baptists	Metho-dists	Presby-terians	All other religious bodies
Alabama	48.5	34.7	4.8	12.0
Georgia	65.2	29.1	2.5	3.2
Kentucky	48.0	16.8	3.6	31.6
Maryland	2.9	19.8	3.1	74.2
North Carolina	58.1	29.8	4.0	8.1
South Carolina	64.2	24.4	6.2	5.2
Tennessee	45.2	31.0	8.6	15.2
Virginia	30.7	35.1	7.9	26.3
West Virginia	20.0	36.5	6.7	36.8
Total mountain region	40.0	31.2	6.0	22.8

On the basis, therefore, of numbers, the Methodist and Baptist may be called the dominant Churches of the mountains. This state-ment is intended, of course, to apply to these two denominations considered in their entirety. Their several divisions vary greatly in strength in different areas. Of the various divisions of the Metho-dist Church, that of the Methodist Episcopal Church South is by far the largest, considering the mountains as a whole, although the northern branch of the Church is stronger in Maryland and West Virginia. Some reference should be made to the Holiness sect, known sometimes as the Holiness Methodist Church, but not affili-ated with the Methodist denomination. While not listed, probably because of its lack of organization, this Church through its super-emotionalism makes from time to time a strong appeal in different parts of the mountains.

The largest number of Baptists now in the mountains are what are known sometimes as Missionary or Regular Baptists, but more generally as Baptists without descriptive adjective. They are represented by the Northern,[1] Southern, and National (colored) Conventions, distinguished on the basis of locality and race rather than of doctrine. So great, however, are the number and variety of the divisions of this Church in the more remote areas, that one is reminded of Hawks' description quoted earlier in this chapter, of the differences in doctrine among the early Baptists. Nowhere is the individualism of the Highlander more in evidence. For example, while the census classes under the head of Primitive[2] Baptists the Old School, Regular, Anti-Mission, and Hardshell Baptists, and describes their doctrine as strongly Calvinistic, yet in the High-

[1] The Northern Convention is practically confined to West Virginia; 62,249 of the 62,451 listed in Table 7 are in this state.

[2] "The Primitive Baptists arose in 1836 in opposition to the various organizations for Christian work, by which as they felt, the Church was vacating its own duties and privileges."—U. S. Census: Religious Bodies, p. 44. 1906.

".The Warwick Association of New York issued a circular letter in 1849 which shows that a warm controversy was then in progress. This letter, which was written in behalf of the 'new Ideas' charged the Primitive Brethren with holding hyper-Calvinistic doctrines, and insisted that their predestinarianism was such as practically to deny any responsibility in man for his conduct or condition. It attributed to them statements to the effect that God carries on His work 'without the least instrumentality whatever,' and that 'all the preaching from John the Baptist until now, if made to bear on one unregenerate sinner' could not 'quicken his poor dead soul.' The Primitive Baptists do not oppose the preaching of the gospel, but believe that God will convert the world in his own way, and own good time, without the aid of missionary societies."—Carroll, H. K.: Religious Forces in the United States, Enumerated, Classified, and Described, p. 12. New York, Charles Scribner's Sons, 1912.

A relic of this controversy is reflected in one of the old hymns:

There is a reprobated plan;
　Come how did it arise?
By the predestinated clan
　Of horrid cruelties.

The plan is this—they hold a few
　Who are ordained for heaven;
They hold the rest a cursed crew,
　That cannot be forgiven.

They do believe God has decreed
　Whatsoever comes to pass,
Some to be damned—some to be freed—
　And this they call free grace!
* 　* 　* 　* 　* 　* 　* 　* 　* 　*

But we do say God's holy word
　Doth no such doctrine teach,
For if it do, then why do you
　Attempt his word to preach?

For if God has foreordained
　All things to be just so,
Then do we say, all cease to pray,
　And to a-fishing go!

But my friends all, on you I call,
　To mind this doctrine well;
It has its birth, not on this earth,
　But in the pit of hell!

—The Sweet Songster, No. 212, p. 240. Edited by Edward W. Billups, D.D., Catlettsburg, Ky., C. L. McConnell, 1854.

lands some of the Old Regulars believe in Free Will, although they are not Free Will Baptists, and attribute the doctrine of predestination to the Hardshells. Some of the Hardshells are more liberal in giving and in communion than some of the Old Missionary Baptists, who are Anti-Mission in practice. Some of the Primitives deny that they oppose Sunday schools and education, while others preach openly against them; numbers believe in the practice of washing the saints' feet in church and are known as "Foot-washing Baptists," while other Primitives do not practice this rite.

An idea of the strength of these various divisions is but inadequately gained from the census returns, for in addition to the fact that many scattered congregations are situated in parts of the mountains most difficult of access to the enumerator, churches are often without organization or records of any kind.

If, indeed, we have regard to the remote rural areas of the mountains, as well as to those that are more accessible and to all the various sects which are designated as Baptist, as well as to the Baptist Church in the usual acceptation of the term, it must be said that the Baptist Church is the predominant or, if the term be allowed, the "native" church of the Highlands. This is the more true in that certain other denominations found in the mountains, though not affiliated with the Baptist Church are essentially Baptists in practice, and differ no more in belief from some of the branches of this denomination than these branches differ one from another. Among them may be mentioned the Disciples of Christ, Brethren, Dunkers, and Churches of Christ.

Should one be permitted to coin a term, "Immersion Church" would express more nearly the idea we have sought to convey by the statement that the Baptist Church is now the native Church of the mountains. So generally are the mountaineers immersionists that the wisest ministers in churches that practice another mode of baptism use this method if the prospective communicants desire it. It must be remembered, however, that in any general statement made later as to the native Church of the mountains, the term will apply not only to the "Immersion Church" but to any churches which have been long established locally and which in a limited way may also be called "native."

Keeping in mind, then, the somewhat arbitrary distinction be-

174

tween native and foreign churches and ministers, and remembering always that there are urban and rural sections of the mountains well served by their churches, we may proceed to a discussion, inadequate though it may be, of the religious life of the rural mountains today.

CHAPTER IX

THE RELIGIOUS LIFE OF THE RURAL HIGHLANDS

IN NO part of our country will one find a more deep and sincere interest in matters of religion than in the Southern Highlands. The "infidel" is so rare that the term is almost anathema. Even he who is confessedly "wicked" believes in the Deity, and has a rather definite theory of life and of the course necessary for salvation—a state to which he intends in a general way to attain some day. The fact that as one of the old hymns[1] suggests, he may put off the day, though conscious of his evil state, cannot be considered an evidence of his peculiarity.

Come think on death and judg-ment, Your time is al-most spent—

You've been an aw-ful sin-ner, 'Tis time that you re-pent.

I know I've been a sin-ner, And wick-ed all my days, But

when I'm old and fee-ble, I'll think u-pon my ways.

[1] With one exception the words of the hymns quoted in this chapter may be found in The Sweet Songster, a collection of the most popular and approved songs, hymns, and ballads. Ibid.

In the meantime he is well-disposed toward church, which he attends regularly or as regularly as is possible, for preaching in many rural sections still is held but once or twice a month. He does this not only because the occasion is one of the few when he may meet his friends but to listen to the sermon, in the analysis of which he is an expert. Were theological students privileged to hear the criticism of sermons at the mill on "grinding day" following "the last preaching," many valuable suggestions would be received.

The "foreign" preacher who looks down on his right into the attentive faces of the men, and on his left to the women, motionless save as a mother tries to still the restless baby in her arms, little knows the critical faculty that is being focussed upon his discourse. It is well for him if he has refrained from expounding doctrine and has preached frankly and freely against open sin. The Highlander's heart holds no resentment against the outsider who tells him to his face of his shortcomings; but woe betide the foreigner who talks of his failings behind his back, or who endeavors to enter with him into the intricacies of theology. He who attempts the former may follow in the steps of those who have been invited to leave their fields hastily and without ceremony; while those who pursue the latter course will find their adversary no mean opponent in the splitting of doctrinal hairs. The true Highlander, indeed, like his Calvinistic ancestors, delights in theological debate; and assent to doctrine being, theoretically at least, the way to salvation, he finds an unfailing interest in the discussion of foreordination and election, free-will and immersion, and kindred topics. The essential thing for the individual is to believe, the complement of right belief—ethical dealings with one's neighbors—being too little dwelt upon. Like many a professed Christian elsewhere, the mountaineer has not learned the lesson of self-effacement. He is not willing to decrease that others may increase. Self-preservation here is a large factor in determining his ethical standards; and self-preservation hereafter a part of his religion.

For one so little versed in reading he has a remarkable knowledge of the Scriptures. He "loves" to "read after" them, and to "study on" them. Even when nearly illiterate he often has a real appreciation of the beauty of their language and of human nature as revealed in their pages, as well as ingenious interpretations or deductions to draw from the context. The compelling fashion in which an old patriarch of the Highlands recounted the story of Abraham is not easily forgotten:

"Abraham went out in the wilderness on a four days' journey, and he took with him several camels and she-asses and built hisself an altar unto the Lord. And he packed wood hisself for the altar. And Isaac said unto Abraham, ' Pap, whar's the ram?' And Abraham said unto Isaac, 'Son, you needn't be worritted about the ram. The Lord will pervide a sacrifice.'

"Then Abraham took his son and stripped him, and he drew his knife——" here the old man paused and his voice grew unconsciously tender, "Kindly slow-like, don't you reckon, cause hit were his boy, and turned away his head. And the Lord stationed his arm. And there was a ram, catched by his horn in the grapevine!"

"I've studied a right smart, and I've asked a heap of men learned in books. What do you reckon would have happened if Abraham had killed Isaac? *I* reckon there wouldn't have been no need to kill Christ. The Scripture says we must be saved by blood, and we would have been saved by the blood of Isaac."

The Scriptures are the source from which arguments are drawn for every important discussion of Church or State, or of life in general. To bolster up a cause or an opinion the Highlander is able to quote disassociated texts—"textes" as he would say—and often, too often, the Book of Books becomes a cudgel for the head of an opponent rather than a "lamp unto the feet."

It was the writer's experience upon one occasion to deliver a sermon at the same meeting with two mountain preachers. It had been the custom for the school pastor to preach in a distant neighborhood on those Sundays when there would be no other service. On this Sunday he, being ill, dispatched the "Professor" to take his place, but unfortunately he had mistaken the day, and his substitute arrived to find not only a large congregation assembled but two preachers native to the region already present, the one a young man new to the calling, and the other an older man of considerable reputation throughout the countryside. Despite the efforts of the latest comer to withdraw, it was held by the two first on the field that all three should preach, for the Brother had traveled a long distance; he was a learned man; and the audience was expecting to hear him. They decided, furthermore, after some consultation, that he should speak second—a convenient middle, as he afterward discovered, upon which pressure could be exerted from both sides. The young man began. He introduced his discourse by saying that there was present that day a stranger who would speak to them. He was a very learned teacher. He came from——; all the audience knew——; it was the greatest institution of learning in the county. However, in the second chapter of Matthew the Lord Jesus had said, "I thank Thee, O Father, because Thou hast hid these things from the wise and prudent and hast revealed them unto babes"; so perhaps he himself would have something worth hearing to say to them. When he had finished, the writer spoke briefly and as well as he could after his inauspicious introduction. Thereupon the old man rose. Stroking his long white beard, he thus addressed his audience and completed the work so well started by his companion: "I take my text from Deuteronomy (just where he did not disclose). 'The Lord said not to listen to them that has smooth faces, but to hearken unto them that has gray hairs.'"

A common misconception as to the mountaineer is that he is a stolid person. What passes for stolidity when he is in an environment other than his own, or with strangers, is a self-protective attitude—an "on guard" frame of mind. In point of fact he is very emotional, easily moved and easily led by those who have his confidence. Moreover, despite the lack of connection often existing between his religious ideas and ethics, he feels himself accountable to a Higher Power for the deeds of his life, and he has, too, a sense of responsibility for his neighbor's soul. This sense of responsibility for another in the hour of stress was strikingly illustrated in a county which the writer visited with a friend in whose field it occurred. The leader of one of the worst feuds in the mountains, in a moment of anger shot a man to whose house he had gone for liquor, because he assumed that the refusal to give it to him was due to unwillingness rather than to lack of whiskey. As his victim fell fatally wounded and endeavored to speak, the murderer bent over him and said, "I'm right sorry I had to kill you." Then turning to the bystanders, he asked someone to offer prayer for the dying man. As no one volunteered, he himself, declaring "It ain't right to let this man's soul go naked into the presence of his Maker without prayer," knelt beside the man whom he had wounded unto death and offered prayer in his behalf.

This is, of course, a paradoxical case, but no one who has attended the big religious gatherings of any native church in the mountains and has witnessed the pleadings of neighbor with neighbor, the old with the young, and often the youth and maiden with companions of their own years, can fail to see that concern for others has a part in their religious life.

Usually the "conversions" have, or are supposed to have, some impressive preliminary experiences, and when these do not occur it is sometimes a matter of deep anxiety to the waiting one. A pathetic memory is that of a saintly old man of eighty-five, who had been "rassling in prayer" for years for the assurance of salvation. Often he had sent for a friend, a young pastor, to pray with him. But notwithstanding the pastor's assurance, the old man was going to his grave hopeless because he had not experienced certain emotions or seen certain visions expected as an earnest of redemption.

Visions, dreams, and omens have a part in the life of the people, especially in the life of the older women. An elderly woman, known to the writer, was deeply affronted because the preacher who had officiated at her son's funeral had taken the occasion to emphasize his own convictions on baptism. The soul of the boy, he said, was lost, because although he had been a mighty good boy and had prayed on his death-bed, he had never been baptized. The mother thereupon had a vision, in which her son appeared and declared that he was not going to have any preacher standing over his grave saying he was lost, when his soul was shining bright as any star. The offices of a new and young preacher must be secured, who should preach another sermon and tell the assembled people of the mother's experience. These directions were followed.

A little later the mother had a second vision, which conveniently enabled her to do some electioneering for a living son. "Do you believe in the Lord Jesus Christ?" said the vision, "Well, this is his spirit a-talking to you." Whereupon she was advised to per-

suade the man who was an obstacle to her son's election to go away
by telling him that the disease which was affecting him was "heart
dropsy." If he should go away he would be cured, but if he should
stay and fight her son his dropsy would wear him away "drap by
drap, drap by drap, drap by drap, till he was all gone." The
authority of the vision was irresistible, and the man left the country.

The older mountain preachers play upon these beliefs and
doubtless many share in them themselves. One preacher who had
opposed the Sabbath school as an innovation subversive of sound
doctrine, told in a dramatic way of his vision of a roaring lion seeking to enter the "church-house" door, but put to flight by a beautiful spirit robed in white. The roaring lion symbolized the Sabbath school, eager to destroy the young of the parish, and the beautiful figure in white was "the spirit of the old-time religion."

At the risk of seeming to give the impression that these are the
only types of native ministers found in the mountains, special
reference should be made to these older men, not only because of
their numbers through the rural sections but because they represent
one of the strong links with the past which here in the Highlands
have not yet been broken.

Most of the older ministers have an extremely limited education;
very few have received any scholastic training for their calling.
They are usually men of native ability who still have much influence over the older people—influence which they exercise by
reason of the fact that they have received what they themselves,
and their people as well, believe to be a divine call to preach.
Their mission is not that of the priest but of the prophet, serving
often with little or no pay. Occasionally one assumes the rôle of
a political Jeremiah, warning his people to escape impending doom
by electing him to the county office to which he aspires. A minister of this sort in a section which the writer visited some years
ago, offered to deliver on Sundays the funeral sermons that had
not been preached, of all "departed relatives and friends" in the
district. During the rest of the week he carried on his campaign
for office. His opponent, a "tooth-dentist," followed on his trail.
At the end of each funeral oration the tooth-dentist was wont to
announce that he would pull aching teeth free of cost during the
following week. There being more aching teeth than departed

relatives with unpreached sermons, the tooth-dentist was elected county clerk.

Among these preachers are many who have grown tender through experience and have a firm hold on the deeper things of life. They have, too, keen insight and a knowledge of human nature, dramatic power, and an ability to touch responsive chords in the hearts of their hearers—a combination of endowments which makes them leaders not to be ignored in any effort for betterment. Such men, riding or walking year by year the many miles of their wide circuit, have so endeared themselves to their people that a memorial service will be indefinitely delayed until the desired preacher can be present. Characteristic was the act of one of these ministers who, in his journey across the mountain from one day's preaching station to the next, spent the night in a home where a baby had died the previous year. It was impossible for the visitor to remain another day, so to comfort the mourning mother he climbed by night the steep hill above the house to the cemetery, and there in the moonlight preached to the little family group the baby's funeral sermon.

The real humanity of men like this is often singularly at variance with the harsh theology of their preaching. In their sermons there is usually little of the love of God and the beauty of holiness, but much of the worm that never dieth and the fire that is not quenched —themes which are developed with masterly detail. At times the sermon is largely a disconnected succession of unrelated texts delivered in an almost unintelligible sing-song which rises at intervals to a shout, and is interspersed with occasional direct remarks uttered in a natural tone and containing the actual substance of the discourse. While delivering his address the preacher strides to and fro, now in front of, and again among his congregation, appealing collectively and individually to the different members.

This type of preaching, so marked as to have elicited much comment and to have led to the mistaken impression that it is characteristic of all mountain preaching, is in point of fact purely conventional, and probably almost as much a matter of tradition[1] as

---

[1] Newman, the Baptist historian, writing of conditions among Baptists in the early nineteenth century, says:

"Many men * * * * * devoted a large amount of time to private study

the old songs and ballads. Its inherent power to stir the emotions is seen in its effect upon the audience, some of whom are usually thrown into a state of great religious excitement. Protracted meetings[1] and funeral preachings in particular, are marked often by a high intensity of emotional expression. It is indeed the office of the preacher on such occasions to stir the audience to tears and repentance, and his success is measured somewhat by the extent to which he accomplishes this. The Highlander, moreover, is so accustomed to emotional preaching that he is wont to characterize the more restrained methods of foreign ministers as "not real religion."

The emotional appeal of the sermon is greatly heightened by the hymns. Through large sections, modern evangelical hymns are now used by both native and foreign churches, although they are often sung in the old manner, with marked and arbitrary rhythm and inserted slurring half-notes. A marked partiality is

and became good literary and theological scholars; but a large proportion undoubtedly fell very far short of attaining to such a grasp of the truth as would have made them instructive preachers. Noisy declamations in unnatural tones, accompanied by violent physical exercises and manifest emotional excitement, in too many cases took the place of intelligent exposition of the truth made vital by the indwelling power of the spirit. The latter part of the preceding period, and the beginning of the present, produced a large number of Baptist preachers of the highest grade; but the average of ministerial culture was low, and the large amount of illiteracy in the ministry, and the widespread satisfaction with an illiterate ministry, furnished an obstacle of the most serious nature to the onward and upward movement that had characterized the recent history of the denomination."—Newman, A. H.: A History of the Baptist Churches in the United States, p. 382. New York, The Christian Literature Co., 1894.

[1] "The annual protracted meeting was an establishment by which the time of other events was reckoned, and is still reckoned so in many places. Things happened three weeks before, or a month after the 'big meeting.' The meetings were usually held in August, during the period of comparative leisure after the crops were 'laid by.' They continued for one or two weeks, and consisted of a service each forenoon, and one at 'early candle light' in the evening. In these meetings the pastor, if we are to indicate by that term the pioneer preacher in his once-a-month or fewer regular visits to the church, was nearly always assisted by one or more visiting preachers, who did the preaching. During the meeting the pastor went to see the people, here for dinner, and yonder for the night, the visiting preachers foregathering with him to enjoy the winsome and whole-hearted hospitality of the people. It was the only visit made for the whole year by the preacher to most of the homes, but its infrequency was partly balanced by the generous open-heartedness with which the visitors were taken into the family circle. From these meetings came the converts and church members,—nearly all who came at all."— Masters, Victor I.: Baptist Missions in the South: A Century of the Saving Impact of a Great Spiritual Body on Society in the Southern States, pp. 24-25. Baptist Home Mission Board, Southern Convention, 1915.

shown for those having a chorus, or much repetition, such as:

> There's a beautiful land, far beyond the sky,
>   And Jesus, our Saviour, is there.
> He has gone to prepare us a place on high,
>   Oh I long, Oh I long to be there.

Chorus:

> In that beautiful land, where the angels stand,
>   We shall meet,——shall meet,
> We shall meet,——shall meet,
>   We shall meet in that beautiful land.

In some places the music is printed in shaped notes, by which the singer reads the note from its peculiar shape rather than from its place on the staff.

There are, however, still sung in certain neighborhoods the tra-

184

The Swannanoa River Valley, near Asheville, North Carolina

Clay County Salt Works, Manchester, Kentucky

Branch of Carr Creek, Kentucky

"The poorness of mountain roads was probably not as much a deterrent to travel at this time, as later."

When the Creek is up over the Road

"Conjectures have been many as to the ancestry of the Southern Highlanders."

"The social aspect of the Red Cross meetings."

"There is something magnificent in many of the older women."

Cecil J. Sharp collecting Old English Ballads and Folk-Songs

"In the center is the home itself."

"Such a sled as may be seen today on almost any mountain farm."

Grist Mill

In Process of Distilling

The Crushing of Sorghum Cane and Boiling Down

A Highland Horse-Swapping

A Speech on Patriotism from the Court House Steps on Registration Day

"Men who carry out the letter of the law."

"The mountaineer is not a person to be pushed where he does not wish to go, nor is he submissively responsive to a shaping process."

A Maker of Guns, with Gun Made Thirty Years Ago

A Highland Soldier of the Civil War

The boy of this daguerreotype had "heart and cravin' that our people may grow better," and in his old age gave all he had to found in his remote community, a school which should teach the children "books and agriculture and machinery and all kinds of labor and to learn them to live up as good American citizens."

Four Brothers in One of the Mountain Schools
(Average height 6 feet 2 inches. Average weight 199 pounds)
"The type that has come to be called American."

A Prominent Feudist in One of Kentucky's Past "Wars"

A Mountain Preacher

County-seat in the Kentucky Mountains, Showing Congestion of Population in a Narrow Valley

Logging in East Tennessee

Cradling Rye on a Hillside Farm

Public School

County Teachers Taking Examination at the Court House

Visiting a Mountain School Sixty Miles from a Railroad

The Appeal of the Children is Strong

The Mountain Store is the Gathering Place of the Neighborhood

"Most of his journey was taken over roads impassable to automobiles."

ditional tunes of older hymns, the words alone being printed and "lined out," that is, read or recited from memory, line by line, by the preacher. Some of these tunes with their unfamiliar and old-time intervals, possess a strange and somber beauty which strikes to the heart even of the unregenerate foreigner.

Others suggest the old carols[1] and ballads[2] in their semi-narrative form, and the long telling of Bible stories:

There was a lit-tle fam'-ly   Lived up in Beth-an-y,

Two sis-ters and one brother,   Composed that fam-i-ly.

With pray'r and with sing-ing, Like   an-gels in the sky,

At morn-ing and at eve-ning,   They raised their voices high.

Still others, in accord with the spirit of the sermon, are mournful in the extreme, with their emphasis upon the uncertainty and wickedness of life and the certainty of death and judgment.

[1] Several versions of the old Cherry Tree Carol have been collected. See Campbell and Sharp: English Folk Songs from the Southern Appalachians, No. 13. New York, G. P. Putnam's Sons, 1917.

[2] Words may be found in A New and Choice Selection of Hymns and Spiritual Songs for the Use of the Regular Baptist Church, by Elder E. D. Thomas, No. 449. Catlettsburg, Ky., C. L. McConnell, 1871.

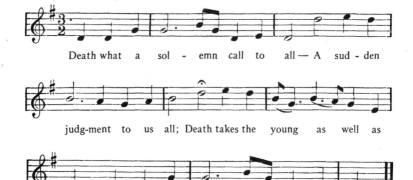

Death what a sol - emn call to all — A sud - den judg-ment to us all; Death takes the young as well as old; And in the wind - ing sheet doth fold.

I spied a youth the other day,
Just in his prime, he looked so gay;
His time is come, his days are past,
And he must go to the grave at last.

His father and mother standing round,
With tears a-falling to the ground;
Saying, father, father! pray for me,
For I must go to eternity.

His faithful sisters standing by,
Saying brother, brother! you're going to die;
You've trifled all your days away,
And now must go to eternity.

And when the corpse was brought to the ground,
His friends and relations standing round,
With sorrowful hearts and troubled mind,
To think his soul's in hell confin'd.

A story, late, has just been told—
A warning for both young and old,
For to prepare to meet the Lord,
That we may hear his happy word.

O ye young, ye gay, ye proud, You must
Time will rob you of your bloom, Death will
Then you'll cry, I want to be, Hap - py

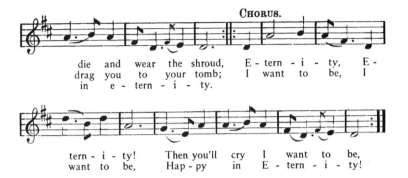

Will you go to heaven or hell?
One you must, and there to dwell—
Christ will come, and quickly too,
I must meet him, so must you;
Then you'll cry, I want to be
Happy in eternity.

Chorus.

The judgment throne will soon appear,—
All this world shall then draw near,
Sinners will be driven down,
Saints will wear a starry crown;
Then you'll cry, I want to be
Happy in eternity.

Chorus.

Until one has heard these hymns, sung in a little mountain church dimly lighted by smoking, flickering pine torches, he cannot know how powerfully they grip the listener. The congregation sways to and fro, in part to the rhythm of the music, in part to express the inner surge of feeling aroused by the exhortations of the preacher and the tense emotional atmosphere. It is but a step from this to sobs and tears, to shouting, screaming, jumping up and down, and even to more violent manifestations.

Miss Miles, herself a mountaineer, writes:

No attempt is ever made to check the excitement, although its excess has been known to result in insanity and even death, for whoso dies shouting happy is held to have met a fortunate end. I hesitate to say much of this, for there is a tendency among certain classes of city people to make a jest of these peculiarities, to which we of the mountains are becoming more sensitive year

by year. It ought not to be so—God knows what the old ceremonies mean to those who take part in them; but such is the
persecution in some places where the curiosity of the town is
pressing close in on us that even after a congregation has met
together to hold a foot-washing, if any city people are present
who are not well known and trusted, the occasion will be quietly
turned into an ordinary preaching.[1]

As the young people come under the influence of schools, the
shortcomings of the native preachers and practices are brought
into sharp relief. Usually there are Sabbath schools in connection
with the church and independent schools and in their outlying
stations. Frequently, too, the denominations which are maintaining educational work in the mountains send ministers to these
fields. These men are better educated than the older native
preachers, who not infrequently are displaced in such neighborhoods by younger mountain men of their own church, better trained
to meet the competition of the "foreign preacher." The inevitable
change of attitude on the part of the young people is attributed by
the old ministers to education and to the Sabbath schools, and
rightly so. Consequently, many of them, as they see their former
leadership waning, oppose such innovations. The day of these
men is passing, though slowly in some sections and new men, many
of them having the little knowledge which is so dangerous a thing,
are taking their places. The problem of support will for some time
yet limit such new men largely to centers of influence, although
even here in some instances new preachers, too advanced theo-
logically for their constituency, have met with as little success as
have some of the "foreign" ministers. We have in mind a number
of such cases, especially that of a young native minister of exceptional character and ability who was endeavoring to work in harmony with all helpful agencies, native and foreign, but who was
forced to leave the field because his congregation failed to maintain
him.

It is to be remembered that all churches, whatever their denomination, that have ministered long to remote communicants
of the mountains, are extremely conservative and are not to be

[1] Miles, Emma B.: The Spirit of the Mountains, pp. 133–134. New York, James
Pott and Company, 1905.

taken as the measure of the denomination in more accessible regions within and without the Highlands. Their strength and their weaknesses are those of rural churches served by men intimately acquainted with their people, but illiterate or having a limited education and holding to the older theological conceptions, especially those which emphasize the futility of personal effort. With all its limitations, however, the mountain church has been a conserver of the best in mountain life and is yet the best organized mountain agency for the promotion of spiritual growth.

It is not an easy matter to estimate the influence exerted by the foreign churches as a whole. Apparently the coming into the mountains of the ministers of these denominations has awakened the native churches to the need of better trained preachers for themselves. If this be the only result attained it has been worth the effort made, though the foreign churches must give a share, and probably the larger share, of the credit for this change to the church schools. It is almost impossible to disassociate the influence of these churches from that of the church schools through their Sabbath schools and other religious organizations, which are carried on in many places, without a church or pastor. The same may be said of the Christian activities of the independent schools. If the questionable standard of numbers and increase in membership be employed as a measure of success, these foreign churches have been unsuccessful, and beyond question the spiritual influence of the schools and their allied Christian organizations is far greater than that of these churches considered alone.

The reasons for limitation in influence are many. Prominent among them is the shortness of the term of service of pastors on the field. Young men who feel the call to the mountains are of necessity forced out ere long unless they forego all thought of a home of their own, have an independent income, or are willing to attempt to bring up a family on a salary barely sufficient for one person. Those who remain are often expected to help in the school, as well as to be pastor of the church, and in addition to carry the work of one or two men. At times where there are both pastors and school principals on the same field, differences of view cause both church and school work to suffer. It is difficult in such places to draw the line between the so-called religious and the so-called secular work of the schools, and with final authority indefinite, there is not infrequently a crossing of purposes.

A too general tendency prevails on the part of both pastors and teachers to force upon the mountain people modes and methods natural in other regions but unnatural to the mountaineer. Too many sent to this field have felt it necessary to bring the mountaineer to adopt their point of view and their forms. Those who send, and those who go, regard their mission altogether too much as one of "teaching the people better ways"; that is to say, "their ways." Too seldom the question is asked, "May we not learn?" It is perhaps because many have been unwilling to learn, that the foreign churches have failed in number and in influence. More intelligent tolerance is needed; more of Christianity and less of its by-product, denominationalism. It is usually the enforced nonessential that bars the church door. If foreign ministers would follow so far as they conscientiously could the practices that have through long association become somewhat sacred to the mountaineer, and beautify rather than abolish these, there would be an increase in church membership and prestige.

In one field some years ago a denomination deservedly noted for the excellence of its school work, took officially a position in regard to baptism that seemed to the mountaineer and to some of his friends inconsistent, more inconsistent than that taken by the illiterate mountain preacher. He holds that there is but one true method of baptism for all believers. The particular church in the field mentioned, though holding the more consistent belief that any mode is valid, insisted upon its own form when the mountaineer would join it; or forced him to satisfy his conscience by receiving baptism at other hands before it would admit him into church fellowship.

In another denomination noted for the freedom of action it allows the individual, a technicality of belief forbids the mountain preacher, who is used to speaking where he will, from occupying its pulpits. While visiting a school of this denomination the writer was at one time asked, as is the usual custom in the mountains, to address the students in chapel on some religious subject. The question then arose as to whether as a layman and of a different denomination, he could be permitted to speak in the church building where chapel was to be held, the momentous decision being finally concluded in the affirmative when it was remembered that the building had not been as yet officially set aside for religious purposes.

Another block of stumbling is placed in the way unintentionally, by supporters at a distance. A strong, promising young man of a denomination not dominant in the mountains is sent to the field, and "results" are looked for by the end of the first year and confidently expected the second; these results being measured usually by the number of communicants added to this "foreign" church, and by the local contributions made to its support. Such results may even be demanded as prerequisite for additional funds.

The natural reaction of the Highlander, accustomed to a ministry which derives its support mainly from labor like his own, is to look with suspicion at these efforts for numbers and support from the field, and it usually culminates in active antagonism. Religion thus becomes increasingly a matter of controversy.

Would that there might be sent into this rural mountain field, and to other rural fields as well, men instructed by their denominations, native or foreign, to forget that they are anything but Christian ministers whose definite purpose is to reinforce, not to compete with, all Christian forces on the field—men more anxious to win followers of the Great Leader than to make more of the twelve kinds of Presbyterians, fifteen kinds of Adventists, four kinds of disunited United Brethren, or Congregationalists, Episcopalians, or any others of the 143 denominations in our country listed under different titles by the Census Bureau. The church that in practice gives evidence of such a belief and will continue to sustain men who also believe it, has a future in the mountains and elsewhere.

One hesitates even to mention a third cause of failure, or to seem to pass judgment upon any group of men who have sought service in fields so remote. The hesitancy is the greater because there are among them men of large vision, trained intellect, and genuine spirituality, who have been dominated in their choice of a field simply by its need and their desire to be of service. These men would have succeeded anywhere. Exception must be made of them in any statement that would seem to call in question the influence of the group. Unhappily, however, the pull to the city has affected the conception of the relative values of city and country church work, and perhaps unconsciously the thought has grown up that men unfitted for service in the city will succeed in a rural community. Acting upon this assumption, or, it may be, through the necessity of taking those that could be had, church boards have too often sent into the mountains ministers entirely unsuited to the needs of the region but who "might do some good in the country." On the other hand, men of ability have been sent but not supported, and their intelligent initiative for rural betterment has been crushed by the dictum of a superior officer, who knew nothing of rural conditions but who was supposed to know more about them, even about local ones, than a pastor living in the small country parish he was serving.

"When they send us the right kind of a preacher," said one Highlander, "they don't keep him here, and too often the man who stays is below the level of his congregation, and unable, and his wife is unable, to mingle with the people." There was no intimation that the speaker, a person of education and influence, had any feeling of superiority. He simply regretted that men of originality, progressiveness, and winning personality, as well as of deep spirituality, could not be retained. In a more forceful and direct way, somewhat the same thought was expressed by the father of one of the most noted feud leaders. "You are wondering," said he, "why the missionaries among the Highlanders are a failure. I will tell you. Their missionaries are failures because the men the church sends were failures before they came. They have sent to us ministers who have no brains or gumption—ministers who could not get a church anywhere else. If you are to touch the hearts of these Highlanders you must send us the bravest men, the most able and consecrated women you can find. Give us the men and women who can make a success in any place, and they will make a success here."

A similar feeling as regards city and country values has prompted many a well-intentioned ladies' sewing circle to send worn-out, misfitting, and out-of-date garments to the mountain field. The practice is commendable enough on the ground of making some use of remnants or misfits, but as a theory of rural reconstruction in any form it is fallacious and mischievous. The writer recalls one out of the many mission barrels he has met—for which, rather, he has met the freight bill—and the good that it really did do. This barrel, which stands out conspicuously among other barrels, contained two pairs of frayed duck trousers, a battered silk hat, and a dress-coat with stains upon the lapel, which indicated that it had not been worn in a prohibition state. There were in that barrel, also, a great many cigarette cards with pictures of battleships, of famous race-horses, and of notorious actresses. Sprinkled as leaven in this mixture, were Bible cards with the injunction to "Remember now thy Creator in the days of thy youth." Seemingly these things had not been held as serviceable in the cultured city from which they were sent, so were shipped to the writer with the thought that they might do some good "down there." It cost him $3.63 in freight, and he needed the money, too, to try out another's theory that discards might do somebody some good.

In times of discouragement, when he could not convince the board secretaries that more money was needed, or when local perplexities loomed large, he would imagine himself clad in frayed duck trousers, a wine-stained dress-coat, and battered silk hat, distributing pictures of battleships, of race-horses, and of actresses clad in gaudy pink and blue raiment, none too plentiful, to the children of the primary department for "busy work," as suggested by the kindly disposed lady who sent the barrel but who forgot to pay the freight. But while misfits and discards may serve humorously at times, the humor is too often of the pathetic kind, in which the tear falls to meet the trembling smile.

Inferiority and mediocrity are not qualifications for leadership in rural communities. The best place to send a man of mediocre ability, to insure a measure of success, would seem to be into urban communities, at least into the smaller ones, where there would be a number of people to assist and advise him. Live men are wanted in the rural ministry; not dead ones from what a mountain friend called "them thar theological cemeteries." A live native minister, though illiterate, wields a wider influence than learned, dead imported ones. Little patience is due the sophistry that because a man is good, inefficient, and a failure elsewhere he is qualified for the rural ministry. The country needs men who are not only good but who are good for something.

More men are needed in the mountains who have the large social conception of the ministry, or, shall we say, the sociological conception of the ministry. People leave the country for the city because they believe that in the city they have a fuller life. It is the province of the country church and of its leader to make rural life fuller.

The writer realizes that he is on dangerous ground when he intimates that a pastor should give time to the consideration of those things by which men must live. He may be charged by those who hold that the pastor has only to do with spiritual things, with putting him on the plane of the material when he urges that pastor and church should have much to do with economic and social conditions. He would not, however, have the pastor materialize the spiritual, but spiritualize the material, and a minister must come into close touch with the lives of men in order to accomplish this. In doing it he is but following the example of the Great Teacher from whom we all seek to learn.

In all probability the general falling off of candidates for the ministry seriously affects this most remote field, but there is little doubt that if the same appeal were made for the "home field" and for service in rural communities as is made in the colleges and theological seminaries for the highest type of young men and women for the "foreign field," there would be the same inspiring response. There is as much heroism in the hearts of young men as there ever was. They need only to feel that the work of a country minister is a man's work; and that if they do a man's work they will have moral support, a fair consideration of such plans of betterment as their experiences have taught them are practical and promising, and enough financial return to enable them to maintain a home and provide for the future of those dependent upon them.

Doubtless certain church policies and forms will gain a readier entrance in the Highlands than others, but the measure of success is in the man. Personality is greater than method. Consecrated ability and sanctified common sense in brave men and women are the solution for all our problems.

CHAPTER X

LIVING CONDITIONS AND HEALTH

ONE cannot travel far in the mountain country without facing the fact that romance is not necessarily synonymous with comfort, nor is the beautiful perforce wholesome. If one's point of view be that of the traveler merely, he enjoys the pleasures of the journey and tries to disregard as far as possible the less agreeable aspects; but if one stays in the mountains he cannot long remain indifferent to the various considerations which bear upon the welfare of the people. Sickness is of too frequent occurrence, the need to relieve suffering too obvious, to permit matters of hygiene and sanitation to become obscured.

Much as one may rejoice in all that is picturesque in the manner of life and in the independence which is so outstanding a trait of mountain character, he comes to feel that where the health, at least, of the people is affected, these must give place to or be transformed into more salutary, albeit less interesting virtues. That the changes which must necessarily accompany a movement to relieve suffering are far-reaching he soon discovers. At times they involve the loss of things not only worthy of preservation, but in and of themselves without relation to the health problem of the mountains. With the large question of prevention are concerned some of the most familiar and characteristic features of Highland life.

Even the log cabin of the pioneer, symbolic as it is of the history of our country, harmoniously as it fits into the mountain landscape, is destined in time to disappear as the Highlander improves the conditions of his living. Not only is the log cabin home becoming a costly luxury, as the sawmill gives its cheaper substitute of boxhouse or the more commodious frame dwelling, but from the standpoint of housing it has its deficiencies. Hewn with a narrow axe on two sides, the logs are rough and warped. The pioneer builder had no time to dry his timber, nor broad axe nor adze to smooth it off; and his descendant, can he afford in these days to use logs, builds much in the same way even though his tools be more modern. Green timber, it is true, is heavy to handle but it is easier to hew. Besides, as a Highlander remarked with characteristic humor, "The young folks are marrying too fast to wait for it to dry."

Little attention is given to exterior or interior finish. The walls are roughly chinked with mud and clay, which hardening, crumble out onto the floor. Often they are pasted over with newspapers, varied wherever possible by gaily colored prints cut from flower catalogs or other advertising matter. Such luxuries as smooth floors, closets, and shelves are almost unknown in remote sections. Lumber is hard to obtain and planers are few. In addition, the Highlander has had little opportunity to become a skilled workman. Some men, indeed, are building better houses, and where dressed lumber is not available are dressing it by hand. Very many homes, however, are still close to pioneer needs and far from standards set by sanitary experts.

One sees in these days fewer of the "typical" windowless one-room cabins. Windows, although often they do not open, have been inserted even in the older buildings, but window space as a rule is very inadequate. Light and air are furnished during the day by the door which is swung hospitably wide throughout winter and summer. At night the door is closed, and the chance traveler through the darkness can mark the cabin site only by the fitful glow of the hearth-fire through the window, or when there is no window, by the sparks and flames which spurt upward through the low chimney.

The open log cabin, however, through whose chinks and apertures air circulates more or less freely, is more conducive to health than is the tighter house of more recent times, where ventilation can be and often is, especially at night, reduced to a minimum. If the fireplace still persists in the latter a certain amount of fresh air is provided, but if the stove has superseded the fireplace, conditions in this regard are usually much worse.

The situation is aggravated by the number of people living in the home. One faces in the Highlands the problem of congestion within homes rather than that of congested neighborhoods. It may seem strange in a country where timber and land are plentiful that

196

houses should not be enlarged to meet the enlarging family. One does, it is true, pass many a rambling old cabin and many a painted new frame house with the little outgrown cabin by its side; but habit is strong, and even when the necessity for crowding has passed, through the occupancy of a larger and better built dwelling, previous conditions of congestion frequently remain. Large families, many times surprisingly large, occupy one or two rooms. There is little understanding, even in those households which are scrupulously clean, of ordinary hygienic and sanitary precautions. Old and young, sick and well, sleep together and use in common the scanty toilet articles. The spread of contagious and infectious diseases is naturally rapid.

Nor are such diseases confined to the home, even if this be comparatively isolated. Neighbors flock to the afflicted household both to give help and because they feel they are not showing a proper interest if they do not do so. Moreover, waste of all sorts, though sometimes burned, is more often thrown out and scattered about by hogs and chickens, or finds its way into the nearby creek or branch to be carried on to other households below.

No attempt is made to safeguard drinking water, which is still, for the most part, from springs or shallow wells which run dry in time of drought. Both wells and springs are frequently polluted through seepage from nearby barn or outhouse, if there be one. Outhouses are the exception, however. Even in the public schools of the remoter sections they are almost universally lacking, and too many of the schools under private auspices, which should set an example in this regard, by the untidy and unsanitary condition of these provisions make their absence almost more to be desired than their presence.

How general is the lack of sanitary provisions in the rural Highlands was brought to public notice a few years ago by the findings of the survey made by the Rockefeller Sanitary Commission for the Eradication of Hookworm Disease. Nor has the matter been disregarded by health authorities. Some of the remedies, however, suggested for its correction have been pathetically humorous. In one community, distant from the railroad several score of miles, a state sanitary expert held forth on the desirability of a certain kind of septic tank. He displayed blueprints, beautifully drawn, showing just how these tanks were to be made, but he forgot that the bricks had to be hauled nearly fifty miles from the railroad and that the minimum cost was prohibitive for all but the wealthiest mountain families. Lest the reader regard this as an exceptional instance, we may add that many similar cases in this and in other phases of mountain life might be cited where the advice of well-meaning experts, brought in to stimulate local initiative, has served but to discourage even the most progressive of those who listened to it.

It is an easy matter to sit in a steam-heated city office and hold forth upon the deficiencies in mountain households and to suggest or plan remedies for them. If, however, one has spent some winter days in a mountain home, and, sharing its labors as he ought in so democratic a household, has helped to cut wood for the many fireplaces and "toted" it in, he can more easily understand why there is congestion in sleeping quarters; and if he has helped to blast a well through resisting strata of rock, be it only to a depth of twenty-five feet, he is strongly inclined to be a believer in the predestinarian theory of disease, whether it be called typhoid or mountain fever. He may even view with a lenient eye certain shortcomings in cleanliness, and, if he helps the housewife to carry in and out the water used, he reverts fondly in thought to the days of his childhood, when he was comfortable in mind and body with a Saturday night bath by the kitchen stove. He admits that he has fallen, but

"Facilis descensus Averno . . . , sed revocare gradum . . . , hoc opus, hic labor est."

However philosophic the visitor may be as to matters of housing and sanitation, he is less apt to be indifferent to the question of food. No detail, probably, of the Highlander's living has been more severely criticized than his diet, and inasmuch as it has been held responsible for many of his ills, it is perhaps worth while at this point to see in some detail what food is eaten in the ordinary rural home in the mountains.

While diet varies somewhat in different sections, the staples through most of the rural portion of the mountains are corn and pork. The reasons for this are simple. Corn can be grown throughout the Highlands and used to feed both family and stock; and

198

hogs can be raised—at least until recently and even now in many places—with little trouble or expense by turning them loose in the forest to forage for themselves. Corn, moreover, is easily stored and ground as needed, and hog meat can be salted or cured and the fat used in every form of cooking.

The curing of meat is necessary because there is no way to keep it fresh. Speaking generally, the spring-house is the only means of refrigeration in the Highlands, and this is usually confined to the more prosperous families. It is customary, when a cow or sheep is to be killed, for the owner to go about among his neighbors and dispose of the various portions before proceeding to slaughter it. The use of beef or mutton, however, is not common in the rural districts, nor is the meat particularly appetizing when served. There is little pasturage, and animals are allowed to wander about in forlorn search of such vegetation as they can find. In certain sections of the mountains a distinct step forward has been taken by putting the steep slopes into grass and making the beginnings of a profitable dairy and cheese industry; but the usual mountain cow has a lean and hungry look. Her milk is poor and thin and her flesh tough and hard. The keeping of sheep is far less frequent than in early days, owing to the pest of dogs. A few are kept here and there for the wool, but with the advance of prices in wool the flesh is too valuable for ordinary consumption. Poultry is the only meat commonly used besides pork, and this is less common than the reports of fried chicken would lead one to expect. Eggs are comparatively cheap but do not form so great a factor in the diet as they should.

Variety is occasionally secured for the table by the addition of rabbit, squirrel, or 'possum. Reserves, stocked by national or private enterprise, are tempting to the poacher, but game no longer offers an inducement for settling in the mountains. Sawmills and the practices of seining, harpooning, and dynamiting, have played havoc with the fish supply, and although fishing is a favorite diversion, fish as an article of diet is negligible.

A welcome addition to the spring diet is furnished by "sallets" of cress, poke, bear's lettuce, and various other young greens, and every family has its fenced-in garden patch which helps to furnish the summer table. Beans, white potatoes, and onions are the common vegetables, but cabbages, beets, sweet potatoes, and turnips are also raised, with a few cushaws,[1] pumpkins, and melons. Tomatoes are becoming more common every year. Sweet corn is seldom found, but young field corn is often eaten, "roasting ears" being considered a great delicacy.

Usually there is also available an abundant supply of wild blackberries, and in places wild strawberries, huckleberries, and grapes. Peaches are plentiful is some sections, and apples are found more or less freely throughout the mountain region. Little or nothing is done in the way of spraying or pruning, but the trees bear abundantly unless caught by frost, as happens every few years. The covered wagon with its load of crimson winesaps or big green "horse apples" is a familiar sight in many a mountain metropolis, while the fame of the Albemarle pippin has reached to foreign shores.

But while the season's crop offers possibilities of variety for the winter diet, it does not affect the winter diet as much as it should. For one reason the Highlander has little storage space. The larger houses have lofts or plunder rooms; but in the smaller cabins reserve food must be strung from the rafters or stacked upon the floor. Outside cellars are not understood or used to any great extent, and potatoes and other root crops, of which there may be a plentiful supply in the autumn, seldom last through the winter.

A real attempt is made to provide a winter supply of vegetables and fruit. Beans are dried in the pod, together with onions, peppers, and savory herbs, and pumpkins are sliced and dried before the fireplace or in the sun. Apples usually are spread out on the roof of shed or cabin, or cured, as are peaches, with the fumes of sulphur. Among the more prosperous families and even in the poorer homes, especially in the southern part of the mountains where fruit is more abundant and climatic conditions less severe, much is done in the preparing of jellies, apple-butter, and pickles. Canning, particularly of tomatoes, is becoming more common in recent times, due in large part to the activity of canning clubs fostered by government and private agencies. Where peaches and berries are put up it is often simply with boiling water, sugar being scarce and expensive.

[1] A kind of squash.

A visit to a pupil of the writer in one of his early schools found the mother baking pies. She was rolling out the crust, not on a molding board but on a piece of cloth spread on the table, her rolling-pin being a round bottle. Having no sugar, she sweetened the apples with a little sorghum syrup, and for want of cinnamon spiced them with berries gathered in the woods, dried and ground. When ready, the pies were baked, not in the oven but on the stone hearth before the fire. All mountain housewives are by no means reduced to such substitutes, but there is still room in many homes for pioneer ingenuity.

Autumn brings the making of sorghum which, with honey, supplies much of the sweetening used. Bees are kept very commonly, sections of the gum-tree serving as hives. A good deal of mountain honey is dark in color and strong, but sourwood honey is famous for its light color and delicate acid flavor. Maple sugar is found only occasionally, hard maple having been pretty well cut out of large sections of the mountains. The autumn traveler is not likely to forget the pawpaws and persimmons, nor the chestnuts, walnuts, and hickory nuts scattered along the road which winds up the mountain through forests of gold and mahogany. A store of nuts is frequently gathered by the household and put away for winter use.

When, however, the crop is finally gathered and winter closes in the family diet is very much restricted. It is probably safe to say that the main sustenance of many a rural household a good share of the winter is fat pork, beans, potatoes, and cornbread, with the addition of sorghum or honey and strong cheap coffee. Soda biscuit of wheat flour, and "grits" are also used extensively among families in better circumstances. "Light-bread," or raised white bread, is very unusual.[1]

Many mountain families have milk through the entire year, but numbers are without it during the winter and sometimes the summer as well. Where there is milk, butter is churned every day. Often it has a curious white flaky appearance, due probably to the fact that the tall earthen churn is left to stand close to the fire where its contents become scalded. Little is known of working the butter

[1] In one locality raised white bread was known as "Presbyterian bread" because baked by the Presbyterians for Sunday use, no cooking being allowed on the Sabbath.

sufficiently or of salting it, and its keeping qualities are poor. Buttermilk is a favorite beverage, referred to usually as "milk." If the guest wishes "sweet milk" he must so designate it.

Food is usually poorly prepared. Frying and boiling are the common methods of preparation, the former predominating largely. Cornbread and biscuits, of course, are generally baked, although hoe-cake may be cooked in a skillet on top of the stove and sometimes by the hearth. Starchy foods are rarely boiled or baked sufficiently, but whatever is fried, is fried a long time, large quantities of grease being used both in preparing and serving.

That the Highlander is not immune to this diet, one may gather from the frequency of sallow complexions and the great prevalence of "risings"—a comprehensive term which may apply to anything, from a minute swelling to a carbuncle. The mountaineer himself is frank to admit that he suffers from "stomach trouble," and while he frequently makes complaint of "heart trouble" one is inclined to suspect that this, too, may be another name for indigestion.

It would seem likely that to the limitations of diet are due also some of the inertia and even apathy that are evidenced by many. Tall and lean the Highlander seems to have, when interested, plenty of endurance; he can walk long distances without apparent fatigue, and he is indefatigable on a hunting or camping trip. He often appears, nevertheless, to lack energy and initiative and that he succumbs rather quickly to disease has been claimed by many, a claim corroborated by a number of physicians who had experience with mountain soldiers in the recent war. By some, however, the indolence of the mountaineer is laid to lack of purpose, while others attribute it to hookworm.

As to the effect of restricted diet in causing pellagra, which is being found in the Highlands today, there seems to be little doubt.[1] Unfortunately, it is impossible to know at this time how extensively the mountain people suffer from this disease, but physicians of the writer's acquaintance have met, they say, an increasing number of such cases in the late years of their practice.

[1] Goldberger, Joseph, and Wheeler, G. A.: Experimental Pellagra in the Human Subject brought about by a Restricted Diet. Reprint No. 311 from the Public Health Reports, U. S. Public Health Service, Washington, Government, 1915.

An interesting side-light on diet in the mountains is furnished by the country store. Here one may purchase salt, vinegar, molasses, soda, coffee, sugar, white flour, and usually some kind of canned goods—"salmons," tomatoes, and peaches. Eggs, too, are quite generally found, as they serve as a medium of barter in the mountains. Chicken and egg men make regular tours of some sections, collecting at a low price supplies to sell in urban centers. Salt pork is kept occasionally and plain crackers. Often there is a small supply of cheap candy. Cooking utensils are exceedingly scarce, though one has no difficulty in procuring saddles, hame strings (rawhide thongs), leggings, cheap shirts (woolen and cotton), calico, nails, spurs, gauntlet gloves, paper tablets, kerosene, and usually cheap shoes and hats. The owner's profit would seem sometimes to be derived largely from tobacco, despite the fact that the Highlander so frequently raises his own. A storekeeper in one community asserted that he bought every seventy or eighty days $200 worth of a popular kind of tobacco, exclusive of all other brands.

In how far the very large use of snuff and tobacco in the mountains, mainly in dipping and chewing, may be accounted for by the monotony of the diet and poor cooking it is difficult to say. The need of stimulants, seemingly felt by many, is probably due at least in part to this cause. It cannot be charged against the Highland people as a whole, however, that they drink excessively.

The Highlander has been used in the past to brewing his own liquor and partaking of it when he pleased. Mr. Combs, to whose Life in the Kentucky Mountains from a Native Mountaineer's Viewpoint reference has been made, says:

"A great many of the mountaineers drink whiskey, but the per cent of those who can 'take a dram' and stop at that, is large. It is thought no harm to drink a little—sometimes more. The story is told of a man in Knott County who 'turned off' a whole quart of moonshine before taking the cup from his head. 'Won't you have more?' he was asked. 'Nope, it might fly to my head.' In many families the children drink whiskey sweetened with sugar."

Unhappily, in these days of highly doctored moonshine, the effects of such drinking as there is are very violent. In the words of a mountain friend, "It drives a man plumb crazy."

203

The rural Highlander is by no means indifferent to the many ills which are resultant upon his manner of living. Forced from early times, however, to face almost without help the grim certainty of suffering and death, he has come to assume toward them the only attitude which makes life endurable under such circumstances—a belief that they are ordained and therefore to be borne with what display of stoicism one may command. "'Pears like hit's bound to go plumb through a family," said a mountain girl wistfully when approached as to treatment for tuberculosis, from which five of her brothers and sisters had died. In her mind there was no help for her.

There is, too, in the attitude of many, the natural conservatism and the suspicion of strangers and new methods which are characteristic of all isolated peoples. And when it happens, as it so often does, that modern theories of disease interfere with the absolute freedom of action so dear to the mountain heart, it is to be expected that they will be viewed with scepticism, if not with actual hostility.

Not long ago, during a health rally held within a few miles of one of the larger mountain cities, a young boy appeared well broken out with smallpox. When protests were addressed to the father, with the request that the child be taken where he could not spread the contagion, he became highly indignant and declared that the boy had been looking forward to this occasion for several weeks, and he did not aim now to have him disappointed.

The incident recalled to the writer a campaign he led in his earlier years to have the stock law enforced in a mountain community where typhoid was epidemic. "Professor," returned a prominent citizen when appealed to on the materialistic score that hogs running loose in the streets were a menace to the growth of the town and to the success of the "college." "The hogs were here before the college. If you don't like them, move the college."

The indifference to the rights and welfare of others manifested in the cases cited, while selfish like many other aspects of individualism, was not intentionally so. The mountaineer does not really believe that disease will be spread through such causes, and he does most thoroughly believe that no one has a right to interfere with

204

his personal liberty.   He has, moreover, certain time-honored remedies of his own.

All dwellers in the remote Highlands are more or less familiar with the use of teas made from common herbs and roots,[1] such as boneset, camomile, sassafras, and pennyroyal; and turpentine taken externally and internally, alone or in combination with various other ingredients, is a favorite household remedy.   The prevalence of patent medicine advertisements in small isolated country stores suggests that, in places at least, these must be used to a considerable degree.   There is not a little faith among many that the performance of prescribed rites under prescribed conditions will drive away certain ailments.   There is in a neighborhood generally some older woman who is recognized as peculiarly gifted in the matter of charms.

When his own knowledge and the offices of those near at hand fail, the Highlander goes for the doctor, if there be one within reach; but usually it is not until the patient is "dangerous"—so dangerous often that the efficacy of help is past.   His delay in seeking medical advice is due in large part to the great scarcity of physicians, which has existed from early days in the Highlands, but the unreliable character of some of the native doctors and the high charges made—$15 to $25 a visit being not uncommon—have doubtless been discouraging factors.

Much must be said for the native mountain physician.   At the best it is a hard life, riding by day and night the rough trails that lead along creek, branch, and over mountain to the isolated homes; and there is little reward save in the knowledge of duty performed. The oft repeated criticism, "He won't come unless he knows he can get his money," must be tempered by adding that his field is far too large for him to serve, and that he may easily spend a whole day going ten to fifteen miles and back to see one patient.

After all is said, however, for the devoted men who serve their countryside to the best of their ability, it must be admitted that

---

[1] A list of teas given by an old man experienced in their use included wild cherry, black cohosh, black and white walnut, slippery elm (white better than red), Indian hemp, bitter-sweet, yellow sarsaparilla, pink-root, yellow dock, boneset, white horse-mint, spignet, pennyroyal, Seneca snake-root, black snake-root, Samson's snake-root, Indian turnip, ginseng, yellow lady's slipper, "lin" (linden) bark and root, Solomon's seal, and lobelia.

much of the more rural Highland region, where supplied at all with physicians, is served by men who have had little or poor training, sometimes none at all. Many of them are men of good sense, who even with their limitations are useful; with proper leadership and co-operation they would be helpful in bettering conditions. But unfortunately it is also true that the mountains have proved a retreat for so-called doctors who are morally and intellectually unfit to minister to the communities which they are supposed to serve. Some, once able physicians in other sections, have been forced from their original fields of service through addiction to drugs or drink.

The effects of the practice of such men on the suffering people are sometimes pathetic in the extreme. Many instances might be cited, some of which have come under personal observation, of gross ignorance and criminal neglect both in medical and surgical practice. Strict laws for the granting of physicians' licenses and the education of the people to a knowledge of what real medical aid means, are gradually reducing the influence of this group; but progress cannot be rapid as long as there is such a large deficit in the number of trained physicians, or indeed, of physicians of any kind.

To recommend an increase in the number of trained physicians, however, is easier than to determine how an adequate number of such men can be supported in a section where the population is not only poor but widely scattered. Doubtless many of the people can pay more than is generally supposed, but even so, the well-trained physician, especially if he have a dependent family, can scarcely afford to settle in remote regions, however altruistically inclined he may be, unless his living be partially underwritten by some philanthropic agency, at least until such time as he shall have gained the confidence and co-operation of his neighborhood or unless medical aid becomes the concern of the state.

In a study made by the United States Children's Bureau in 1918, the following conditions were found to exist in one mountain county in North Carolina. That they are duplicated in many other counties within the Highland region may be safely assumed. Probably they are far worse in certain areas:

Facilities for the care and treatment of sickness are strikingly lacking in this county. Only five physicians,—four at the county seat and one in a village where a normal school is located —over-burdened almost to the breaking point, are the dependence for medical service of a population of 13,718. This is an average of 2,744 persons to a physician, which is over four times as many as the average (691) for the United States. The concentration of physicians at the county seat is to be expected, for social and financial reasons; but, because of rough roads, at times almost impassable, and an absence of telephone communication, also because of the prohibitive expense of a day's trip from physician to patient, the greater part of the country is practically cut off from medical service. There is no physician resident in either of the three townships of the survey, and the families live from 3 to 25 miles from the nearest doctor.

The county has no hospital, the nearest being located at the county seat of the adjacent county, reached once a day by mail stage across the roughest of mountain roads. No trained nurses are resident in the county, and patients are entirely dependent upon the well-meaning but untrained services of neighbors and relatives.[1]

How serious has been the effect of all these conditions upon the mortality rate of the Highlands is not easy to determine with accuracy. Until recent years a large part of the mountain region has not been included within the United States registration area for births and deaths. The first of the mountain states to be included in their entirety in the United States registration area for deaths were Maryland and Kentucky, admitted in 1906 and 1911 respectively. Virginia followed in 1913, North Carolina and South Carolina in 1916, and Tennessee in 1917. Alabama, West Virginia, and Georgia[2] are still without the area. Only five of these states— Maryland, Kentucky, North Carolina, Tennessee, and Virginia— were included in the registration area for births in 1917.

Even now registration cannot be said to operate altogether satisfactorily in the remote mountain sections of those states included within the registration area. State officials are earnestly endeavoring to remedy this condition and great progress has been made,

[1] Bradley, Frances Sage, and Williamson, Margaretta A.: Rural Children in Selected Counties of North Carolina, pp. 67–68. U. S. Department of Labor, Children's Bureau, Publication No. 33, Washington, D. C., 1918.

[2] At the time of writing there were indications that Georgia would soon be admitted.

but the collection of vital statistics under conditions prevailing in the mountain country is at best very difficult. In how far the data returned indicate true health conditions in the mountains it is unsafe to hazard an estimate, but it would not be surprising were they to indicate a lower death rate than is actually the fact. In any case the obstacles in the way of the accurate reporting of vital statistics should be taken into account in considering them.

Table 9 shows the death rates for the mountain region of six states in 1916, the latest year for which data for all were available. The construction of the table has been attended by many difficulties. As in the case of areas and population it has been necessary to base the computations on county figures, and as these were not always published, recourse was had both to federal and to state officials, who kindly furnished manuscript data when printed reports proved inadequate. Where there has been disagreement between figures furnished by state boards of health and the Census Bureau, the figures of the latter have been used. The lack of uniformity in listing diseases in the different states has also been a source of confusion.

The table shows death rates for the rural population, but they are computed on the basis of an urban minimum of cities of 10,000 inhabitants—that used by the Census Bureau in computing mortality statistics. They therefore apply, as in the case of the homicide rates in Chapter VI, to about 90 per cent of the population instead of to the approximately three-quarters of the population with which we are especially concerned in this study. The comparison of the rates for the three mountain belts, on this account, will reflect such differences as are induced by the more urban character of the Valley, as well as the possible differences resulting from topographic and climatic peculiarities in the three belts.

When one considers this table in the light of the many obstacles in the way of good health in the Highlands, one cannot but be struck with the fact that, so far as these data show, the death rate for rural portions of the mountain region, 11.2 per 1,000, is nearly 2 per 1,000 less than that for the rural portion of the entire United States registration area. In all of the six states the mountain sections, except the small upland region of Maryland, compare

TABLE 9.—RURAL DEATH RATES FOR THE MOUNTAIN REGIONS OF SIX SOUTHERN HIGHLAND STATES. 1916

Region	Deaths per 1,000 population. All causes	Deaths per 100,000 population					Infant deaths	
		Tuberculosis (all forms)	Pneumonia (all forms)	Measles	Typhoid fever	Puerperal state	Per 100,000 population	Per 1,000 living births
Blue Ridge Belt								
Maryland	14.9	373.5	137.9	11.9	4.7	16.6	187.9	74.7
North Carolina	11.0	106.6	83.2	4.0	26.9	15.7[a]	276.9[a]	78.7[a]
South Carolina	11.4	109.9	100.6	10.9	33.9	18.8	..	..
Tennessee	11.0	115.3	100.3	13.0	34.8	14.3	221.6	74.4
Virginia	12.1	122.1	102.0	24.6	20.7	17.8	..	..
Total	11.5	123.1	95.8	12.0	26.9	16.6	..	..
Greater Appalachian Valley								
Maryland	14.6	104.6	108.4	52.3	33.5	7.5	340.1	115.2
Tennessee	12.0	166.4	104.4	6.9	33.5	10.3	195.1	80.4
Virginia	12.1	144.1	104.2	11.1	22.2	15.9	..	..
Total	12.1	155.1	104.4	10.1	28.8	12.5	..	..
Alleghany-Cumberland Belt								
Kentucky	9.9	121.3	80.2	9.6	32.9	7.2	260.1	79.3
Maryland	12.1	78.8	97.7	9.4	15.8	7.9	264.9	103.4
Tennessee	9.2	121.0	75.8	8.5	25.6	11.9	145.3	57.5
Virginia	11.3	111.0	103.4	9.7	25.5	13.2	..	..
Total	10.1	117.1	84.3	9.4	29.1	9.3	..	..
Total mountain region								
Kentucky	9.9	121.3	80.2	9.6	32.9	7.2	260.1	79.3
Maryland	13.5	176.9	112.7	18.9	15.9	10.6	255.6	97.4
North Carolina	11.0	106.6	83.2	4.0	26.9	15.7[a]	276.9[a]	78.7[a]
South Carolina	11.4	109.9	100.6	10.9	33.9	18.8	..	..
Tennessee	11.1	144.5	75.6	8.4	31.5	11.4	185.7	74.6
Virginia	11.9	128.5	103.2	15.2	23.5	15.9	..	..
Total	11.2	129.5	93.8	10.5	28.3	12.7	..	..
Rural portion of United States registration area	12.9	124.7	111.3	10.3	15.6	15.1	211.1	97.0
Total United States registration area	14.0	141.6	137.3	11.1	13.3	16.3	229.9	101.0

[a] Includes Asheville.

209

favorably with the United States rural registration area. Specific death rates for the mountain area, except in the case of typhoid fever, also compare favorably with United States rates. The natural conclusion would seem to be, therefore, even allowing for the possible incompleteness of statistics, that the Highland stock is not less resistant to disease than is other rural stock, despite impressions to the contrary.

One would have a fairer basis for conclusions as to the strength of Highland blood were it possible to eliminate from these rates the effect of Negro deaths. Data are available in the case of North Carolina to indicate the effect of the Negro rate. The following table has been constructed in order to show the comparison between colored and white death rates in the Highlands and Lowlands of this state.

TABLE 10.—WHITE AND NEGRO DEATH RATES PER 1,000 POPULA-
TION FOR RURAL NORTH CAROLINA. 1916

	White	Negro	Total
Mountain region	10.6	16.5	11.0
Non-mountain region	11.2	15.8	12.9
Total	11.1	15.9	12.6

That the Negro death rate would be much higher than the white rate was to be expected, as well as that it would be higher in Highlands than in Lowlands. It is to be noted, however, that although this rate is high, it raises the total Highland rate very slightly owing to the small number of Negroes in the mountains. Its effect is less in the mountains than in the non-mountain portion of the state.

In case of tuberculosis especially it would be interesting to know what part Negro deaths play in the high rate found in the mountains. This rate, 129.5 per 100,000, is slightly higher than the rate for the rural portion of the registration area. The death rate for tuberculosis is especially high in the Greater Appalachian Valley of Virginia and Tennessee. This is a fact for which the more generally urban character of the Valley may be responsible. The total urban and rural death rate from tuberculosis for the entire registration area, however, is only 141.6 per 100,000 as against 166.4 for the Tennessee Valley, and 144.1 for the Valley of Virginia. It would seem possible, therefore, that the high rates in these sections may be due at least in part to the larger number of Negroes there who it is well known are peculiarly susceptible to this disease.

On the whole it would seem that tuberculosis is more widespread in the Allegheny-Cumberland than in the Blue Ridge region. This bears out our own observations and the observations of physicians, that this disease is much more common in the narrow fog-hung valleys of the Kentucky mountains, where the greatest congestion of population is found, than in the higher and less densely populated areas of the Carolinas.

Throughout the mountain area indications point to a high mortality from diseases of the respiratory tract in general. The fact that children walk long distances to school, one to three miles, without adequate protection in stormy weather and remain all day without facilities for drying themselves, suggests one reason for such affections. Men, too, are accustomed to walk many miles under all sorts of conditions, to and fro from the "public works," as railroad, logging, and similar operations are called. The death rate from pneumonia, as shown in the table is, however, in every instance save in that of the Blue Ridge of Maryland, materially lower than that for the total or the rural portion of the United States registration area.

It may be surprising to many to know that measles are responsible for a large number of deaths in the Highlands, a result probably of exposure during convalescence. Although the rate given in the table for the entire mountain region, 10.5 per 100,000, is but slightly higher than that for the entire rural area, one questions, after many years of experience in the Highlands, whether it indicates the extent of mortality which has its inception in this cause. In this disease as in others a better basis for judgment would be had were there data available for a number of previous years, and were the causes of death as returned more accurately determined.

The single case in which the mountain death rate is conspicuously higher than the rate for the entire country is that of typhoid. The rate from this disease in the mountains is 28.3 per 100,000 as against 15.6 for the rural portion of the United States registration area. It has been suggested that typhoid fever, tuberculosis, and numerous other communicable diseases, notably hookworm, were brought into the mountains by soldiers returning at the close of the Civil War,[1] and that wells, springs, and soil were well infected at that time. It is, of course, true that in pioneer days, when homes were few and scattered, the effects of stream and soil pollution were not widely felt, but in the latter half of the nineteenth century there was a considerable population in the Highlands. The theory that communicable diseases began to spread rapidly from the close of the war is therefore tenable. In any case the high rate from typhoid cannot be a matter of surprise when one realizes that the disease is endemic in the mountains, that no sanitary measures are known for preventing infection of streams and drinking water, and that summer brings myriads of flies which swarm about unprotected food. It is especially prevalent in the autumn when springs and wells are low, sometimes as many as seven or eight in a family being stricken at one time.

Other communicable diseases affecting the mortality rate of the mountains more or less seriously, but for which data were not secured, are diphtheria, scarlet fever, and smallpox. The first is perhaps the malady most dreaded by the mountaineer, who considers it practically fatal. Scarlet fever, too, is greatly feared. Smallpox, however, while present every year in some areas, is so little feared that mountain mothers have been known to expose their babies deliberately in order that the malady might be taken early in life when its effects would be less marked. The isolation of the country does not, unhappily, prevent the inroads of such epidemics as infantile paralysis and influenza, which make their appearance in the most remote homes.

Another cause markedly affecting the death rate is the lack of care afforded women in childbirth. The rate for causes of this nature have been entered in Table 9. The mountain death rate from causes attendant on childbirth is not high, 12.7 per 100,000, as compared with that of 15.1 for the rural registration area. While the rate for South Carolina, 18.8, should be considered in connection with the cotton-mill development and the larger Negro population

[1] It was claimed in one remote mountain section that syphilis was first introduced there at the close of the Civil War.

of the Piedmont strip which it has been necessary to include with the mountain belt, in general the rates of the different states and belts vary too markedly to permit of conjecture as to possible factors. It seems especially probable that low death rates for puerperal causes may be due to failure to report properly causes of death.

The more prosperous and accessible families are coming to demand the services of a physician and nurse, where these may be secured, but a large proportion of the remoter families—just how large is of course impossible to say without a detailed study, county by county—still depend upon the midwife[1] or such help as can be secured from neighbors. Few of the midwives have any knowledge of infection and the means to prevent it; comparatively few hold licenses from the state boards of health. Methods employed are primitive in the extreme, and include little or no pre-natal or post-natal care. Even when a physician of the better class is employed, he seldom sees the mother except at the time of birth; and when an untrained "doctor" is in attendance, both mother and child may be sacrificed by the brutal ignorance of his practices.

To failure to report deaths fully is probably due the low rate for infant mortality shown for the mountain region. It has been possible to obtain data on which to compute these rates for only four states, Kentucky, Maryland, North Carolina, and Tennessee. Of these only Maryland was included in the United States registration area for births in 1916, and rates for the others are therefore based on data obtained directly from state sources.

Table 9 shows the infant death rates both per 100,000 population and per 1,000 living births. In the case of the latter, except for Maryland, the rates obtained for the mountain region are distinctly lower than that for the United States as a whole. This rate for Maryland, 97.4, is practically the same as that for the rural portion of the registration area and is less than the urban and rural rate for the United States.

The infant death rates in terms of population, however, do not compare so well with corresponding rates for the entire country. Only Tennessee, with 185.7 infant deaths per 100,000 population,

---

[1] "Over half the mothers were attended in confinement by a neighborhood midwife."—Bradley, Frances Sage, and Williamson, Margaretta A.: Rural children in Selected Counties of North Carolina, p. 95. U. S. Department of Labor, Children's Bureau, Publication No. 33, Washington, D. C., 1918.

has a better rate than that for the rural United States. The rates found for Kentucky, Maryland, and North Carolina are distinctly higher. In fact deaths of infants under one year of age appear to constitute from one-fourth to one-fifth of the total number of deaths in these three states, while for the entire United States they are about one-sixth of the total number. That the mountain region compares poorly with the rest of the country when infant deaths are compared with total population, but well when they are compared with the number of births, means only that the birth rate is high.

In the study of one mountain county of North Carolina,[1] to which reference has been made, a county in which the rate showed a loss of one out of every thirteen children born, it was found that prematurity here, as often elsewhere, was the most important cause of infant loss, and that nearly half of the infant deaths had occurred within the first two weeks. Similar findings would probably result from a study of many of our distinctively Highland counties.

Indiscriminate feeding is another prominent cause of infant loss. While breast feeding is practically universal, almost from the beginning the baby is also given a taste of all that the family table affords. Consequently digestive disorders are frequent; probably they constitute one of the highest causes of mortality among young children. By some it is claimed that the common practice of permitting little children to sit and crawl about upon damp ground and cold draughty floors results in a higher rate of mortality among those old enough to move about than among infants in arms.

It may be added here that it seems to be the verdict of those acquainted with Highland conditions that the mountain baby is physically well born. Whatever the ills that afflict the older child, they are largely of a preventable nature. Social diseases are found, but the experience of some doctors points toward their greater prevalence near urban centers, or where large logging, sawmill, and other industrial enterprises are in operation. Physicians who have had charge of mountain schools say that the boys are unusually free from infections of this nature. One finds, however, in the mountains practically all that one finds elsewhere. It is not diseases that are lacking but the means of combating them.

[1] Ibid.

While specific data are wanting on many aspects of the health problem in the mountains, an opportunity to observe some of the effects of existing conditions upon the rural child and thus indirectly upon the general health, is offered in the various boarding schools maintained throughout this region by church and independent agencies. Naturally a large number of the pupils who come from little isolated homes show many evidences of the want of ordinary care of the person. Not only are they often in need of a thorough cleaning up, but not infrequently are suffering from neglected sores and skin diseases of various kinds.

The teeth, too, usually need attention, the only attention indeed commonly given them in very rural districts being to pull them out when they ache. In past days this was accomplished by means of crude home-made "tooth-pullers" wielded by some man who had obtained a reputation for skill along this and other "surgical" lines. As a result, the Highlander has been frequently deprived at an early age of these very necessary assistants to his digestion, or, if they remain, it is in such condition as to subject him to the results of dental infection. A first preparation made by one outside physician before he entered a mountain field was the purchase of forceps, and several lessons in their use. He declares that he has pulled teeth indoors and out, on the porch and in the middle of the road, on foot and on horseback, and that no new place for this operation is now likely to surprise or disturb him.

Another common condition found among school children is "sore eyes," or what, in its most serious form, has proved to be trachoma. That this dangerous eye affection should exist so commonly among native Americans, isolated almost entirely from foreign infection, came as a great surprise to health authorities. So many indeed were the cases of trachoma reported in a clinic held at one of the independent schools of the mountains, as to lead to an investigation by the United States Public Health Service and the establishment in 1913 by this service in co-operation with the state boards of health of a number of trachoma hospitals, first in Kentucky and later in infected districts of other states. The heaviest infection was found to be where the states of Kentucky, Virginia, West Virginia, and Tennessee are adjacent, and in this region, at Pikeville, Kentucky, a hospital is still maintained.

Dr. John McMullen, who has charge of the trachoma work of the United States Public Health Service, thus writes in the *Southern Medical Journal:*

> A survey made by the Service in 23 counties in eastern Kentucky, showed that 1,280 out of a total of 18,000 people examined, were suffering from trachoma, that is, about 7 per cent of the total number examined had trachoma. Of the number examined, in the survey, 16,696 were school children. The type of the disease found was severe and its mutilating effects are seen everywhere. It would be difficult to appreciate the suffering and disastrous effects of the disease in Appalachian America without actually seeing these cases and witnessing the pathetic sights they present. It is here that most of the cases have gone without proper aid, and many without any at all.[1]

To no disease found in the Highlands, however, has greater publicity been given than to hookworm. One hears at times from enthusiasts that if the Highlander could only be rid of hookworm his ills would disappear. He would have the vigorous, energetic physique naturally expected in one so near to pioneer ancestors, and so would acquire without further assistance all the accompaniments of better living.

That hookworm infection is widespread throughout the mountains the investigations of the Rockefeller Sanitary Commission have demonstrated beyond question. It would be easy to cite many instances observed in schools where severe cases of hookworm infection, when treated, have shown such marked improvement as to establish this cause as a prominent one affecting the mental as well as the physical condition of the mountain child. But while it would indeed be interesting to know whether Highland life would be transformed by the elimination of this disease, the variation in the percentage of infection[2] shown by groups examined in selected counties, and the many possible explanations for the variation would seem to suggest that blame for some of the existing conditions can-

[1] McMullen, John: "Trachoma: a Disease of Equal Importance to the Ophthalmologist and Public Health Officer and what the Government is Doing to Eradicate and Prevent its Further Spread," pp. 130–135. *Southern Medical Journal*, February, 1917.

[2] See Reports of the Rockefeller Sanitary Commission for the Eradication of Hookworm Disease, 1912, 1913, 1914.

not be laid to hookworm alone. More definite conclusions must await fuller data.

As suggested in a previous part of this chapter, many conditions existing in the mountain child are probably due in part to a poorly balanced diet. A large number of the children are insufficiently nourished, and it is not uncommon for some to gain within a comparatively few months twenty or more pounds under the better prepared and more regularly served meals of a school.

Marked changes for the better have also been effected by the removal of adenoids and diseased tonsils. The story of such a case was recently brought to the writer's attention. A pupil in one of the mountain schools had been so backward in his work as to be considered by some of the teachers mentally deficient. So far was this from being the fact that after the removal of adenoids and tonsils he proved to be one of the keenest pupils of the school. Unfortunately, he developed at the same time such a propensity for mischief that his distracted teacher earnestly inquired if there was no way by which the adenoids and tonsils could be returned.

There are, of course, deficient children in the mountains, although one sees comparatively few in the schools. When data are entirely lacking upon deficiency and mental disorders of any kind, it is idle to hazard a statement as to their extent. One meets occasional cases; and there are, far removed from the ordinary routes of travel, certain limited neighborhoods containing what is apparently a high percentage of defectives. Little is being done for these neighborhoods by schools or other beneficent agencies. Philanthropy too often seeks out their more promising individuals as future leaders, leaving the less promising to multiply because of isolation and inadequate state and county provision for their care. An effort is often made to provide temporarily for some of the more desperate cases in the county jails, but the average county jail is not a remedial institution, and conditions in many are deplorable.

The court house, with its annex the jail, is usually the most prominent public building in the rural county-seat of the mountains. In the newer buildings there are decided improvements. Riding into a county-seat forty miles from a railroad at the end of a warm day, and inquiring if there might be a hotel where he could secure a bath, a travel-worn horseman received the reply that the

217

only bathtub in the county-seat was in the new county jail. The only person therefore privileged by reason of his confinement to enjoy a bath, was a lone prisoner from Boston. In fairness to Boston it must, however, be said that the prisoner was originally from the mountains of this section, but having shot a man "accidental" he fled north to lose himself in that distant metropolis. Unfortunately for him he became, like most exiled mountain dwellers, homesick for his native mountains. Returning, he was apprehended, and was awaiting the decision of the jury as to the degree of chance in the accident.

In some of the mountain states public attention is being challenged by a number of able and determined Southern women, who are seeking to put an end to the indiscriminate herding not only of criminals but of defectives, and sometimes of insane and epileptic of both sexes, in county jails and county homes.

It must not be inferred that state health officials and others in authority are unmindful of the need of public care for defectives, nor that the more thoughtful citizens of these localities ignore them. There is a ready response to appeals to personal benevolence; but here, as is so often the case in rural sections elsewhere, public opinion needs to be awakened to a recognition of public responsibility. The need of help is naturally greatest in weak counties for which some of the states are now seeking to provide more adequate educational funds. Taxation is, however, a bugaboo in well-to-do rural communities, as well as a burden in those that are not, and will continue to be so until life is placed on a sounder economic basis.

To many who have endeavored to provide in past years the educational opportunities lacking in so many remote mountain sections, the evident need of help in matters of health has become more and more prominent, until it often seems the most pressing of mountain questions. Where public funds were non-existent it was useless to apply for aid to state or county officials, and little could be expected from the people themselves, who were not only poor but unfamiliar with possibilities and methods of relief. It was necessary, therefore, for the various agencies at work to meet the local situation as best they could. A number of church and independent schools have for some years employed nurses, who not only superintend the health of the school children but endeavor to serve as much of the neighborhood as possible. One of these nurses, early recognizing that the need of education in health matters was quite as great as the need of relief, held health classes not only for the children of the school but for the mothers of the neighborhood. She attended when she could mothers in confinement, with the cooperation of the local physician. Limited as such a single effort must needs be, in a number of years it succeeded in revolutionizing many conditions in the little community in which the school was situated. Another nurse who has been particularly helpful is a graduate of a nursing school which lays especial emphasis on obstetrics and midwifery. Her situation in a community far from the services of a physician makes her aid invaluable, and her presence, in fact, is cordially welcomed by the nearest physician, who is greatly overburdened with the extent of his territory.

In several schools, patients requiring special attention, particularly eye, ear, and nose cases, have been gathered together once or twice a year for clinics administered by public-spirited specialists and nurses from urban centers. During one short clinic at a school in eastern Kentucky which has been foremost in this work, there were 10 major and 608 minor operations.

A number of the private schools in the mountains maintain small and very simple hospitals where clinic patients may be cared for and emergency cases brought. Ordinarily, these hospitals are used simply for the pupils and are in charge of the school nurse. Private aid has also been found to send individual cases to cities for treatment, in one state the railroads co-operating by furnishing transportation. In other places physicians have been sent in, supported entirely or in part for a number of years by church or other philanthropic agencies. Their relation to the native doctors, whose income is threatened by their presence, is sometimes perplexing, especially if the local doctor be of an inferior type. Tact and a kindly spirit will usually, however, solve such problems, and when the people have once profited by the benefits of trained help, they are not willing to do without it.

In a few places well-equipped hospitals have been established with resident physicians and nurses. The possibilities of these as centers of influence, medical and co-operative, is illustrated by one

219

built and equipped by a church board, which has a resident physician and two nurses working in co-operation with a Red Cross public health nurse supported by the same board. Recently, with the assistance of the State Board of Health, an adenoid and tonsil clinic was held here for children of the whole county. Two nurses from the health department of the state, together with the Red Cross public health nurse, gathered up the cases, which were operated upon by a specialist and assistant from the nearest urban center, assisted by the local doctor and by leading physicians of surrounding counties.

The great benefit of all these various independent and unrelated efforts can be appreciated only by those who have known conditions as they were, and who actually see, day by day, the need and suffering of isolated families and communities which have little or nothing in the way of help. But great as has been their effect, they might be duplicated many times without appreciably affecting the health problem as a whole. The success and continuance of these efforts depend, moreover, largely upon the personality and exertion of individual mountain workers who have gained the confidence of their boards or of the giving public. In addition, the suffering in the mountains has been so intense that effort for the most part has been directed to its immediate alleviation rather than to preventive measures. The need of this kind of work is not less today, but it should be accompanied by a widespread educational movement for public health. As long as the congested home conditions of the Highlands persist, and as long as there is such general ignorance of hygienic and sanitary measures, it is useless to hope for permanent improvement in the health situation.

In the arousing of interest for better public health, the campaigns of the Rockefeller Sanitary Commission against hookworm in the South have been of inestimable value. One of the direct outcomes has been the establishment of county health organizations with full-time health officers in North Carolina, the first Southern state to meet its rural health problems by organization on a county basis. While such county organizations in this state are as yet limited in number, in places in the Highlands the creation of a county health unit, financed by state, county, and the United States Public Health Service, is already a possibility. Such a unit would consist of a full-time county health officer and a public health nursing corps working under a county board of health. Recent state campaigns with wide publicity as to causes of disease—especially hookworm, pellagra, and typhoid—and the free injection of typhoid vaccine, have done much to prepare the way for as well as to dispel prejudice concerning vaccination and inoculation.

Through large rural areas of the Highlands, however, state, county, or local forces will for a long time be unable to minister adequately to health needs. The hope for such areas would seem for some years to lie, therefore, not in isolated efforts valuable as these are locally and individually, but in a public health service, national in scope, working so far as possible in co-operation with local and state agencies.

The activities open to such a service are many. Prominent among its features would be a nursing corps. The proposed extension of the Red Cross Public Health Nursing Service naturally suggests itself in this connection, and a beginning is further indicated by the presence in the Highlands of a few Red Cross nurses of this Service, who are working in conjunction with and through the support of denominational and independent boards or under mining corporations. More support of this sort can undoubtedly be furnished, and in some places where there are local Red Cross Chapters, or sufficient local interest to organize chapters, further support may be secured. It may even be possible to make a beginning toward health centers, as recently outlined by Red Cross officials in post-war activities possible for the Red Cross. The influence of returned soldiers would doubtless make this feasible in certain localities where it would otherwise have been delayed for many years. Often, however, where the need is greatest, there is no local agency nor immediate prospect of one able to furnish support, and no public consciousness of the need. In such sections a "pioneer nursing corps" could revolutionize existing conditions, if maintained by some private organization until such time as support could be assumed in whole or in part by local, county, or state agencies.

Objection will probably be made that a rural nursing corps of this sort will be almost as difficult to secure as an adequate number of physicians. It is not our purpose here to indicate what national agency should undertake this work; nor can we enter into the vexed question of the small training hospital as a source of supply. We would, however, urge the possibility of nursing centers in the Highlands, in charge of nurses who are qualified by education and training and by experience in rural mountain needs to superintend and direct the activities of nurses less well equipped. To such centers might also be sent nurses who wished to go into rural service for the practical rural part of their public health training, or even medical students for a knowledge of rural sanitation and health.

While it is perhaps unnecessary to outline the work of such a nursing service, we cannot refrain from calling attention to the wide opportunities open to public health nurses not only through the homes but in the little rural public schools of the mountains, and through health talks given in remote districts. One public health nurse in the remote Highlands has already outlined a program whereby she will devote a part of her summer months to short stays of perhaps a week at a number of very isolated communities. A course of lectures on various health topics has been planned with especial reference to the care of babies and instruction of midwives. To vary the monotony of such a program she purposes to take with her at different times people who will be able to give demonstrations in domestic science, or canning, gymnastics, or recreational features of one kind or another. During the year she will keep in touch with such communities and gather up the cases that need attention for the nearest doctor or clinic.

The work of the Public Health Service suggested would not, of course, be confined to a nursing corps. Working always with state authorities as far as possible, it would be ready to send into localities which asked for help specialists who would study the health situation and outline a program which the central organization would be prepared to further by lectures, slides, and propaganda of one sort and another. In places a trained dietitian and home economics worker might do an invaluable service, especially with children. It is, indeed, impossible in so brief a study as this to more than suggest a few of the many lines of activity open to a service of this kind.

That many of the local physicians would welcome such a service has been amply evidenced. Moreover, experience in certain localities has shown how easily local rural physicians may be brought not only to co-operate with nurses but to practice under the direction of the best medical authorities of the state. Throughout our investigations we have found national and state officials and experts both sympathetic and eager to assist, if only connection could be established and the way opened. The president of the state board of health in one of the Southern Appalachian states, recognizing the weight of Biblical texts in the mountains and the influence of the native preachers, called upon some of the pastors and physicians of the state to help him outline sermons on health topics, based upon suitable texts. These were to be sent into mountain and other rural communities with personal letters urging pastors to preach sermons on health topics, and to set aside certain Sabbaths in the year when subjects of a like nature were to be discussed. It is through the insight of men such as this health officer, that plans will be worked out that will result in benefit to the mountain people.

Several years ago the writer had the pleasure and privilege of traveling through the Kentucky mountains with the executive secretary of the National Society for the Study and Prevention of Tuberculosis. Arrangements were made in advance for conferences with physicians, teachers, county superintendents of education, and others of influence. At one county-seat court was in session, and upon the request of the people the judge courteously gave an hour of the afternoon session for a lecture on "Tuberculosis and its Prevention." The prisoner as well as most of the male inhabitants of the county-seat and others from outlying communities, had the benefit of the lecture. As a result some of those whose families were afflicted came to the lecturer for advice, and in one instance treatment was begun with marked benefit under the direction of the school nurse. A few such practical demonstrations of benefit received quickly educate a community. Good results have followed upon this expedition in all schools and communities visited.

The experiences of this trip reveal the possibility of utilizing for health instruction those periods during which the people are gathered together for one purpose or another. Court week, for example, is a notable week in the mountains. At such times the county-seat is filled with men from all parts of the county. They come even when they have no direct interest in a case, drawn by the opportunity to meet friends, transact business, and listen to discussions on topics of interest.

The county teachers' institutes held in the early summer are occasions when most of the county teachers meet for a one or two days' session. These institutes have a social as well as an educational side in which others than teachers are interested.

In late July and in August, depending somewhat upon the region and season, is "laying-by time," a period of respite from farming after the crop has been worked over sufficiently to warrant leaving it until the fall labor preliminary to "gathering time." This is an interval of leisure in which people come together, especially for "camp meetings" and "protracted meetings."

If during court week, at teachers' institutes, and at the various large gatherings of laying-by time, lectures could be given on general health topics and upon such diseases as tuberculosis, typhoid fever, and hookworm, their causes, prevention, and cure, with suitable illustrations and exhibits practical for the mountains, much might be done to lessen the ravages of these diseases and to improve the general health situation. The striking posters used in cities, illustrating the ways and dangers of contagion and infection, would have effect in the mountains if placed along the lines of travel, especially after campaigns for health have been carried on in some such way as suggested.

The specialists who come upon request and remain only temporarily would encourage the better type of mountain physician, and the poorer type would be forced into improved methods, or be gradually excluded from practice when the people see the improvement in cases formerly held as hopeless. The need for county organizations of physicians and for registration of births, deaths, and diseases would be made apparent and be likely to follow such co-operation.

Another opportunity to advance the cause of health is offered by the county fair. Prizes for the largest variety of vegetables raised, and for the best exhibition of canned goods, jellies, and light-bread, would tend to a larger and better diet as well as to better farming. Baby shows in connection with some of these fairs have already proved their value.

The stimulus given by lectures, exhibits, and similar methods, however, may die out. Patient teaching through wise educational measures is the only remedy. It must awaken the altruistic co-operative spirit, rather than the self-centered spirit which has too generally characterized the education of the past,—an education which gives to the relatively few so-called "advantages" and leaves the many poor in condition and resources.

CHAPTER XI

RESOURCES OF THE MOUNTAIN COUNTRY
AND THEIR DEVELOPMENT

TO ONE attempting to summarize the assets of the mountain country, there is suggested, first of all, the human asset as represented in its children. However widely opinions may differ as to the extent of the material resources of the mountains and the possibility of their development, there cannot fail to be unanimity of opinion as to the wealth of children. To some, doubtless, they will seem an embarrassment of riches, for even the most destitute homes abound in them. The psalmist's song, "children are an heritage of the Lord," and "as arrows in the hand of a mighty man," and "happy is the man that hath his quiver full of them,"[1] touches a responsive chord in the heart of the mountaineer. The assumed higher criticism of decadent cliques in modern society, rich in material things but willingly paupers in paternity, has not yet reached him to make him sceptical of the olden belief that it is right to increase that his seed may possess the land. It is easy to argue that he, like the poor man elsewhere, would be richer with fewer children; it is easy, too, to charge him with unworthy motives, but despite imputation and argument—did he hear them —he would seem to regard children as a greater blessing and a surer stay in old age than the treasures that moth and rust may corrupt and thieves break through and steal.

Scriptural as to size of family, the mountaineer has followed all too literally another Bible injunction—to take no thought for the morrow. In the past the rifle, hoe, axe, and loom, supplying his simple needs, have kept him from anxious thought for food, shelter, and raiment. The traits of the pioneer, still largely his, have fostered hospitality, generosity, and wastefulness, and today it is a question in the minds of many whether his misinterpretation as to forethought in material affairs, and his orthodoxy as to the increase

[1] Psalms CXXVII.

226

of his kind, have not brought his children to a point where, by the force of circumstances that might have been prevented, they are to be dispossessed of the land of their fathers and driven among strangers.

He who travels day by day through regions where seemingly all level and fair-lying land, however small the tract, is occupied and sees the ragged clearings extending far up the steep slopes, cannot but wonder as to the future of the many children who watch him pass. Whether there is enough in the mountains to maintain its population is a fair question that thinking people are beginning to ask. Already it is a subject of debate as to whether in a certain number of areas the population is not greater than can be sustained by the resources of these areas. Some even have advocated the removal of the whole mountain population to more promising regions because the resources in the mountains will never be sufficient for adequate support. How easy it would be to carry out such a plan is suggested by the comment of a woman who, having dwelt for three-quarters of a century in one of the most beautiful and remote parts of the Southern Highlands, amid clear streams and tall forests, was taken for a pleasure trip to the nearest city. Looking out upon the stark sordidness of a new industrial development, she exclaimed with the fervor of conviction: "I would rather be a knot on a log in Laurel than live in that place."

Leaving out of the discussion the practicability of moving a mountain population deeply attached to its environment, the question is not whether all the mountain people should be moved from the mountains or all forced to remain. A certain proportion will always go; it is right that they should, and they are needed in our urban civilization. Many, however, will wish to stay if a fair living is possible for them and their children. The chief question here is whether the resources of the Highlands are such as to furnish suitable and sufficient returns for such of the present and future population as wish to remain.

An inquiry as to the support of population raises many questions, but in any consideration of the resources of the Highlands, the great variety of the country, so often called to mind, must play a prominent part. The three regional belts into which the mountain section is divided have in themselves certain differences which are already showing in their life, and are destined to have a marked effect upon their future development. Moreover, local areas within the belts differ greatly, and the character and development even of certain resources which are common to all areas and belts are strongly affected by different topographic and climatic conditions. Speaking generally, the Greater Appalachian Valley is pre-eminently suited to agriculture, and its accessibility has made it the seat of many cities; the western, or Allegheny-Cumberland Belt is a coal belt—part of the greatest coal field in the country; and the eastern, or Blue Ridge Belt, while possessing some mineral wealth, is famous for the magnificence of its forests and for its water power.

Forests

It is of the forests perhaps that the majority of people think first in any inquiry into the natural resources of the Southern Highlands. The forests of the Highlands are part of that great hardwood area which extends throughout our territory and on to the north into the mountain and hill region of Pennsylvania, New York, and New England. Although spruce and pine are common, and there are in the southern stretches along the edges of the Piedmont Plateau in Georgia scattered colonies of long-leaf pine, the field is on the whole a region of hardwoods, of which it furnishes the largest and most valuable supply left in the United States.

Abused and neglected by the Highlander, desecrated and ruined in many sections by the operations of logging companies, the remnants of these magnificent forests still sweep over the crests of the mountains in indescribable beauty. Their great variety is at no time more apparent than in spring, when the varied greens of the many oaks and hickories are contrasted with the red fruit of the maples, the yellow tassels of the chestnuts, and the myriad bloom of the towering tulip poplar—the whole shot through with a lower tracery of dogwood blossom and fringed with a border of redbud. But not even the glory of the autumn which covers the slopes with a glowing mass of color for mile on mile as far as the eye can reach, can surpass the winter beauty of these great trees in all the silvery majesty of their naked outline, the delicate network of their upper branches melting into a haze which is but a part of the blue veil that ever hangs above the Highlands.

The eminent botanist, Professor Gray, is quoted as saying that in a thirty-mile trip through western North Carolina, he encountered a greater variety of indigenous trees than could be observed in a trip from Turkey through Europe to England, or from the north Atlantic coast to the Rocky Mountain Plateau.

An idea of the great variety of the mountain forests may be better obtained from the following paragraphs, taken from a report of the Secretary of Agriculture in relation to the forests, rivers, and mountains of the Southern Appalachian region.

At the eastern foot of the Blue Ridge, in North Carolina, the typical flora of the Piedmont Plateau abounds, and follows up the river gorges into the mountain valleys, where it associates with more characteristically Appalachian species. Thence up to the tops of the higher peaks there is a constant succession of changes—an intermingling and overlapping of the lower species with those which belong to greater elevations or more northern latitudes.

Thus, in ascending any of the higher mountains, as Mount Mitchell, which, with its elevation of 6,711 feet, is the loftiest of them all, one may penetrate, in the rich and fertile coves about its base, a forest of oaks, hickories, maples, chestnuts, and tulip poplars, some of them large enough to be suggestive of the giant trees on the Pacific Coast. Higher up one rides through forests of great hemlocks, chestnut oaks, beeches, and birches, and higher yet through groves of spruce and balsam. Covering the soil between these trees is a spongy mass of humus sometimes a foot and more in thickness, and over this in turn a luxuriant growth of shrubs and flowers and ferns. At last, as the top is reached, even the balsams become dwarfed, and there give place largely to clusters of rhododendron and patches of grass fringed with flowers, many of them such as are commonly seen about the hills and valleys of New England and southern Canada.

In such ascent one passes through, as it were, the changing of the seasons. Halfway up the slopes one may see, with fruit just ripening, the shrubs and plants the matured fruit of which was seen two or three weeks before on the Piedmont Plateau, 3,000 feet below; while 3,000 feet higher up the same species have now just opened wide their flowers. Fully a month divides the seasons above and below, separated by this nearly 6,000 feet of altitude.[1]

[1] "Message from the President of the United States transmitting a Report of the Secretary of Agriculture in relation to the Forests, Rivers, and Mountains of the Southern Appalachian Region," pp. 22–23. Washington, Government, 1902.

As a rule the forests are more luxuriant on the northwestern side of the Blue Ridge Belt, where the slope is less abrupt and the conditions of moisture and soil such as to produce "the best examples of the superb hardwood forests which abound in this region—the finest on the continent."

There have been in the United States four great areas of hardwoods—the Ohio Valley, the Lake states, the lower Mississippi Valley, and the Appalachian section. Recent data are lacking for a statement of the comparative output of these various sections, but a survey published by the Forest Service in 1907[1] disclosed that the states of Ohio, Indiana, and Illinois, which as late as 1899 produced 25 per cent of the hardwood cut, in 1906 produced only 14 per cent, and that Ohio and Indiana had dropped 50 per cent in output. It was estimated at that time that the Lake states and lower Mississippi Valley had probably reached their maximum output, with their many woodworking industries making great demands on what remained. Moreover, as much of the land from which this hardwood was removed was eminently suited to agriculture, reforesting in many sections was not taking place, even swampy lands such as parts of the lower Mississippi Valley being drained and used for farm purposes.

The importance of the fourth and last hardwood area, the Appalachian section, much of which was not suited to agriculture because of slope and elevation, was therefore recognized as an available source and probably a permanent source of hardwood supply if properly conserved and lumbered. In 1906 the Appalachian states[2] from Maine to Alabama were estimated to contain 75,000,000 acres, or fully half of the country's supply of hardwood, and to be producing 48 per cent of the total cut.

In the Southern Appalachians, as the name is here used to cover the Southern Highland region, there were estimated to be 58,583,000

[1] The following data are taken from Circular 116 of the United States Forest Service: "The Waning Hardwood Supply and the Appalachian Forests," Washington, Government, 1907; and from "Report of the Secretary of Agriculture on the Southern Appalachian and White Mountain Watersheds," Washington, Government, 1908.

[2] The Appalachian states as here considered include Maine, New Hampshire, Vermont, Massachusetts, New York, Pennsylvania, Maryland, Virginia, West Virginia, Kentucky, Tennessee, North Carolina, South Carolina, Georgia, and Alabama.

acres of timber, 17 per cent unlumbered or slightly culled and 83 per cent cut over and in all stages of growth and reproduction, which at a conservative estimate[1] should yield annually 2,343,320,-000 cubic feet, or 76 per cent of the annual cut of 3,000,000,000 cubic feet for the entire Appalachian region.

How accurately these estimates represent the forested areas and the annual hardwood output of the Southern Highlands in more recent years there are no data to indicate, but they serve to suggest the great value of the hardwoods of this section, even when one keeps in mind the heavy cutting that has gone on in the Highland area since this survey was made, the devastation caused by forest fires,[2] and the turning of forested into agricultural lands to support the increase of population.

The increasing scarcity and value of hardwood timber would seem great enough in themselves to insure care of what forest is left; and when one sees the industrial and agricultural possibilities of the mountain country that await development, and realizes that only through a proper care of its forests will the full benefits of such development be secured to the future, one dares to be hopeful, for surely wisdom and regard for the rights of posterity must both guide and stay the hand of the man of today. But something of discouragement fills the traveler's heart when in contrast to the primeval grandeur of the remote forests, he encounters sections of the mountains where the axe of the woodman, forest fire, commercial short-sightedness, and greed have conspired to do their worst. The tendency on the part of lumber companies to disregard the future is painfully brought home to one as his horse stumbles and falls amid the logs, branches, and shattered tree trunks left to be enkindled by the careless camper, hunter, or mountaineer. The lumberman gathers the best and goes his way.

It is perhaps true that because of the carelessness of the mountain farmer and neighboring loggers in the matter of fires it does

---

[1] Studies by Forest Service, which covered both the virgin and cut-over lands in east Tennessee, led to the conclusion that with proper care there should be an annual yield of 50 cubic feet of wood per acre. A conservative basis of 40 cubic feet was used in making estimates for the whole area.

[2] The damage done by forest fires in the mountains of North Carolina alone during 1912 was estimated as amounting to $651,981, exclusive of $5,916, estimated as the cost of fighting fire to private individuals.

not pay a lumberman, even so disposed, to seek to insure a second growth. Doubtless, too, uneconomic methods of taxing standing timber and its increase give the logging companies some warrant for reaping a quick harvest.

The mountaineer himself is doing much to lessen the value of these forests. Despite the high value placed upon woods of such scarcity as black walnut, in one mountain home visited the meal was being cooked over glowing coals of black walnut. In the yard were many logs of the same wood ready to be cut into fireplace lengths. The owner of the house was amply able to buy a cook-stove, but his wife preferred the old-fashioned ways. In reply to a protest against the burning of such valuable wood, she replied that it was "a right smart of trouble to haul timber down the branch," and that there were "several walnut trees" (a goodly number) about there, and moreover, they "didn't need the money nohow." The needlessness of this waste was the more apparent as one saw on all sides cheap timber suitable for firewood; and in addition, not ten yards from the cabin door were outcroppings of coal laid bare by the brook, so abundant in quantity as to require but little work to yield a fuel supply sufficient for months. Timber buyers and inspectors report walnut and beautifully figured timber, which as trees would have brought high prices, split into rails and firewood.

Much of such wastefulness is probably due to difficulties of transportation. Still more may be attributed to ignorance of values, some to antagonism toward trees in general, and not a little to a certain contentment with things as they are. This is particularly the case with those in middle life and older. "What more does a body need?" said an old lady to the visitor, pointing to her little corn field and garden. "Yonder is a right smart chance of corn and a heap of cushaws, and the shoats will be big enough to kill for meat after the mast is gone."

In response to the need of measures for insuring a good forest growth for the future, strong movements were launched by public-spirited officials and citizens which have resulted in the setting aside of certain areas in national forest reservations. The relation of such reservations and their forest cover to the control of leading rivers, the headwaters of which lie within them, was an essential consideration in their location and importance. There have been approved up to the present time for purchase within the Southern Highlands, 1,337,076 acres in national forests, distributed by states as follows: Virginia, 407,554; North Carolina, 347,674; Tennessee, 241,697; Georgia, 148,556; West Virginia, 114,985; Alabama, 52,526; South Carolina, 24,084. New areas should, it is believed, be reserved especially in West Virginia, and in Kentucky, which has now granted the Federal Government the right to acquire lands for national forests within its borders.

In the administration of the national forests it is the object to serve the interests of all the people. Where conditions permit, mineral rights are leased, timber is cut, and cattle grazed. On a tract of less than 100,000 acres of forest range in the Shenandoah National Reserve in Virginia, 2,000 head of cattle were supported during the season of 1918–1919. During the same period the receipts from the sale of resources from the national forests in the Appalachian states jumped 36 per cent, according to the report of the National Forest Reservation Commission[1], and this at a time when the scarcity of labor and of equipment greatly handicapped the lumbering industry everywhere. The belief, moreover, is expressed that these national forests, purchased primarily for watershed protection, will without danger to this function yield annually in a few years in excess of half a billion board feet of timber in addition to large amounts of pulp wood and tannic acid stock.

It is purposed, too, that definite provisions for recreation shall be made besides the usual rights granted to campers. The recreation problem, however, is not a simple one in these areas which are small as compared to many of the western parks and fairly accessible to a large population. The suggestion that more or less permanent camp or summer communities, possibly with hotel accommodations, be permitted within restricted areas seems reasonable, in view of the many objections in the way of leasing home sites to individuals.

But three of the mountain states own reservations: North Carolina, with 1,225 acres along the summit of Mount Mitchell; Kentucky, with 3,400 acres along the south side of Pine Mountain

[1] Annual report of the National Forest Reservation Commission for the fiscal year ending June 30, 1919. Washington, Government, 1920.

in Harlan County;[1] and Maryland, with four reserves in Garrett County covering 2,628 acres. Tennessee owns about 2,500 acres of land in the mountainous part of the state, but this is held mainly for its timber, coal, and fish, and is not set apart as a forest reservation.

Water Power

A consideration of the forests of the Southern Highlands naturally raises an inquiry as to the water power dependent so largely upon their conservation. The importance of the Southern Appalachian forests to the development of water power within the Southern states will be the more evident when one realizes that practically all the rivers which flow through these states to the Atlantic or to the Mississippi and Gulf of Mexico have their sources in the Highlands; and that inasmuch as there are no natural lakes for water storage within the Highlands, the exceptionally heavy rainfall of the region must be stored and equalized through the action of the forest cover. Thus upon the proper conservation of these forests depends not only the future industrial development of the immediate section which is dependent upon the use of its water power, but the present and future industries of the Piedmont Plateau as well. The extent of this development through the transmission of electric power cannot yet be estimated.

Table 11 shows the estimated water power of the principal rivers heading in the Southern Appalachians, with the exception of the Big Sandy, the Cumberland, and the Kentucky. These estimates were the result of a seven-year field investigation of the United States Geological Survey, as revised by the Commissioner of Corporations in his report, "Water Power Development in the United States in 1912."[2] The table shows both the potential water power and the water power which has been developed for the Southern Highland states and for the total United States. The minimum potential power represents the power which could be developed from the average stream flow for the lowest fourteen-day period in each year. The maximum potential power represents the amount that could be developed from the average flow for the six-month period of highest stream flow during the year. The table shows

[1] Gift of the Kentenia-Catron Corporation of Harlan, Kentucky.

[2] U. S. Senate Document No. 316, 64th Congress.

that 672,000 horse power, or only a fifth of the potential power at minimum stream flow, had been developed at the time these data were secured. Were only half of the total minimum power to be regarded as commercially available, this would represent at the conservative annual rental of $20 per horse power an annual income of $33,880,000.

TABLE I I.—ESTIMATED POTENTIAL AND DEVELOPED WATER POWER OF THE RIVERS OF THE SOUTHERN HIGHLAND STATES.[a]

State	Potential horse power		Developed horse power
	Minimum	Maximum	
Alabama	509,000	943,000	26,446
Georgia	374,000	627,000	111,501
Kentucky	83,000	197,000	5,841
Maryland and D. C.	48,000	133,000	16,889
North Carolina	578,000	875,000	110,203
South Carolina	460,000	677,000	221,492
Tennessee	463,000	761,000	37,396
Virginia	492,000	870,000	123,079
West Virginia	381,000	1,051,000	19,181
Total	3,388,000	6,134,000	672,028
Total United States	29,943,000	53,905,000	4,870,320

[a] Exclusive of the Big Sandy, the Cumberland, and the Kentucky Rivers.

The proper control and use of this enormous water power, about one-sixth of the total potential water power of the United States, will mean much to the entire South. A tendency to concentrate the control of this water power is being evidenced, however, just as lumber syndicates are seeking control of the timber lands. This effort has been apparent during the last few years. For example, in North Carolina it was reported by the state geologist in 1918 that 75 per cent of the developed water powers were controlled by corporations, and that 94 per cent of the potential water powers of the state were controlled by only eight corporations.[1] Only 1 per cent of the water power was controlled by 49 municipalities in the state.

[1] Biennial Report of the State Geologist, North Carolina Geologic and Economic Survey, 1917–1918, p. 75.

The large supply of hardwood timber in the Blue Ridge Belt is already inviting wood-working plants. If the water power could be rightly controlled and utilized, and a reasonable rental and systematic treatment of the forests assured, there should be a great increase in wood-working and other industries. It is likely, also, that the difficulties of transportation throughout the mountain section would be met more economically through electric power here generated than through the present means of rail locomotion.

The possibility of generating electricity from the smaller streams to do the farm and home tasks has as yet scarcely been considered.[1] Eventually it would seem that in many regions the heavier burdens of rural life—pumping, washing, churning, sawing of wood, and other activities—might be lightened in this way. The cost of installation of any apparatus is at present prohibitive for the majority of people, but it is not unreasonable to anticipate that much of the labor of the Highlander of the future will be lessened in shops and homes lighted and run by electricity.

Bituminous Coal

As has been indicated, our western belt, the Allegheny-Cumberland, is pre-eminently a region of coal which extends into western areas of the Greater Appalachian Valley. There is no coal in the Blue Ridge Belt.

For the sake of convenience, the coal areas of the United States are divided into two great divisions—anthracite, and bituminous and lignite. The anthracite field is confined almost exclusively to an area of about 500 square miles in eastern Pennsylvania. The workable bituminous fields are scattered widely over the United States and include an area of more than 300,000 square miles. These fields are divided primarily into six provinces. The coal field of the Southern Highlands is part of the eastern province, which in its entirety includes all of the bituminous areas of the

---

[1] An electric plant, operated by water power and installed in one of the mountain schools at the cost of about $125 per horse power, is used for lighting school buildings and some of the neighborhood homes. In the work of the school five motors are used, not all at the same time, however. With these they run machines in shop, separators, and milking machines, and grind corn and wheat. Electricity is utilized also in heating and cooking, and for ironing in the laundry. The expense of running the plant is said to be small.

Appalachian region, the Atlantic Coast region, and also the anthracite region of Pennsylvania.

The known area of workable coal within the Highlands is 42,215 square miles, containing an estimated original supply of coal of 344,456,900,000 net tons. In 1917 the production of coal within this area was 145,159,553 net tons. The total production to the end of 1917 was 2,074,343,738 tons.

If no other coal fields be discovered or come to be workable, there is a bituminous coal supply in the Southern Appalachians sufficient for almost 2,360 years, if the rate of production be that of 1917, and a supply for 165 years if the annual production equal the total exhaustion from the beginning of mining to the close of 1917. As mining methods improve, however, the waste of coal, which, according to the United States Geological Survey, has amounted in the past to as much as 50 per cent of the total amount mined, in the future may not run more than 10 or 20 per cent, thereby materially increasing the length of life of this coal field.

The largest area of workable coal in the Highlands is in West Virginia, with Kentucky and Alabama ranking second and third respectively. Table 12, which has been compiled from figures of the United States Geological Survey,[1] compares the coal areas of the mountain regions of the several states and also shows the production in 1917 and the number of miners employed. The mountains of North and South Carolina are without coal areas, and in Georgia, which has only two counties with working mines, coal mining does not rank as an important industry. In the other six states, both in point of coal produced and the number of miners employed, coal is important. The table also shows the total figures for the United States for bituminous mines. The Highland area of 42,215 square miles of workable coal is about one-eighth of the total coal areas of the United States. In point of operation the Southern Highlands produced in 1917 more than a quarter of the total bituminous production of the United States and employed more than a fourth of the entire number of miners.

[1] Mineral Resources of the United States, 1914, Part II, p. 29. Mineral Resources of the United States, 1917, Part II, pp. 903–1409. Washington, Government.

TABLE 12.—COAL AREAS, COAL PRODUCED, AND MINERS EMPLOYED
IN THE SOUTHERN HIGHLANDS, BY STATES. 1917

State	Coal areas in square miles	Coal produced		Miners employed
		Tons	Value	
Alabama[a]	8,373	20,068,074	$45,616,992	28,386
Georgia	167	119,028	301,391	281
Kentucky	10,270	17,503,548	43,386,990	23,503
Tennessee	4,400	6,194,221	13,592,998	10,421
Virginia	1,550	10,087,091	20,125,713	11,168
West Virginia	17,000	86,441,667	200,659,368	88,422
Maryland	455	4,745,924	11,667,852	5,919
Total mountain region	42,215	145,159,553	$335,351,304	168,100
Total United States (bituminous mines)	339,900	551,790,563	1,249,272,837	603,143

a Includes data for two counties, Bibb and Tuscaloosa, lying just without the
mountain region.

The rapidity of development in different areas of the field has
varied greatly, West Virginia and Kentucky showing the greatest
recent increase. In 1917 West Virginia showed a gain over 1914
of 14,734,041 net tons output, and Kentucky a gain of 5,081,789 tons.
The development of certain local areas within these two states can
be fully appreciated only if one has as a basis of comparison the
conditions existing in these regions but a few years ago.

It would be interesting to know how many of the total number
of miners are native mountaineers. At present they appear to constitute a minority. Estimates have been made that in some of the
Appalachian states the native mountaineers comprise about one-
third of the miners in those states. As a general statement for the
entire region this would probably be too large a proportion. The
mountaineers follow naturally the work to which they have been
accustomed, such as lumbering, hauling, and farming; but as they
become acquainted with mining operations, numbers of them attempt mining, and a fair percentage become good miners. They
would seem to work largely in the newer smaller mines, the foreign
element increasing rapidly as operations are extended. In one
newly opened area where many mountain miners were employed,

some of these men were said to be earning in 1919, $15 a day, and some as high as $500 a month in contrast to the $300 of the mine superintendent. Speaking generally, however, the returns to the mountain people from the opening of coal mines are, and probably will be for some time to come, indirect returns from the sale of produce from their farms and from business undertakings other than mining that spring up as a result of the opening up of new territory.

The many problems connected with betterment of conditions in mining communities in the mountains are primarily those of an industrial development, but they cannot be viewed entirely apart from the rural mountain problem, for mountain life in the vicinity of mines has already been greatly affected from a social as well as an economic standpoint. How to fit the Highlander to take his place in this development, and how to equalize the reaction of industrial conditions upon rural regions adjacent and entirely unprepared for such changes, are questions which must concern all who are interested in the Highlander and his homeland.

Coke, Oil, and Natural Gas

Closely allied with the bituminous coal industry is the production of coke, in which West Virginia and Alabama lead the other states in our field. Among the 22 coke producing states of the United States in 1917, Alabama ranks second, West Virginia fifth, Virginia seventh, Kentucky twelfth, Maryland fifteenth, Tennessee eighteenth, and Georgia twenty-second. The output of coke for these seven states in 1917 was 11,379,376 tons, and its value at the ovens $61,293,417.

About two-thirds of the output was used in 1916 within the states which produced it—largely in the manufacture of iron. There being little production of iron in West Virginia, most of its coke goes to supply markets without the mountain region.

West Virginia ranked first in 1917 among the states producing natural gas, and eighth among those producing petroleum, these outputs being valued at $57,389,161 and $27,246,960 respectively. Other gas and oil producing states are Kentucky, Tennessee, and Alabama, the gas and oil in Alabama lying mainly in the region adjoining the mountains rather than within them. In Kentucky and Tennessee during the last few years oil development has been rapid—Kentucky in 1917 marketing 3,088,160 barrels of petroleum, the largest part of which was produced within the Highland region. Much of this development is, however, likely to be short-lived, some of the eastern Kentucky wells being already exhausted after two years of operation.

Iron

Iron is an important mineral deposit of the Southern Highlands. The Southeastern Iron District, within which most of the iron producing states considered in this study lie, includes the Virginias, eastern Kentucky, east Tennessee, North Carolina, Georgia, and northeastern Alabama. The ores of Maryland are not included in this group. This Southeastern District ranks second in importance among the iron districts of the United States in the amount of iron produced. The total amount of iron ore shipped in 1917 from the mines of Alabama, Georgia, North Carolina, Tennessee, and Virginia[1] was 8,396,841 gross tons, valued at $16,437,775. Including ores from the mines of Maryland—10,730 gross tons valued at $40,423—these six states produced 11 per cent of the total amount of iron ore shipped from the mines of the United States in 1917.

Accessibility and mining conditions are the two factors which most affect the cost of delivering ore at the furnace. Distance from fuel is a more serious drawback than the absence of transportation lines. Many of the deposits of the Southeastern District are near the fuel supply, and it is noticeable that in times of depression when the output of iron falls off in other districts, there is less of a falling off in sections of this district, and at times even an increase. This is especially marked in Alabama, where the fuel supply is readily available. The close juxtaposition of fuel and ore would seem to offer in the future an advantage to the lower grade of ores of this district over the high-grade ores of other districts more remote from fuel supply.

According to estimates made by C. W. Hayes, of the United States Geological Survey in 1908, there was in this field an available supply of iron ores, including magnetite, hematite, brown and carbonate ores, of 538,440,000 tons, and the estimates of ores not

[1] The ores of West Virginia are not included, as separate estimates are not available.

yet available were 1,276,500,000 tons. These are, of course, only approximate estimates.

Other Mineral Deposits

In addition to the minerals mentioned previously there are numerous other mineral deposits within the mountains. Some of these, such as gold, copper, marble, mica, emery, chromite, feldspar, corundum, asbestos, talc, slate, barytes, and kaolin, have been mined profitably. Many others have never been developed.

Gold has been found in different parts of the field. The gold region of Georgia was famous before the discovery of that metal in California in "forty-nine." So important was this field that a government mint was established at Dahlonega in Lumpkin County in the decade after 1830. Although there is no longer a mint there, gold mining is still carried on profitably in this region.

The most important copper district is that of Ducktown, Polk County, Tennessee.

The marbles of Tennessee and Georgia have a deserved reputation.

Mica is worked profitably in North Carolina. There are also deposits of value in Georgia, likewise asbestos of commercial importance.

Among the building stones other than marble are limestone, granite, sandstone, dolomite, soapstone, and others. Many of these as yet undeveloped are of a grade equal and often superior to those now quarried in the more accessible parts of the field.

Clay for brick, the fire clay of the coal measures, together with kaolin and other deposits, await better transportation facilities and more economical methods of production to bring from this region a rich return to labor and capital alike.

Transportation Facilities

In the development of the mineral resources of the mountains, capital, trained labor, and transportation are essential.

The transportation facilities of the mountain region as a whole are poor. Many of the sources of supply are far from railroads. Within the last decade, however, much territory hitherto difficult to reach has been made more accessible through the building of railways. In Kentucky especially, a number of short railway branches in connection with the coal development have penetrated the mountains, opening up territory which had been isolated for fifty or one hundred years. Other extensions are now building which will give access to new mountain fields and outlets for these fields to the north, east, south, and west.

A strong movement has been initiated looking to the provision of water transportation through the locking of some of the forks of the mountain rivers. Some of this work has already been done, but as yet the development has not been such as to divert traffic from the railroads.

It is likely that in the future this region will be made still more accessible by means of well-built highways. The Highlands have suffered in the past, economically and socially, from exceedingly poor roads. In some sections, roads are practically impossible to travel at any time of year except by horseback or the heaviest of wagons, drawn sometimes by several teams of mules. Travel in the winter season is very difficult throughout a large part of the rural mountain country. The Ford car has made accessible many areas which previously were shut off; but in places where the population is poor, where natural resources are such as to offer no great inducements to capital, and where the expense of road building is high because of lack of road-building material and the difficulties of topography, it will probably be many years before travel is possible even to these "great civilizers."

In many sections, however, and even in some remote counties, the good-roads movement is being advanced rapidly, under the stimulus of state and federal aid. A plan advocated in some states to connect all county-seats by good roads, would be of untold benefit to the rural population.

A highway known as the Dixie Highway is at present under construction, which is to offer a through route from Sault Ste. Marie and Detroit to Savannah, Georgia. While this route passes for the most part through valley areas and territory already opened up by railroads, one portion which turns east from Knoxville, Tennessee, through North Carolina into South Carolina, traverses one of the most beautiful and rugged portions of the Blue Ridge. Branches will eventually connect this main highway with a road along the crest of the Blue Ridge by Grandfather Mountain, and other branches will connect it with highways through the valley and mountain sections of Virginia.

By reason of this greater accessibility the Southern Highlands are likely to become more and more the recreation fields of the South, the East, and the Middle West. This great upland tract is but a short distance from the urban centers of the Southern states, and but a day's journey from many of the cities of the East and of the Mississippi Valley. Lack of proper accommodations and transportation facilities have kept it from being more extensively explored by pleasure and health seekers, although parts of it, especially the Blue Ridge section, have long been considered peculiarly favorable for the treatment of certain diseases, and the region in general has been for many years increasingly used as a refuge for those who wished to escape the extreme heat of the lower country surrounding it and the long cold springs of more northern climes.

Climate

The idea is sometimes held that because this region is situated in the South, it must necessarily be warm in winter and hot and enervating in summer. Surprise and doubt are expressed when it is heard that blankets are needed almost every summer night, and that in winter below-zero temperatures are occasionally registered for a day or two at a time.

As a whole the Highlands are much cooler than the surrounding regions, but as might be expected, in view of their extent and the great variety of their topography, marked differences are found in different areas. Naturally, the northerly reaches are likely to be cooler than the southern, and the ridges, of course, than the Greater Appalachian Valley, or the intramontane valleys. The temperature varies in summer from 40 degrees on the tops of the mountains to from 70 to 85, and occasionally even 90 degrees in the valleys. It is always cool at night, and cool in the shade even on the warmest days. In the direct rays of the sun it is warm. Winter temperatures of from 11 to 20 degrees below zero have been registered, but usually the winters, while cool enough to be bracing, are not severe. It is common for the thermometer to drop 15 to 20 degrees below freezing at night, and to rise to several degrees above freezing during the course of the morning. Snow seldom lies long on the ground except on the northern sides of the higher mountains. Outdoor sports and activities of all kinds are possible throughout a large part of the year.

The country is drained through most of its area by an abundance of swift-flowing streams, which carry off the heavy rainfalls with amazing swiftness. Considering that the amount of rainfall is exceedingly high in parts of the mountain section, especially the southeast slope where it is exceeded only by that of the northern Pacific slope, the average of humidity is not so great as might be expected. It is, in fact, not so great as that of the Gulf Coastal Plain or Interior Lowlands, where the average of wind movement is less.

It would seem, indeed, that the healthfulness of the climate and the great beauty of the country were in themselves resources sufficient to lead to its development.

Unfortunately, the opening up of a country is at times of questionable benefit to a native population. Even good roads, as has been seen, are not an unmixed blessing. In some rural sections they have already served as easy avenues by which to leave the country for the city. In others the vices of the city have found a quick approach to the heart of regions which, with all their limitations, had preserved a certain sturdy vigor. Industrial development has brought in its train both good and evil, as may be quickly recognized where a new railroad has accompanied the recent opening of mining or other industrial operations.

Better transportation, higher wages, a market at hand for the sale of produce, more recreational opportunities, and a wider view of life are among the features which in many ways are of advantage. On the other hand, lumber and mining operations not permanent, as is the case with many, leave a region not only poorer in material resources but vitiated by association with types of criminality not native to the region. When operations are of a more permanent character, class distinctions appear and extremes of wealth and poverty tend to make these distinctions rigid. "It seems like folks don't live as well now that the railroad has come in as they did in the old days when everyone raised enough for himself," is the plaint one frequently hears. The increase in certain types of crime, "bootlegging" especially, has been suggested. Moreover, in mining and mill communities, unless the corporation is far-sighted and liberal in expenditures, sanitary conditions are bad. Unsanitary conditions of living which in isolated places have proved dangerous, under the congestion of the industrial town become fruitful sources of disease and death. In a like manner an attitude which for lack of a better word may be called "unmoral" in isolation, becomes often actively immoral in the mining town.

The industrial development of the mountains has been dependent largely upon urban and extra-mountain capital. It is doubtful if in the past the mountain people as a whole have profited largely by their mineral or timber holdings. Individuals have become very wealthy, but too often the people have sold to outside companies for a nominal sum rights which should have been held for a higher price, or better, should have been leased on a royalty basis.

The condition of many of the Highland people would seem to be discouraging—with timber cut, water and mineral rights gone, minerals in some cases already exhausted, and health and sometimes moral stamina impaired. Even the agricultural resources, as we shall see, have suffered serious deterioration. The picture is a dark one, yet there has never been a time when so much intelligent interest was manifested in the safeguarding and proper development of resources.

The situation is not to be improved, moreover, by decrying industrial development. It is not possible, nor is it desirable to arrest this. The store of treasure is of value only as used, and ability, if dormant, is useless. In places it may even be desirable that capital be invited to the field, and equitable terms offered as well as trained labor provided. In order that such a condition be brought about, the states should individually and collectively and in cooperation with the Federal Government and with disinterested private associations, from time to time take the action that is needed to encourage private enterprise, and also to check the excesses which grow out of such enterprises when but little restricted.

Many as are the possibilities of industrial growth, for much of the mountain country the future development lies probably in agriculture, for which large areas are eminently suited, and most kinds of mining do not necessarily interfere greatly with the tilling of the soil.

Agriculture

Fundamental in any discussion of agricultural resources is the question of soil. The Southern Highland country lies within the two soil provinces[1] designated by the United States Bureau of Soils as the Appalachian Mountain and Plateau Province and the Limestone Valley and Upland Province. Within the first[2] are included the Allegheny-Cumberland and Blue Ridge Belts, and in the second the Greater Appalachian Valley. In both these provinces the soils are derived from the disintegration and to a certain extent the decomposition of rocks in place, but the classes of rocks underlying the soils and the manner of their disintegration are very different.

The entire western, or Allegheny-Cumberland Belt, may be regarded in a very general way as cut from an enormous block of sedimentary rock, sloping to the northwest and so deeply eroded as to have lost in sections all semblance to a plateau, save in the prevailing level of the resistant rocky hill crests. The soils are predominantly the weathered residuals of sandstone, shale, and conglomerate, and are sufficiently deep in most places to support a good forest growth. The rocks of the Blue Ridge Belt are more varied and difficult of classification. They are in large part igneous and metamorphic—granites, gneisses, schists, and quartzites. Their great age and long weathering have resulted in the formation of a soil which while very deep in places is, when exposed to the action of the atmosphere, peculiarly subject to erosion. The rocks of the Greater Appalachian Valley are largely of sedimentary

[1] "For purposes of soil classification, the United States has been divided into thirteen soil provinces and regions, the soil region being more inclusive and embracing an area which may for further study be resolved into several soil provinces. A soil province is defined as 'an area having the same general physiographic expression, in which the soils have been produced by the same forces or groups of forces, and throughout which each rock or soil material yields to equal forces equal results.'"—United States Department of Agriculture, Bureau of Soils, Bulletin No. 96: Soils of the United States, pp. 7–8. 1913.

[2] The first also includes the eastern and western belts of the Appalachian Province in Pennsylvania, the Onachita and Boston Mountain region of the Ozark uplift west of the Mississippi River, and the area of coal measure rocks in western Kentucky and southern Indiana. The second also includes the Central Basin of Tennessee and the Bluegrass region of Kentucky.

origin. Unlike the valleys of the belts to east and west, which have been formed by the leveling action of streams, the valley character of this belt is due to the rapid weathering of soft limestones and shales, the resistant sandstones and conglomerates being left as long ridges in the Valley.

There is little question in the minds of most people as to the agricultural possibilities of the soils of the valley sections of the Greater Appalachian Valley, but to some the topography and soils of the adjoining belts—the Allegheny-Cumberland and the Blue Ridge—present insuperable obstacles to any extensive agricultural development.

During the seasons of 1904 and 1905, under the direction of the United States Geological Survey, an examination was made of the Southern Appalachian region, and in 1907 of the Monongahela Basin in West Virginia and Pennsylvania, for the purpose of studying the effect of deforestation and consequent erosion of the steep mountain slopes on geologic, hydrologic, and economic conditions both in the mountain region itself and in the surrounding areas through which the many streams that rise in the high Appalachians flow on their way to the Mississippi, the Gulf, or the Atlantic. An area comprising some 35,000 square miles, including parts of south-western Virginia, the eastern borders of Tennessee, the western part of North Carolina, the northwestern part of South Carolina, the northern part of Georgia, and a portion of northeastern Alabama, was examined in detail. A cursory examination was also made of an additional area of 15,000 square miles likewise in the Southern Appalachians. The following is quoted from the report of these surveys:

> The clearing of virgin forests for agriculture is going on steadily from year to year to replace worn-out, eroded, and abandoned lands. When the region was settled, the more level lands along and near the streams were first cleared and those that have been properly cared for and out of the reach of the stream floods have remained in cultivation and are in good condition today. After these lands had been largely cleared the steeper slopes were next invaded by the axman, and then still steeper slopes, so that very much of the land now being cleared is too steep for cultivation under present farm practice and should be kept in forests.

Numerous attempts have been made to estimate the percentage of the area of these mountains that might safely and profitably be cleared for cultivation. These estimates average about 15 per cent. It is difficult to give any definite idea of such area, for the allowable limit of slope of lands that may be safely cleared—which is generally put at 10 degrees and which alone has usually been considered—is not the only factor of the problem, for the nature of the soil, which is dependent on the geology of the underlying rock formations, and the intelligence and care of the cultivator should also be considered. On some soils 10 degrees may be the maximum slope for safe cultivation; on other soils slopes of 20 degrees do not wash. Slopes themselves may be changed by terracing, and education may so greatly increase the intelligence and care of the cultivator that estimates of cultivable area that consider these varying factors must of necessity vary, and the variation tends to increase the estimate of cultivable area as time passes. The increase, however, must be slow, and for present methods of cultivation 18 to 20 per cent is probably a liberal estimate for the area that may be cleared safely. The present area, 24 per cent, is undoubtedly in excess of the limit of safety under the existing conditions of agriculture.[1]

As to the agricultural problem of the region, we quote from the same source:

The agricultural problem involves the selection of the areas best suited for agriculture because of fertility of soil and moderate slope of surface and the study of the ways in which such areas may best be handled to prevent their destruction through erosion and the destruction of other lands and property by the waste they yield and the floods they help to generate.

Much of the mountain area is properly agricultural land, and as the population increases more and more of this area must be brought under cultivation. This means that steeper and steeper slopes must be cleared, and that danger of erosion must increase unless improved methods of agriculture are introduced. Terracing, contour plowing and ditching, crop rotation, sodding to pasture or meadow, as well as the crops best adapted to the region, especially those most helpful in holding soil on steep slopes, should be studied, and to be of practical value, this study must consider all these things as they are directly related to the

[1] Glenn, Leonidas Chalmers: Denudation and Erosion in the Southern Appalachian Region and the Monongahela Basin, pp. 11–12. United States Geological Survey, Professional Paper 72, Washington, Government, 1911.

specific and sometimes peculiar climatic, rainfall, soil, slope, labor, and other natural and economic conditions in the region. It can not profitably be a long-range or general study.

The study of the agricultural problem should also include a consideration of practicable methods of reclaiming eroded and abandoned lands, and of the effectiveness of brush, straw, or other filling for gullies, or brush, log, or rock dams across them, and of tree, vine, or other vegetative covering for bare areas. Such a study should also include a consideration of methods of regulating and restraining both the wild headwaters or torrent reaches, and the lower, but still rapid and easily changeable courses of the mountain streams along whose banks lie the most fertile agricultural lands of the region—lands that are now at the mercy of their uncurbed destructive activities in times of flood.

In studying these problems much could be learned of Europe, where for hundreds of years man has slowly won to agriculture area after area of steeper and steeper slope, as population has pressed hard upon subsistence. Doubtless the methods employed in Europe should not be exactly followed, because of differences in climate, crop, soil, labor, and other factors, but, warned by their failures, and profiting by their achievements, we can adapt their successful methods to our own peculiar conditions. . . . The agricultural lands of the Appalachian Mountains are generally fertile, and if wisely handled will support safely and permanently a much greater population than now inhabits the region.[1]

Inasmuch as the statements above apply primarily to the eastern or Blue Ridge Belt, with its bordering Valley and Piedmont Plateau strips on the west and east, the writer sought information from Dr. L. C. Glenn, author of the report just quoted, in regard to the agricultural problem of our western belt, the soils of which are held by many to be unsuitable for farming. Dr. Glenn's reply forms part of a personal letter:

North of the cotton belt on Sand Mountain, Cumberland Plateau section, the soil though thin will grow good fruit— apples, peaches, grapes, strawberries and other small fruits; part will produce field crops of corn and other grain, especially along the flood-plained streams and on certain shaly or clayey belts, while much of it is suitable for sheep raising. The agricultural problem is by no means a hopeless one—indeed I do not

[1] Ibid., p. 30.

feel that it is even a serious one. The worst part is that adjacent to the cotton belt margin. As you go northward into Kentucky and on into West Virginia the surface topography changes from the flat plateau type to the deeply dissected type with sharp ridges and deep narrow valleys, but the soils on these very steep slopes of Carboniferous rocks are often surprisingly fertile and they do not erode as badly as the equally steep slopes in the Old Crystallines of western North Carolina. There are areas of poor soil, it is true, but such is far from being the rule. The problem of whether that country will produce food for its inhabitants may be answered affirmatively.

The problem there to my mind is to fight against the isolation nature has imposed on those people. You probably know how steep and high as well as how intricately winding the ridges are, and how cabins perched far up in the heads of coves have an isolation that is painful. This tells on the people, and especially on the women who stay at home.

It is possible to approximate the amount of land admittedly agricultural within our territory. Under government direction a reconnaissance survey[1] was made of the non-agricultural lands of the Appalachian region lying south of Pennsylvania and within our field. The centers of these lands are the more mountainous regions of the Allegheny-Cumberland and Blue Ridge Belts, which are the roughest and wildest of the principal mountain regions. Though called non-agricultural lands they include some agricultural areas. From such a survey on the basis of our present knowledge, it is of course impossible to determine accurately the extent of the agricultural lands lying within the non-agricultural areas or within the field as a whole. Furthermore, it has been seen that lands now called non-agricultural may become available for cultivation if new methods adapted to environment be introduced. From these data, however, we may approximate the area of lands suited, to some extent at least, to agriculture under present conditions.

The total acreage of non-agricultural lands as indicated in the report of the survey is 23,310,000 acres, or 36,422 of the 111,609 square miles of our territory, leaving 75,187 square miles which by inference are agricultural. Omitting from consideration the

[1] Report of the Secretary of Agriculture on the Southern Appalachian and White Mountain Watersheds. Washington, Government, 1908.

Greater Appalachian Valley, which is agricultural throughout most of its area, and deducting all the non-agricultural lands from the areas of the other two belts, there are left within the two upland belts 49,710 square miles, or 31,814,400 acres, with agricultural possibilities.

Under present agricultural methods a hundred-acre farm affords a family support, measured by existing standards. For example, a certain mountain farmer whose prosperity was somewhat above the average, had this much land but worked only about ten acres, the yield from which he called a "one-man crop." Putting about three months' labor on this acreage he expected to produce about 200 bushels of corn to carry the family through the winter. Much of the remainder of his holding was in woodland, the residue worn-out mountain slopes, "resting."

The average size of the farms as reported by the United States census of 1910, appears in the Allegheny-Cumberland Belt to be a little above and in the Blue Ridge Belt a little below 100 acres. Taking 100 acres as the typical size of mountain farms, our estimate of the total area of agricultural land in these two belts gives us 318,144 farms. The total number of farms in the two belts in 1910 was recorded by the census as 416,738, or 98,594 more than the number available from strictly agricultural land. It is true, however, that the ordinary hundred-acre farm is only in part improved and under cultivation. Were farms improved to their utmost capacity by means of proper adaptation of crop to soil and suitable cultivation, many of the present farms could be divided, thereby increasing the total number. When reinforced by agricultural tracts in the areas estimated as non-agricultural lands, but capable of improvement by scientific methods of farming, there is little doubt that the acreage of agricultural land within these two belts of the mountain country would be sufficient to support a considerable increase of population.

With right influences set in motion there should come about a distribution of population within our territory to the better agricultural lands. Those who would remain necessarily on the less promising areas, with proper training might make them yield more abundantly.

The hindrances to agricultural development lie in the disregard of wise methods by the average farmer. The topography of the country, the most important influence affecting the soil province within which most of it lies, has been generally ignored. Doubtless some have had to take what land they could get, despite the slope; but many a mountain farmer of the past, and of the present as well, has worked against rather than with the forces of his environment. As long as he could supply his needs from game, fish, and the virgin fertility of the soil, and as long as he could obtain more land when his holdings were worn-out, he gave little care to the soil itself. In fact he did little to retain the soil. With pioneer and characteristically American disregard of the future, he girdled the trees to "deaden" them, thus furnishing sunlight for his crop. He planted the crop that fed him and his stock, namely corn, and when the virgin fertility of his clearing was impaired because of successions of the same crop, or, as was more often the case, because the humus and the underlying soil itself were washed away, he would "deaden" another field and plant corn again. Scores of such "deadenings" may be found in a short journey through the mountains, the stark trees still standing in abandoned and gully-furrowed fields as sad monuments of ignorance and neglect.

Today crops of corn are seen on slopes so steep as to make easy of belief a fiction writer's statement that a mountain farmer broke his leg falling out of his corn field. In places, especially in the northwestern part of our area, where the plateau has been minutely dissected, the mountain cabins are clustered in deep, narrow valleys and overshadowed by steep hills cultivated to their tops. In some places it seems impossible to work the fields even with the hoe. One mountaineer who owned such a farm, being asked how he planted and gathered his crop, gave the jocose reply that in the spring the seed was shot into the hillside from the opposite slope, and because of the difficulties of harvesting, the corn was carried down in a jug in the fall.

Even in large areas of comparatively level land, suitable so far as surface is concerned for agriculture—such, for instance, as the Cumberland Plateau of Tennessee—the mountaineer has worked against success. He has been wont to burn the underbrush, thus destroying not only all the coarser grasses and the seedling trees

252

but the humus as well, which is of great importance to the texture of the soil and to its composition.

Little use has been made of fertilizers. The amount of manure available on the average farm is small, owing to lack of knowledge as to its value and to uneconomical methods of storing. What there is, moreover, is generally utilized for the garden or the small wheat crop. Commercial fertilizers, when bought, often in small amounts through the country store, are a fruitful source of indebtedness. Sometimes they mean a mortgaging of the crop in advance, rather than an increase in profits. It is simpler for most farmers remote from a market to clear new fields than to try to improve the old ones. A newly cleared slope, even if it be steep, will without fertilizer yield from 35 to 40 bushels of corn per acre the first year. From 15 to 20 bushels per acre would probably be a good average yield for many hillside farms. The acreage put in other grains is comparatively small, especially on hillside farms, and the yield is lower.

The mountaineer is not lacking in humor, nor is he blind altogether to the futility of some of his attempts at agriculture. A friend, thinking to buy a home in the mountains but questioning the title, was informed by the owner that while he might be unable to give him a clear title, yet as some evidence of his right to sell the land he could show him the grave of the man from whom he bought it—the man having starved to death in attempting to cultivate it.

For the future, however, the care of the soil, such as it is, must be the mountaineer's concern if he is to maintain himself by agriculture in the mountain country. The crop best suited to a specific locality can be determined only by study and experimentation. In places, especially along the streams, there will be an increase in the growing of different kinds of grains, but in more places other staple crops better adapted to the respective regions should be planted. Much of the mountain country is peculiarly suited to fruit. The apples of Virginia and western North Carolina have long been famous, and during the last ten years there has been a rapid increase in orchards in these regions and in northern Georgia. Peaches, too, have been grown for many years throughout the Highlands, although the crop is subject to frequent loss from late frosts and has therefore been replaced in a number of localities by the apple. Small fruits and berries do particularly well in the plateau belt, and strawberry culture has been developed very successfully in this part of Alabama and Tennessee. Potatoes and garden truck in general are also adapted to certain soils. Legumes do especially well.

Transportation and a market are vital factors in determining what to plant. Production in the past has been limited sadly by the lack of them. The mountaineer has had little use for what his family could not eat. In very many places still where conditions are good for the culture of fruits and vegetables, only such as will stand the long rough journey to market will return a profit above the costs of raising and transportation.

The activities of canning clubs, when connection is made with the market, are offering a partial solution for the utilization of certain products. In one remote mountain section the canning agent, a community worker under one of the denominational boards, induced the club to put up a high grade of the native blackberries, which were selling at that time at 10 cents a gallon when anyone could be induced to pick them. These canned blackberries took 22 first prizes and 13 second prizes at the county fair, and more prizes at the state fair, at the Eastern State Division Fair, and at Washington. Through the state university, connection was made with a prominent hotel in an eastern city which took 500 cans on trial, then sent for 3,000, of which only 300 could be supplied. Another state sent for 15,000. The girls of the club cleared about 45 cents a gallon over all expenses. In a similar way the output of tomatoes of another canning club brought a fair profit to the members.

Much might be done with grapes. A horticulturist of long experience has proved that with proper care they grow luxuriantly in the mountain country; and he points to the demonstration work done by the Department of Agriculture in preparing syrups, conserves, preserves, and marmalades from the grape, as suggestive of the way in which such mountain produce might be marketed.

The output of canning clubs would not be able to compete in the open market with the large commercial product, but special brands of a high grade will find a ready market, and there are larger opportunities in co-operative canneries. The drying of fruit and vegetables offers another avenue to market.

Attention has been called to the practicability of growing hardy shrubs native to the mountains such as azaleas and rhododendrons, of which the large part of our commercial supply is imported. Bulbs, too, hyacinths, tulips, and narcissus, grow as readily in the mountain soil as they do in the little home gardens abroad, where they furnish a substantial reinforcement to the family income.

The possibilities of tree farming have not yet been adequately tested. The Chinese chestnut grafted on the chinquapin gives a fruit which, as food for man, and also, in connection with the improved persimmon, mulberry, and acorn, as food for hogs, has been enthusiastically advanced as a solution of the agricultural question on steep slopes.[1]

As yet little has been done in raising goats,[2] which would seem, in steep areas, to have a number of important advantages over cattle as milk, cheese, and meat producers. Their pasture must, however, be fenced and wired securely, as they do great harm to young forest growth when allowed to range freely.

Sheep have always been kept in small numbers throughout the Highlands, in large part for the household use of the wool. They might be very profitable in large numbers, if properly cared for and if the Highlander could be persuaded to reduce the number of his dogs. Certain sections are making a definite publicity campaign toward this end, a high tax on dogs being advocated and in some places levied.

The raising of poultry and the keeping of bees also offer sources of profit in the mountain country.

A large part of the more rugged mountain region, however, seems destined to become a cattle and dairy country. In sections where roads have been poor and transportation facilities few, the advantages in the past of raising such products as could take themselves to market is obvious. Hogs, sheep, and turkeys have thus been driven to the railroad for many years, and since early days the

[1] Smith, J. Russell: "Farming Appalachia," in American *Review of Reviews*, March, 1916.

[2] The Department of Agriculture has been experimenting with the crossing of various breeds in the endeavor to produce a hardy stock with a high milk production. Individual experiments are also being made in various parts of the mountains.

grassy balds of some of the higher mountain and some of the plateau areas as well, have been used for grazing purposes, the cattle being driven later to the lowlands and sold.

Milk, however, has had no local market; and butter, usually of an inferior quality, has brought but small return even when it could be sold. In many places natural pasturage has been small and it has been generally believed that grass would not grow. Silos were unknown, and the difficulties of raising enough grain and hay for winter feeding have been very great. As a result the number of cows kept has dwindled, and they are allowed to go dry during the winter to save trouble and expense.

That certain grasses will grow freely in many regions formerly considered unfavorable has been proved, and the possibilities of co-operative dairying in these and other regions where there is a large amount of natural pasturage, and where a reasonable amount of some forage crop can be raised, would seem great. The initial difficulties lie in arousing the interest of the people to a point where they will improve and increase pasturage and stock and will transform their independence into a spirit of co-operation.

The United States Department of Agriculture stands ready to help. The Dairy Division, in co-operation with the state agricultural colleges in each of the Southern states, maintains specialists who are available without cost to the farmers to advise concerning dairy problems—the improvement of herds, better breeding, better feeding and management of dairy cattle, construction of silos, provision of feed, butter-making, etc. In some of the states specialists are also available to give instruction in the making of factory butter. Efforts to start co-operative cheese making have already had far-reaching results.

The history of some of the co-operative cheese factories which have been established in North Carolina, Virginia, Tennessee, and West Virginia during the last five years reads like a romance. The first of these factories was established at Sugar Grove on Cove Creek, Watauga County, North Carolina, in 1915. At an initial cost of $400 it returned almost $1,500 the first year, making a return of more than $1,200 over the usual profit on butter. The second year it was doubled in size and more than quadrupled its business. Other factories speedily followed, and owing to careful selection of favorable localities, all have prospered.[1] The expense of highly trained cheese makers was avoided by training a man from each neighborhood who, with the aid of the field agent, was able to manage the business. Local expense was lowered by the elimination of ice, cold springs being used to cool the milk. The use of the by-product, whey, to fatten hogs, proved a further source of profit. Among the many benefits which have followed are improvement in agricultural methods and milk production, farm buildings, and life, and not least the spirit which has grown out of the fact that the enterprises are local and co-operative.

It is to be remembered that certain requirements of altitude, coolness, cold springs, and so forth, are desirable for successful cheese-making; but the movement is one of great promise to some of the mountain areas. In certain other areas, co-operative creameries may be started.

The greatest agricultural possibilities of the mountain country, indeed, can only be realized through the growth of the co-operative movement. Until the farmers of a neighborhood far from market join in some definite co-operative undertaking, or can agree to raise crops best suited to the soil in such quantity and of such quality as to bring the market to them, the efforts of the individual farmer will fall far short of their desert, no matter how excellent his method. This failure has been especially evident in the case of isolated orchards in the mountains which, although they produced apples and peaches of high quality, could not command railroad rates. Wagon loads of perfect fruit taken to the railroad have been left many times to rot at the track by the discouraged producer.

Most helpful would be a special study of the co-operative societies of Denmark, which in connection with the educational sys-

---

[1] "In 1916 about $30,000 worth of cheese was made in North Carolina alone, and during the year 1917 more than $125,000 worth of cheese was made in the 34 factories now in operation in the mountain districts of North Carolina, Virginia, Tennessee, and West Virginia. Twenty-six of these factories were organized in 1916. All have been successful and each has shown a rapid growth from the day it opened. The cost of operation, added to what the farmers would probably have received for the milk if there had been no cheese factories, would amount to about one-fourth of the gross receipts; therefore it is fair to infer that three-fourths of the $125,000, or a little more than $90,000, is newly created wealth."—Doane, C. F., and Reed, A. J.: "Cheese Making Brings Prosperity to the Farmers of the Southern Mountains," p. 8. No. 737 Separate from the Year-book of the Department of Agriculture, 1917, Washington, Government, 1918.

tem have raised that country from a small poverty-stricken nation to one of the richest in per capita wealth in Europe. The Irish co-operative movement, too, which under the leadership of Sir Horace Plunkett and George W. Russell has triumphed over difficulties harder in many ways to combat than the topography and individualism of the mountains, furnishes valuable examples of what may be done to solve local problems in remote rural communities.

It is impossible here to enter into a discussion of steps by which the co-operative movement gained its foothold in these countries, and by which farmers were brought to see that only by combining could they effect an economy in the buying of seeds, fertilizer, feed, and expensive farm machinery, command a credit which the average individual was powerless to secure, meet competition, and control market prices. Nor can we dwell upon the many kinds of co-operative societies—agricultural, dairy, poultry, bacon, home industries, and numerous others—each holding itself responsible, not alone for marketing but for the quality of the products of its members, for upon the quality of the product will depend eventually its market.

We may, however, illustrate the power of the co-operative movement by a brief mention of the now famous region about Dungloe in northwest Donegal, Ireland, where through the efforts of Patrick Gallagher—familiarly known as "Paddy the Cope" from his interest in the cause of co-operation—an entire revolution in the economic life of the region was accomplished.

This section, described as one of the poorest and wildest in Ireland, a region of rocks and bogs and little cabins, was completely under the control of the gombeen man, as the local usurer is called. Seventy-five per cent of the farmers were born in debt and had never been free from it. The people were intimidated and hopeless. Into this district was injected the co-operative seed, in the form first of a co-operative bank, and then of the Templecrone Agricultural Co-operative Society. The instigator of this movement was Gallagher, himself a poor boy who had left the country, come under the stimulus of co-operative leaders, and returned to try the new theory in his old home. Beginning as a tiny store in the hill region, the society grew and branched out into the selling of eggs for its members, Gallagher meeting the aroused hostility of the bosses with fearless strategy. So greatly indeed has the society flourished that its members now control the producing, buying, and selling of most of the necessities of life.

Citing this instance of co-operation in an address delivered to the American Commission of Agricultural Inquiry at the Plunkett House, Dublin, in 1913, George W. Russell, or "A. E." as he is usually known, the "nature mystic and poet" as well as the "journalistic mouthpiece and champion of the agricultural co-operative movement in Ireland," continued:

> You see what a tremendous advantage it is to farmers in a district to have such organizations; what a lever they can pull and control! You will understand the difference between a rural population and a rural community, between a people loosely knit together by the vague ties of a common latitude and longitude, and people who are closely knit together in an association and who form a true social organism, a true rural community. I assert that there can never be any progress in rural districts or any real prosperity without such farmers' organizations and guilds. Wherever rural prosperity is reported of any country, inquire into it and it will be found that it depends on rural organization. Wherever there is rural decay, inquire into it, and it will be found that there was a rural population, but no rural community, no organization, no guild, to promote common interests and unite people in defence of them.[1]

It is the belief of the writer that the people of the mountains and their children will play a large part in the development of their native land. Within certain areas men native to the Highlands have already demonstrated their ability as leaders in industrial progress. Without the Highlands men of ability have found the mountaineer who has left his own country a worthy competitor.

If the belief that there is much latent ability within the Highlands, needing only opportunity for training to become active in developing mountain resources, be an unsound belief, the resources yet remain. If the children of the mountaineer cannot or will not develop them, others will. The right and limit of possession will eventually be determined by fitness to serve through the use made of the things possessed.

---

[1] Reprinted in *Rural Manhood*, March, April, 1914.

CHAPTER XII

EDUCATION[1]

RURAL problems in the Highlands, difficult because they are in such a degree problems of intense isolation, are made more difficult because of the prevailing illiteracy. Those who know the mountain people know that illiteracy is not necessarily synonymous with ignorance, and that an ability to pass written or oral tests is after all an inadequate measure of knowledge. If we accept as a definition of education, adaptation of life to environment, many a Highlander would compare favorably with some of the college graduates who have come into his community to educate him. Yet whatever the defects of our present educational system, which seeks too much to shape men in the same mold, it gives to them if they will have it, the power to break away from the dominance of its defects. While freedom remains, environment will not conquer easily men who read intelligently, and who have the initiative to prove their powers in the new ventures of which they have read. They learn, too, in the doing.

The illiterate man of the mountains is limited in his knowledge to what has come down to him, to what experience in a circumscribed neighborhood has taught him, and to what a chance voice from without brings to him. There has been enough of struggle with pioneer conditions to make him self-reliant while those conditions remain, and if his mountain barriers have shut out many things that are good, they have also shut out some things that are evil. He has not, however, a wide enough outlook to give him the proper perspective. Like many an individualist elsewhere, he prefers to learn through personal experience with all the attendant risks rather than from the accumulated experiences of others.

[1] Much of the information contained in the latter portion of this chapter is published separately in pamphlet form under the title: "The Future of the Church and Independent Schools in Our Southern Highlands."—Campbell, John C.: Russell Sage Foundation, New York, 1917.

Consequently he must pay the penalties of individualism as well as of illiteracy. The penalties he pays may be the growing-pains necessary to the best manhood. Whether or not they be so, they are less painful to him than the chafing bonds of conventionality. But the education which sufficed to meet the requirements of the past will not suffice for the future. Conditions are changing, and unless the mountaineer be prepared for the necessary readjustments he must fail in the adaptation of life to environment.

Though not a fair measure of knowledge, literacy is still the accepted standard by which the educational status of a region is judged; and of necessity we employ the accepted standard. The United States Census Bureau classifies as illiterate any person ten years of age or over who is unable to write, regardless of ability to read. It is to be regretted that the extent of illiteracy as thus defined must be measured in the Highlands by figures for 1910. The efforts of state and county, and of public-spirited citizens through moonlight schools and educational campaigns of one sort and another, will probably result in lower figures in the 1920 census returns.

According to the census for 1910, of 3,856,420 persons of ten years of age and over within our Southern Highland area, 515,131, or 13.4 per cent, were illiterate.

TABLE 13.—PER CENT OF ILLITERACY FOR PERSONS 10 YEARS OF AGE AND OVER IN THE SOUTHERN HIGHLANDS, BY RACE AND BY BELTS. 1910

Belt	Native white	Foreign-born white	Negro	Total
Blue Ridge	13.6	5.0	33.1	16.5
Greater Appalachian Valley	9.0	12.2	26.6	12.4
Allegheny-Cumberland	11.0	22.0	26.9	12.4
Total	11.0	19.5	28.5	13.4

Table 13 shows the percentage of illiteracy in each of the mountain belts for the three racial groups, native and foreign-born whites, and Negroes. It shows that for the entire mountain region, 11 per cent of the native whites over ten years of age were illiterate on the basis of the census definition, while 19.5 per cent of the foreign born and 28.5 per cent of the Negroes were illiterate. The foreign born constituted less than 2 per cent of the population of the Highlands in 1910, but the Negroes were nearly 12 per cent of the total. They were sufficiently numerous to materially raise the illiteracy rate for the general population.

The relative numbers of the three race groups must also be kept in mind in comparing the rates for the several belts. The foreign born are least numerous in the Blue Ridge, and most numerous in the Allegheny-Cumberland Belt where their illiteracy rate is highest and where they constitute about 3 per cent of the total population. On the other hand, the Negroes are least numerous in this belt. They are most numerous in the Greater Appalachian Valley where they constitute over 18 per cent of the population. Their illiteracy rate is highest in the Blue Ridge Belt where they represent 15 per cent of the population.

The general rates do not indicate the degree of illiteracy existing in many remote rural areas, where the foreign and Negro elements are negligible. Thus the mountain region of North Carolina, containing some of the highest and roughest areas of the Blue Ridge Belt, has a rate of illiteracy of 15.4 per cent for native whites of ten years of age and over; the contiguous Blue Ridge Belt of Tennessee has a native white illiteracy rate of 16.2 per cent; while the Kentucky Highlands, lying wholly within the Allegheny-Cumberland Belt and until recently very much shut off, have a native white illiteracy rate of 18.2 per cent.

That the illiteracy rates for the native whites shown in Table 13 are relatively high is emphasized by a comparison of the rates for the mountain regions with the rates for the total population of these states. This has been done in Table 14 for native white males twenty-one years of age and over. The rates are conspicuously higher for the mountain territory than for the entire state.

The high percentage of illiteracy, 12.2, for the mountain region as a whole, as against 10.6 for the nine states, or 3.5 for the United States, probably both overstates and understates educational conditions in the Highlands. The rate of illiteracy even for many rural areas was undoubtedly considerably below the rate indicated for the whole mountain area and for the mountain regions of the several states. On the other hand, the average rates, as has been suggested, do not indicate the extent of illiteracy that prevails in many shut-off areas.

TABLE 14.—PER CENT OF ILLITERACY FOR NATIVE WHITE MALES OF VOTING AGE IN THE SOUTHERN HIGHLANDS AND SOUTHERN HIGHLAND STATES, BY STATES. 1910

State	Mountain region	Total state
Alabama	10.6	10.6
Georgia	13.8	8.7
Kentucky	19.5	11.9
Maryland	3.9	3.4
North Carolina	17.1	14.0
South Carolina	14.1	10.8
Tennessee	14.1	11.3
Virginia	12.8	9.7
West Virginia	7.5	7.5
Total	12.2	10.6

As an example of the wide disparities that exist in different parts of even the same regional area may be cited the Allegheny-Cumberland Belt of Virginia. The rate of illiteracy for native white males of voting age for this region of the state is 16.2 per cent, yet the four northernmost counties next to West Virginia range from 2.6 per cent in Craig to 8.8 per cent in Alleghany; while the four most southwesterly counties bordering Kentucky range from 16.3 per cent in Dickenson to 34.8 per cent in Buchanan. The four intermediate counties range from 12.9 per cent in Bland to 20.6 per cent in Russell.

Similarly, in the Blue Ridge Belt of this state, which has an illiteracy rate of 13.8 per cent for native white males twenty-one years of age and over, Greene County lying among the spurs on the eastern side of the mountains has a rate of 32.0 per cent, while Albemarle County, which adjoins it and is the seat of the State University, has a rate of only 8.8 per cent. To the north, Madison and Rappahannock Counties, with rates of 15.6 per cent and 23.3 per cent, lie next to Fauquier and Loudon with rates of 6.0 per cent and 4.5 per cent; and to the south Nelson with a rate of 16.3 adjoins Amherst with a rate of 8.6 per cent. The rates for the rocky plateau still farther southward range from 10.8 per cent to 22.7 per cent. Such contrasts might be multiplied many times in the other states. The danger in drawing conclusions from averages would therefore seem as great as that of generalizing from local instances. When allowance is made, however, for the diversities existing in different parts of the Highlands, it yet remains true that deplorable educational conditions still exist over large rural areas.

The public schools are generally ungraded and with the exception of Maryland, which has a ten-months school law, are in session from three to six months only. Often local conditions result in an even shorter term and sometimes in none at all. The terms depend upon weather and crop conditions. They are not always taught through consecutive months nor by the same teacher. Buildings are as a rule one-room structures poorly lighted and very inadequately heated. Sanitary provisions are quite generally lacking. Little is provided in the way of equipment—in places not even desks, blackboards, or chalk; and as pupils are usually required to furnish their own textbooks, the supply is noticeably deficient.

Most of the teachers are inexperienced, untrained, young, and unformed in character. Some of the "little young girls" are manifestly unequal to maintaining order among their pupils, who have a wide range in age and size. Few, either men or women teachers have had normal school training, and a large number have only the education they have been able to acquire in such elementary schools as they are now themselves teaching. In many of the remote public schools the best teachers have been trained in the church and independent schools. Those who are trained remain but a very short time, for various reasons.

The difficulties in the way of securing and keeping competent teachers are many. Salaries are meager—too small, many times, for support. In a Statistical Study of the Public Schools of the Southern Appalachian Mountains made by the U. S. Bureau of Education in 1915, this statement is made about salaries:

> The median of the county average is $237. That is, in 108 counties the average salary is more than $237, and in 108 counties the average salary is less than $237. This figure is probably very nearly the average salary in this region. With an average term of 112 days, the average pay for a teacher is therefore very

nearly $2 per day. The nature of averages, however, is such that there are probably many more teachers who receive less than $237 per year than there are who receive more than that.[1]

There is, too, a strong pull to Lowland or urban areas where not only are inducements larger but living conditions easier. Moreover, the shortage of teachers which has existed during recent years in the teaching profession everywhere, is felt with peculiar keenness in the Highlands, where a sufficient number of trained men and women has never been available even for such communities as wished them.

At a conference of mountain workers in 1915,[2] the following statement was made by the president of one of the leading state normal schools within the Southern Highlands:

> In the three years past [prior to 1915] there were graduated from this school [the only normal school in the mountain section of this state] about 200 teachers, while the public schools in the mountain section of this state alone demanded the services of more than 3,000 teachers. From 700 to 1,000 new teachers are needed each year to take the places of those leaving the field of teaching.

The need is as great, if not greater, in the mountainous section of some of the other states.

Even when trained teachers are available local officials often favor incompetent local applicants in preference to trained applicants from without the district, or at times when their judgment approves the application of outside teachers they yield to popular clamor and poor teachers who have local support or who are connected by ties of kinship to influential families receive appointments. Small as the salaries are there is frequently great competition for the positions, which offer one of the few ways in the region to earn money. Schools therefore may be "cousined" to death, this being the mountain equivalent for nepotism. Cases have not been infrequent in the past where a term of from three to four months has been divided among a number of teachers; where money has been paid for teaching never done; and where teachers have been appointed to several schools all supposed to be in

[1] Frost, Norman: "A Statistical Study of the Public Schools of the Southern Appalachian Mountains," p. 19. U. S. Bureau of Education, Bulletin No. 11, 1915.

[2] Third Annual Conference of Southern Mountain Workers, Knoxville, Tennessee, April, 1915.

session at the same time. Such cases, however, would naturally occur only in very remote areas.

Occasionally trained teachers are too progressive to suit the notions of patrons and local school officials. An instance of the kind came under personal observation. Two qualified mountain girls were placed in charge of a large mountain school. There was every promise of success until it was learned that the teachers were teaching that the world was round "contrary to the Scriptures, which say that the *corners* of the earth are the Lord's!" In order to drive away the heretics various petty persecutions were practiced, well water was defiled, and covert attempts made to blast the character of the young women. The lack of orthodoxy in the teachers was the argument that had most weight, but doubtless the failure of local applicants to secure these positions was a contributing cause. This school was not in an isolated part of the mountains, but in a hamlet on a line of railway long traveled. A majority of the school trustees sustained the teachers, but many of the former patrons of the school looked askance and withdrew their children, notwithstanding that the teachers were themselves mountain women who came from an adjoining county.

The situation is complicated in many states by the political nature of the office of county superintendent, resulting too often in the election of men who have little knowledge of educational methods, and who through their anxiety to hold their constituency sometimes show favoritism in the granting and grading of teachers' certificates as well as in the awarding of appointments. Even if the county superintendent earnestly desires the improvement of school conditions, as is generally the case, the extent of his field and the difficulties of travel are such as to prevent him from efficiently overseeing the teachers. In the study by Mr. Frost, just quoted, it was found that it was practically impossible for the county superintendent to visit each school oftener than once or possibly twice during the school year, and that by the time a superintendent had attended to the work of his own office he was fortunate if he could spend more than two or three hours in each school during the entire year.

A detailed study of school supervision in seven counties in North Carolina was made in 1916 by L. C. Brogden, the Supervisor of Rural Schools in that state.[1] Conditions in many areas of the mountains are undoubtedly more extreme than those found in these counties, but the study illustrates interestingly the difference in the problems of school supervision in rural sections and in the larger county-seats. In Table 15 significant data from this study are compared for the white schools of three counties, Buncombe, Forsyth, Mecklenburg. Of these counties only one, Buncombe, is within the Highland region and this, moreover, is the seat of the only city of over 10,000 inhabitants in the Blue Ridge Belt of this state. Forsyth and Mecklenburg Counties lie just to the east of the Blue Ridge Belt in the Piedmont region. Data are given for the county-seats, which range from 17,000 to 20,000 population, and for the remaining rural portions of the county.

TABLE 15.—SCHOOL SUPERVISION IN URBAN AND RURAL DISTRICTS OF THREE NORTH CAROLINA COUNTIES. 1916

	Buncombe		Forsyth		Mecklenburg	
	Ashe-ville	Rest of county	Winston-Salem	Rest of county	Char-lotte	Rest of county
Schools per superintendent	6	93	7	82	9	75
Teachers per superintendent	85	167	110	140	127	164
Per cent of teachers college graduates	52	19	60	15	85	44
Per cent of teachers teaching first session	3	18	10	18	2	9
Per cent of teachers teaching three or more years in same school or grade	9	11	25	20	90	14
Length of school term in days	185	125	180	121	180	125
Per cent of total school fund spent for supervision	7.1	2.75	12.5	1.8	5.	2.1
Area in square miles of superintendent's district	6.7	639	5.5	376	12.8	597

Commenting upon the conditions illustrated by this table Mr. Brogden says:

[1] Brogden, L. C.: "More Intensive Supervision of Rural Schools in North Carolina," University of North Carolina Record, No. 159, p. 108. October, 1918, North Carolina Club Year Book.

Two conclusions seem inevitable, viz.: (1) that in the present situation the country child is not receiving, nor indeed can hope to receive anything like equality of opportunity with the city child from the standpoint of having his school work properly directed and supervised, and (2) that while the average city school is probably not spending as large a proportion of its total school fund for the supervision of the work of the city children as their needs demand, yet the county is lagging far behind the city in the per cent of its total school fund it is now spending for the supervision of the work of the country child.[1]

And he adds that until the county puts forth in the form of local tax for the education and training of its children even approximately the same amount of effort that the cities are putting forth, we shall continue to see the same educational inequality between the country and city child as exists today.

Great credit must be given to the public schools of the mountains for what they have done to teach the rudiments, but instances are only too frequent where students have attended session after session without learning how to read. Because of inefficiency and also because of the illiteracy of many of the parents, the benefits of education are not realized. Children are very generally allowed to follow their inclinations in the matter of school attendance, which is therefore often irregular. Moreover, at certain seasons of the year both boys and girls must take their part in making the crop. Often, too, children live many miles from school, and the state of roads, bridges, and foot-logs is such as to prevent their going regularly, or to militate against their going at all no matter how eager they are to do so. A small percentage of children have no school whatever accessible.

Under all these conditions the question of compulsory attendance is a serious one, the more so because, should all children of school age attend, accommodations, equipment, and teaching force would rarely be sufficient to care for them. Most of the states have some kind of compulsory attendance law, but that it would be difficult to enforce in many remote Highland sections is evident. Obvious hindrances to enforcement—scattered population and poor roads in particular—also stand in the way of consolidated schools. The movement for consolidation has gained rapidly, but

[1] Ibid., p. 109.

in certain sections the natural conditions are such as to impede and perhaps entirely prevent its progress.

It must be borne in mind that the following statements apply to the average conditions in remote country districts throughout the mountains, and that exception must be made of many public schools in more accessible rural areas. The causes that have produced these conditions were largely beyond the control of the Highlander, and the initial efforts for betterment must find their beginnings in the co-operation of leaders within and without the mountain territory. Good schools free to all are needed, and the two great means by which they can be attained are better economic conditions and a more general sentiment favoring public schools.

In recognition of the necessity for the upbuilding of a good rural public school system to dispel illiteracy and to secure better ways of living and of earning a living, federal and state officials have been making every effort to provide means to meet the obstacles that exist in all country sections, and to such a marked degree in the rural mountain region. The press, whirlwind campaigns, conferences, and institutes have been some of the methods used to arouse and educate public sentiment.

Prominent among national educational measures which have in them possibilities of much good for the mountains is the Smith-Hughes Act, which "provides a scheme of co-operation between the Federal Government and the States for the promotion of vocational education in the fields of agriculture, trade, home economics, and industry." A notable example of recent state educational legislation is the law passed by the General Assembly of North Carolina in 1919, to provide a six-months school term in every public school district of the state.[1] A tax levied and collected throughout the state is to be applied to a public school fund, in the disbursement of which it is purposed to equalize conditions between rich and poor sections. It is provided that a fixed proportion of each county's school expenses may be met from the fund, but

[1] Other special enactments of the General Assembly of North Carolina in 1919 having to do with public schools, provide a minimum salary for teachers and maximum expense fund for incidentals and buildings, compulsory attendance of children between eight and fourteen years for the entire school term, provision of two privies at each school house, physical examination and treatment of school children.

in order to secure this assistance a county must first levy a special school tax to meet the remainder of its school expenses. If this tax amount to 35 cents on every $100 valuation, and funds are still not sufficient to bring the school term to six months, the necessary extra amount will be supplied from the public school fund in addition to the amount automatically secured from the fund. The value of this act will be more evident if we may use the illustration recently given by the state superintendent of Tennessee:

> The State should be a unit for educational purposes. Only last year did Tennessee have a state-wide school tax, but the law added that the money should remain in the county where it was collected. That was because we did not recognize the need of an equal chance for education throughout the State. The State is a unit in production. The men who cut the trees up in the mountains are quite as truly employes of the furniture manufacturer as the men who work in his factory in the city, and their children should profit by the taxes collected in Chattanooga as much as the children of the factory employes in that city.[1]

In some states in recent years state supervisors of rural schools have been appointed whose knowledge of conditions and plans to meet them promise much for rural education. Their duties are many, and bring them into close touch with all existing agencies for rural educational betterment. By means of assistants, demonstration schools, teachers, and school officials—in fact, through every possible agency—their purpose is to make the whole content of school life more vital and to awaken communities to wholesome activities. County supervisors have also been appointed whose special interest lies in making the rural public school not only the cultural but the social and recreational center of the community.

The establishment of public county high schools is as yet attended by difficulties in many sections. A law passed some years ago in Kentucky, calling for a high school in every county-seat, was found to be premature. The chief obstacles lay, then as now, in the fact that the common public schools of the mountains which should be feeders to the high schools were not and will not be able

---

[1] From address by Albert Williams, State Superintendent of Public Instruction, Tennessee, before the Eighth Annual Conference of Southern Mountain Workers, Knoxville, Tennessee, April, 1920.

for some time to fit students for high schools which are organized on a state-wide uniform system. Another obstacle is the difficulty of securing competent teachers at salaries dependent upon local taxation.

It is evident, indeed, that many measures which have in them much of promise for the public school of the future and for which certain sections are now ready, cannot as yet and probably will not for some years become effective in many rural sections of the mountains. How to meet the present emergency becomes therefore a pressing consideration.

The question of how to provide in the best and most speedy way educational opportunities for the people in the rural Highlands is of concern not only to state and federal officials and to all public-spirited citizens within and without the mountain country, but is of very real importance to a group of agencies already at work in the Highlands. These agencies are known popularly in the North and in the Lowland South as "mountain mission schools" to distinguish them from the public schools and from the self-supporting or well-endowed private schools which have a more general patronage. The title "church and independent schools" is more appropriate, however, than that of "mission schools" because the latter term is associated generally with denominational work, and a number of the most influential of these schools in the mountains are not under denominational auspices.

The church schools are conducted under the auspices of denominational "mountain mission boards," of denominational bodies other than mission boards, and of individuals or groups that trust for the great part of their financial support to the denominations with which they are sympathetically affiliated.[1] The independent

---

[1] The denominations maintaining church schools within the Highland region are:

Baptists, Southern Convention	Congregationalists	Presbyterian in the United States
Seventh Day Baptist	Methodist Episcopal	
Brethren	Methodist Episcopal South	Presbyterian in the United States of America
Christians (Christian Connection)	Associate Presbyterian	Protestant Episcopal
	Reformed Presbyterian	Reformed Church in America
Churches of Christ	United Presbyterian	
Disciples of Christ		Seventh Day Adventists

Data for 1920–21 on the school work of these boards is published in: Southern Highland Schools Maintained by Denominational and Independent Agencies, compiled by Olive D. Campbell, Russell Sage Foundation, New York, N. Y.

schools are free from denominational connection or control but have the same general purpose as have many of the church schools. For convenience the two are here considered together, although there are certain differences between them, especially in administration. It is true, as a general statement, that the independent schools adapt themselves to changing conditions more rapidly than do the church schools, and that a number of them have from the beginning foreseen the needs of the future more clearly than have many of the church schools. While some have been under the administrative control of organizations without the field, the most influential are those whose policy has been determined and guided by a strong individual or individuals upon the field, untrammeled by outside restrictions. Their weaknesses arise, however, from this very element of their strength; namely, from a too great dependence upon the strong characters who have given their impress to the work and who, in the mind of the supporting public, are inseparably connected with it.

The church schools as a whole have been longer in the field than the independent schools, and have followed more closely the academic traditions that prevail outside of the Highlands. This is due no doubt in large part to absentee control in shaping policy and management. Like the independent schools, however, their most successful work has been under the guidance of strong individuals on the field, who have been long in control of local work and in whom non-resident officials have had such confidence as to allow them large liberty in developing their plans. But although some of the church boards, under the able leadership of nonresident officials well acquainted with the mountains are shaping their work admirably to meet changing conditions, yet when one views as a whole the work of the 17 denominational boards sustaining schools in the mountains, it is not overstating the case to say that the church schools suffer from long-distance control and from the submergence of strong personalities familiar with the mountain people and conditions, under policies formulated and usually directed by officials whose point of view is that of an entirely different environment. Nor can such a point of view in the very nature of things be changed by infrequent or hurried journeys through the mountain country.

There are approximately 200 church and independent schools in the mountains, the church schools outnumbering the independent schools ten to one. Some of them, as has been shown, began their activities in pioneer days,[1] and many have existed for a score or more of years and represent a large investment in property.

They are not all of the same character. There are day schools—almost invariably of elementary type—boarding schools of elementary-secondary type, and a few colleges.

The term "college" is misleading. There are a number of so-called colleges whose name is evidence of the hope of their founders rather than indicative of the work being done. A mountain "college" may combine all three of the types of schools indicated previously, and even those doing four years of college work with few exceptions have preparatory departments that, on the basis of numbers, place them in the class with boarding schools of the second and preparatory type.[2] In their college departments, however, small though they are, such colleges attempt to do good work of the traditional kind, and some are succeeding admirably. On the basis of their effort to give mountain boys and girls the advantage of collegiate training they constitute a group to which the name "mountain colleges" is applicable. Several of them maintain special departments in which a strong effort is made to adapt education to mountain environment.

As the number of secondary and college preparatory schools increase in the mountains, preparatory courses will be eliminated from these mountain colleges which will then be likely to develop into the conventional colleges foreshadowed in their collegiate departments. It is to be hoped, however, that some will resist the

[1] See list, Chapter VIII, p. 163.

[2] Data are taken from Campbell, John C.: Future of the Church and Independent Schools in Our Southern Highlands. New York, Russell Sage Foundation, 1917.

Recent data indicate that there are some 30 distinctively mountain institutions known as colleges. A fifth of them give four years of college work; a third are ranked as junior colleges; while the rest give more or less collegiate work, with the exception of two or three which offer no courses above secondary grade. The data indicate, furthermore, a decided decrease during the last few years in the number of day schools. A score or more of influential stations at which such schools were maintained until recently have been changed to centers of community activities other than scholastic. Other day schools have been taken over in whole or in part by the public school authorities.

temptation to develop along traditional lines and be willing to evolve, through experimental stages, into higher institutions especially emphasizing a training that will meet regional needs.

The day schools are usually small and are situated in remote or more or less inaccessible communities. As a rule they are regarded as of temporary character, to be abandoned as soon as the community can supply a good public school. Often they merely supplement the short public term, under arrangements variously adapted to suit the locality. A common arrangement in the past has been for the private day schools to accept the public school funds of their districts, with the agreement that they would teach a free school for the three or four months permitted by the scanty public funds. At the end of the free public term an additional "pay term" was supplied by the church board and financed through tuition fees and scholarships. It was taught sometimes by the public school teacher and sometimes by a teacher sent in from the outside.[1] By this method a good public school was secured, with which the pay term could be easily co-ordinated.

In some states it is now against the law for denominational agencies to administer public school funds. In others the serious objection to the administering of public funds by church or private groups has been met in various ways. One of the most successful plans has been brought about through the co-operation of a county superintendent and one of the church boards, represented in the community by a local worker. By mutual consultation and agreement a qualified teacher is selected for the four-months public term, and when this is over she is retained by the board to complete a term of eight months, the board's payments passing through official channels. A home is furnished to her by the community worker.

---

[1] Where teachers from the outside have been employed to teach the public term, he mistake has often been made of not insisting that they fulfil the requirements of the law by taking state and county examinations to which they are liable when they teach a public term supported by public funds. This has not always been due to unwillingness on the part of the teachers (though naturally they are not zealous in the matter) but because the examinations were held during their vacations when they were absent in their distant homes. Moreover there were often no provisions enabling them to take examinations when they were on the field, and sometimes it has seemed that there was little readiness on the part of local and county officers to accommodate such "foreign" teachers.

But while similar arrangements provide educational opportunities to certain remote neighborhoods and solve one phase of the
question of co-operation between church and state agencies, they
do not necessarily hasten the upbuilding of the public school. In
some cases, indeed, the presence in a community of a day school
under church or private auspices would seem to have a tendency
to weaken local initiative. An instance suggested is that of a certain community which through the efforts of one of its citizens had
begun to take steps toward securing an adequate public school.
Land had been bought, plans matured for a new brick school house,
and even a kiln built to burn the brick. A church board became
interested, and feeling, doubtless, that such enterprise deserved
help, offered to supply a school free of expense. Today this community, which is able financially to administer its own schools, will
neither vote money nor contribute to the support of a good public
school, although the church board has withdrawn its help. This
instance is not to be taken as typical, either in the circumstances
under which the board entered the field or in the almost complete
paralysis of local initiative. It serves, however, to illustrate the
dangers that may attend a policy based upon a real desire to help.

Much can be done in various ways by church boards working
in mountain communities to foster opinion in favor of improving
the public schools that already exist, and to hasten the time when
church day schools shall not be necessary as substitutes for them.
In illustration, an experiment may be cited which is now being tried
by a denomination whose day schools were an influence in awakening a desire for the public school. When the time seemed ripe for
the realization of this desire the church day schools were closed.
The denomination, however, at once undertook other public service
and now maintains community work at the old stations, endeavoring
through public-spirited men and women to develop still further the
self-reliant neighborhood spirit which was manifesting itself. The
different communities are kept in touch with one another and with
the outside world and their influence widened locally by a corps of
workers—physician, nurses, agricultural expert, domestic science
teacher, boy scout master, pastor, and others—all, as it were,
circuit riders of education in its broad sense, serving their own and
other neighborhoods in the way in which they are severally pre-

pared to serve them. As ambassadors of co-operation they seek to link their respective communities together for the common good, and to enlist the aid of the broader civic and educational forces of county, state, and nation.

The policy of this denomination has been to abandon its day schools when districts could support their own public schools, even when such districts protested vigorously against the abandonment; and its policy with reference to community work is to bring its many phases to self-support as early as possible.

As an outgrowth of the influence thus exerted, several districts have united in establishing a consolidated public school at one of these centers, and plans are under way by the board to meet the educational needs of those beyond school age, as well as other general needs[1] of the community for which provision had not otherwise been made.

There are still many inaccessible regions where topography and poor roads, and consequent public inability and inertia, conspire against even good one-room, one-teacher public schools, to say nothing of consolidated schools. The appeal of the children in such regions is strong. Probably for some time to come denominations new in the field, or those whose work is just beginning to be centralized, will feel this appeal strongly,[2] but there is much of practical value for the future work of denominations which still support day schools, in a careful consideration of the wider community service to which reference has just been made.

The boarding schools include 117, or more than half of the church and independent mountain schools, and enroll over two-thirds of the total 25,000 students. A criticism is sometimes heard to the effect that these schools, administered largely by people from without the mountain region, are neither desired nor necessary, the in-

---

[1] A very interesting development in self-support and self-management in mountain church and school activities is seen in the organization by another denomination of a Highland ecclesiastical district, composed of the mountainous areas of several states with authority vested in officials living within this district.

[2] There is a marked activity on the part of at least one of the leading denominations in establishing new day schools in small and remote communities where the public school of the district is difficult of access for the children, or where the school term is so short or instruction so poor that school privileges are almost negligible. To the credit of this denomination it should be said that it does not establish schools except at such isolated or inadequately equipped places.

ference being that they have intruded where they were not called for or wanted. The injustice of such a reflection is obvious, the more so because in a large majority of cases such schools were established in specified localities in response to appeals for help from the locality. So anxious have communities been for assistance that in order to secure it pledges of land, lumber, and labor have usually been made in advance. The reason for the failure of many of the schools to hold in succeeding years the enthusiasm of this initial effort are many. In places it is doubtless due to the incompetence and short-sightedness of local workers. In large part, however, the cause is that which has affected rural schools elsewhere—the failure to adapt education to life.

Most of these schools have followed very generally the type of education which existed without the mountains at the time of their establishment, and which exists too commonly today both within and without the mountains. They have been shaped under urban influences and under the preparatory requirements of college and professional life. A number do undertake, in addition to the regular academic courses, to give the girls a little domestic science and sewing, and the boys a certain kind of industrial work through their doing the necessary chores about the property. An increasing number are laying emphasis upon industrial and agricultural training and on home economics, and a few maintain more or less adequate courses in agriculture, dairying, poultry raising, wood and iron working, dress making, home nursing, and general home making. The expense and the difficulty in securing good teachers in these subjects, however, have often led to ineffective work. Moreover, such work is considered frequently more in the light of a method whereby scholarships may be earned than as a training which will fit boys and girls to live better in their home environment.

This scholarship system, it may be said in passing, if not wisely managed acts to the injury of the pupils for whom the provision is made. Scholarships are solicited by the school and usually credited to individual pupils needing help. The pupils in turn are supposed to "work out" the scholarships. Usually the number of such students is so large and the work so limited that the student does not give an equivalent in labor, and the school in its endeavor to provide for the many, increases indirectly its own expenses. One great need at present is some provision whereby promising students may earn their education without being pauperized or being taught that poor work or insufficient work receives recompense equally with work done well and thoroughly. Some schools are solving the difficulty by refusing to credit scholarships to specified individuals. A scholarship provides for one pupil, but all pupils do an equal share of work, subject to limitations of age and ability, and are credited with payment in proportion to their labor.

There is need of greater emphasis in all schools upon the various phases of work that fit for life in the mountains. The location of the school will have much to do with the subjects upon which emphasis is laid. But schools which have in mind in such work the interest not only of their students but of the region within which their students live, must demonstrate the worth of what they teach. One cannot, for example, expect the Highlander to get a great deal of practical benefit from agricultural instruction accompanied by arduous labor on a poorly managed school farm, and often farms owned and operated in connection with schools admittedly have not paid for themselves under a wasteful system of student labor or poor agricultural methods. The failure of such farms may be said to be almost complete, whether regarded from the point of view of school support, of knowledge acquired by the pupil, or as a demonstration in good farming to the community.[1] Where school farms have paid, it is usually because the school has been so fortunate as to possess good bottom land for a main crop or is itself situated in a rich valley area, rather than because of its management. The value of bottom land or valley farming, however, to the average mountain student whose farm at best will probably contain little such land, is questionable. Students need to learn what crops are adapted to the land which they themselves will be likely to own and till, and how such crops may best be raised and marketed.

In a similar way girls need to know how to prepare well the things that are available in their home neighborhoods. Unfor-

---

[1] A few schools are making every effort to improve poor land, with the object of making a demonstration through its final productiveness. Such land will not, of course, pay for a number of years.

tunately, domestic science courses in mountain schools have frequently left out of account the materials at the disposal of the average housewife or even of the school housekeeper if the school be situated in a rural community. Thus there is often a wide disparity between the demonstration work of the domestic science class and the food served at the school table, despite the fact that the preparation of some or all of the meals is usually a part of the domestic science program. Class instruction which teaches the use of foods with which boys and girls are not familiar will hardly be helpful when such foods are not used at meals served to the students, or when they are monotonous and unsavory or entirely out of reach of the average dweller in a remote neighborhood. Not only should class work teach the best use of materials at hand but especial attention should be given to a balanced and varied diet at the school table. It is in these two points that many of the schools fail, in part because of the manifold difficulties in using student labor, and in part because of lack of connection between farm or garden and home-making departments. The writer remembers, for example, seeing parsnips and oyster-plant thrown out from one school garden because, he was told, those in charge of the kitchen did not know how to prepare them, and moreover it was believed that the boys and girls would not eat them if they were served. Yet this was a school where the table was sorely in need of just the variety and elements these vegetables would furnish.

Neither can it be assumed that students will learn much of the value of cleanliness, order, and thrift when school premises, buildings, and fences are ill-kept and out of repair. Whatever else may be said of the Highlander he is a keen observer, and instances are not lacking where he has watched, listened, smiled, and gone his own way.

Another cause which has sometimes affected the influence of church schools has been an undue stress upon denominationalism. So keenly has this been felt that it has even been contended that church schools were established to further the interests of the denominations which support them. Generally speaking this is not true, although one or two boards have pursued methods which have laid them open to this charge. As a whole, the schools have been remarkably free from proselytism. The varied personnel of the faculties, however, has naturally included sometimes individuals who laid more or less emphasis upon certain denominational beliefs and practices. One prominent school, for example, has for many years required its pupils, who are quite generally of a different faith from that of the board under which the school is maintained, to learn a statement of belief usually associated with that denomination and to contribute toward the support of its missionary societies and the services held in connection with the school. The reasons assigned for this policy were that the statement of belief was a moral code which would benefit any child, and that all young people should learn to contribute out of their little to the support of the church and to the need of others. Resentment, however, has been keen among the pupils, even though the content of what they were obliged to learn did not conflict with the tenets of their own persuasion. The impression became established that the school was trying to change the native faith, an impression strengthened by the activities of the same board in the home neighborhoods of many attending the school.

In another section similar methods employed by the principal of a church school were a very potent factor in bringing about within its community the establishment of a second church school by the denomination predominant in that region. "They have provoked us to good works," said a leader of a sect strong in the Highlands concerning another sect which has done some of the best and most extensive educational work in the mountains. Unfortunately, the two denominations have provoked each other locally to work that is not good. In the case last mentioned the two church schools continued to compete with each other for some years, and as they were situated in a county-seat, in course of time they came into competition with a county high school. The first school not only had the right of precedence but large property investments and was, moreover, the better school. Both were better than the struggling public school. The situation was partially solved at length by the withdrawal of the first denomination after a futile attempt to reorganize its work, but it was not until the community was rent by factions which for many years will impede the growth of a healthy community spirit necessary to the proper support of a good public school system.

Such duplication of work is fortunately not common,[1] and where it has occurred has not for the most part been long-lived. It is usually evidence merely of misdirected zeal. In a very few instances, however, there are indications of shrewd calculation and sharp practice. Where such is the case, jealous local constituents rather than the authorities themselves are often most at fault.

Difficulties arising from denominational emphasis have naturally been fewer in the case of the independent schools, but the lack of emphasis in some of these schools upon evangelistic methods has led to a strong contention, both from within and from without the mountains, that they are not religious.

It would seem difficult to avoid falling upon one horn of the dilemma. A study of the various cases, however, suggests that the main cause of criticism arises from the failure of a school, whether church or independent, to make connection with the life of the people of the community and region within which it is situated; it is not a community school. A solution in most instances would probably come if the school were made a real part of its neighborhood, in which all people of all denominations and interests could have a share and an opportunity for self-expression. Some criticism of religious methods might be avoided by allowing pupils to attend on Sunday mornings the church of their choice. In the afternoon, at the school, vesper services might be held for which special music had been prepared and in which all of the community were invited to share. Addresses by local ministers of different denominations would tend to give to all a sense of personal participation, and at other times ministers could be invited to come in from the outside. Such a plan would meet with obstacles and would need adjustment to local conditions. But the close interrelation of school and com-

---

[1] Data gathered some years ago showed that only 22 of the 247 counties in the Highlands exclusive of Maryland and two counties in Alabama, had church schools of more than one denomination. It is probable that the number is less at this time. Only three or four communities had more than one church school, and in two cases it is known that one of these has withdrawn. In the counties having a number of church schools, but not more than one in any community, there were a few church schools near enough to one another to be regarded as competitors, but usually the roads are so poor and the country so rough as to give a separate field to each school.

munity in what should be an expression of the highest in life should if possible be secured.

The question of the relation of the boarding school to the community within which it is situated, raises the question of its relation to the public school. It may be truly said of these schools that they have, in spite of their weaknesses, been pioneers of progress in the mountains. The establishment of not a few public schools has been hastened by their presence and their activities. It is, however, also true that just as the day school has at times stood in the way of a good public school, so a good public school system which should have existed several years ago has been, and still is in some places, retarded by the presence of a church or independent boarding school. As long as there is in a community a good school which teaches the public school grades and has better teachers, better buildings, and better sanitary provisions than those of the usual public school, the need for establishing or improving the public school will not be evident to the Highlander. He is, as has been frequently observed, a good trader. He may easily argue, if this school from the outside accepts the public money for teaching the public term, that at a minimum of expense all the children are having better educational opportunities than they would otherwise secure. If the private school does not teach the public term, parents who can afford the low tuition (and they would naturally be those most interested in the maintenance of a better public school) may send their children to it. The other children will certainly be in no worse condition than before. As a result little improvement is seen in the public school situation in such communities, and instead a growing tendency is manifested toward social distinctions. If the church or independent school, truly anxious to be of most service, broaches to its patrons the question of its withdrawal and the possibility of the community assuming its own responsibilities there is an immediate and strong protest, for it is evident that such a procedure means not only higher taxes but lower efficiency, at least for some time. Moreover, the community unconsciously has come to lean upon the school even while it may find fault with some of its practices.

The question as to whether in a certain locality a specified church or independent school should continue to teach the same grades as are or should be taught in the public school, can only be determined with reference to local conditions. That there are communities which will from an economic standpoint if from no other be unable to afford adequate public schools for some years, is undoubtedly true. It would seem that church and independent schools situated in such sections should make a careful study of the natural resources and foster means whereby the economic side of life may be improved and the community lifted out of the "field of missions."

But while there is great need of emphasizing far more than in the past methods of securing a better economic life, the Highlander can generally do much more for the support of good public schools than has been supposed either by outside agencies or by himself. The truth of this has been borne out by personal experience. A church board which supported for many years a mountain school with which the writer is familiar made several efforts to transfer the responsibility of the elementary grades to the community in which it was situated. On each occasion when the question was submitted, the townspeople declared that it was impossible for them to assume the expense necessary to the transfer and declared, moreover, that should they do so the result would be a very inferior school. When at last, however, the board refused to carry the lower grades longer, the community rose to the situation and before many years had not only built a good school house but was able to afford a graded school which compared very favorably with its predecessor.

A number of similar instances might be quoted. It is possible that a close examination would show that in most cases the public schools were not entirely comparable with the church schools which preceded them. The training, however, that comes from an effort to assume responsibilities is a better preparation for citizenship than that which comes from leaving such work for outside forces to do, even when it is granted that the outside forces might in the beginning do it much better. It must be remembered, too, that great changes have taken place within the Highlands in the last ten years—changes destined to become more marked and rapid within certain areas during the coming decade. Many communities which were small and backward when the church or independent school came into their midst are now centers of populalation more or less active and flourishing. Sometimes this has been due to industrial development, but often the presence of the school has played its part in the material progress.

Of the 117 boarding schools, 33 per cent are in county-seats, 31 per cent in other growing communities whose importance has been increased by the presence of these schools, and 36 per cent in less important places or in the open country. Thus nearly two-thirds of the boarding schools are in centers in which the best public schools permitted by present circumstances should exist and from which should radiate influences to establish others elsewhere.[1] The general arguments which are advanced to justify the continuance on the present basis of these schools at strategic centers, despite the fact that their work duplicates in large part that of the existing elementary public school and the proposed high school curricula, have already been indicated in part and may be summarized as follows: The state law for establishing county high schools cannot yet be put in force in most mountain counties because adequate funds are not available. Even if sufficient money were available there would not be enough students to warrant the maintenance of a high school because so many mountain students do not receive in the elementary public schools the training requisite for entrance to a high school.

These arguments seem to be put forward by church and independent schools which maintain only elementary courses as well as by those maintaining high school courses, their object being to make sure that pupils shall be thoroughly prepared in elementary schools before entering high school. If one has in view primarily the interests of the individual pupil, and secondarily the larger community and regional needs, the arguments find some justification.

[1] Only two of the county-seats in which boarding schools are located are above the urban minimum of 2,500 population; of the others, 5 are under 2,500 inhabitants and over 1,500, 14 are under 1,500 and over 500, and 15 have less than 500 inhabitants. Of the places other than county-seats in which boarding schools are located, 1 has more than 2,500 inhabitants, 1 has less than 2,500 inhabitants and more than 1,500, 4 have less than 1,500 and more than 500, and 30 have from 500 to 150 inhabitants.

284

The mountain work of the past, however, has been based too much upon the need of the individual. It is difficult for one who has not been a mountain teacher to understand the appeal of these young people with their eager eyes and thirsty minds. The stories of the rapid progress of many of the boys and girls in spite of the limitations of early environment and poverty are worthy to rank among the accomplishments of great men of the day. But in helping the individual, sight has been lost of the community in which the individual dwelt.

It must not be assumed that those in charge of mountain schools have been consciously neglectful of community and regional needs. They provide for them theoretically on the assumption that the promising students whom they train will after graduation settle in mountain communities as leaders of their own people. Like all theories, this one has its strength and its weakness. The great weakness, as proved by practice, is that leaders so trained, with rare exceptions, do not go back to become leaders in the mountains. The fault has not been that of the church boards. Our school system has been such as to train away from the country rather than to train for leadership in the country.

It is probable that the pupils who have attended practical short courses available at a few mountain institutions have more often remained in the mountains. They have received a vision less wide, it is true, than would have been theirs had they completed the entire school course, but it is at least the vision of an ambition attainable within their home environment.

Heroism of a fine kind is needed in a student who has felt the limitations of mountain life to go back into the mountains to give his life to his people, after having had a taste of the things that he has not had before and to which his education, lacking much that is practical, gives undue emphasis. Some mountain men and women have had this heroism and have returned to be prophets without honor in their own country; others who would gladly go back have dependent upon them younger brothers and sisters who can obtain an education only through their efforts; others, in receiving their own training, have incurred debts which necessitate the seeking of remunerative positions without the mountain country.

Those who are familiar with the pioneer work done by church and independent schools of the boarding type, under the guidance of men and women devoted to the interests of the Highlands, will not fail to appreciate fully the purposes and efforts of these schools and their effect upon the lives of individuals and communities. It is our belief that hundreds, even thousands, of lives have been enriched and that the tone of many communities has been raised by their influence. Whatever their shortcomings, whether resulting from the kind of education they have supplied, from failure to meet changing conditions, or from duplicating the public school curriculum, their sole purpose has been to help the mountain student. Persons who feel that this can be done best by furthering denominational interests through denominational schools for denominational ends, or that only the church school can give the best preparation, will probably continue schools of the kind they have maintained in the past. If one may judge from experiments of this nature elsewhere, it is likely that a few will develop into denominational academies or preparatory schools for denominational colleges, but that many will disappear as good public schools become more widespread. In regard to the independent schools that duplicate public school work, they have not even such justification as denominationalism offers.

To those, however, who realize that on the one hand these two groups enroll but 25,000 pupils annually, a large percentage of whom remain but a short time in school, that the number of graduates is relatively small, and that out of this small number a certain percentage from necessity or choice leave the mountain country, and that on the other hand there were, according to the United States census for 1910, nearly 2,000,000 children of school age in the Highland country, the truth is forced home that for the mountains, as elsewhere in a democracy, free public education is a necessity.

For those in charge of church and independent schools who recognize these facts, the question resolves itself into one of ways and means of helping to bring public schools into places where they do not exist; of making them better where they do exist; of re-organizing their own educational work from time to time; and without interfering with a public school system ever growing better, of pointing the way to the realization of higher rural ideals; of helping to realize these ideals through developing a type of school which may not be possible of attainment for generations in the public school system; and perhaps of finally working toward the ideal of a better rural life through church or other community activities rather than through purely academic ones.

It should be said here that some church and independent schools are greatly helping the public school to become better by recognizing it, weak though it be, as an essential link in the educational system of the state, by not competing with it in the grades which it teaches, and by supplementing its work, but only until the public school itself is able to include these supplementary courses in its curriculum. In some communities the question of the relation of the private to the public school has been met by selling the plant for the use of the public school. Elsewhere school work has been given up or not begun as planned. In a few places where public county high schools have been established but dormitories not built, the somewhat difficult experiment of providing dormitory conveniences for the girls and establishing courses in household science has been tried as a temporary arrangement until the county can provide for these from the public fund. Another form of service undertaken by one independent school is the employment of a teacher who acts as an assistant supervisor to the county superintendent. With his co-operation she oversees a group of public schools lying within reach of the independent school, helps in organization and equipment, does demonstration teaching, and stimulates in every way possible sentiment for better public schools.

Other plants might be converted into rural social settlements to undertake neighborhood activities or to become centers of study for prospective teachers and workers in more remote schools. Such opportunity for observation and study would prevent many a mistake which might injure the school with which the innocent offender was connected officially. The methods of the social settlement of the city, working as it does with Christian, Jew, Greek, and the unchurched, would need to be adapted to mountain conditions and more of opportunity given for religious expression than is possible in the city with its varied races and sects.

Summer schools to which public school teachers might come, extension courses, the establishment of what may be called small extension stations in communities which need assistance but lie too far from the central mother school to profit directly from its activities, are some of many other ways in which the church or independent school may reach out and touch the life of the larger region outside the community in which it is situated. Such work would be planned to meet the needs of the particular community, but in every case a prominent end in view would be to foster sentiment for the maintenance of a good public school.

Another possible field of activity in which church and independent schools may aid the public schools is suggested by the lack of good teachers in the rural schools of the Highlands. A few of the boards maintain normal schools which compare favorably with state institutions. The question not unnaturally arises as to whether they might not further help to meet the emergency by providing teachers for the elementary schools through what might be called junior normal courses, adapted to meet the needs of students who have had only elementary or secondary work. In making this suggestion we do not lose sight of the fact that thoroughly equipped teachers are needed most for elementary schools, but a condition, not a theory, confronts us.

Should the church and independent schools establish supplementary training courses, something should be done in addition to counteract the strong pull which tends to draw student teachers thus prepared away from the schools in greatest need of them. Most of the church and independent schools in the mountains provide scholarships, some of which are large enough to meet from 50 to 75 per cent of the annual expenses of a fair number of pupils. It does not seem unreasonable to condition the giving of these scholarships upon service of one, two, or three years of teaching in the country schools of the mountains, with the promise of assistance in securing positions. At present the general practice is to grant unconditioned scholarships, and some schools pride themselves on having carried through their own institutions by such means certain promising students, and on having provided "a way of permanent escape from a limiting environment" by securing for them scholarships in higher institutions far away from the mountains. This practice in particular instances may be justified, but the institutions whose work will tell most for the mountains are those that work out practical ways and means for the welfare of the many, rather than those that tend to retard the general welfare by robbing the mountains of gifted or exceptional pupils.

A very admirable service, too, might be done for certain classes of pupils and for adults. Many of the older boys and girls cannot attend school except every other year, or but a short time each year, and where families are large, as is usually the case, even all of the younger ones cannot attend school regularly because their help is needed at home. The amount of schooling these pupils receive is therefore limited, and if perchance their absence is necessarily seasonal and the public school work be fairly well graded, they return to take up the same studies that they pursued the year before. One rural teacher within our knowledge, though not in the mountains, has met this situation by conducting special classes for seasonal pupils, and by an arrangement of studies suited to the need of each she enables the student eventually to complete the public school course in less time as measured by weeks, though it extends through more years than the average school course.

In the teaching of adults beyond school age, as well as the many grown pupils in the mountains who feel themselves too old to enter the lower elementary grades, may be found another fruitful though temporary field of service.

Helpful as the church schools may be in assisting the public school to become a better one of the type that prevails, their greatest service will be to find through experiment and to inspire by example a new type of school which will serve the country. This truly rural school will meet more effectively the economic needs of the Highlands, will point out the possibilities of a richer, fuller life in the country, and will impart the spirit of altruism and the training necessary to make these possibilities real. Economic betterment is absolutely essential to the development of self-supporting social, educational, and religious institutions. Church and independent schools, as well as public schools, have failed to meet this need, even when they have realized its existence. They have, however, endeavored to give the vision and have in many instances imparted a spirit of altruism, but the training necessary to make this spirit effective in the mountain country has been too generally lacking. They can, if they will, realize their dream of thoroughly equipped, altruistic, rural leaders for the mountains. The effort to make it real is, for some generations to come, the special field of service for church and independent schools.

For those who would undertake this special service there is suggestion and inspiration in the folk schools of Denmark, and in the adaptation of these schools in Norway, Sweden, and elsewhere. The vision of Bishop Grundtvig, "poet, priest, historian, reformer," of a school that would regenerate Denmark and the history of its realization are well known through many recent publications, but its application to the rural school problem of the United States, and of the Highlands in a special sense, is of such promise that a brief review of its outstanding features may well be given here.

The defeat of Denmark in 1864 in her struggle against Germany marked the lowest point in her national life. She had lost that portion of her territory which was richest, and much of that which remained was poor and in part considered even worthless. The farming population was depressed by poverty and almost in a state of serfdom. The whole country was exhausted and hopeless. The wonderful recovery of this people, the rise of the farming class to a prosperous life and a dominating share in the government, and the growth of a co-operative system which is an inspiration to the world, are all held to be in large part the result of Bishop Grundtvig's vision and its application by Christian Kold and others in the folk high schools of Denmark. The psychology underlying the folk school idea is expressed by Christopher Bruun,[1] its champion in Norway, as follows:

> Every school must find its explanation in its relation to the human life. The life of the child is characterized by beauty and joy and faith, and these should be preserved as long as possible from the care and worry that presses the race into the dust. This rule must govern the elementary school. Then there comes the transition period, the early adolescence when the boy will be anything else than a child. He wants to be manly, but he succeeds only in being mannish. He imitates men, but chiefly their faults. This period manifests an unevenness in bodily

[1] Bruun, Christopher: Folkelige Grundtanker, 208 p. Christiania, Norway, Albert Cammermeyer, 1898.

growth which produces extreme awkwardness. The features lose their childish beauty. The soul-life corresponds with the exterior. Coarseness of thought, word, and feeling, dominate. Violent likes and dislikes chase each other through his sympathies. The manly in strength and daring appeals to him. He has an inclination for manual labor, and shows considerable dexterity and ingenuity in work. He delights in physical exercise, hunting, and skating. This indicates that the boy at this time ought to use and train his body—a plain hint nature gives to educators. Least of all is he fitted for uninteresting drudgery in the school-room. He will probably leave school, and if he stays he will most likely devote his energies to mischief rather than to learning. But another life shift comes. The later adolescence begins at seventeen or eighteen. Firmness in bearing, grace in movement, curves in form take the place of their late opposites, and this is only the radiation of the inner beauty world which possesses every life whose development has not been arrested. When the plant blossoms, it gathers all the beauty it has of delicacy and color together in its corolla. Youth is this apple-blossom period of life, when the soul dwells on the fair pictures a strong imagination paints before his inward eye. It is a natural thing for every young person at this time to have at any rate some freedom from physical labor, some leisure to cast a glance at the inner world of ideas and to think over what he sees. When the young have no such freedom or have no opportunity to use it aright, it will not be easy to escape the danger of the whole life getting an impress of materialism, for youth is, par excellence, the time of poetry. It is an age of ideals when we form a picture of reality not as we have met it in our surroundings, but as we ourselves would have formed it if we could —a picture of reality as it *ought* to be. It is a time of longings, the beautiful time of the dreams of youth. And the dreams deal more than anything else with one's own future life towards which the mind, full of expectation, turns looking forward to a time when oneself in manhood's strength shall break his own way, build his own house, and forge his own future. And this life in the future the imagination paints with the finest colors each individual possesses; his life-work, his home, and the woman who shall accompany him through life. But the most important moments in youth in which the life-forces culminate are the great hours of enthusiasm when all the gathering strength of our ideals like Ganymede's eagle bears us aloft. For all, both those of the first rank and humbler ones, these hours of enthusiasm are the highest and most important hours of their youthful years. These are the moments which determine what their later human

291

life shall be, for the floods of manhood's energy seldom go beyond the high water mark of the freshets of youth's enthusiasm. What a person did not glow for in his young days, he will not easily work for as a man.

At this point I may be permitted to speak a word regarding the Common People's High School. It is intended to be a school for young people—most immediately established for young peasants. It means to offer them a place where, in the time they have free from physical labor, they can live a life of genuine youth, where they can have leisure for an inward-turned life in thought, and dream. But the chief purpose of these schools is to arrange for the young to meet the aforesaid eagle of enthusiasm sweeping past on outspread wings. To that end, we lead them to the greatest poets we know, and we present particularly those of the poets who speak most immediately to our own minds, and we try to let them speak to the young peasant lads.

Among the characteristic features of the Folk High School is its emphasis upon all that tends to stimulate idealism and patriotism —the old Danish myths and sagas, Denmark's language and literature, her geography, her accomplishment in history, and her potentialities. Much is made of song,[1] folk-song and patriotic songs in particular. Emphasis is largely on the cultural, but lessons are given in those branches of natural science which promote an understanding of agriculture in its practical aspects, as well as those which add to its dignity and significance. Gymnastic training is also given a prominent place.

As to method, the school does not underestimate the value of accurate knowledge and the development of the reasoning powers to clearness and keenness; but its purpose is nevertheless chiefly "educative." The development of the feelings and the will has for it a greater significance than that of the memory or reason. It would be for democracy what the church is for Christianity. Therefore it must emphasize the concrete, the living, the stimulating, and the hour it succeeds in addressing the sense for the higher and nobler in human life, or spurs someone on to real active work to further this higher, that hour has for the high school greater significance than the hour in which there is added a new mass of knowledge to that previously existing, or even the hour in which the reason has followed a

[1] Music and gymnastics have also a very prominent place in the elementary public school system of Denmark.

new grammatical explanation or reached a new mathematical conclusion. Learning is here for life and not for the school. That they may leave us with a desire to take part in the work of life, the spiritual not less than the temporal, and with judgment to use the means life offers, that is what we wish for our students.[1]

The school does not teach religion in dogmatic forms, nor is influence exerted to lead the student in certain religious directions. Political agitation is avoided, but effort is made to awaken judgment in political matters by teaching the constitution of the state and its chief laws, and by explaining political principles and picturing the historical struggles of society.

In the conduct of the school, books play a very subordinate part. Instruction is imparted largely by word of mouth. The teacher must inspire through the "alchemy of personality." It is a fundamental principle that all intellectual influence must be personal. Everything depends upon how education is given and this is dependent upon who gives it.

No examinations are required for admission, nor does work end with examinations. Neither is there admission certificate to any higher institution. It is held that such examinations, or any advantage gained otherwise than by increased inner worth, would destroy "the free and fertilizing communication and appropriation of knowledge, which is the basis of the power and authority of the school."

All the pupils board at the school and live as a large family during their school life with their teachers and comrades. The elevation of character and the progress made are held to be due to this practice and to the fact that those who come are physically and mentally mature, have a desire to learn, and are under the compulsion of their ideals.

The terms are two: usually a winter term of five months for young men, and a summer term of three months for young women. Strong opposition exists to lengthening the terms, as this would tend to exclude pupils of limited means and to further the idea of

[1] Extract from Sofus Rogsbro, quoted by John Robert Swenson, "Grundtvig and the Common-People's High School: Denmark's Contribution to the History of Education." Course Thesis in Education 5, February 29, 1904, University of Texas.

study for the sake of study rather than for life. At times courses are so arranged that a pupil may return on the following year to take up new work. It is not uncommon for a pupil to take courses in other folk schools in subsequent years, and those who have a desire for further study go to the Extended Popular High School at Askov on the German border, where more emphasis is given to the acquiring of knowledge and training for professions. Offsprings of these popular or folk high schools are hundreds of lecture societies throughout the country doing work somewhat similar to our own university extension movement. Every fall people from country and town assemble for several days at the various high schools to receive instruction through lectures by the principals and by others.

Several attempts have been made to combine folk school and agricultural school, or to transform folk school into agricultural school. Such experiments have not generally met with success. It has been found more satisfactory to keep the two institutions separate. Let the student get his view of life and his spiritual stimulus from the folk school, and then afterward his detailed and exact knowledge from the agricultural school or other institution.

From these folk schools permeated with cultural and religious influences have gone forth men and women who have been leaders in winning the barren heath lands of Denmark to fertility; who have made Europe the market for the dairy products of Denmark, and who have been a vital influence in making the life of this little kingdom as spiritually rich as it is economically independent.

Sir Horace Plunkett, in his investigation of the co-operative movement, examined carefully the work of the Danish folk schools and concluded that the extraordinary national progress of the Danes was due to them. He says:

A friend of mine, who was studying the Danish system of state aid to agriculture, found this to be the opinion of the Danes of all classes, and was astounded at the achievements of the associations of farmers, not only in the manufacture of butter, but in a far more difficult undertaking, the manufacture of bacon in large factories equipped with all the most modern machinery and appliances which science had devised for the production of the finished article. He at first concluded that this success in a highly technical industry by bodies of farmers, indicated a very perfect system of technical education. But he soon found another cause. As one of the leading educators and agriculturists of the country put it to him: "It's not technical instruction, it's the humanities."[1]

With few exceptions the folk schools of Denmark are privately owned, and sustained in large part by the small tuition fees received. The state is empowered, however, to aid such as especially commend themselves.

To those who have struggled to conduct a school of high grade in the mountains and have been conscious of the fact that the requirements turned away in his "apple-blossom period of life" many a mountain youth who had been forced by the "culminating of his life-forces and the gathering strength of his ideals" to seek an education, this type of school will appeal.

Many a teacher has the haunting memory of a mountain youth of eighteen or more applying for admission to school but unable to pass successfully any form of oral or written examination for entrance. If he persisted and were classified on the outcome of the test, his classmates would be children of eight or ten years of age who, living in the village, had had school opportunities from their early years. The progress of the few who persevered gave evidence of the development possible to those beginning school so late. More frequently the youth turned from the closed door discouraged or hardened, to swell before long the ranks of the voters who see no good in taxing themselves to give others education which is "no account nohow."

Before the mind of the writer rises the face of a youth of twenty, who stood before him years ago when he was principal of a little academy in the mountains.

"Can you read, Jim?"

"No, sir."

And there followed the usual farce of a required examination in order to know where the boy was to be placed. He should have gone into the second grade, but by a stretch of conscience the principal

---

[1] Plunkett, Sir Horace: Ireland in the New Century, p. 131. New York, E. P. Dutton & Co., 1904.

put him among the children of the third, where his six feet towered strangely above the little heads.

Troubled in mind, the principal turned to the young man.

"You will have to do your reciting with that grade, Jim," he said, "but you may sit in my room."

There was a pause, and then the eyes met his squarely.

"I reckon, Professor, I'll sit where I belong."

Jim stood the test, and by reason of his maturity advanced quickly through several grades. The pity was not in the situation he was forced to face nor in any failure of his to meet the standards of the school, but that for all his effort he got so little of what he needed. Years of night work and summer work found him struggling on in a vain race between health and knowledge. He would not borrow money, and the principal could find few ways to ease his path. The last the writer knew of Jim, when he himself was leaving the little town, the boy, a man then of twenty-five or six, had been earning money for the coming term by acting as motorman during the day in the nearest urban center, and from midnight to morning as watchman for a big building. Between times he ate, slept, and attended night school. He was very thin, and looked years beyond his age, but he was still moving on, though more slowly now, in the losing race.

The needless cruelty of this struggle stands out in sharp relief against the possibilities which would have been open through a folk school. In such a school, adapted to mountain conditions, Jim might have gained in a few terms something of the larger culture to which he aspired and which he could never hope to attain under the present system. He would have mingled with those of his age, not alone in study but in healthful exercise and recreation. There would furthermore have been open to him practical means whereby he could exercise in life in his own environment the faculties he had gained. In such a school the beauty of the Highland country, its part in the pioneer life of the nation and the great advance to the Far West, its native culture, which has been too much ignored, and its folk-song in particular, would all be given expression.

It may be contended that, though such an educational ideal be desirable for the mountains, there are practical objections arising from lack of money. The annual budget of the church and independent schools is over $600,000; the property investment nearly $4,000,000. One denomination alone has during the past score of years spent in a limited mountain area over $2,000,000. It would be far better for the ultimate good of the many in the mountains if a number of the church boards would dispose of their property holdings, especially those in county-seats, or give them to the public school authorities and concentrate upon a few of their boarding schools best located rurally for development on folk school lines. The influence of a few institutions of the kind described would, we believe, be far greater and more extensive than that of a larger number of such schools as are maintained at present.

It is not to be expected that a foreign institution could be transplanted without change to the mountains; there would need to be a readjustment to conform to generally accepted American ideals and to meet the special needs of the particular environment in which the school was established. Such readjustment would be less experimental in character if picked men and women, long acquainted with the mountain field, should be given opportunity to study the folk schools in countries where they now exist, and then be placed over selected schools to direct their work in the light of their past experience and recent study.

Furthermore, to insure success the organizations or trustees under whose auspices this new work is undertaken must give assurance of full support—a support that provides adequate funds for the school and sufficiently large salaries for the workers to enable them to satisfy their legitimate official and personal needs.

The most serious mistakes that have been made in school as well as in agricultural work—the fundamental occupation in the Highlands—have arisen from the assumption that what was good for the city school, or the school in the Lowland rural sections, or for agriculture elsewhere, was without change good for the Highlands. Transplanting exotics that die and exterminating the indigenous would eventually leave even a land of promise—as is the mountain country—a barren waste.

The folk schools, with their extension systems, might be adapted readily to meet the changing and varied needs of this land. In such a pioneer educational movement for the mountains the church and independent schools are better able to take the lead than are public agencies, because the latter require the support of an awakened and progressive public opinion before they feel justified in expending public funds. The difficulties of finding persons possessing the proper spirit and personality to conduct folk schools, and of training and sustaining such persons, are not underestimated; nevertheless, such workers can be found and they can be trained.

It is just here, in the solving of the problem of a richer rural life, that the church and independent schools have a unique opportunity to influence for generations to come the life of the mountain people, and thus to find their own highest service.

CHAPTER XIII

AVENUES FOR CONTACT AND PROGRESS

A MOUNTAIN realm rich in forests, streams, mines, and soil awaits development. A mountain population with latent possibilities awaits opportunity that it may share in this development and in what it may bring. That commercialism on the one hand, and individualism on the other, may not war further against the welfare of the Highlander, equal foresight and intelligence must characterize the efforts of all agencies working in his behalf.

What is to be done with this people? What is to be done for them? These two forms of inquiry, put by many who seek to help in the solution of mountain problems, are indicative not only of perplexity but of certain attitudes of mind. Those who employ the first form appear to regard the mountain people either as social encumbrances or material to be cast into whatever place they may fill or fit, or into which they may be packed or fitted. The second group of questioners, actuated by the highest motives, seem to feel a responsibility of kinship to all in need. Some of the efforts they have made to answer their question have resulted in great good. Not a few of this class, however, are inclined to believe that a benevolent overlordship, at times a philanthropic despotism by some board or organization, is the only guarantee of success.

The social salvation of the mountains will not be won by putting its people forward as pawns to advance others, nor by using them as filling to make the highway of progress smoother, nor will compulsion from without, however benevolent, ever be a substitute for self-direction under the impulse of ideals voluntarily accepted.

In the desire to give a clear and definite answer to the question as to what can be done to awaken this impulse where it does not exist, and to indicate ways and means to give it expression, the tempting lure of dogmatism presents itself. Certain kinds of work have proved of great local benefit, and their extension to all mountain communities would seem to offer a ready solution of the problem. Communities, however, differ as do people, and the needs of the mountaineer are as diverse and as numerous as the needs of humanity. No one nor any definite number of methods will meet them all. Insistence by rural workers upon specific measures is no less irritating and obstructive than complacency or bigotry in matters of religion.

This much may be said at the beginning: whatever the place, whatever the method, the people themselves must first be considered. While they differ one from another as do members of other groups, there are certain general characteristics that need to be kept in mind if unnecessary misunderstandings and mistakes are to be avoided.

The mountaineer is extremely sensitive and independent. He is not a person to be pushed where he does not wish to go, nor is he submissively responsive to a shaping process. Although often appreciative of efforts made for his good by those who have won his regard, he is yet somewhat distrustful of innovations or of new people trying old methods. Furthermore, he is not altogether an easy person with whom to work, for his individualism leads him to disregard the thoughts and plans of others and to consult only his own wishes, which today may differ widely from those of yesterday. His sensitiveness renders it very difficult for his best friends to make public any statement regarding him, even by way of clearing up misrepresentations or to suggest measures of promise for his country and his people. Those who have his confidence may guide him and may tell him his shortcomings face to face, but frequently he turns upon the leaders whom he has followed because they have set forth his need to the public. Many an attempt for community betterment in the mountains has failed because those who planned it have not duly regarded this sensitiveness. There is, however, more of hope for people who feel thus than for such as are ready to be exploited and willing to be held up, or to hold themselves up, as cheerful recipients of "missionary effort."

The wisest plans for betterment are those that take the people themselves into account as contributors to their own welfare. Preliminary steps must often be taken by others, and perhaps for a long time co-operative efforts will need to be furthered; but the ultimate aim must be to enable the individual to so shape his life as to make him a contributor to, as well as a sharer in, the benefits of the general social welfare. In all measures designed to bring about this end the initiative and co-operation of the mountaineer should from the beginning be invited and welcomed.

If the largest success is to attend efforts in behalf of particular peoples within a specified section, the feelings of that section as a whole cannot be ignored or passed by without fair consideration. It is not our purpose to call into question the growing belief that the peoples of the different sections that make up our common country are coming to understand one another better. Certain indirect influences, however, arising from sectional misunderstandings and the mistakes growing out of them, have affected work done by denominational and independent boards in the mountains.

These influences emanated on the one hand from a feeling that Northerners who were contributing to the support of work for certain peoples in the South were lacking in sympathy toward Southerners whose knowledge and leadership are essential to the solution of Southern problems. In addition it was felt, often, that these charitably disposed outsiders conceived the way of betterment to lie in fashioning the section where work was done into the likeness of their own section, because they felt the latter had more to contribute in the way of ideals. It was also claimed, often justly, that pleas made in the North for the support of such work were based upon past differences between North and South, in the presentation of which the peculiar geographical conditions of the two sections and consequent economic, political, and social differences were little touched upon.

On the other hand, many Northerners held that this resentment was often unwarranted and generally unjust, and that there was in the South a lack of proper appreciation of the genuine interest which prompted thousands to deny themselves in order to give a little toward the generous total donated for educational purposes. It was furthermore alleged that there was a failure to perceive that the needs of each part of the country must be the concern of all, if the right kind of national life is to be developed.

Many of the misunderstandings were no doubt inevitable. The

mass of people in the respective sections knew one another only through the observations of others. If these observations chanced to be superficial—conditions being measured merely by the tradition and customs of the observer's home neighborhood rather than interpreted in the best spirit of the section itself—false impressions would be disseminated widely, particularly if the critic were of sufficient prominence to shape public opinion in his own part of the country.

Despite many of the retarding influences which had their beginnings in misunderstandings, one cannot but wonder whether their effects would not have been felt less had there been a more sparing use of the word "missions." After all, there is much in a name. The mountaineer resents this term as applied to him. He feels he is being classed with the heathen.

Localities and sections respond as do individuals when pride is wounded. Regions ready to respond to the call of need elsewhere are loath to believe that there may be a somewhat similar need in their own remote rural townships. They resent such a suggestion in terms no less emphatic than those used by the mountaineer. Doubtless many dwellers in the metropolis of America would deny that among the hills and mountains lying less than twoscore miles from its center exist conditions that rival the extreme conditions in the Southern Highlands. Other localities could also be pointed out where similar conditions obtain. In the Southern Highlands the problems are only larger in extent and more intense. If churches would recognize the fact that these problems are rural, and would place mountain work under general social service and rural departments instead of under mission boards, larger and better results would follow. If this is impossible a softening of the emphasis upon the word "mission," where it cannot be removed from the names of church boards, is worthy of careful consideration by those who desire to have the work done, and only to the glory of the Inspirer of all good work.

If one may judge from questions asked, numbers of people wonder why measures for betterment cannot be best secured through state legislation. Those who make the inquiry seem to have lost sight of certain facts and not to have followed the development of beneficent state activities elsewhere. New and great changes are taking place within the South which are taxing her energies and demanding her attention. Only one who has lived in this part of the country can appreciate the remarkable progress that has taken place during the last twenty-five years. It should be remembered, however, that in states which since the time of their organization have never borne the strife of warring armies, most of the corrective and preventive agencies, now a part of the state machinery, were first inspired by the success of private enterprises along these lines. Only after public opinion had awakened to the need of making such benefits general and free to all, did the state assume these activities, even such states as were abundantly able financially to maintain them.

It would be expecting too much to look for immediate remedies through special legislation for the mountains. It has already been seen that the upland areas of the South are largely a country within a country, and that the mountaineer's political allegiance often differs from that of the Lowlander. In the Lowland South a number of prominent educational, agricultural, industrial, and political leaders have affirmed that they have not been able as yet to secure the necessary legislation and appropriations for the promotion of the interests of the section where most of their constituents live. Before much can be done for the remote mountains, measures immediately applicable to the Lowlands and Valley will probably receive consideration. Such a course is in the natural order of things.

The attitude of some of the Lowlanders toward the mountain people may be set forth in the statement of a prominent leader in welfare work for a Lowland group which would correspond, somewhat, to our third group of Highlanders. "We know," said he, "that there are mountain problems needing solution, but we are a people of sentiment. In the past the mountaineer has differed from us on important questions, and in this state the mountains were the retreat of the bushwhacker and the traitor. Our resources and our strength are limited, and as we cannot yet care for all, we care first for the children of those whose fathers with our fathers shouldered the musket and suffered and died for what they believed to be right." There was no bitterness of feeling expressed, no resentment for what had been done for the mountaineer, no implied wish that efforts should not be made on his behalf, but a very natural and straightforward statement of a universal truth that people first take care of their own.

Some of the mountain areas have possessed, it is true, enough political influence to be of importance, and certain counties are among the wealthiest in their states. As yet, however, too many so-called "pauper counties" pay into the state tax fund less than is required to carry on the necessary activities in the county to permit an aggressive political movement from within the region for its own betterment. Moreover, if legislative measures be furthered for the welfare of the entire state, they would very likely be of a kind little suited to the immediate and special needs of the mountains, unless legislators should be far-sighted enough to allow for variation in a general method based on the need of the majority.

There are people in the mountains who see the needs. There is also in the Lowland South a rapidly increasing number of thoughtful men and women who know that the different peoples of the South cannot rise or fall alone, but that all must rise or fall together. Fortunately, too, many of the social workers in the South, who are not native to it but are striving earnestly for its welfare, are coming to understand that no attempt to improve conditions has in it much promise of ultimate success that fails to enlist the co-operation of these mountain and Lowland leaders.

In the working together of all these forces for betterment there should be on the one hand evidence of sympathy for the South in its struggle for right adjustment, and on the other the recognition that many of its problems, while in a sense special and sectional, are national in effect and call for the best thought of the nation in their solution. All people of a country are responsible to a degree for the difficulties in any section, and for their removal, though leadership in their solution falls naturally upon those nearest to the problems.

The movement that would have in it the greatest promise of success for the Highlands would be part of a national rural movement to improve country life throughout the nation, and having, perhaps, as its guiding force, a rural life commission or bureau under whose leadership all state and private activities could co-operate in studying conditions and in setting in motion corrective measures.

The recently organized American Country Life Association[1] offers a possible beginning within which may develop a nucleus of leaders who can advise and stimulate and perhaps in time direct definite experiments in rural work along lines that seem promising. The fact that life in the Highlands is so generally rural and so little complicated by differences in race and religion, would make this field peculiarly fitted for experiment, and difficult enough, because of topographical conditions, to test any effort made.

There are many national, state, church, and philanthropic agencies that ultimately will be co-ordinated in a general movement of the kind indicated, and which even now are intended to benefit the whole country. The attention of the executive officers of such organizations should be directed to the Highlands, and the attention of leaders within the field should be called to these agencies. Connection is often all that is needed, and once established would give assurance of ultimate success. Remedial efforts would then be heartily welcomed, as they would not be were they advertised as specifics for the peculiar ailments of a "peculiar people." To make the remote mountain sections of each state more vital parts of the state and of the nation is the task that confronts all who have the interests of the Highlands at heart.

Education in the fullest meaning of the term is the solution. Eventually, the right kind of public school will fit the people of the future for better citizenship, but the people of today and tomorrow, who have not been through any kind of school and therefore do not properly value education, must be taught that there is need for good schools with trained teachers and with adequate administration and supervision—and that the only fitting way to secure them is through local taxation.

The right kind of a public school for the mountains is not a thing of the immediate future. The difficulties in the way are many, not the least being the lack of sufficient examples in other rural regions. Agencies now at work, however, will ultimately devise a system of public training that will provide for the needs of the state and will allow, also, for the variations and special instruction demanded

[1] Organized January, 1919, Baltimore, Maryland.

by the needs of different localities and individuals. It is not too much to hope that in the mountain country, as in rural sections elsewhere, elementary schools will instruct in the fundamentals necessary for citizenship, that high schools will prepare for still higher institutions which themselves will be adapted to modern needs; and that supplementary or continuation schools will train for his life work not only the youth unable or unwilling to enter the high school or university but the man already at work. The emphasis in such continuation schools would naturally be upon training for the prevailing industry of its particular region. It would be expected that in the border belt of the mountains and Piedmont Plateau occupied by the cotton mills, textile schools would be part of the system. In them teachers, mill operatives, and mill officials, as well as the public, would be interested to work together not alone for a better product of the loom but for a better manhood and womanhood in the producer. In other regions to which the forests have drawn the lumber interests and wood-working factories, training would be given suitable to the development of these industries, while in the coal and iron sections instruction would be offered in mining, metallurgy, and similar subjects. In all of these schools the natural sciences, agriculture, and allied studies would be taught. A way will be found to so teach all of these subjects and to so train for life, as not to leave the impression upon the mind of the pupil that he is one of an inferior class working with his hands for the benefit of a leisure or professional class. This better way will inspire the pupil and awaken in him a love for his work by showing that it has a place not only in the economy of the world but in its esthetic and spiritual life; that his task is God-given, and if well done is of service not alone to his brother man but to his Creator.

The bane of the present public school system is that it gives to the mountain youth, as well as to many another country boy, the impression that work with the hands is an inferior kind of work and therefore degrading; that the lawyer, the teacher, the doctor, and the minister are, by their callings, superior social beings. With such an impression, he seeks too often to avoid manual labor and to live by his wits, content to be a pettifogging lawyer, a quack doctor, a poor teacher, or a ministered-unto minister rather than a first-class artisan.

In educating the people of the remote Highlands to a desire for a good system of free schools, civic improvement, better health, social and economic conditions, and for a catholic spirit in matters of religion, outside agencies may for many years exert a wide influence. No general statement is possible as to which lines of activity will be best to promote. Certain measures would seem necessary in all communities, but as a rule plans must be determined in view of local conditions.

As a basis for estimating the value of certain kinds of work in relation to general conditions prevailing within designated areas, and for disclosing possibilities and points of contact for cooperation, surveys will be found useful. The mountain field should be studied at close range, regional and local differences taken into consideration, the views and findings of individual investigators corrected and checked by the views and findings of others, and publicity given to the results.

Already numbers of individuals and some organizations have undertaken studies of particular counties or communities. The value of data gleaned in this way would be greatly increased were there preliminary conference with those experienced in surveys, in order to determine the principal lines of investigation and to bring about uniformity in details so that a comparison of findings may be possible. It is questionable whether in matters of health, soil possibilities, and other such subjects of inquiry which call for scientific training in the investigator, data gathered by men not thus trained will be of value. Where earlier investigations have already been made by experts, these data could of course be secured by later investigators not scientifically trained. The United States Bureau of Soils has, for example, made a number of soil surveys covering certain mountain districts and counties, and the United States census also gives much helpful information. Material of great value may likewise be found in county and state records.

The most promising attempt known to the writer to gather and publish facts concerning conditions in certain counties, is that of the Georgia Club and other state clubs which have followed its plan. The Georgia Club was an outgrowth of the ideals and enthusiasm of Dr. E. C. Branson, former president of the State Normal School at Athens, Georgia. From faculty meetings assembled to consider economic and social questions pertaining to school life the club was enlarged to include students, and a program was outlined whereby a careful study was to be made, county by county, of the entire state. Members of the club surveyed their home counties, securing information on resources and general conditions; and the findings, with conclusions, were made public through the local papers, in order that people might become familiar with the possibilities and deficiencies of their home environment and be able to work toward better conditions.

As an example of the scope of such clubs we quote some of the subjects studied during 1917 and 1918 by the North Carolina Club, organized at the State University of North Carolina, where Dr. Branson is now Professor of Rural Economics and Sociology. Under the main topic for the year—the County in North Carolina—special attention was given to the history of the county government system, taxes, fee and salary system, finances, supervision of rural schools, county health work, public health work, county high schools, farm demonstration work, poor relief, the care of children, and other phases of county welfare. Addresses upon these subjects were published in the yearbook of the university.

The making public of disagreeable facts is at best a delicate task and is attended with grave risks to the constructive efforts of those making the investigation. This is the more true if such investigators and organizations are not native. It is too much to hope that future publicity will not be met with resentment, but a growing consciousness is evidenced in both Highlands and Lowlands that facts, however hard, must be acknowledged before remedial undertakings can be begun. If surveys of home counties could be made by mountain students in institutions of higher learning, it would seem that some offense might be avoided and a more genuine desire aroused among the people themselves to improve conditions.

Various lines of effort possible for outside agencies have already been discussed in previous chapters. In general it may be said that church and independent boards in their educational work should concentrate rather than diffuse their efforts. Schools which would best serve the interest of a particular community or of the mountain country as a whole, must cease to compete with the public school system by refusing to take public funds and to teach grades taught in the public school. Some should be closed entirely. Others, while willing to supplement public school work for a time in certain localities and under certain conditions, should as rapidly as possible transfer their activities into lines of work which for some years cannot be a part of the public school system or be carried on through state or county agencies; such, for example, as courses in rural sociology, dietetics, and home making; kindergarten classes, music, physical training, and the furnishing of recreational activities; agricultural experiment, demonstration, and extension work; forestry; public health work; the encouragement of co-operative enterprises of different kinds, such as dairying, stores, buying, selling, borrowing, and banking. We might prolong much further the list of methods and movements intended to better living conditions in community and section.[1] Which of them will be most helpful to a given community and how they can be initiated most successfully will depend upon the needs and the resources of the community and region under consideration and upon the temper and character of the people who live there. The institution or agency which wishes to adapt its work to local needs must take into account all these factors. Certain lines of effort which are feasible in one locality will not be desirable in another for various reasons, and in all cases the right kind of leadership is more important than specified courses or methods.

[1] In a population with so large a percentage of illiteracy, the use of stereopticon and motion pictures might be greatly extended to give stimulus to all helpful influences and agencies. A minister serving a mountain field of considerable extent, recently used a motion picture machine on a circuit which included a number of community centers to bring a crowd together and secure pledges for the Red Cross and for various enterprises of general benefit to the community. Films of travel, industry, comedy, and war were shown with marked success, even though regarded only from the point of view of pledges secured. It was felt, moreover, that the effect upon the community was wholesome, as evidenced by the hearty laughter of the children and the new topics of conversation afforded the older people.

The machine used had attachments either for direct or indirect lighting. Where there were electric lights the plug was inserted in a socket; where there were no electric lights a current had to be supplied. Storage batteries did not prove satisfactory, but fortunately the main road through the county had been improved and was passable for automobiles a good part of the year. With the acquisition of a Ford the lecturer was able to generate electricity by jacking up the hind wheels, starting the engine, taking the current from the headlights and running it to the lamp house of the picture machine. The sheet he tacked on walls of school houses, churches, and even on the outside of bunk houses at logging camps. The machine was set on anything available—boxes, oil barrels, blocks of wood, organs, and tables.

Deserving of particular study and attention by agencies which wish to adapt their educational work more closely to the needs of the mountain country, is the Danish folk high school. There are, too, in certain foreign countries, a number of interesting movements for carrying instruction in household and farm management to outlying homes and farms, which through study and adaptation have promise for the mountains.

Until national or state government provides for a corps of experts in rural education, subject to the call of rural workers needing advice, some plants now run as schools might be used as centers to which those who wished to become informed on mountain conditions might go for study. The great danger in calling in outside experts is that their experience, gained in a different environment, prompts them to suggest methods and measures impracticable and often impossible in the average mountain home or on the mountain farm. In a center such as suggested, advice and assistance could be obtained from resident experts who had actually tried out locally many of the measures they would advocate.

With this center might co-operate national organizations for the promotion of public health, state boards of health, departments of agriculture and education of state and nation, and other scientific and philanthropic agencies. Assurance of such co-operation and even definite examples of co-operation with individual schools have already been given by state, government, and national agencies. Here, too, might assemble at certain seasons of the year the teachers of the public schools of the mountains to be themselves taught by teachers of rural subjects from Southern teachers' training schools, who through special provisions would form as it were a peripatetic faculty.

Such a center or settlement, financed in part by an inter-denominational group, in part perhaps by national and private organizations which were endeavoring to meet the rural side of their particular problem, and supplemented possibly by contributions from philanthropic boards, may seem the vision of the dreamer, but is, we believe, possible of realization.

For the improvement of health conditions in the mountains, the work directed by one of the national associations for the promotion of public health would seem most promising. Especially useful would be a "pioneer" public health nursing corps co-operating with state and local agencies; the building of rural hospitals in needy centers where local physicians are competent; and the bringing in of experts and specialists for clinics, lectures, and health propaganda of various kinds. Movements of this sort would not arouse hostility as would a definite campaign to place better physicians in the mountains, supported from without, in competition with the native physicians depending upon local fees.

Better health requires better food, better cooked. This means greater variety in what is raised and better methods of raising it, better stock better cared for, as well as innumerable other accessories of wholesome life, many of which depend upon the soil, the desire to till it, and better methods of tillage.

It was shown in the chapter on Resources that large areas of the mountains are suited to agriculture. There is, too, a quite general desire to till the soil. A connection with the country which has been lost elsewhere and which many are seeking personally to re-establish, has never been severed entirely. The old plantation system of the South and the rural character of its life have tended to preserve the idea of "the country gentleman"—a worthy idea not yet eradicated by an extended public school system whose influences tend cityward. The lawyer, the doctor, and other professional men have in many instances not yet been won away from the soil, but keep in touch with it through residence on or ownership of farms worked under their general oversight. The word "farmer," which in some other regions carries with it a certain suggestion of inferiority, in the South retains its dignity. This holds true in Highlands as well as in Lowlands, and the repugnance that many elsewhere who most need help feel toward country life need not here be overcome.

Students who have been forced from the mountains to the city by overcrowding on the soil or by the compulsion of urban ideas stimulated by their academic training, have professed a preference for the farm if a better living might be made there. This desire in the hearts of many of the best mountain youth would seem to indicate that suitable methods of agriculture and marketing and provisions for acquiring land on easy terms would bring about a great increase in farming in the Highlands.

In the South, if anywhere, agricultural schools should succeed. It is true, however, that although a wide desire for land ownership exists, the need of better training to develop the possibilities of the soil is not so generally accepted as it should be. The feeling exists that agricultural schools are schools for the sons of farmers—schools in which they may get what the sons of other men get elsewhere. Often, therefore, students attending such institutions elect the purely academic studies. The tendency now evidenced in a very few of our agricultural schools to emphasize the cultural through the agricultural rather than through disassociated courses, should be encouraged. If the impression be given that an agricultural school is merely to train students to raise produce for the consumption of social classes too much occupied in the pursuit or promotion of finer things to engage actively in the production of the material essentials of life, agriculture will not call a high type of man. Here, as everywhere, men must find the better things of life in and through the work they do to live.

As yet, agricultural schools are not numerous enough in the mountains to permit a just criticism of their work. In a few state institutions visited, that have in the personnel of the faculty the promise of success, meager equipment wars against growth. In others the effects of the palsying touch of politics are seen. The false idea, too prevalent, that the quality of a school is determined by numbers—that a large school is a good school, and only large ones are good—has sometimes led to the selection of leaders because of their popularity in order to draw students and thus swell local pride. The name "agricultural and mechanical," so commonly applied to such schools, prompts the query as to whether the call of the industrial world has not forced the emphasis to be placed upon the mechanical work of these schools at the cost of the agricultural.

Some of the state universities in their agricultural colleges, especially in their agricultural extension departments, are doing a work of wide usefulness; and though their efforts are restricted by lack of funds, they have outlined a program which eventually will aid greatly in solving the agricultural problem of the Highlands. Particularly promising is the co-operative extension work in agriculture and home economics now carried on in the different states by federal and state departments of agriculture, boards of education, state universities in their colleges of agriculture, and various other agencies.

In this connection reference should be made to the county agricultural agent, supported in part by federal and state funds under the Smith-Lever Act, and in part by county appropriations. Such an agent, with expert training in agriculture, having an office in a county-seat or other influential center where he can be found at stated times, and holding himself ready at other times to go with farmers to examine soils, to give advice as to seed, stock, and marketing, and furthering movements for better roads and innumerable other useful projects, would be invaluable in remote mountain sections. Most helpful, too, would be the farm bureau movement to form associations of farmers built primarily about the county agent, and now so strong in parts of the country as to be amalgamated into state bureaus, and recently into the American Farm Bureau Association.

It must be remembered, however, that both county agents and county farm bureau associations presuppose either that the interest in the county toward improving agriculture is sufficient to warrant an appropriation of funds for that purpose, or that the county is already producing crops of importance for market. Through a large part of the remote rural areas neither of these suppositions is true. There is therefore still need for the help and co-operation of outside agencies in promoting the agricultural development of the mountains.

Some of the best church and independent schools teaching agriculture are in the Greater Appalachian Valley or other valley areas. They are valuable in training for rural life on soil and in surroundings similar to those where the instruction is given. They should be encouraged in every way, for they contribute greatly to rural life as a whole even though the students do not return to the mountains proper.

The agricultural instruction, however, needed for the Highlands is such as suits training and tools to the varied mountain topography and soil. Elevation, slope, and other conditions must be reckoned with if success is to be won. It is important, therefore, that if agricultural schools be established by church and independent boards, they be distributed on a regional basis, or provision be made whereby the central school may have outlying stations regionally distributed where instruction suited to location may be given at stated times. Schools that take the mountain youth from his home environment, however well they may train him, do not help to solve the problems of the mountains unless they send him back equipped with a training that will enable him to make use of the resources of his home locality.

In the various courses for the farm youth, and in courses in the many household, dairy, and farm activities in which women have a large part and for which provision should be made likewise, instruction should aim to show the best thing to do under existing circumstances, the best way to do it, and the changes necessary to bring about better conditions. The nearer instruction is brought to the different localities, communities, and homes, the better.

With a discussion of methods for the developing of agriculture, the matter of farm tenancy needs also to be considered. The Highlands in the past have been regarded as a good "poor man's country" because of the low price of land which permitted ownership by purchase; but tenancy is increasing. Figures are not available to show the extent of increase, but it is known that in certain areas of the mountains it is growing. In approximately one-half of the counties of the mountain region more than 30 per cent, and in some counties more than one-half of the white farmers are tenants.[1] Among the tenants some are shiftless, but others should not be so classed. The latter need only assistance to place them where they belong—among freeholders.

A few owners of large tracts of mountain land feel their responsibility for the native population of their estates. The women have been taught better ways of weaving, lace making, and similar home industries. Instruction in dairying, better stock, examples in road building and forestry have been helpful to men and women alike. Schooling is provided for the children. It is quite generally true, however, that these benefits are enjoyed only by tenants or employes.

If what might be termed a family unit school could be begun on one of these large estates, in which the tenant farmer and his sons

[1] United States census for 1910, Vols. VI and VII.

314

could be given agricultural training, his wife and daughters instruction in home keeping, fireside industries, dairying, household nursing, care of children, and so forth, and the children taught in a school adapted to rural needs, a good beginning in corrective measures would be made. In such a school the owners of large estates, the federal and state departments of agriculture, state boards of health, nurses' associations, and associations for the betterment of health and the eradication of disease, as well as the educational forces of the state, might unite. It would seem that some of the expense necessary for such an undertaking could be met by the tenants through increased yields from the farms, a third or half of which is usually the tenant rate of rental.

If hope of ownership of the land he tilled, or of other land upon which he was placed after being trained, and the prospect of paying for this upon equitable terms could be held out with a guarantee of his ownership, despondency in the tenant would give way to hope. Some method looking to the increase of the number of small landholders is worthy of careful experimentation.

How co-operative societies in Denmark and Ireland have freed a population from debt and general agricultural depression has already been discussed in the chapter on Resources. It would, however, be unfair to leave this subject without reference to the wider effects and possibilities of co-operative undertakings. In Denmark, for example, we find that as a result of the co-operative development, which can hardly be dealt with here apart from the educational system, the rural people have become the potential factor in the politics of the nation. In Ireland, too, the co-operative movement is acting, slowly but steadily, to give to a farming population growing in intelligence the power of directing the destinies of that country. Especially interesting is the organization of the United Irishwomen, a co-operative society which plans to do for the women what the Irish Agricultural Organization Society does for the men, and which lays special emphasis upon enlarging the social life of the community without which, as Sir Horace Plunkett says, "all but the dullards will fly to town."

Great indeed as are the possibilities in co-operation of improving the material life of the country, the aims of this movement are far beyond mere economic well-being. May we quote once more from

Mr. Russell[1] who, better than anyone else, describes the scope of the co-operative ideal:

> I would like to exile the man who would set limits to what we can do, who would take the crown and sceptre from the human will and say, marking out some petty enterprise as the limit: "Thus far can we go and no farther, and here shall our life be stayed." Therefore I hate to hear of stagnant societies who think because they have made butter well they have crowned their parochial generation with a halo of glory and they can rest content with the fame of it all, listening to the whirr of the steam separators and pouching in peace of mind the extra penny a gallon for their milk. And I dislike the little groups who meet a couple of times a year and call themselves co-operators because they have got their fertilisers more cheaply and have done nothing else. Why, the village gombeen man has done more than that! He has at least brought most of the necessaries of life there by his activities; and I say, if we co-operators do not aim at doing more than the Irish Scribes and Pharisees we shall have little to be proud of. A poet interpreting the words of Christ to His followers who had scorned the followers of the old order made Him say:
>
> > "Scorn ye their hopes, their tears, their inward prayers?
> > I say unto you, see that your souls live
> > A deeper life than theirs."
>
> The co-operative movement is delivering over the shaping of the rural life of Ireland, and the building up of its rural civilisation, into the hands of Irish farmers. The old order of things has left Ireland unlovely. But if we do not passionately strive to build it better, better for the men, for the women, for the children, of what worth are we?

That co-operative societies are not impossible in the mountains despite the Highlander's individualism, has already been demonstrated by the success of the cheese factories previously cited and by isolated instances of co-operative canning, buying and selling, personal credit societies, and so forth. These movements merely need initiation in local centers and a little wise fostering to prove their immense value as agents in neighborhood well-being, not only material but social and moral.

[1] Russell, George W.: "Ideals of the New Rural Society," in The United Irishwomen, their Place, Work, and Ideals, by Horace Plunkett, Ellice Pilkington, and George W. Russell ("A. E."), p. 39–40. Dublin, Maunsel and Co., Ltd., 1911.

The writer has in mind a certain co-operative store, started through the efforts of a worker in a remote community, which paid 5 per cent dividends on the amount of purchases in addition to the 4 per cent interest on investment the first year. The second year business was doubled, and plans are now under way for a new building and increased stock. When one realizes that the mountain store is the gathering place of the neighborhood and in a sense the arbiter as well as the reflector of its standards, he will realize that the effects on the community of a clean building in which a more generous variety of stock than is customary is offered, in which order and a strict business integrity are preserved, and in which all the community has a real interest, cannot be measured in dollars and cents. Among the results most apparent have been the variety introduced into the diet of the community, improvement in dress, increasing demand for higher classes of goods, more careful management of other business enterprises, and a growing co-operative spirit. It is the hope of those who are the guiding spirits of the enterprise that this co-operative store may gradually become the center of a healthful social community life.

When we remember the small beginnings of the Templecrone society, described in a previous chapter, undertakings such as the above seem fraught with large promise for the mountain country.

Matters of church cannot be dealt with so directly without great risk. A sympathetic spirit toward all churches and workers seeking to impart a deeper knowledge of things spiritual is essential. If some have a wide vision and others narrowness of view resulting from limiting circumstances, it is incumbent upon those with the wider vision to exercise a broader charity. Men and women with this larger spirit, sent to minister through the foreign and native churches and schools of the mountains, will serve as beacons to dispel any darkness that may exist. The Highlander like other men "must needs love the highest when he sees it." He has the power of vision, but he needs more beacons to illumine his way.

Although the field is so large and inaccessible as to make overlapping of effort in school work rare, and in church work not general, there is already enough of overlapping—and a possibility of more as the field opens—to call for a consideration of questions of federation and division of territory. Such matters must be left to the organizations best able to deal with them and least affected by local influences; namely, the Federal Council of the Churches of Christ in America, religious foundations, and other bodies whose object it is to promote federation, union, and comity among denominations. Representatives of such bodies, speaking at mountain conferences and meeting leading men of the various churches already at work in the mountains, would probably effect a greater service than would movements for union or church federation attempted alone by individuals within particular communities. In a rural community in need of breadth of spirit, suspicion is often aroused if a particular church or minister seeks union or federation. Unhappily, the church most needing the benefits of such effort is wont to assume that the body setting it in motion has some hidden motive and will reap the sole profits.

There are, however, in every community certain activities in which all churches can unite—activities that do not bear in any way upon church polity, doctrine, or practice—such as the suppression of vice and the enforcement of laws drawn for the good of the community. These are points of beginning. The likelihood that jealousies and suspicions will obstruct if one church or a particular minister begins the movement, will decrease with the increase of men who see that true leadership does not necessitate prominence in the movement. Wise ministers will keep in the background and put forward laymen in whom the community has confidence, or permit the minister of the predominant faith to take the lead.

Too great praise cannot be accorded the splendid men and women who have remained year after year, broadening local community life by the contagious inspiration of their wide vision and broad charity. Adequate compensation cannot be given such laborers, but the churches, and independent boards as well, must pay larger salaries than they do in order that the qualified workers who remain with efficiency increased by long experience and wide acquaintance may grow in numbers. Self-sacrifice is a splendid thing, but when the constituency of so-called mission work imposes sacrifice upon those at the front when such sacrifice is unnecessary, it is something akin to crime. With many of the necessities of life excessively high in accessible markets, doubled in price because of the long, hard cross-country haul, it is idle to argue that the cost of living is low in the remote rural sections. There are few so-called "social demands" entailing personal expenditure, but calls to relieve others more needy are numerous and urgent.

The day should be past when workers for rural welfare are forced because of waste, indifference, mistakes, mismanagement, or over-heavy cost of administration to accept their wage largely "in the consciousness of disinterested service to the needy," supplemented by an occasional "mission barrel" containing clothes they cannot wear or theological books from the attics of our great-grandfathers. They should be supported well, even if it is necessary to close some activities already begun. No loss to the Kingdom would ensue if some other Christian denomination should come in and take the outposts thus abandoned.

Among the religious bodies not denominational that may have a direct and active part in constructive measures in the mountains, are the Young Men's and the Young Women's Christian Associations. These organizations through their county work have a rich field, and if they were properly manned they could be the stimulators of various federated activities. It would be wise, in the mountains, to emphasize the non-denominational character of the Young Men's Christian Association, but to avoid giving the impression that it has come to do a work that the county churches are failing to do. If there be in the state or section a federation of churches, the Association would do well to show that it was at work with the knowledge and sympathy of the denominations which have local churches in the mountains and representation in the federation. When there is no such federation, or where the strong local denomination has not yet joined the church federation movement, it would seem advisable to select broad-minded Young Men's Christian Association secretaries whose church connection is with the denomination strongest in the county.

The Young Men's and the Young Women's Christian Associations might also find a special field for service in supplying and stimulating recreation. The young people of the mountains as a whole do not know how to play. They need to be directed into lines of wholesome vigorous activity. No definite program can be suggested. Here, as elsewhere, it will not be enough to supply the means. There must be definite fostering and supervision, and in places a traditional and religious opposition must be overcome sympathetically and tactfully. The greater use of music—of community singing in particular—would be helpful, as well as the encouragement of games in which all may take part, folk dancing, and sports of various kinds.

There are other movements not needing financial assistance from a philanthropic board that would be of benefit. The industrial departments of railroads, for example, might be brought to see the advantage of promoting industry not alone in communities on their lines, but in territory that might easily be tributary to their lines through a better system of county roads.

The immigration departments of different states, interested in populating uninhabited regions or reclaimed lowlands, might find it worth while to locate people familiar with upland culture on mountain lands. Too often such colonization schemes conducted by private enterprise have as their ruling motive the selling of inferior tracts to unsuspecting foreigners at exorbitant prices, and one colony at least in the Highlands has suffered such exploitation. The success after years of struggle of its few colonists without direction, upon poor mountain land, gives ground for the belief that people accustomed to labor would win great and early success in the Highlands if from the time of their settlement they might be directed by trained men and women in farming, dairying, and marketing.

Up to this point we have dwelt largely upon a number of things that might be done. Inasmuch as the region is a varied one and there are particular needs in particular places, the fewest mistakes would be made if frequent conference and interchange of ideas might take place between those outside the mountains who are attempting new lines of rural work which might be suited to this section, and those within the mountains who are striving to adapt their work to meet local needs. Advice and counsel should also be sought from those workers who by long residence in the mountains have an intimate knowledge of their respective sections. Not the least benefits of such a plan would come through mutual understanding and sympathy between public, private, and church organizations.

In the furtherance of such a plan, an interdenominational Conference of Southern Mountain Workers has been held in Knoxville, Tennessee, for the last seven years. Before this conference have been brought speakers who by knowledge and experience were fitted to discuss certain phases of mountain life and work, and representatives of state, federal, and national organizations, as well as of denominational and philanthropic agencies especially interested in the improvement of rural conditions. Workers in the mountain field, native and foreign, many of whom would not be able because of the small salaries received to attend larger national conferences, have thus had an opportunity to learn something of measures that have proved successful both within and without the Highlands. Such workers shut off in small communities during the greater part of the year, and giving largely of their mental and physical strength, require the inspiration that comes from the vision of leaders who see the needs of the individual and community, but see them as part of a larger whole for whose advancement all are co-workers. The peculiar value of the conference has been its small size (generally not over one hundred and fifty) and the frank and thorough discussion of all methods, educational, agricultural, and social, which has taken place from the floor.

There are ways, also, in which through the establishment of local connections helpful measures may be introduced without any great preliminary conference. As has been indicated, there are times and seasons in the mountains when people can be reached in large groups—"court week," county teachers' institutes, and "laying-by time," the especial season of "protracted meetings." Through bringing experts and men of prominence, ministers, educators, and laymen by local invitation to such gatherings, much can be done to awaken a right public opinion without creating the impression that pressure is being exerted from without.

It seems needless to dwell upon the many influences that may be set in motion. Innumerable adaptations of methods now in use elsewhere suggest themselves as helpful, but in the way of organization all that seems necessary has been indicated: study, counselors, local centers, and some means of connection between helpful men and women and associations and movements within the mountains, and helpful men and women and associations and movements without the mountains.

Such a plan of continuous study and connection would eventually result in the greatest good to the mountains as a whole. The work as outlined is not the work of a year nor of a decade, but of a generation, perhaps of several generations. It will often be necessary to feel one's way. Not infrequently progress will seem very slow, but the end in view will make the effort worth while. Measures found to be wise and made operative through a long period of time will bring the longed-for results. Emphasis will be placed at one time and in certain localities upon one thing; and at other times and in other places upon another; but the movement, though leaning now this way and now that, if wisely controlled will go on as a movable equilibrium to the goal.

CHAPTER XIV

THE NEW BASIS OF APPEAL

A FEW months ago the writer was traveling up the lovely Valley of East Tennessee, out from the early capital, past the spot where grew the first institution of learning west of the Alleghenies, and on to that region where, one hundred and fifty years ago, was raised the cabin of the first white settler in the wilderness beyond the mountains.

He had just come from a mountain conference attended by almost two hundred people, among whom were representatives of thirteen denominations doing work within the Highlands, state and federal officials interested in advancing in various ways the prosperity of the Highland country, and many individuals—Highlanders, Lowlanders, Northerners, and Southerners—all of whom were present because they had at heart the welfare of the Highland people.

His mind was upon the meeting which to him had been an inspiration. It seemed a great thing that all these people of different sections, different faiths, and different training, could come together and discuss frankly the educational, religious, social, and economic measures which had in them promise for the Highlands of the future.

A long time he sat silent, scarce seeing the green valley which unfolded on either hand, his thought dwelling on the gathering and on the assurance that it seemed to give of increasing understanding and co-operation which could result only in progress. Many as had been the changes of the last twenty-five years, the coming years were to bring far deeper and, he hoped, more fruitful changes for the mountain country. It should indeed "blossom abundantly, and rejoice, even with joy and singing."

He was aroused from his reverie by a man's seating himself beside him. He proved to be a minister who had been present at the conference, and who belonged to a denomination doing much good work in the Highlands. Turning to him the writer commented upon the spirit of comradeship and good-will that had been manifested in the meeting, upon the evident desire to get at the truth, whatever it might be, and to apply such remedies as the truth demanded and added, "If those who go out to raise money would only qualify their statements, and say first that they are speaking of the section where they are working, not necessarily of all the Highlands, and tell of the changes which are taking place and what the Highlanders themselves and the Southern states are doing to bring about these changes, as well as what is being done by denominational agencies, there would be fewer misunderstandings."

It was a subject close to the writer's heart, and he may have spoken more emphatically than was necessary when he denounced the unfairness of citing local and particular instances in such a way as to give the impression that they were universal and typical.

The minister shook his head.

"It is all very well to talk in that way," he said, "but it doesn't raise money. The instances cited by workers who come before us are true, whether they are true of the whole mountain section or not. The contributing public doesn't want to hear about change and progress, and about improvements other people have made. It wants to hear the pathetic and the picturesque—to feel that the mountaineer is dependent upon its charity. As far as I am concerned, I believe it is right for the speakers to say such things if it will bring them money. They might as well. Everybody is doing it!"

The arrival of the train at a junction put an end to the discussion which had come to an impasse. The minister stepped back into his Pullman reservation, and the writer stopped to make connections for the railway point nearest a remote section which he had not visited for ten years.

It must be admitted that he was both stirred and disheartened. If a minister of intelligence could attend a gathering such as had recently met, and come away, willing for the sake of getting contributions to perpetuate general impressions which were not generally true and consciously to give offense, and could justify his position by the statement, "Everyone is doing it," what hope would there be of ever securing real understanding and sympathetic co-operation?

Subconsciously he realized that the attitude just expressed did not represent that of most of the people who had attended the conference nor that of the majority of those working in the mountains; yet he had to admit that it was the attitude of some who delivered, and many who went to hear addresses on the Southern Highlands. After all, were these speakers and listeners so fundamentally honest as the talented young Highland politician who had sought him at the close of a church address to admit that he had played politics and bought votes to secure his last office? "Everyone is doing it, but it's like you said," he confessed. "I had a little boy born the other day, and I couldn't look him in the face if he grows up and finds his father is dishonest."

Deep in reflection, he crossed the city to the station from which he was to leave for his more distant destination. The little Valley metropolis he had not seen for some years had changed almost beyond belief; it had indeed shown an increase of almost 100 per cent in population in the decade between 1900 and 1910. Two railroads now passed through it, competing for transportation of the vast stores of coal hidden away in the mountains to north and west; and to the east extended a narrow-gauge railway which followed the gentle valley of the Watauga and tapped the iron deposits of those lofty ridges which Daniel Boone had crossed on his way to "Kaintucke" from his home on the Yadkin in North Carolina.

It was a beautiful, warm spring day, and he stood on the platform to watch the narrow-gauge engine with its train of miniature cars puff away toward the mountain wall. A tall lean Highland boy, on the shoulder of whose army coat was blazoned a wildcat, limped across the track and leaned against the station in the sun. He had a handsome reckless face, and keen eyes that vouched for the sharpshooter's medal on his breast. Visible on his sleeve were three gold stripes. His story was that of many others. Volunteering early, he had seen much service, killed seven Germans he knew of, and had fallen at last in a hand-to-hand encounter, wounded in arm, side, and back. Another soldier loitered by, a big cheerful fellow on his way home—home being the community to which the writer was going. Further conversation revealed the fact that he was a graduate of one of the larger mountain schools.

"And what are you going to do now?"

"I reckon I'll stay home and farm awhile."

A short ride brought us to the little town from which the writer ten years before had started into the remote mountains. It was now paved and built up with trim frame houses. A china factory had recently been located here which was using the fine clays native to the region. Here, too, was a silk mill where raw silk imported direct from China was spooled.

Climbing into a Ford car we swung on out into the country. The old road which once had found its way along the margins of the creek bottom had been replaced by a new highway which the county had taxed itself the previous year to build at the cost of $200,000. It had taken, before, almost a day to ride by muleback the twenty miles to the journey's end, crossing the winding stream twenty-one times in its course. Now our Ford covered the distance in an hour.

The returned soldier was leaning out to greet the many friends whom he passed, but the writer as he watched the loops of the new highway curving ahead in the old landscape could not but wonder what the minister would have said. Probably he would have seen only the mud holes which undeniably did exist, the log-houses that still remained here and there, and the single razor-back hog that viewed the car suspiciously from a vantage point on the hill.

The country was indeed a strange mingling of new and old, whose contrasts were not less striking in that once remote part of the mountains where at last we reached our destination. As in our national capital the young and prosperous lived side by side with the old and humble; the modern was close to the pioneer. The mother who ran to greet her soldier son from overseas, left quilting frame at the challenge of the automobile horn. A father whose boy had taken advantage of a motor truck to slip away to the city, could only pursue him on horseback, but he made up for lack of speed by warning the sheriff by means of the rural telephone.

In a nearby settlement a mountain funeral brought people on foot, on horse and muleback, riding single and riding double, or seated in chairs set in the beds of hacks or wagons; but also waiting beyond the new cement bridge which spanned the main stream were twelve automobiles, and not all Fords either. At this point, however, the triumph of the ancient over the modern was complete, for the automobile travelers were forced to descend, cross the branch by a foot-log, and walk up a rough track to the old log-house, whose great squared timbers bespoke their survival from early days. The dress of the company gathered—some hundred strong—showed a preponderance of city clothes and hats, but mingled with them were garments of homespun and the old-time sunbonnet. And when at last the "fotched-on" casket was lifted to the shoulders of six strong men, the long procession wound up through a steep grove of white pines to the hill-top, where county and city preacher together conducted the simple service.

On another day a good-roads meeting drew our household and many of our neighbors to the county-seat. The morning was one of April sunshine. Peach and feathery plum bloom lined the road, and the mountain slopes on either side the creek were all aflower with "sarvice" and red-bud, and carpeted below with blood-root, violets, anemones, Culver's root, and cinquefoil. Groups of walkers were overtaken who had passed the house before it was light on their twenty or more mile trip to the court house. Among the many who rode were women cross-saddle, one whose bright red fascinator was curiously out of keeping with her modern divided skirt.

The town itself had assumed the appearance incident to court day. Men thronged the street corners and leaned against the fence about the court house. Within the building every seat was taken, and when after a number of speeches the motion was put to endorse the good-roads bill, the resolution was passed by a unanimous vote without ceremony of discussion.

From the eastern belt of the mountains the writer recrossed the Valley to the western region of coal development. Six years before he had been able to approach by railroad only within seven miles of the gorge where the Big Sandy breaks through the walls of the Cumberlands, and that on a logging train. The friendly "captain" refused to sell him a ticket, lest in case of accident the company be held responsible for damages, but he advised him to sit near the edge of the piles of lumber where he could jump if the car broke away. Now the traveler thundered along at the base of the sheer cliffs on a well-equipped train.

At the little station where he again changed cars he talked with the waiting group—a miner who was taking his sick daughter to one of the camp hospitals, a mine manager returning from the great outer world, an Italian from Turin whose knowledge of English scarce permitted him to explain the difficulties which a free drink of moonshine had brought upon him, and many others, men and women whose lives were now a part of the changed life of the mountains.

We would not leave the impression that all is change and progress even in the coal belt of the Highlands. Continuing his way on horseback from the bustling mining town at which he left the train, the writer drew rein within a few hours' ride at the top of a long lonely hill and looked far down to the hollow at its base. There, undisturbed by the rush of industrial life drawing ever nearer, nestled an old log-house among the flowering fruit trees. In defiance of the coal banks close at hand, the wood smoke curled in a thin blue line from its chimney, and borne up to him clearly against the echoing hills, where families plowed and planted as steep slopes as of yore, rose the quavering measures of an old song.

Most of his journey was taken over roads impassable to automobiles, and only to be traversed by horseback or by the slower wagon or mail-hack. As of old he saw much that was backward, but it is equally true that he saw much quite as disheartening where material progress had swept upon a people unprepared for its coming. There is sometimes more hope in the old than in the new. Help is often most needed where changes have come most rapidly. But the changes are not to be ignored.

The Highland country is in truth a land of paradoxes and contradictions, because here in a restricted area are taking place all the changes that are going on in the world elsewhere; so that when one seeks to give a general statement that will hold true of remote areas, the close juxtaposition of ancient and modern, of extreme conservatism and extreme progressiveness make constant qualification necessary.

The writer knows only too well the conditions under which the average mountain worker has had to raise money in the past—ten minutes to state his cause, before church service, after the sermon, or to the children of the Sunday school; and out of the money raised he often must pay his own expenses. Gathering his energies for the brief time at his disposal, he puts forth his best efforts. Even if he is familiar with the changing conditions he cannot take time to educate his audience. He makes the most effective appeal he can, without at all intending to deceive, realizing subconsciously that most people give through feeling and sentiment. He is compelled to do this even when he is aware of the diversity of the country and of conditions within the country. Oftentimes, however, he is not aware of them, and does not qualify his statements because he cannot. He knows his own circumscribed field and how greatly it needs help—and necessarily in his plea he dwells upon the picturesque and stirring. If he be a speaker from without the mountains he has the further handicap, or it may be the advantage, of not being able to measure how simple mountain needs really are, for what are necessities to him are often luxuries to the Highlander. In later days, since boards have disbursed their charities through the apportionment plan, both independent and church workers who seek to raise money must put their cases more strongly than ever because of the businesslike way in which apportionments are made.

Because of these conditions there has grown up a certain kind of appeal which has come to be conventional and expected. More and more secretaries of boards are studying the fields under their supervision. To some of these far-sighted earnest students of mountain needs is due the initiation of a new policy, which aims at an understanding not only by the workers but by the supporting constituency of the conditions of the field and the methods that have in them most promise. Appeal, however, is still too often made by throwing on the screen pictures of the past. This is not to say that there are not similar conditions and even greater needs than those which existed before, but petitions for help should be coupled with a statement of what is being done by the Highlander himself, by the Southern states, and by the Federal Government. And the advance that has taken place should not be attributed to "mission work" only.

Let the plea be changed to the basis of the rural plea. Admit frankly that there is a need, a great rural need throughout the United States, and that it is especially great in the mountains because conditions are intensified by topography. The South would welcome help put on such a basis.

Let surveys be made and let us hear their findings. Let us be sure, if possible, that we have the facts. If we cannot get facts, let us be sure we have presumptive evidence, and so state. Let us make fewer sweeping statements, and not justify a thing that is inherently wrong in the words "Everybody is doing it, and we won't get any money if we do not follow suit."

More things are possible than we now dream of, if denominations and agencies sustaining work in the mountains will give convincing evidence of a willingness to work together. It will be convincing if we actually co-operate and do not stop at organizing for co-operation. Aside from the visible educational and material benefits will be the invisible benefits arising from an assurance of oneness in purpose.

Too many schools and individuals in the past, who have honestly sought the good of the Highland people, have antagonized other institutions and agencies, native and foreign, and limited the sphere of their influence by assuming the role of "star players." Others seemingly forget that the ultimate solution of mountain problems must come through convincing the individualistic mountaineer that he cannot live for himself alone, and through enlisting him in co-operative service to create an environment that will breed in his children the community spirit. Co-operation in Christian effort, which emphasizes the essential and minimizes the non-essential, and ultimately finds full expression in united effort, is what we all so much need.

There is discouragement in all work. One great source of discouragement comes from the desire for quick tangible results that can be tabulated. All great social changes are in their initial stages slow. It is only when they begin to move by their own momentum that they are recognized.

There are encouragements in all work. May the writer close with a scene and lesson that he has never forgotten? Lost in the forest late one afternoon, hungry, tired, and discouraged, he gave rein to his horse, which found the trail and brought him to the head of a mountain cove after night had fallen and just before the full moon broke through the clouds that had obscured it. On a sudden that which appeared dark and forbidding became marvelously beautiful, as the slopes dotted with mica flashed back the moonbeams. There is the solution that we seek—light!—light reflected from the true Light shining in obscure places, that what is native in obscure places may, itself illumined, help to dispel the darkness.

APPENDICES

APPENDIX A

REGIONAL DESCRIPTIONS OF STATE MOUNTAIN AREAS

ALABAMA

THE topography of Alabama is somewhat confusing inasmuch as the three belts of the Appalachian Province terminate in this state and merge with one another and into the Gulf Coastal Plain. We may perhaps get a clearer idea of the topography of the mountainous section of this state if in imagination we take our stand on some lofty detached lookout in the northeast, where Georgia, Alabama, and Tennessee join their borders.

Facing the southwest and giving imagination sway, we see before us the much divided Greater Appalachian Valley as an inland sea. On our right to the west is an archipelago whose nearer islands are sharp and irregular, while its more remote ones are smooth and flat. These represent the isolated peaks, mesas, and remnants which make up that part of the Allegheny-Cumberland Plateau north of the Tennessee River. The large island directly before us, with comparatively level surface, is Sand Mountain, and the reefs to the southwest of it represent the rough, low-lying lands of the Warrior Basin into which Sand Mountain and its spur, Blount Mountain, merge beyond the southwest border of Blount County. The large island on the left, toward the south and east, with central depression and elevated rim cut in a few places by inlets, represents Lookout Mountain. Farther to the southeast, on the mainland that marks the southeastern border of our fancied midland sea, is a coastal range, the Talladega Mountains, the southernmost member of the Blue Ridge Belt.

All the valleys of the mountain region of Alabama, with the exception of the Valley of the Tennessee from Guntersville, where the river leaves Browns Valley,[1] have a northeasterly-southwesterly trend, and may be regarded as parts of the Greater Appalachian Valley Belt. The valley of the Coosa, or "Coosa Valley," as the Greater Appalachian Valley sections

---

[1] In Tennessee, Sequatchie Valley is regarded as a valley in the Cumberland Plateau. In Alabama, Browns Valley, its continuation, is regarded as an outlier of the Coosa, as the main part of the Greater Appalachian Valley is here called. This seeming inconsistency may be explained by the statement made later in our Tennessee section that the Sequatchie Valley is in reality an outlier of the East Tennessee Valley, as the Greater Appalachian Valley is there called, and would be so viewed did not Waldens Ridge show so many of the characteristics of the Plateau section lying to the west of the Sequatchie.

of Georgia and Alabama are wont to be called, has in Alabama its main valley in the counties of Cherokee, Calhoun, Etowah, St. Clair, Talladega, and Shelby, and extends into Chilton which lies in the country of our indefinite southwestern border. It is closely furrowed with many northeasterly and southwesterly parallel ridges. Its outliers are the Cohaba Valley in the counties of St. Clair, Jefferson, Shelby, and Bibb, which is also in the vague southwestern border; Roups Valley in Jefferson, and in Tuscaloosa and Bibb, of our undefined zone; Wills Valley in DeKalb, Etowah, and St. Clair Counties; Murphree in Etowah and Blount; and Blount Springs or Browns Valley in Blount, Marshall, and Jackson Counties.

The Allegheny-Cumberland Belt of Alabama includes Sand Mountain[1] and its spurs in Jackson, Marshall, Etowah, Morgan, St. Clair, and Blount Counties, Lookout Mountain in DeKalb, Cherokee, and Etowah, and the detached spurs of the Plateau northwest of the Tennessee, in Jackson, Madison, and Marshall Counties. To these should be added half the area of Cullman County, which partakes of the characteristics of both the tableland and the Warrior Basin.

A considerable part of the area northwest of the Tennessee River is not strictly tableland. There are, especially in the northeastern part of this division, deep, narrow coves and valleys with low-lying areas between the spurs. Some of these spurs partake of true mountain proportions. With the exception of this area northwest of the Tennessee River and one or two localities on Lookout Mountain, the edge of the tableland has been cut but little by streams.

The western part of this subdivision merges into the so-called Barrens, which extend from northeast of Huntsville, Madison County, as far south as Athens and west to the Mississippi line.

The Talladega Mountain range, as previously indicated, is the southernmost member of the Appalachian Mountains, though separated by an interval of a hundred miles from the main body which terminates in Georgia. It is a narrow range with a central ridge bordered by low hills. The three Blue Ridge counties, Clay, Cleburne, and Coosa, might perhaps better be called border counties, in which the Piedmont Plateau and the terminus of the Appalachian Mountains merge.[2]

---

[1] In Lawrence and Franklin Counties is an elevated rim overlooking the Tennessee River. Locally this rim is known as Sand Mountain. It is the border of the Warrior Coal Field, and may better be considered with it. The main body of the tableland, known as Sand Mountain, with its spur, gradually sinks into the Warrior Basin beyond the southwestern line of Blount County.

[2] The belts of the Appalachian Province differ not only in surface features but in structural features as well. The Blue Ridge Belt is largely a region of meta-

Except for the northwestern portion of the Allegheny-Cumberland Belt, which is drained by the Tennessee and its tributaries, the drainage is to the Gulf through the Coosa and Warrior Rivers.

While more territory might be included with the mountainous area of Alabama—especially the rough country of the bordering Warrior Basin and the southwest counties into which parts of the Coosa Valley project—it has seemed best to limit our territory as indicated.

GEORGIA

The mountain region of Georgia lies northwest of a line drawn from the Georgia-South Carolina boundary, through Toccoa in Stephens County and Cedartown in Polk County, to the Georgia-Alabama border. The section thus defined is subdivided into the so-called "ten counties of Northwest Georgia" and the fifteen Blue Ridge or northeast counties. With the exception of one county, Dade, which we list in the Allegheny-Cumberland Belt, the counties of northwest Georgia lie within the Greater Appalachian Valley.

The Allegheny-Cumberland Plateau section, or Dade County, lies in the extreme northwestern corner of the state, and consists of a part of Sand Mountain, as the severed remnant of Waldens Ridge is known, a part of Lookout Mountain, and its spur Pigeon Mountain. Lookout Mountain, which enters the state from Alabama and terminates abruptly at Chattanooga, may be viewed as dividing the Greater Appalachian Valley into two parts, the smaller division of which lies between Sand Mountain and Lookout and extends well into Alabama. The average elevation of this flat-topped group of the Allegheny-Cumberland Plateau Belt is about 1,800 feet above sea-level, with points reaching 2,300 feet. Their slopes are precipitous with bold sandstone cliffs attaining in places a height of 200 feet. Sand Mountain is broader and more level than the others.

The eastern escarpment of Lookout and its spur, Pigeon Mountain, form the western boundary of the Greater Appalachian Valley section of the state. The eastern boundary of this belt is the southwestern escarpment of the great mountainous plateau made by the division of the Blue Ridge in lower Virginia. The fronts of this plateau, the Unakas on the northwest and the Blue Ridge on the southeast, terminate in Georgia, and

morphic rocks. The metamorphic region of Alabama lies within an irregular triangle, the base of which is that part of the Georgia-Alabama line between the northern boundary of Cleburne and the southern boundary of Lee County. The approximate apex of this triangle is the northeastern corner of Chilton County. Practically all of this area, except the northwestern border, lies in the Piedmont Plateau. This northwestern border is roughly traced by the Talladega Mountains, which separate this region from the Coosa Valley.

the escarpment referred to as bounding the Greater Appalachian Valley section on the east may be considered somewhat as the final cross-range which connects the termini of the fronts.

In the northern part of this bordering escarpment the altitude is much higher than in the south. This is especially true in the Cohutta Mountains. Coves and ravines cut up this section so that mountains are encountered in all parts for a distance of ten or fifteen miles between the base and summit of the escarpment. Farther south the rim of this border is from 500 to 600 feet above the average elevation of the Greater Appalachian Valley Belt to the northwest, but is approximately of the same general level as the country to the south.

The part of the Greater Appalachian Valley lying between the Lookout-Pigeon Mountain front on the west and the Blue Ridge-Unaka Plateau escarpment on the east, is composed of minor valleys separated by sharp or well-rounded ridges. In the northwestern part of this area the streams flow northward into the Tennessee. Elsewhere they take a more direct route southward into the Gulf of Mexico.[1]

The Blue Ridge counties form an irregular triangle with the escarpment facing the Greater Appalachian Valley as its base. The northern boundary of the state forms one side, and Chattahoochee Ridge—the continuation of the Chattooga Ridge of South Carolina, which is the southeast extension of the Blue Ridge *not* bearing the main divide—the third side of this triangle and the natural southeastern boundary of the mountain section of the state. The Blue Ridge bearing the main divide, which turns to the northward at the North Carolina-South Carolina line, enters Georgia from North Carolina between Rabun and Towns Counties, continues southward, and in Habersham County resumes its general southwesterly course southeast of the Chattahoochee River. The main ridge sends off a number of spurs known by various names.

The general elevation of this region is from 1,600 to 1,800 feet above sea-level, with mountains ranging from 2,000 to 3,000 feet above the general elevation. The sides of the mountains are often so steep as to be almost inaccessible. · There is within this mountain section a considerable area of broken country resembling the more hilly parts of the Piedmont Plateau.

The mountain section of northeast Georgia is the terminus of the mountainous region of the Blue Ridge Belt (except the limited area within the Talladega Mountains of Alabama). The highest elevation of the state, 5,046 feet, is reached in Sitting Bull, the middle peak of the Nantahala cross-range in Towns County.

[1] In the extreme eastern part of the Blue Ridge Belt the drainage is to the Atlantic through the headwaters of the Savannah River.

Nacoochee Valley in White County, and the Little Tennessee Valley in Rabun County, are among the larger of the intermontane valleys. Most of the valleys are narrow, with rapid streams and with falls many feet in height.

KENTUCKY

The "mountain country" of eastern Kentucky, in its usual acceptation, is the name given to the region lying east of a line drawn from Portsmouth on the Ohio River to the junction of Clinton and Cumberland Counties, which lie on the Tennessee border; or, on a county basis, those thirty-seven counties which lie east of a line drawn from the point where the western line of Lewis County touches the Ohio to where the western line of Clinton touches the Tennessee line. The true mountain country of eastern Kentucky, however, occupies but a comparatively small area in the southeastern portion of the state, and includes the Pine, Black, and Cumberland Mountains, with the intervening valleys.

Our field is the larger territory which lies east of the boundary above mentioned. This entire field is within the Allegheny-Cumberland Belt. The general character of this region is that of a deeply dissected plateau, which is highest on its southwestern side. Here the Cumberland Mountains, on the state line between Virginia and Kentucky, rise in the crest of Big Black Mountain to a height of 4,100 feet and form the watershed between the Cumberland and Tennessee Rivers.

The western side of the Plateau is bordered by an irregular line of low hills and knobs known as the "Knob Region," in which terminates the Eastern, or Appalachian, Coal Field of Kentucky, with which our territory is almost identical. The general surface elevation along the western margin of this Eastern Coal Field is about 1,000 feet.[1] The eastern boundary of our territory is formed by the Big Sandy River, and the northern boundary by the Ohio.

In describing this region we avail ourselves of the classification of counties into districts as made by the Forest Service of the United States Government and of the state of Kentucky. These districts are the drainage basins of the Big Sandy, the Cumberland, the Upper Kentucky, and Upper Licking Rivers, all of which drain into the Ohio. Small areas of some of

---

[1] At Rockcastle County a division is effected in the escarpment, part sweeping around toward Louisville as Muldraughs Hill, and part continuing to the southwest. The region lying south of Muldraughs Hill, east of the Western Coal Field and west of the southwesterly continuance of the escarpment above mentioned, is closely allied with the mountain section of eastern Kentucky, which, however, is more noted on account of a certain picturesqueness that attaches both to people and scenery.

these districts lie without the drainage basins in which they are classed, but we follow the convenient arrangement above given.

The Cumberland District includes the southern and southwestern counties. The Cumberland River has its main sources in Harlan County, flowing hence in a generally southwesterly direction through narrow, deeply cut valleys with ridges often more than 1,000 feet above its waters. At Pineville, for the first time in over 100 miles, it breaks through the Pine Mountain barrier, which continues to the southwest and passes from Whitley County into Tennessee. Toward the western part of this district the country as a whole becomes more open and rolling, especially in the north, with gentler slopes and broader ridges, broken in places by valleys sometimes reaching a depth of 550 feet.

The northern and northeastern counties fall within the Big Sandy District. Letcher County marks the divide between the Cumberland and Big Sandy Rivers. North of this divide the general surface slopes gently toward the Ohio. Gradually the narrow bottoms and precipitous hill slopes that are characteristic of the southern portions of this district give way to a country somewhat less rough, and from an altitude of 2,000 to 3,000 feet above sea-level we descend to an elevation of 1,000 feet or less.

HIGHLAND COUNTIES IN KENTUCKY, CLASSIFIED BY DRAINAGE BASINS [a]

Cumberland District (south and south-west)	Big Sandy (north and north-east)	Upper Kentucky (central and west)	Upper Licking (northwest)
Bell	Boyd	Breathitt	Lewis
Harlan	Carter	Clay	Magoffin
Jackson	Elliott	Estill	Menifee
Knox	Floyd	Lee	Morgan
Laurel	Greenup	Leslie	Rowan
Pulaski	Johnson	Owsley	
Rockcastle	Knott	Perry	
Wayne	Lawrence	Powell	
Whitley	Letcher	Wolfe	
	Martin		
	Pike		

[a] Clinton and Madison Counties are also Highland counties, but do not lie within the drainage basins above mentioned.

The counties of the Upper Kentucky District are those of the central and western part. This whole country is very rough. The hills are steep, the valleys narrow, and there is comparatively little bottom land. The land slopes to the northwest, growing gradually somewhat less rugged.

Near Beattyville the three forks of the Kentucky River unite with the Red River to form the main Kentucky.

The Upper Licking District includes the northwestern counties. On the whole this district is somewhat less rugged than that of the Upper Kentucky. The ridge crests rise only from 1,000 to 1,500 feet above sea-level, and there is more bottom land. The general surface features, however, resemble those of the other counties.

MARYLAND

Maryland, with only four counties in its mountain region, covering in all an area of 2,250 square miles, has the smallest Highland area of any of the nine Southern states within which our territory is included. It embraces all three belts of the Appalachian Province.

The easternmost, or Blue Ridge Belt, is narrow. The main ridge follows for most of its course the boundary line between Frederick and Washington Counties, reaching its highest altitude, 2,145 feet in Quirauk Mountain, in the northeastern part of the latter county. By some, however, the Catoctins, the most easterly range in Frederick County and separated from South Mountain, as the main range is here known, by the fertile Middletown Valley, are considered to mark the topographic boundary between the Piedmont and Appalachian Provinces.[1] The larger part of Frederick County, though necessarily listed on the basis of the county unit as a Blue Ridge County, lies largely without our territory.

The Allegheny Front, or Dan's Mountain as it is known in this state, crosses Allegany County just to the west of Cumberland. The extreme western part of this county, and the whole of Garrett County, thus fall within the Allegheny-Cumberland Belt, which constitutes almost exactly half of the entire mountain area of Maryland. This region contains the highest land in the state and is traversed by four prominent ridges. One of these, Backbone Mountain in the southwestern end of Garrett County, reaches an elevation of 3,400 feet, and with its continuation, Big Savage, an average of almost 3,000 feet. It forms for about half of its length the divide between the drainage of the Potomac and Youghiogheny systems, or between waters flowing to the Atlantic and to the Ohio.

The Greater Appalachian Valley occupies the narrowest portion of the state. In its eastern or distinctively valley portion it is known as the Cumberland or Hagerstown Valley. Its western or Valley Ridge section, lying in the western half of Washington and eastern half of Allegany County, is divided by Tonoloway Mountain into two varieties of mountain topography. To the west of Tonoloway Mountain the country is very

[1] Maryland Geological Survey so holds.

rugged, cut by long narrow valleys and by ridges which rise in places to an elevation of over 1,900 feet. East of Tonoloway, while extremely dissected, it manifests more of plateau and less of mountain character.

NORTH CAROLINA

North Carolina, with its 10,101 square miles of upland in the mountainous part of the Blue Ridge Belt, is worthy of extended notice. This mountain area is bounded by the Blue Ridge on the southeast, which traverses the state in a southwesterly direction, and on the northwest by the mountains known collectively as the Unaka Range. This region is, in fact, a mountainous plateau with the Blue Ridge and Unakas as its fronts between which extend massive cross-ranges.

The Blue Ridge, viewed from the east, presents the appearance of a rampart overlooking the Piedmont Plateau. Though some of the counties near this border are made very rugged by monadnocks, and by the Piedmont valleys which separate them from the Blue Ridge proper, we include only those lying to the west within the main front of the Blue Ridge or crossed by it.

Viewed from the west the Blue Ridge seems often a low, ill-defined ridge, its horizon line almost unbroken, but in places it lifts itself into bold prominence. It has a number of peaks over 4,000 feet and a few over 5,000. In Grandfather Mountain, its highest point, it attains an altitude of 5,964 feet, descending gradually to 2,700 at the Virginia line and to 2,200 near the border of South Carolina.

The Blue Ridge is very ancient, and has from early times formed the divide between waters to east and west. Streams rising on its eastern slope plunge in their upper courses 1,000 feet or more to the Piedmont Plateau below. Gradually they are carving their way back through the range, pushing the divide ever westward and capturing as they go the headwaters of streams which once flowed to the Gulf. Such a river is the Linville, a branch of the Catawba, which has cut its way back until its headwaters now lie to the west of Grandfather Mountain. The Yadkin, whose waters likewise reach the Atlantic, rises but a few yards distant to the east. A few miles west are the sources of the Watauga and Nolichucky, which empty into the Tennessee, while to the north rises the New or Kanawha River which flows north to Virginia and thence to the Ohio. Farther south the Saluda and Savannah make their way south and southeast across the Piedmont Plateau, and the French Broad flows in an opposite direction into the Tennessee.

Those rivers which rise on the western slope of the Blue Ridge and flow west across the Blue Ridge Plateau to the Tennessee, have during the course of ages cut their channels into deep canyons through the high Unaka Mountains which lie athwart their courses and have divided this range into a number of segments. The term Unaka Mountains is a source of confusion unless it is remembered that it is used to designate the range collectively as well as two of its segments. South of the Pigeon River most of the summits of the Unakas are above 5,000 feet, while north of this river few are above 5,000 feet but many above 4,000 feet in height.

Among the prominent cross-ranges which extend between the Blue Ridge and the Unakas, the Black Mountains, although a single range but fifteen miles long, have a dozen peaks above 6,000 feet in elevation. In Mount Mitchell, 6,711 feet above sea-level, it reaches the highest point east of the Rocky Mountains. The Pisgah range, interrupted by a depression of a few miles and continued as the New Found Mountains, extends to the Tennessee line and attains in Mount Pisgah a height of 5,750 feet. The Balsams, extending in unbroken continuity, save for two high narrow gaps, cross the state from the South Carolina line to the Great Smokies. This range has a mean average elevation of 5,500 feet and fifteen summits exceeding 6,000 feet. They are succeeded by the Nantahala and Valley River Mountains, which lie closely parallel for a distance on the Georgia line, then separate. One branches westward and unites with the Unakas in Cherokee County, and is known as the Long Ridge. The other, under the name of Cheowah, turns to the northeast and ends in isolated peaks and ridges.

These dominant cross-ranges, which have had as their fronts the Unakas and the Blue Ridge which border the plateau, serve in turn as fronts for minor cross-ranges, extending between and sometimes connecting them.

In all this mountain section there are over forty peaks of 6,000 feet and upwards, over eighty which exceed 5,000 and approximate 6,000 feet, and many more above 4,000 feet which approach 5,000 feet in elevation. Several of these in the Great Smoky Mountains are close rivals of Mount Mitchell.

Among the more noted valleys are the French Broad and the Mills River Valleys of Henderson and Transylvania Counties, the Swannanoa in Buncombe, the Pigeon River, the Richland and Johnathan's Creek flatlands of Haywood County, and those of the Valley River and Hiwassee in Cherokee County. The Valley of the upper Linville, Mitchell County, should also be mentioned.

SOUTH CAROLINA

The mountain area of South Carolina is small, being only 450 square miles larger than that of Maryland, the smallest of all the mountain areas of the Southern states.[1] It is included roughly within the northern halves of Oconee and Pickens Counties, the northern third of Greenville County, and the northwestern corner of Spartanburg County.

The boundary line between North and South Carolina is formed in part by the Blue Ridge and its spur the Saludas.[2] The main divide of the Blue Ridge, which maintains a general souıhwesterly direction throughout North Carolina, turns to the north at the South Carolina line; and the Blue Ridge, not bearing the main divide and known as the Chattooga Ridge, crosses the northwestern corner of the state in Oconee County. All of these mountains rise abruptly from the Piedmont Plateau and reach a considerable elevation. Mount Pinnacle in Pickens County is the highest elevation in the state, being 3,436 feet above sea-level. The whole region drains southeast into the Atlantic through the Santee and Savannah River systems.

TENNESSEE

The Tennessee mountain section is of especial interest, as the three belts of the Appalachian Province are very well marked therein. Each belt embraces a comparatively large area, having both the major and minor features of the respective divisions.

The Greater Appalachian Valley Belt in this state has the true valley character especially prominent and extensive, but decreases in width from north to south. Some of its minor valleys are very long, several with a width of a mile extending for a distance of 150 miles, or the entire distance from Virginia to Alabama. There are numerous other minor valleys.

The ridges of the Greater Appalachian Valley are of various kinds. Clinch Mountain, Bay Mountain, and White Oak Mountain, on the western side, are examples of the narrow ridges of great length parallel to the side of the valley. Their crests are almost perfectly horizontal, forming an even sky line like the neighboring plateau escarpment, which

---

[1] The Piedmont Plateau region of South Carolina has a number of mountain masses separated from the main range by Piedmont valleys. Though this Piedmont area, like the mountain region of South Carolina, is comparatively limited, the development of its water power has led to a marvelous industrial growth which must be reckoned with as an influence affecting the nearby "Alpine Region" of South Carolina and the mountain regions of adjacent states.

[2] The Saludas should be included properly in the group of disconnected mountain masses mentioned in the note above, but being less completely isolated are referred to as a spur of the Blue Ridge.

King's Mountain Range, an extension in York and Cherokee Counties of the range of the same name from North Carolina, is a subordinate range and one of the mountain groups of the Piedmont Plateau. Though perhaps subordinate as a physical feature of the state, this range is of the greatest historical interest to the country as a whole.

they also resemble in height. On the southeastern side of this Valley Belt along the base of the massive Unakas, is another type of ridge, represented in the Chilhowee Range which includes the Holston, Iron, English, Chilhowee, Starr, and Beans Mountains. These are of greater height than the Clinch, Bay, and White Oak type, are less regular in crest, and under the name "Chilhowee Range" are referred to at times as a subordinate range of the Unakas. The ridges that make up the minor irregularities of the valley surface constitute the third group.

The Allegheny-Cumberland Tableland, whose eastern escarpment bounds the Greater Appalachian Valley on the west, is strikingly marked in its plateau character. Though flat over much of its surface, it has high elevations and ridges rising as mountains on the tableland. Some of these reach a height of 3,100 feet above the sea. Again, its surface presents the appearance of a gently rolling country with hills and shallow valleys. Its margin is higher than the general interior surface. The eastern front facing the valley is a curving line little broken. Its western front toward the Interior Lowlands is very irregular. Here its streams flowing to the west have cut their channels backward, forming deep coves between the remnants of the plateau. Often these finger-like spurs are cut entirely from the main plateau mass and left as isolated flat-topped hills or mesas.

Among the most interesting and peculiar topographical features of the plateau are the coves of the Crab Orchard Mountains. The largest of these is Grassy Cove, containing an area of eight square miles lying far below the level of the range from which it was eroded. Its stream flows to the northeast, disappears in a cave, and doubling in its underground course reappears in the head of Sequatchie Valley, eight miles to the southeast. There are other such coves, but smaller, and the process of cove making is still going on in the Crab Orchard Mountains.

Sequatchie Valley is a trough-like valley about four miles wide and sixty miles long cut lengthwise out of the plateau. It heads about midway between the northern and southern boundaries of the state and opens to the south in Alabama. Walls of stone a thousand feet high enclose it. Its eastern wall, which lies between it and the Greater Appalachian Valley region, is known as Walden's Ridge. Were it not for the fact that this ridge partakes of the character of the main plateau west of Sequatchie Valley, this Valley might be regarded as a part of the Greater Appalachian Valley.

The Blue Ridge Belt of Tennessee is represented by the main Unaka Range and its subordinate ranges. This range extends for 200 miles along the eastern border of Tennessee, and its axis forms the line between Tennessee and North Carolina, about equal areas of the range lying in each state. A fuller description of the mountain plateau of which the Unakas form the western boundary will be found under the Blue Ridge Belt (Ch. II, p. 13) and in the description of the State Area of North Carolina (Appendix A).

Shut in within the various ranges and mountains of this belt are many coves and valleys. In Johnson County, the extreme northeast county of the state and highest in altitude, are a number of such valleys and numerous coves. From some of the valleys of this county many coves of greater or less extent penetrate the bordering mountains and contain hundreds of acres at a higher level than the valleys into which the coves open.

The drainage of the mountain region of Tennessee is into the Ohio, in the northwestern part largely through the Cumberland, and in the eastern and central parts through the Tennessee system. The Tennessee, which is the trunk stream of the Greater Appalachian Valley to the Georgia line, not only receives all waters of the Valley and nearby ridges south of the New River divide in southwestern Virginia, but all the waters to the east and south of this divide which have their rise on the western slope of the Blue Ridge.

VIRGINIA

The section of Virginia included within our territory consists of the three divisions of the state which are known locally as the Blue Ridge country, the Valley of Virginia, and the Appalachian country.

The name "Valley," as used locally, applies to the comparatively ridgeless strip in the eastern part of the Greater Appalachian Valley, and extends from the Blue Ridge on the southeast to the frontal ridges of the much broken Allegheny Ridge section to the northwest.

The Valley, though continuous in outline throughout the state, is made up of five minor valleys named from their rivers—the Shenandoah Valley, the James River Valley, the Roanoke River Valley, the Kanawha or New River Valley, and the Valley of the Holston or Tennessee. The part of the Valley occupied by the Shenandoah is little diversified. About the headwaters of the Shenandoah, however, and the headwaters of the James and Roanoke, and in the region of the New River the ridges become extremely numerous and much broken. Farther to the southward they gradually become fewer in number and of less importance.

The western part of the Greater Appalachian Valley is made up of the Allegheny ridges and their intervening valleys, which extend from the frontal ridges before referred to as facing the ridgeless strip, westward to the main front of the Allegheny Mountains. The Greater Appalachian Valley is thus higher on its western than on its eastern side.

The natural division of Virginia called "Appalachia" lies for the most part within the western, or Allegheny-Cumberland Plateau Belt, of the Appalachian Province. This section is crossed from northeast to south-

346

west by the Alleghenies with their spurs, and by minor and dividing ridges. Though a strictly geological division might necessitate the inclusion of parts of some of these counties within the Greater Appalachian Valley Belt, the rugged character of the twelve counties as a whole, which justifies the name Appalachia, warrants our placing them on the basis of predominant characteristics among the Allegheny-Cumberland Plateau counties. This region contains many long, narrow, and trough-like valleys within its confines, and ranges in elevation from 1,000 to 3,000 feet and more.

The Blue Ridge country, which receives its name from the range which gives it its chief characteristics, is a varied landscape of much beauty. The general elevation of the range is about 2,500 feet, arising from 1,400 feet at the Potomac River gorge to the highest point in the state, 5,719 feet, in Rogers Mountain, Grayson County. It is a single range and comparatively narrow as a whole, but expands in lower Virginia, forming the Floyd-Carroll-Grayson Plateau. The eastern front of this Plateau continues under the name of the Blue Ridge as the eastern and southeastern boundary of the mountainous section of the Blue Ridge Belt, while the western front is continued in the various segments of the Unakas, whose crests mark the Tennessee-North Carolina boundary. Both these fronts, the Blue Ridge and the Unakas, increase laterally and vertically southward from the point of their division.

It will be recalled that the mountain portion of Virginia which lies north of the New River divide is technically a part of the northern Appalachians. Its northern part is drained by the Shenandoah, which flows northward along the trough of the Valley to join the Potomac at Harper's Ferry. The Potomac itself, however, like the James and Roanoke to the southward, rises behind the Allegheny Front and cuts diagonally across ridges and Valley through gaps in the Blue Ridge to the Atlantic. In exactly the opposite direction New River, rising in the Blue Ridge of North Carolina, pursues its ancient course northwest across the Valley and passes through West Virginia to the Ohio. The region south of the New River Divide drains southward through the Holston and the Clinch into the Tennessee.

WEST VIRGINIA

West Virginia with an average elevation of 1,500 feet, the highest average elevation of any state east of the Mississippi, may be considered in its entirety, in a popular sense at least, as a mountain state. It lies for the most part in the western belt of the Appalachian Province. The Allegheny Front, the western boundary of the Greater Appalachian Valley, passes through Mineral, Grant, and Pendleton Counties. If we hold strictly to the Allegheny Front as the western boundary of the Greater Appalachian Valley, the eastern part of the three counties mentioned, together with the counties to the east of them, lie in the Valley Belt of the Appalachian Province.[1]

Of these five Greater Appalachian Valley counties, the most easterly, Berkeley and Jefferson, have the valley features especially well marked. The more westward counties of this belt have comparatively narrow valleys and have the ridge features more prominent as they approach the Allegheny Front.

The Allegheny-Cumberland Plateau Belt in West Virginia is divided into what are known as true mountain counties and hill counties. The true mountain counties[2] lie west of the counties of the Valley Belt and east of the hill county group, or, in general, east of a line drawn through the middle of the state from the junction of Monongalia and Preston Counties on the northern state line, to the junction of McDowell and Mingo Counties on the southwestern boundary of the state.

Within the limits of these counties, which have the folded and deeply dissected mountain character, the ridges run from northeast to southwest and contain many upland plateaus and meadows. They rise from a base line of approximately 1,500 feet to the highest elevation in the state (and also in the Alleghenies) 4,860 feet in Spruce Knob, Pendleton County. The county of highest average elevation is Pocahontas County, which is approximately 3,000 feet above sea-level.

Westward from the line which marks the base of the true mountain counties is the so-called "Hill Country," a mountain country in miniature when seen from a high altitude. In the northwestern part of this division, especially along the tributaries of the Kanawha and the Ohio, the hills are exceedingly rough and rise from 400 to 600 feet above the streams. The valley bottoms are very narrow and the slopes often precipitous. As they approach the main rivers the hills grow a little less rugged, and descending a few hundred feet, extend with nearly level tops to the brink of the river gorges.

The state as a whole slopes in three directions—to the east where the Potomac River leaves the state at Harper's Ferry, to the north where the Cheat empties into the Monongahela at the Pennsylvania line, and to the southwest where the Big Sandy joins the Ohio.

[1] Some of our authorities hold that Jefferson and Berkeley Counties alone lie in the Great Appalachian Valley, and that the valleys to the westward as far as Monongalia County are intermontane valleys. This seeming difference of opinion may perhaps arise from a different use of terms.

[2] At times reference is made to the "thirty-five mountain counties of West Virginia." This number is obtained, apparently, by including with the counties east of the line above mentioned, the bordering hill counties immediately to the west, into which the mountain counties merge.

APPENDIX B

A MISAPPLIED THEORY OF MOUNTAIN ORIGIN

FISKE'S theory of the origin of the "poor whites," "sand-hillers," and "crackers" of the South has been so widely accepted as an explanation of the origin of the mountain population that it is fair to him to include here a statement of what he actually does say.

It must be remembered that before 1719 the strong stocks of the Germans and Scotch-Irish had not yet made their appearance as a definite frontier people, and the backwoodsmen were recruited more from the less wealthy classes of the English emigrants. "In its early days," says Fiske, "North Carolina was simply a portion of Virginia's frontier; and to this wild frontier the shiftless people who could not make a place for themselves in Virginia society, including many of the 'mean whites,' flocked in large numbers."[1]

For the state of society he accounts as follows:

> In the character of this emigration [by which North Carolina was first peopled] we find the reasons for the comparatively democratic state of society. As there were so few large plantations and wealthy planters, while nearly all the white people were small land-owners, and as the highest class was thus so much lower in dignity than the corresponding class in Virginia, it became just as much the easier for the "mean whites" to rise far enough to become a part of it. North Carolina, therefore, was not simply an Alsatia for debtors and criminals, but it afforded a home for the better portion of Virginia's poor people. We can thus see how there would come about a natural segregation of Virginia's white freedmen into four classes: 1. The most enterprising and thrifty would succeed in maintaining a respectable existence in Virginia; 2. A much larger class, less thrifty and enterprising, would find it easier to make a place for themselves in the ruder society of North Carolina; 3. A lower stratum would consist of persons without enterprise or thrift who remained in Virginia to recruit the ranks of "white trash"; 4. The lowest stratum would comprise the outlaws who fled into North Carolina to escape the hangman. Of the third class the eighteenth century seems to have witnessed a gradual exodus from Virginia, so that in 1773 it was possible for the traveller, John Ferdinand Smyth, to declare that there were fewer cases of poverty in proportion to the population than any-

---

[1] Fiske, John: Old Virginia and her Neighbors, Vol. II, p. 311. Boston, Houghton, Mifflin, and Co., 1897.

where else "in the universe." The statement of Bishop Meade in 1857, which was quoted in the preceding chapter, shows that the class of "mean whites" had not even then become extinct in Virginia; but it is clear that the slow but steady exodus had been such as greatly to diminish its numbers and its importance as a social feature. Some of these freedmen went northward into Pennsylvania, but most of them sought the western and southern frontiers, and at first the southern frontier was a far more eligible retreat than the western. Of this out- ward movement of white freedmen the governor of Virginia wrote in 1717: "The Inhabitants of our frontiers are composed generally of such as have been transported hither as Servants, and being out of their time, . . . settle themselves where Land is to be taken up . . . that will produce the necessarys of Life with little Labour. It is pretty well known what Morals such people bring with them hither, which are not like to be much mended by their Scituation, remote from all places of worship."[1]

As society in North Carolina became more and more orderly and civilized, [after the entrance of the Scotch-Irish and Germans, 1730] the old mean white element, or at least the more intractable part of it, was gradually pushed out to the westward. This stream that had started from Old Virginia flowed for a while southwestward into the South Carolina back-country. But the southerly movement was gradually turned more and more to the westward.

Always clinging to the half-savage frontier, these poor white people made their way from North Carolina westward through Tennessee, and their descendants may still be found here and there in Arkansas, south- ern Missouri, and what is sometimes known as the Egyptian extremity of Illinois.[2]

Specimens of these people, he maintains, are found in the Appalachians today, but distinguished more for shiftlessness than for criminality.

The indisputable facts, in short, about this English frontier class are these:

There is, first, the importation of degraded English humanity in large numbers to the two oldest colonies in which there is a demand for whole- sale cheap labour; secondly, the substitution of black cheap labour for white; thirdly, the tendency of the degraded white humanity to seek the frontier; as described by Spotswood, or else to lodge in sequestered nooks outside of the main currents of progress. These data are suffi- cient in general to explain the origin and distribution of the "crackers," but a word of qualification is needed.

Here Fiske carefully guards himself against any sweeping generaliza- tion in regard to the composition of the mountain population by adding:

It is not to be supposed that the ancestors of all the persons designated as "crackers" were once white freedmen in Virginia and Maryland;

[1] Ibid., Vol. II, pp. 315–317.   [2] Ibid., Vol. II, pp. 319–320.

it is more probable that this class furnished a nucleus about which various wrecks of decayed and broken-down humanity from many quarters were gradually gathered. Nor are we bound to suppose that every community of ignorant, semi-civilized white people in the Southern states is descended from those white freedmen. Prolonged isolation from the currents of thought and feeling that sway the great world will account for almost any extent of ignorance and backwardness; and there are few geographical situations east of the Mississippi River more conducive to isolation than the southwestern portion of the great Appalachian highlands. All these circumstances should be borne in mind in dealing with what, from whatever point of view, is one of the most interesting problems of American history.[1]

[1] Ibid., Vol. II, p. 321.

APPENDIX C

BOONE'S TRAIL

THE trail of Daniel Boone from his home on the Yadkin in North Carolina, through Tennessee and Virginia to Kentucky has, by the agency of the Daughters of the American Revolution in these four states, been marked by stone tablets. The old Wilderness Road, beginning at Sycamore Shoals, Tennessee, had never been lost, but the trail in North Carolina had been forgotten and was established only after two years' work by means of old maps, letters, histories, unpublished manuscripts, and finally by traditions in the Boone family and the memories of old settlers in the region adjacent.[1] One is now able, therefore, to follow from the beginning the pioneer path which for many years was traversed by hundreds on their way to the great West. Railroads and thoroughfares have made parts of it easily accessible, but some of its most lofty and beautiful portions still present many obstacles to the traveler.

There are ten tablets in North Carolina, situated in the following places:

1. Boone's home on the Yadkin River, near Salisbury. (Davie County.)
2. Shallow Ford, where Cornwallis crossed on his way to the Battle of Guilford Court House. (Davie County.)
3. Huntsville. (Yadkin County.)
4. Wilkesboro. (Wilkes County.)
5. Holman's Ford, where Boone's wife Rebecca Bryan once lived. (Wilkes County.)
6. Elksville. (Wilkes County.)
7. Boone, where Boone's hunting cabin once stood. (Watauga County.)
8. Hodges Gap. (Watauga County.)
9. Graveyard Gap. (Watauga County.)
10. Zionville, on the Tennessee border. (Watauga County.)

[1] We are indebted for this information to Mrs. Lindsay Patterson of Winston-Salem, North Carolina, whose great-great-grandfather, Elkanah Bramlette, a companion of Boone on his trip to Kentucky, was murdered at Cumberland Gap. Through the family tradition, Mrs. Patterson became interested in the trail, and it was largely due to her efforts that the North Carolina part of the trail was located.

In Tennessee there are nine markers:

1. Trade. (Johnson County.)
2. Shoun's, nine miles north, along Roan Creek. (Johnson County.)
3. Butler, at the junction of Roan Creek and the Watauga. (Johnson County.)
4. Elizabethton. (Carter County.)
5. Watauga. (Carter County.)
6. Austin's Springs. (Washington County.)
7. Boone's Tree. (Washington County.)
8. Old Fort, south end of Long Island. (Sullivan County.)
9. Kingsport. (Sullivan County.)

From Tennessee the trail, coinciding with the later Wilderness Road which Boone marked out, led into Virginia through Moccasin Gap. The nine Virginia markers were placed as follows:

1. Gate City. (Scott County.)
2. Clinchport, reached from Gate City across Moccasin Ridge and down Copper Creek to the Clinch. (Scott County.)
3. Natural Tunnel. (Scott County.)
4. Duffield. (Scott County.)
5. Fort Scott, an early fort where Boone is known to have spent a night. (Lee County.)
6. Jonesville. (Lee county.)
7. Boone Path Post Office, above Rose Hill. (Lee County.)
8. A spot between Ewing and Wheeler's Station in Lee County where two graves were found, one of which was supposed to be that of Boone's oldest son.
9. Site of old Fort Blackmore. (Scott County.)

Kentucky boasts fourteen tablets:

1. Indian Rock, near Cumberland Gap, used by pioneers as a rude fort and signal tower. (Bell County.)
2. Pineville, on the ford of the Cumberland River. (Bell County.)
3. Flat Lick. (Knox County.)
4. On the farm of C. V. Wilson, near Jarvis's store, where the old trail crosses the new road. (Knox County.)
5. Near Tuttle, on the Knox and Laurel County line, on the farm of Arthur Hunfleet.
6. Fariston, near a pioneer burying ground known as the "Place of Defeated Camps." (Laurel County.)

7. About three and one-half miles from East Bernstadt, where was found an old boulder on which Boone had carved his name. (Laurel County.)

8. Near Livingston, on the farm of Philip Allen. (Rockcastle County.)

9. Boone's Hollow, near Brush Creek. (Rockcastle County.)

10. Roundstone Station. (Rockcastle County.)

11. Boone's Gap. (Rockcastle County.)

12. Berea. (Madison County.)

13. Estell Station, site of Fort Estell. (Madison County.)

14. Boonesboro. (Clark County.)

APPENDIX D

HISTORICAL ESTIMATES OF THE SCOTCH-IRISH AND GERMANS IN THE UNITED STATES IN 1775

ACCORDING to estimates of population made by the Continental Congress of 1776, as a basis from which to apportion the expenses of war, the white population of the thirteen original colonies in 1775 was as follows:

New Hampshire	102,000
Massachusetts (including Maine)	352,000
Rhode Island	58,000
Connecticut	202,000
New York (including Vermont)	238,000
New Jersey	138,000
Pennsylvania	341,000
Delaware	37,000
Maryland	174,000
Virginia (including Kentucky)	300,000
North Carolina (including Tennessee)	181,000
South Carolina	93,000
Georgia	27,000
Total	2,243,000

Bancroft says of these estimates:

The discussion led the members to exaggerate the population of their respective colonies: and the aggregate of the estimates was made to exceed three millions. Few of them possessed accurate materials; Virginia and the Carolinas had never enumerated the woodsmen among the mountains and beyond them. From returns which were but in part accessible to Congress, it appears that the number of white inhabitants in all the thirteen colonies was, in 1774, about two million one hundred thousand; of blacks about five hundred thousand; the total population very nearly two million six hundred thousand.[1]

Hanna,[2] as a basis for his estimate of the number of Scotch-Irish in the colonies in 1775, discusses the estimate of the Continental Congress in some

[1] Bancroft, George: History of the United States of America (author's last revision), Vol. IV, p. 62. D. Appleton and Co., 1916.

[2] Hanna, Charles A.: The Scotch-Irish, Vol. I, Chapter VI. New York, G. P. Putnam's Sons, 1902.

detail. Applying to the period between 1776 and 1790 the average normal rate of increase in America ever since there have been data to strike an average—about 3 per cent a year, the population doubling about every twenty-three years—he finds that the actual population in 1775 would have been about 10 per cent less than the congressional estimate. Basing further estimates upon a state census of New Hampshire in 1782, and the number of taxables in Pennsylvania in 1770, he continues:

> It would seem that we can safely follow this [Bancroft's] estimate and assign 700,000, or one-third to the territory east of the Hudson.

He then proceeds on this basis to apportion the population of the nine states south of the Hudson in 1775 in accordance with their relative population in 1790:

New York (exclusive of Vermont)	202,000
New Jersey	109,000
Pennsylvania	273,000
Delaware	30,000
Maryland	134,000
Virginia (including Kentucky)	325,000
North Carolina (including Tennessee)	206,000
South Carolina	90,000
Georgia	34,000
Total	1,403,000

Now we can safely estimate the proportion of inhabitants of Scottish blood or descent to have been one-eighth of the whole white population in New York; one-fifth to one-fourth in the states of New Jersey, Maryland, and Virginia; more than one-third in Pennsylvania, Delaware, North Carolina, and Georgia; and one-half in South Carolina.

Hanna bases these proportions on the number of communicants in the various churches of New Jersey in 1830; on estimates of congregations computed from information given by Smith in his History of the Province of New Jersey, published 1765; upon the enumeration of taxables in Pennsylvania in 1760 (Colonial Records, Vol. XIV, p. 336), as viewed in the light of historical research (see Proud's History of Pennsylvania, Vol. II, p. 275, note) and the large extent of the Scotch-Irish element in this state and in Maryland, then included in it; upon statements made in Jefferson's Autobiography (p. 31), and the returns of the Virginia militia in 1782, annexed to Chapter IX, Jefferson's Notes on Virginia; upon Williamson's references (History of North Carolina, Vol. II, p. 68); and Ramsay's History of South Carolina (Vol. I, p. 20). He also gives in another chapter long lists of early Presbyterian congregations. He concludes:

> Using the census of 1790 as a basis on which to apportion the popula-

tion in 1775, we find from the foregoing estimates that the number of inhabitants of Scottish ancestry at that time in the nine colonies south of New England (there were probably 25,000 in New England) was close to 385,000, as follows:

New York	25,000
New Jersey	25,000
Pennsylvania	100,000
Delaware	10,000
Maryland	30,000
Virginia	75,000
North Carolina	65,000
South Carolina	45,000
Georgia	10,000
Total	385,000

As may be gathered from Chapter IV (p. 54), there is no comparison possible between the figures of Hanna and the statistics of the Census Bureau. The compilers of A Century of Population Growth based their conclusions on a study of names, and divided the elements of population into English and Welsh, Scotch, Irish, Dutch, French, German, Hebrew, and "all others." No one or group of these is synonymous with the Scotch-Irish.[1] It would seem, therefore, that Hanna's figures must be

[1] "A paradoxical fact regarding the Scotch-Irish is that they are very little Scotch, and much less Irish. That is to say, they do not belong mainly to the so-called Celtic race, but they are the most composite of all the people of the British Isles. They are called Scots because they lived in Scotia; and they are called Irish because they moved to Ireland. Geography and not ethnology has given them their name. They are a mixed race through whose veins run the Celtic blood of the primitive Scot and Pict, the primitive Britain, the primitive Irish, but with a larger admixture of the later Norwegian, Dane, Saxon, and Angle. How this amalgamation came about we may learn from the geography of Scotland.

"The highlands of Scotland begin at the Grampian Hills, and the lowlands extend south from this line to the British border, and include the cities of Glasgow and Edinburgh. The Scotch-Irish came from that southwest part of the lowlands which bulges out towards Ireland north of the Solway Firth. Over these lowland counties, bounded by water and hills on three sides, successive waves of conquest and migration followed. First the primitive Caledonian or Pict was driven to the Highlands, which to this day is the Celtic portion of Scotland. The Britain from the south, pressed on by Roman and then by Teuton, occupied the country. Then Irish tribes crossed over and gained a permanent hold. Then the Norwegian sailors came around from the north, and to this day there are pure Scandinavian types on the adjacent islands. Then the Saxons and Angles, driven by the Danes and Normans, gained a foothold from the east, and lastly the Danes themselves added their contingent. Here in this lowland pocket of territory, no larger than a good-sized American county, was compounded for five hundred years this remarkable amalgam of races."

. . . .

"More than any other race they served as the amalgam to produce, out of divergent races, a new race, the American. The Puritans of New England, the Quakers of Pennsylvania, the Cavaliers of Virginia, were as radically different as

357

accepted as the nearest careful computation of the total number of the Scotch and Scotch-Irish in the colonies. It may be noted that Fiske reckons that between 1730 and 1770 at least 500,000 Irish were transplanted, while the annals of the Scotch-Irish Historical Society claim 600,000 before the Revolution. In the light of these, Hanna's estimate of 410,000 in the thirteen colonies is conservative.

Faust, the German historian, after commenting upon the estimates of Hanna, says that it is just as difficult to get at the approximate number of inhabitants in 1775 who were of German blood. He continues by basing estimates upon a census made by the Rev. M. Kocherthal, of the Palatinates in New York State in 1718, this estimate checked and corrected by other data; by records of the immigration at the port of Philadelphia from 1727, from which Kuhns (German and Swiss Settlements of Colonial Pennsylvania, p. 57) and Rupp (I. D. Rupp: A Collection of Thirty Thousand Names of German, etc., Immigrants in Pennsylvania) have computed the number of Germans landed between 1727 and 1775; by numbers of German churches in some of the colonies, reports of early Moravian missionaries, and various other data. He feels justified, therefore, in apportioning the Germans as below, with the following conclusions:

New England	1,500
New York	25,000
Pennsylvania	110,000
New Jersey	15,000
Maryland and Delaware	20,500
Virginia and West Virginia	25,000
North Carolina	8,000
South Carolina	15,000
Georgia	5,000
Total	225,000

This estimate is very conservative, being based upon estimates of the numbers in known German colonies. The number of scattered German settlers in the large cities, and the number of settlements of which there is no record, must have been quite large. An estimate of two hundred and twenty-five thousand inhabitants of German blood at the outbreak

peoples of different races, and they were separated from each other in their own exclusive communities. The Germans were localized in Pennsylvania and Maryland, the Dutch in New York, but the Scotch-Irish were present in sufficient numbers in all colonies to make their interests felt."—Commons, John R.: Races and Immigrants in America, New York, The Macmillan Company, 1913.

"The term Scotch-Irish was early used in Scottish Universities to designate the students from Ulster. The Ulster student was registered as 'Scotto Hibernus.' "—Ford, Henry Jones: The Scotch-Irish in America, p. 521. Princeton University Press, 1915.

of the Revolution must therefore be regarded as a minimum. It would mean that a little more than one-tenth of the total white population at the beginning of the war of independence was of German blood. In certain localities, of course, the German population was much larger in proportion to the total population, notably in Pennsylvania, where it was one-third of the total number. Future researches in the colonial history of the Germans will undoubtedly reveal larger numbers than have been given above, but the attempt has been made here to confine the estimate within limits that are clearly incontestable.[1]

[1] Faust, Albert Berhardt: The German Element in the United States, Vol. I, p. 285. Boston, Houghton, Mifflin and Co., 1909.

APPENDIX E

TABLE 16.—AREA IN SQUARE MILES OF THE SOUTHERN HIGHLANDS AND THE SOUTHERN HIGHLAND STATES, BY STATES

State	Blue Ridge Belt[a]	Greater Appalachian Valley	Allegheny-Cumberland Belt[a]	Total mountain region	Non-mountain region	Total state	Mountain region	
							Per cent of total mountain area	Per cent of total area of state
Alabama	1,837	5,090	6,745	13,672	37,607	51,279	12.3	26.7
Georgia	4,486	3,219	186	7,891	50,834	58,725	7.1	13.4
Kentucky	...	...	13,302	13,302	26,879	40,181	11.9	33.1
Maryland	663	459	1,128	2,250	7,691	9,941	2.0	22.6
North Carolina	10,101	...	...	10,101	38,639	48,740	9.1	20.7
South Carolina	2,705	...	...	2,705	27,790	30,495	2.4	8.9
Tennessee	3,538	6,918	7,327	17,783	23,904	41,687	15.9	42.7
Virginia	6,864	7,800	5,219	19,883	20,379	40,262	17.8	49.4
West Virginia	...	1,991	22,031[b]	24,022	...	24,022	21.5	100.0
Total	30,194	25,477	55,938	111,609	233,723	345,332	100.0	...
Per cent of total mountain area	27.1	22.8	50.1	100.0	...	...	...	...

a As defined for the purpose of this study this belt includes the total area of certain border counties which are largely, but not entirely, mountainous in character. The figures as given, therefore, are slightly larger than would be shown for the actual Highland area.

b Approximately half of this area may be considered "hill" rather than "mountain" country.

TABLE 17.—POPULATION OF THE SOUTHERN HIGHLANDS AND THE SOUTHERN HIGHLAND STATES, 1890, 1900, 1910, AND PER CENT OF INCREASE FROM 1890 TO 1900, AND FROM 1900 TO 1910, BY STATES

State	BLUE RIDGE BELT				
	Population 1890	Population 1900	Population 1910	Per cent of increase	
				1890–1900	1900–1910
Alabama	44,889	46,449	51,025	3.5	9.9
Georgia	126,778	140,048	147,941	10.5	5.6
Maryland	49,512	51,920	52,673	4.9	1.5
North Carolina	288,427	352,865	394,018	22.3	11.7
South Carolina	134,771	162,059	204,601	20.2	26.3
Tennessee	103,429	123,450	137,566	19.4	11.4
Virginia	250,296	262,712	269,406	5.0	2.5
West Virginia	..	..	..	..	..
Total	998,102	1,139,503	1,257,230	14.2	10.3

State	GREATER APPALACHIAN VALLEY				
Alabama	232,306	302,633	410,511	30.3	35.6
Georgia	128,002	143,479	163,369	12.1	13.9
Maryland	39,782	45,133	49,617	13.5	9.9
North Carolina	..	..	..	..	..
South Carolina	..	..	..	..	..
Tennessee	378,924	443,314	504,523	17.0	13.8
Virginia	315,940	348,708	386,694	10.4	10.9
West Virginia	59,985	62,953	66,593	4.9	5.8
Total	1,154,939	1,346,220	1,581,307	16.6	17.5

State	ALLEGHENY–CUMBERLAND BELT				
Alabama	188,271	225,561	270,199	19.8	19.8
Georgia	5,707	4,578	4,139	−19.8	−9.6
Kentucky	388,364	492,489	580,919	26.8	18.0
Maryland	55,784	71,395	82,516	28.0	15.6
North Carolina	..	..	..	..	..
South Carolina	..	..	..	..	..
Tennessee	165,276	192,701	218,056	16.6	13.2
Virginia	111,806	146,518	181,219	31.0	23.7
West Virginia	702,809	895,847	1,154,526	27.5	28.9
Total	1,618,017	2,029,089	2,491,574	25.4	22.8

TABLE 17.—POPULATION OF THE SOUTHERN HIGHLANDS AND THE
SOUTHERN HIGHLAND STATES, 1890, 1900, 1910, AND PER CENT OF
INCREASE FROM 1890 TO 1900, AND FROM 1900 TO 1910, BY STATES.
—(*Concluded*)

State	TOTAL MOUNTAIN REGION				
	Population 1890	Population 1900	Population 1910	Per cent of increase	
				1890–1900	1900–1910
Alabama	465,466	574,643	731,735	23.5	27.3
Georgia	260,487	288,105	315,449	10.6	9.5
Kentucky	388,364	492,489	580,919	26.8	18.0
Maryland	145,078	168,448	184,806	16.2	9.7
North Carolina	288,427	352,865	394,018	22.3	11.7
South Carolina	134,771	162,059	204,601	20.2	26.3
Tennessee	647,629	759,465	860,145	17.3	13.3
Virginia	678,042	757,938	837,319	11.8	10.5
West Virginia	762,794	958,800	1,221,119	25.7	27.4
Total	3,771,058	4,514,812	5,330,111	19.7	18.1

State	NON-MOUNTAIN REGION				
Alabama	1,047,551	1,254,054	1,406,358	19.7	12.1
Georgia	1,576,866	1,928,226	2,293,672	22.3	19.0
Kentucky	1,470,271	1,654,685	1,708,986	12.5	3.3
Maryland	897,312	1,019,596	1,110,540	13.6	8.9
North Carolina	1,329,520	1,540,945	1,812,269	15.9	17.6
South Carolina	1,016,378	1,178,257	1,310,799	15.9	11.2
Tennessee	1,119,889	1,261,151	1,324,644	12.6	5.0
Virginia	977,938	1,096,246	1,224,293	12.1	11.7
West Virginia	..	..	..	..	..
Total	9,435,725	10,933,160	12,191,561	15.9	11.5

State	TOTAL STATE				
Alabama	1,513,017	1,828,697	2,138,093	20.9	16.9
Georgia	1,837,353	2,216,331	2,609,121	20.6	17.7
Kentucky	1,858,635	2,147,174	2,289,905	15.5	6.6
Maryland	1,042,390	1,188,044	1,295,346	14.0	9.0
North Carolina	1,617,947	1,893,810	2,206,287	17.1	16.5
South Carolina	1,151,149	1,340,316	1,515,400	16.4	13.1
Tennessee	1,767,518	2,020,616	2,184,789	14.3	8.1
Virginia	1,655,980	1,854,184	2,061,612	12.0	11.2
West Virginia	762,794	958,800	1,221,119	25.7	27.4
Total	13,206,783	15,447,972	17,521,672	17.0	13.4

TABLE 18.—COMPOSITION OF THE SOUTHERN HIGHLAND POPULATION BY NATIVITY AND RACE, BY STATES. 1910

State	Total population	White								Negro		Others	
		Native born				Foreign born		Total white					
		Of native parents		Of foreign parents									
		Number	Per cent	Number	Per cent	Number	Per cent	Number	Per cent	Number	Per cent	Number	Per cent
Alabama	731,735	513,485	70.2	16,584	2.3	10,831	1.5	540,900	73.9	190,690	26.1	145	(ª)
Georgia	315,449	267,884	84.9	1,789	0.6	757	0.2	270,430	85.7	45,003	14.3	16	(ª)
Kentucky	580,919	555,685	95.7	4,531	0.8	2,085	0.4	562,301	96.8	18,421	3.2	197	(ª)
Maryland	184,806	151,720	82.1	17,747	9.6	6,193	3.4	175,660	95.1	9,136	4.9	10	(ª)
North Carolina	394,018	356,876	90.6	1,688	0.4	1,129	0.3	359,693	91.3	32,842	8.3	1,483	0.4
South Carolina	204,601	143,450	70.1	982	0.5	612	0.3	145,044	70.9	59,549	29.1	8	(ª)
Tennessee	860,145	762,212	88.6	11,217	1.3	5,684	0.7	779,113	90.6	80,922	9.4	110	(ª)
Virginia	837,319	700,308	83.6	6,913	0.8	6,102	0.7	713,323	85.2	123,880	14.8	116	(ª)
West Virginia	1,221,119	1,042,107	85.3	57,638	4.7	57,072	4.7	1,156,817	94.7	64,173	5.3	129	(ª)
Total	5,330,111	4,493,727	84.3	119,089	2.2	90,465	1.7	4,703,281	88.2	624,616	11.7	2,214	(ª)

ª Less than 0.1 per cent.

25

TABLE 19.—POPULATION PER SQUARE MILE IN THE SOUTHERN HIGHLANDS AND IN THE SOUTHERN HIGHLAND STATES, BY STATES. 1910

State	Blue Ridge Belt	Greater Appalachian Valley	Allegheny-Cumberland Belt	Total mountain region	Non-mountain region	Total state
Alabama	27.8	80.7	40.1	53.5	37.4	41.7
Georgia	33.0	50.8	22.3	40.0	45.1	44.4
Kentucky	..	..	43.7	43.7	63.6	57.0
Maryland	79.4	108.1	73.2	82.1	144.4	130.3
North Carolina	39.0	..	..	39.0	46.9	45.3
South Carolina	75.6	..	..	75.6	47.2	49.7
Tennessee	38.9	72.9	29.8	48.4	55.4	52.4
Virginia	39.2	49.6	34.7	42.1	60.1	51.2
West Virginia	..	33.4	52.4	50.8	..	50.8
Total	41.6	62.1	44.5	47.8	52.2	50.7

TABLE 20.—NUMBER AND PER CENT OF RURAL POPULATION (IN PLACES OF LESS THAN 1,000 INHABITANTS) IN THE SOUTHERN HIGHLANDS AND IN THE SOUTHERN HIGHLAND STATES, BY STATES. 1910

State	Blue Ridge Belt		Greater Appalachian Valley		Allegheny-Cumberland Belt		Total mountain region		Non-mountain region		Total state	
	Number	Per cent	Number	Per cent	Number	Per cent	Number	Per cent	Number	Per cent	Number	Per cent
Alabama	48,910	95.9	218,297	53.2	232,519	86.1	499,726	68.3	1,182,992	84.1	1,682,718	78.7
Georgia	134,527	90.9	131,272	80.4	4,139	100.0	269,938	85.6	1,668,668	72.8	1,938,606	74.3
Kentucky	..	..	..	..	526,703	90.7	526,703	90.7	1,121,915	65.6	1,648,618	72.0
Maryland	37,487	71.2	31,539	63.6	47,855	58.0	116,881	63.2	485,296	43.7	602,177	46.5
North Carolina	353,042	89.6	..	..	..	..	353,042	89.6	1,441,187	79.5	1,794,229	81.3
South Carolina	158,164	77.3	..	..	..	..	158,164	77.3	1,063,921	81.2	1,222,085	80.6
Tennessee	127,705	92.8	363,214	72.0	196,600	90.2	687,519	79.9	973,576	73.5	1,661,095	76.0
Virginia	255,334	94.8	283,114	73.2	160,092	88.3	698,540	83.4	823,984	67.3	1,522,524	73.9
West Virginia	..	..	51,051	76.7	870,198	75.4	921,249	75.4	..	..	921,249	75.4
Total	1,115,169	88.7	1,078,487	68.2	2,038,106	81.8	4,231,762	79.4	8,761,539	71.9	12,993,301	74.2

TABLE 21.—NUMBER AND PER CENT OF URBAN POPULATION (IN PLACES OF 1,000 INHABITANTS AND OVER) IN THE SOUTHERN HIGHLANDS AND IN THE SOUTHERN HIGHLAND STATES, BY STATES. 1910

State	Blue Ridge Belt		Greater Appalachian Valley		Allegheny-Cumberland Belt		Total mountain region		Non-mountain region		Total state	
	Number	Per cent	Number	Per cent	Number	Per cent	Number	Per cent	Number	Per cent	Number	Per cent
Alabama	2,115	4.1	192,214	46.8	37,680	13.9	232,009	31.7	223,366	15.9	455,375	21.3
Georgia	13,414	9.1	32,097	19.6	0	0	45,511	14.4	625,004	27.2	670,515	25.7
Kentucky	..	..	..	..	54,216	9.3	54,216	9.3	587,071	34.4	641,287	28.0
Maryland	15,186	28.8	18,078	36.4	34,661	42.0	67,925	36.8	625,244	56.3	693,169	53.5
North Carolina	40,976	10.4	..	..	..	..	40,976	10.4	371,082	20.5	412,058	18.7
South Carolina	46,437	22.7	..	..	..	..	46,437	22.7	246,878	18.8	293,315	19.4
Tennessee	9,861	7.2	141,309	28.0	21,456	9.8	172,626	20.1	351,068	26.5	523,694	24.0
Virginia	14,072	5.2	103,580	26.8	21,127	11.7	138,779	16.6	400,309	32.7	539,088	26.1
West Virginia	..	..	15,542	23.3	284,328	24.6	299,870	24.6	..	..	299,870	24.6
Total	142,061	11.3	502,820	31.8	453,468	18.2	1,098,349	20.6	3,430,022	28.1	4,528,371	25.8

TABLE 22.—NUMBER AND AGGREGATE POPULATION OF PLACES OF FROM 1,000 TO 2,500 INHABITANTS IN THE SOUTHERN HIGHLANDS AND IN THE SOUTHERN HIGHLAND STATES, BY STATES. 1910

State	Blue Ridge Belt		Greater Appalachian Valley		Allegheny-Cumberland Belt		Total mountain region		Non-mountain region		Total state	
	Cities	Population	Cities	Population	Cities	Population	Cities	Population	Cities	Population	Cities	Population
Alabama	2	2,115	8	12,634	12	17,214	22	31,963	34	55,784	56	87,747
Georgia	3	4,369	5	7,056	0	0	8	11,425	77	120,440	85	131,865
Kentucky	..	..	..	..	16	22,283	16	22,283	43	63,562	59	85,845
Maryland	1	1,054	1	1,571	3	4,092	5	6,717	19	28,260	24	34,977
North Carolina	6	9,476	..	..	..	..	6	9,476	53	84,108	59	93,584
South Carolina	7	10,196	..	..	..	..	7	10,196	36	58,287	43	68,483
Tennessee	5	9,861	12	19,914	10	15,591	27	45,366	23	37,283	50	82,649
Virginia	3	4,799	11	16,297	5	8,555	19	29,651	21	32,908	40	62,559
West Virginia	..	..	2	2,182	44	69,446	46	71,628	..	..	46	71,628
Total	27	41,870	39	59,654	90	137,181	156	238,705	306	480,632	462	719,337

367

TABLE 23.—NUMBER AND AGGREGATE POPULATION OF CITIES OF 2,500 INHABITANTS AND OVER IN THE SOUTHERN HIGHLANDS AND IN THE SOUTHERN HIGHLAND STATES, BY STATES. 1910

State	Blue Ridge Belt		Greater Appalachian Valley		Allegheny-Cumberland Belt		Total mountain region		Non-mountain region		Total state	
	Cities	Population	Cities	Population	Cities	Population	Cities	Population	Cities	Population	Cities	Population
Alabama	0	0	7	179,580	4	20,466	11	200,046	16	167,582	27	367,628
Georgia	2	9,045	4	25,041	0	0	6	34,086	39	504,564	45	538,650
Kentucky	:	...	1	16,507	6	31,933	6	31,933	34	523,509	40	555,442
Maryland	2	14,132	:	...	3	30,569	6	61,208	9	596,984	15	658,192
North Carolina	5	31,500	:	...	:	...	5	31,500	35	286,974	40	318,474
South Carolina	3	36,241	:	...	:	...	3	36,241	22	188,591	25	224,832
Tennessee	0	0	10	121,395	2	5,865	12	127,260	17	313,785	29	441,045
Virginia	2	9,273	12	87,283	3	12,572	17	109,128	15	367,401	32	476,529
West Virginia	:	...	2	13,360	23	214,882	25	228,242	:	...	25	228,242
Total	14	100,191	36	443,166	41	316,287	91	859,644	187	2,949,390	278	3,809,034

TABLE 24.—NUMBER AND AGGREGATE POPULATION OF CITIES OF 10,000 INHABITANTS AND OVER IN THE SOUTHERN HIGHLANDS AND IN THE SOUTHERN HIGHLAND STATES, BY STATES. 1910

State	Blue Ridge Belt		Greater Appalachian Valley		Allegheny-Cumberland Belt		Total mountain region		Non-mountain region		Total state	
	Cities	Population	Cities	Population	Cities	Population	Cities	Population	Cities	Population	Cities	Population
Alabama	0	0	4	166,900	0	0	4	166,900	3	103,306	7	270,206
Georgia	0	0	1	12,099	0	0	1	12,099	8	361,742	9	373,841
Kentucky	..	..	..	..	0	0	0	0	8	403,294	8	403,294
Maryland	1	10,411	1	16,507	1	21,839	3	48,757	1	558,485	4	607,242
North Carolina	1	18,762	..	..	..	..	1	18,762	6	130,283	7	149,045
South Carolina	2	33,258	..	..	..	..	2	33,258	2	85,152	4	118,410
Tennessee	0	0	2	80,950	0	0	2	80,950	3	257,248	5	338,198
Virginia	0	0	2	45,478	0	0	2	45,478	8	336,445	10	381,923
West Virginia	..	..	1	10,698	5	124,828	6	135,526	..	..	6	135,526
Total	4	62,431	11	332,632	6	146,667	21	541,730	39	2,235,955	60	2,777,685

369

TABLE 25.—NUMBER AND AGGREGATE POPULATION OF CITIES OF 25,000 AND OVER IN THE SOUTHERN HIGHLANDS AND IN THE SOUTHERN HIGHLAND STATES, BY STATES. 1910

State	Blue Ridge Belt		Greater Appalachian Valley		Allegheny-Cumberland Belt		Total mountain region		Non-mountain region		Total state	
	Cities	Population	Cities	Population	Cities	Population	Cities	Population	Cities	Population	Cities	Population
Alabama	0	0	1	132,685	0	0	1	132,685	2	89,657	3	222,342
Georgia	0	0	0	0	0	0	0	0	4	301,608	4	301,608
Kentucky	..	..	..	..	0	0	0	0	4	342,666	4	342,666
Maryland	0	0	0	0	0	0	0	0	1	558,485	1	558,485
North Carolina	0	0	..	..	..	..	0	0	2	59,762	2	59,762
South Carolina	0	0	..	..	0	0	0	0	2	85,152	2	85,152
Tennessee	0	0	2	80,950	0	0	2	80,950	2	241,469	4	322,419
Virginia	0	0	1	34,874	0	0	1	34,874	4	257,764	5	292,638
West Virginia	..	..	0	0	2	72,802	2	72,802	..	..	2	72,802
Total	0	0	4	248,509	2	72,802	6	321,311	21	1,936,503	27	2,257,814

TABLE 26.—MEMBERSHIP OF THE NINE LEADING PROTESTANT, ROMAN CATHOLIC, AND ALL RELIGIOUS BODIES IN THE SOUTHERN HIGHLANDS, BY BELTS AND STATES. 1916

	Baptists	Methodists	Presbyterians	Disciples of Christ	United Brethren	Lutherans	Churches of Christ	Protestant Episcopal	Dunkers	Roman Catholics	All religious bodies
BLUE RIDGE BELT											
Alabama	14,395	7,458	401	68	0	47	796	0	0	0	24,024
Georgia	47,805	16,465	848	921	0	0	0	145	0	36	66,825
Maryland	689	5,260	329	0	748	6,187	35	769	976	3,529	23,743
North Carolina	97,865	50,177	6,722	1,107	0	690	0	3,256	774	511	168,450
South Carolina	61,763	23,432	5,994	156	0	392	0	1,075	68	422	96,172
Tennessee	27,821	10,748	2,771	3,497	0	398	633	29	20	157	47,384
Virginia	47,375	30,234	3,092	3,565	90	1,373	180	3,381	3,373	476	95,242
Total	297,713	143,774	20,247	9,314	838	9,087	1,644	8,655	5,211	5,131	521,840
GREATER APPALACHIAN VALLEY											
Alabama	97,279	69,401	9,950	1,255	0	242	873	3,336	0	14,295	202,603
Georgia	36,645	20,728	2,419	366	0	0	796	293	0	0	62,085
Maryland	402	2,310	431	1,329	3,864	4,743	0	0	2,781	1,663	21,737
Tennessee	85,254	62,802	18,973	7,071	0	1,899	1,967	2,820	1,260	3,309	191,754
Virginia	25,265	43,103	14,903	6,628	6,915	11,444	396	2,410	8,809	801	130,347
West Virginia	1,785	10,572	2,570	1,533	4,003	1,647	172	1,338	1,098	1,755	27,727
Total	246,630	208,916	49,246	18,182	14,782	19,975	4,204	10,197	13,948	21,823	636,343
ALLEGHENY-CUMBERLAND BELT											
Alabama	44,188	34,551	5,144	934	0	750	4,616	526	31	1,825	94,668
Georgia	355	660	10	0	0	0	200	0	0	0	1,274
Kentucky	71,744	25,054	5,315	29,059	0	165	2,756	391	374	3,076	149,263
Maryland	1,245	8,621	1,757	35	945	3,606	0	2,130	682	14,880	36,038
Tennessee	23,397	20,118	4,385	937	35	174	9,561	708	0	759	62,898
Virginia	10,983	22,196	3,434	5,422	264	451	205	345	213	1,136	46,610
West Virginia	83,743	145,647	25,975	17,694	25,423	6,365	10,170	5,493	3,581	58,582	399,845
Total	235,655	256,847	46,020	54,081	26,667	11,511	27,508	9,593	4,881	80,258	790,596
TOTAL MOUNTAIN REGION											
Alabama	155,862	111,410	15,585	2,257	0	1,039	6,285	3,862	31	16,120	321,385
Georgia	84,805	37,853	3,277	1,287	0	0	996	438	0	36	130,184
Kentucky	71,744	25,054	5,315	29,059	0	165	2,756	391	374	3,076	149,263
Maryland	2,336	16,191	2,517	1,364	5,557	14,536	35	2,899	4,439	20,072	81,518
North Carolina	97,865	50,177	6,722	1,107	0	690	0	3,256	774	511	168,450
South Carolina	61,763	23,432	5,994	156	0	392	0	1,075	68	422	96,172
Tennessee	136,472	93,668	26,129	11,505	35	2,471	12,161	3,557	1,280	4,225	302,036
Virginia	83,623	95,533	21,429	15,615	7,269	13,268	781	6,136	12,395	2,413	272,199
West Virginia	85,528	150,219	28,545	19,227	29,426	8,012	10,342	6,831	4,679	60,337	427,572
Total	779,998	609,537	115,513	81,577	42,287	40,573	33,356	28,445	24,040	107,212	1,948,779

BIBLIOGRAPHY

BIBLIOGRAPHY

A partial list of the most important authorities consulted in the preparation of this volume. The Russell Sage Foundation Library has published a briefer and somewhat more popular list of books and articles about the Southern Highlands.

HISTORY

Alden, George H. New Governments West of the Alleghenies before 1780. Univ. of Wisconsin Bulletin, Historical Series, Vol. 2, No. 1. p. 1–74. Madison, 1897.

Aler, F. Vernon. History of Martinsburg and Berkeley County, West Virginia. 438 p. Hagerstown, Md., Mail Publishing Co., 1888.

Allen, William B. A History of Kentucky embracing gleanings, reminiscences, antiquities, natural curiosities, statistics, and biographical sketches of pioneers, soldiers . . . and other leading men of all occupations and pursuits. 449 p. Louisville, Ky., Bradley and Gilbert, 1872.

Allison, John. Dropped Stitches in Tennessee History. 152 p. Nashville, Tenn., Marshall & Bruce Co., 1897.

American Atlas, The, or a Geographical description of the whole continent of America and chiefly the British Colonies, composed from numerous surveys. Engraved by Thomas Jeffreys. Philadelphia, Sayer and Bennett, 1778.

Arthur, John Preston. Western North Carolina, a history (from 1730 to 1913). 710 p. Raleigh, N. C., Edwards and Broughton Printing Co., 1914.

Asbury, Francis. The Heart of Asbury's Journal. Edited by Ezra Squier Tipple. New York, Eaton and Mains, 1901.

Asbury, Francis. The Journal of Rev. Francis Asbury, Bishop of the Methodist Episcopal Church, from August 7, 1771 to December 7, 1815. 3 vols. New York, Bangs and T. Mason, 1821.

Ashe, Samuel A'Court. History of North Carolina. Vol. I, 1584–1783. Greensboro, N. C., Chas. L. Van Noppen, 1908.

Atkinson, George Wesley. History of Kanawha County from its organization in 1789 until the present time, embracing accounts of early settlements . . . also biographical sketches of a large number of early settlers of the Great Kanawha Valley. 338 p. Charleston, W. Va., Office of the W. Va. *Journal*, 1876.

Bagenal, Philip H. D. The American Irish and their Influence on Irish Politics. 236 p. Boston, Roberts, 1882.

Bancroft, George. History of the United States from the Discovery of the American Continent. 6 vols. New York, D. Appleton and Co., 1883–86.

Bardsley, Charles W. A Dictionary of English and Welsh Surnames with special American instances. 837 p. London, Frowde, 1901.

English Surnames. Their sources and signification. 612 p. London, Chatto & Windus, 1875.

Baring-Gould, Sabine. Family Names and their Story. 432 p. Philadelphia, Lippincott, 1910.

Bassett, John Spencer. The Regulators of North Carolina, 1765–1771. In American Historical Association, Annual Report for 1894. p. 141–212. Washington, 1895.

Bernheim, G. D. History of the German Settlements and of the Lutheran Church in North and South Carolina to 1850. 557 p. Philadelphia, Lutheran Bookstore, 1872.

Bickley, George W. D. History of the Settlement and Indian Wars of Tazewell County, Virginia. 267 p. Cincinnati, Ohio, Morgan and Co., 1852.

Bittinger, Lucy F. The Germans in Colonial Times. 314 p. Philadelphia, Lippincott, 1901.

Bolton, Charles K. Scotch-Irish Pioneers in Ulster and America. 398 p. Boston, Bacon and Brown, 1910.

Brackinridge, Henry M. History of the Western Insurrection in Western Pennsylvania, commonly called the Whiskey Insurrection, 1794. p. 336. Pittsburgh, W. S. Haven, 1859.

Brewer, W. Alabama; Her History, Resources, War Record, and Public Men, from 1540 to 1872. 712 p. Montgomery, Ala., Barrett and Brown, 1872.

Brown, John Mason. The Political Beginnings of Kentucky. 263 p. (Filson Club Publication No. 6.) Louisville, Ky., John P. Morton Co., 1889.

Bruce, H. Addington B. Daniel Boone and the Wilderness Road. 349 p. New York, The Macmillan Company, 1910.

Buchanan, William. An Inquiry into the Genealogy and Present State of Ancient Scottish Surnames; with the origin and descent of the Highland clans and family of Buchanan. 310 p. Glasgow, Wylie, 1820.

Burk, John Daly. The History of Virginia from its First Settlement to the Present Day. (1781) 4 vols. Petersburg, Va., Dickson & Pescud, 1804–16.

Burnaby, Andrew. Travels through the Middle Settlements of North America in the Years 1759 and 1760; with observations upon the state of the colonies. Reprinted from the 3rd edition of 1798. 265 p. New York, A. Wessels Co., 1904.

Byrd, William. The Writings of Colonel William Byrd of Westover in Virginia, Esquire. Edited by J. S. Bassett. 461 p. New York, Doubleday, Page and Co., 1901.

Caldwell, Joshua W. Studies in the Constitutional History of Tennessee. 183 p. Cincinnati, R. Clarke & Co., 1895.

Carroll, H. K. The Religious Forces of the United States, Enumerated, Classified, and Described. 488 p. New York, Chas. Scribner's Sons, 1912.

Chadwick, French E. The Causes of the Civil War, 1859–1861. The American Nation: A History, Vol. XIX. 372 p. New York, Harper and Bros., 1906.

Cobb, Sanford H. The Story of the Palatines, An Episode in Colonial History. 319 p. New York, G. Putnam's Sons, 1897.

Cole, Arthur Charles. The Whig Party in the South. 392 p. Washington, American Historical Association, 1913.

Collins, Lewis. History of Kentucky. 2 vols. Covington, Ky., Collins, 1874.

Commons, John R. Races and Immigrants in America. 242 p. New York, The Macmillan Company, 1907.

Cooke, John Esten. Virginia; A History of the People. 523 p. Boston, Houghton, Mifflin, and Co., 1883.

Craighead, James Geddes. Scotch and Irish Seeds in American Soil; the early history of the Scotch and Irish Churches and their relations to the Presbyterian Church of America. 348 p. Philadelphia, Presbyterian Board of Publication, 1878.

Crevecoeur, Michel, G. St. J. de (Pseud. J. Hector St. John Crevecoeur). Letters from an American Farmer; describing certain provincial situations, manners, and customs, etc. 355 p. New York, Fox, Duffield, and Co., 1904.

Cuming, Fortesque. Sketches of a Tour to the Western Country through the States of Ohio and Kentucky; a voyage down the Ohio and Mississippi Rivers, and a Trip through the Mississippi Territory and part of West Florida, commenced at Philadelphia in the winter of 1807, and concluded in 1809. 504 p. Pittsburgh, Cramer, Spear, and Eichbarn, 1810.

Davidson, Robert. History of the Presbyterian Church in the State of Kentucky. New York, 1847.

De Hass, Wills. History of the Early Settlement and Indian Wars of Western Virginia; embracing an account of . . . . expeditions in the west previous to 1795, etc. 416 p. Wheeling, W. Va., H. Hoblitzell, 1851.

Denny, Ebenezer. Military Journal of Major Ebenezer Denny, an officer in the Revolutionary and Indian Wars. Historical Society of Pennsylvania, Memoirs. Vol. VII, p. 205–492. Philadelphia, 1860.

Dinsmore, John Walker. The Scotch-Irish in America; their history, traits, institutions, and influence, especially as illustrated in the early settlements of western Pennsylvania, and their descendants. 257 p. Chicago, Winona Publishing Co., 1906.

Doddridge, Joseph. Notes on the Settlement and Indian Wars of the Western Parts of Virginia and Pennsylvania, from 1763 until 1783. 316 p. Wellsburgh, Va., Printed for the Author, 1824.

Doyle, John Andrew. The English Colonies in America. 5 vols. New York, Henry Holt and Co., 1882.

Draper, Lyman Copeland. King's Mountain and its Heroes. 612 p. Cincinnati, P. G. Thompson, 1881.

Dunbar, Seymour. A History of Travel in America; showing the development of travel and transportation from the crude methods of the canoe and the dogsled to the highly organized railway systems of the present, etc. 4 vols. Indianapolis, The Bobbs-Merrill Company, 1915.

Eckenrode, H. J. Separation of Church and State in Virginia; a study in the development of the Revolution. Special Report of the Department of Archives and History. 164 p. Richmond, Va., Davis Bottom, Supt. of Public Printing, 1910.

Ely, William. The Big Sandy Valley; a history of the people and country from the earliest settlement to the present time. 500 p. Catlettsburg, Ky., Central Methodist, 1887.

Fairchild, Henry Pratt. Immigration: A World Movement, and its American Significance. 455 p. New York, The Macmillan Company, 1913.

Farrand, Livingston. The Basis of American History, 1500–1900. The American Nation: A History, Vol. II. 303 p. New York, Harper and Bros., 1906.

Faust, Albert Bernhardt. The German Element in the United States; with special reference to its political, moral, social, and educational influence. 2 vols. Boston, Houghton, Mifflin and Co., 1909.

Filson, John. The Discovery, Settlement, and Present State of Kentucky. See Imlay, Gilbert: A Topographical Description, etc. p. 269–415. London, Debrett, 1793.

Fiske, John. Old Virginia and her neighbors. 2 vols. Boston, Houghton, Mifflin and Co., 1897.

Fleming, Walter L. Civil War and Reconstruction in Alabama. 815 p. New York, Columbia University Press, 1905.

Foote, William Henry. The Huguenots, or Reformed French Church. 27 p. Richmond, Presbyterian Committee of Publication, 1870.
Sketches of North Carolina; historical and biographical, illustrative of the principles of a portion of her early settlers. 557 p. New York, Carter, 1846.
Sketches of Virginia; historical and biographical. 2 vols. Philadelphia, Martien, 1851.

Ford, Henry Jones. The Scotch-Irish in America. 607 p. Princeton, N. J., Princeton University Press, 1915.

Fosdick, Lucian J. The French Blood in America. 448 p. New York, Revell Co., 1906.

Garrison, George P. Westward Extension, 1841–1850. In The American Nation, a History, Vol. XVII. 366 p. New York, Harper and Bros., 1906.

Gilmore, James R. The Rearguard of the Revolution, by Edmond Kirke, pseud. 317 p. New York, D. Appleton and Co., 1886.

Gist, Christopher. Journals, with notes and biographies of his contemporaries. Edited by William H. Darlington. 296 p. Pittsburgh, Weldin, 1893.

Graham, George W. The Mecklenburg Declaration of Independence, May 20, 1775; and lives of its signers. 205 p. New York, The Neale Publishing Co., 1905.

Green, Thomas Marshall. Historic families of Kentucky; with special reference to stocks immediately derived from the Valley of Virginia. Series I. Cincinnati, R. Clarke, 1889.

Hale, John Parker. Trans-Allegheny Pioneers; historical sketches of the first white settlements west of the Alleghenies, 1748–and after. 330 p. Cincinnati, the Graphic Press, 1886.

Hamilton, Alexander. The Works of Alexander Hamilton. Edited by Henry Cabot Lodge. 9 vols. New York, G. Putnam's Sons, 1885–86.

Hanna, Charles A. The Scotch-Irish, or the Scot in North Britain, Ireland, and America. 2 vols. New York, G. Putnam's Sons, 1902.

Hawks, Francis Lister. A Narrative of Events Connected with the Rise and Progress of the Protestant Episcopal Church in Virginia. 286 p. New York, Harper and Bros., 1836.

Haywood, John. Civil and Political History of the State of Tennessee; from its earliest settlement up to the year 1796, including the boundaries of the state. Knoxville, Tenn. 504 p. Heiskell and Brown, 1823.

Henderson, Archibald. The Conquest of the Old Southwest; the romantic story of the early pioneers into Virginia, the Carolinas, Tennessee, and Kentucky. 1740–1790. 395 p. New York, The Century Co., 1920.

  The Creative Forces in Westward Expansion. Henderson and Boone. In *American Historical Review*, XX: 86–107. October, 1914.

Hewatt, Alexander. Historical Account of the Rise and Progress of the Colonies of South Carolina and Georgia. 2 vols. London, Printed for A. Donaldson, 1779.

Holditch, Robert, Esq. Observations on Emigration to British America and the United States; for the use of persons about to emigrate. 100 p. London, Plymouth Dock, the Author, 1818.

Hosmer, James K. Short History of the Mississippi Valley. 230 p. Boston, Houghton, Mifflin and Co., 1901.

Howe, Henry. Historical Collections of Virginia. 544 p. Charleston, S. C., Babcock & Co., 1852.

Howell, Robert Boyle C. The Early Baptists of Virginia. 125 p. Philadelphia, American Baptist Publication Society, 1857.

Hulbert, Archer Butler. Boone's Wilderness Road. In Historic Highways of America, Vol. VI. 207 p. Cleveland, Arthur H. Clark, 1903.

  Braddock's Road, and Three Relative Papers. In Historic Highways of America, Vol. IV. 213 p. Cleveland, Arthur H. Clark, 1903.

  The Cumberland Road. In Historic Highways of America, Vol. X. 208 p. Cleveland, Arthur H. Clark, 1904.

  The Ohio River, a Course of Empire, 378 p. New York, G. Putnam's Sons, 1906.

Hunter, C. L. Sketches of Western North Carolina; historical and biographical, illustrating principally the Revolutionary Period of Mecklenburg, Rowan, Lincoln, and adjoining counties, etc. 357 p. Raleigh, the Raleigh News Steam Job Print, 1877.

Imlay, Gilbert. A Topographical Description of the Western Territory of North America; containing a succinct account of its climate, natural history, population, agriculture, manners, and customs, with an ample description of the several divisions into which that country is divided, and an accurate statement of the various tribes of Indians that inhabit the frontier country. Annexed, a delineation of the laws and government of the state of Kentucky. Includes also, Discovery and settlement of the present state of Kentucky, by John Filson; The Adventures of Daniel Boone; Minutes of the Piankashaw council; An account of the Indian Nations. London, Debrett, 1793.

Jefferson, Thomas. Autobiography. 1743–1790. 162 p. New York, G. Putnam's Sons, 1914.

Johnson, Joseph. Traditions and Reminiscences of the American Revolution in the South. 592 p. Charleston, S. C., Walker and James, 1851.

Johnston, David E. History of the Middle New River Settlements and contiguous Territory, 1654–1753. 500 p. Huntington, W. Va., Standard Printing and Publishing Co., 1906.

Jones, Charles Colcock, Jr. History of Georgia. 2 vols. Boston, Houghton, Mifflin and Co., 1883.

Kemper, Charles E. The Early Westward Movement of Viginia, 1722–1734, as shown by the proceedings of the Colonial Council. In Virginia *Magazine of History and Biography*, XII: 337; XIII: 1, 113, 281, 351. 1905–1906.

Kercheval, Samuel. History of the Valley of Virginia. 486 p. Winchester, Va. Davis, 1833.

Kuhns, Levi Oscar. The German and Swiss Settlements of Colonial Pennsylvania; a study of the so-called Pennsylvania Dutch. 268 p. New York, Henry Holt and Co., 1901.

Studies in Pennsylvania German Family Names. In Americana Germanica, Vol. IV, p. 299–341. New York, 1902.

Lang, Theodore F. Loyal West Virginia from 1861–1865; with an introductory chapter on the status of Virginia for thirty years prior to the war. 382 p. Baltimore, Deutsch, 1895.

Lederer, John. The Discoveries of John Lederer; in three several marches from Virginia over the mountains, made March 1669 to September 1670. 27 p. London, Printed by J. C. for Samuel Heyrick, 1672.

Lewis, Virgil A. History of West Virginia. 744 p. Philadelphia. Hubbard Bros., 1889.

Lodge, Henry Cabot. The Distribution of Ability in the United States. *Century* Magazine, XX: 687–694. September, 1891.

Logan, John H. History of Upper South Carolina; from the earliest periods to the close of the war of Independence. 521 p. Charleston, S. C., S. G. Courtenay, 1859.

MacAfee, Robert B. History of the Late War in the Western Country; comprising a full account of all the transactions in that quarter, from the commencement of hostilities at Tippecanoe to the termination of the contest at New Orleans. 534 p. Lexington, Ky., K. Worsley & Smith, 1816.

MacAllister, W. A. Pioneer Days in Alleghany County. In Virginia *Magazine of History and Biography*, X: 183.

MacDonald, William. Jacksonian Democracy, 1829–1837. 345 p. In the American Nation: A History, Vol. XV. New York, Harper, 1906.

MacLean, J. P. An Historical Account of the Settlements of Scotch Highlanders in America prior to the Peace of 1783, etc. 459 p. Cleveland, Helman-Taylor & Co., 1900.

McCrady, Edward, Jr. The History of South Carolina. 4 vols. New York, The Macmillan Company, 1897–1902.

McGee, Thomas D'Arcy. A History of the Irish Settlers in North America, from the Earliest Period to the Census of 1850. 240 p. Boston, Patrick Donahoe, 1855.

McIlwaine, Henry R. The Struggle of Protestant Dissenters for Religious Toleration in Virginia. 67 p. Johns Hopkins University Studies in Historical and Political Science, 12th Series, No. 4. Baltimore, April, 1894.

Maguire, John F. The Irish in America. 653 p. London, Longmans, Green and Co., 1868.

Masters, Victor I. Baptist Missions in the South: A Century of the Saving Impact of a Great Spiritual Body on Society in the Southern States. Publicity Dept. of the Home Mission Board of the Southern Baptist Convention, 1915.

Mathews, Lois Kimball. The Expansion of New England, the Spread of New England Settlement and Institutions to the Mississippi River, 1620–1865. 303 p. Boston, Houghton, Mifflin and Co., 1909.

Meade, William. Old Churches, Ministers and Families of Virginia. 2 vols., Philadelphia, Lippincott, 1857.

Michaux, André. Travels into Kentucky, 1793–1796. In Thwaites: Early Western Travels, Vol. III, p. 25–104. Cleveland, Arthur H. Clark, 1904.

Mills, Robert. Statistics of South Carolina, p. 47–49, in O'Neall, John Belton: Annals of Newberry, historical, biographical and anecdotical. 413 p. Charleston, S. C., S. G. Courtenay & Co., 1859.

Mitchell, John. A Map of the British and French Dominions in North America, with the Roads, Distances, Limits, and Extent of Settlements. February 13, 1755. London, Jeffreys & Faden.

Moore, John W. History of North Carolina from the Earliest Discoveries to the Present Time. 2 vols. Raleigh, A. Williams Co., 1880.

Moravian Diaries of Travels through Virginia. Edited by William J. Hinke and Charles E. Kemper. In Virginia *Magazine of History and Biography*. Vols. XI, XII. 1903–04.

Newman, Albert H. A History of the Baptist Churches in the United States. 513 p. New York, Christian Literature Co., 1894.

North Carolina, General Assembly. Colonial Records of North Carolina. Collected and edited by William L. Saunders. 10 vols. Raleigh, P. M. Hale, printer to the state, 1886–90.

Perry, William Stevens. Historical Sketch of the Protestant Episcopal Church in the United States of America. 1784–1884. 22 p. New York, Whitaker, 1884. The Influence of the Clergy in the War of the Revolution. 7 p. New York, 1891.

Peyton, John Lewis. History of Augusta County, Virginia. 387 p. Staunton, Va., Yost, 1882.

Pickett, Albert J. History of Alabama and Incidentally of Georgia and Mississippi from the Earliest Period. 2 vols. Charleston, S. C., Walker and James, 1851.

Pooley, William Vipond. The Settlement of Illinois from 1830 to 1850. University of Wisconsin, Bulletin No. 220, Historical Series, Vol. I, No. 4. Madison, Wis., May, 1908.

Pope, John. A Tour through Southern and Western Territories of the United States of North America; the Spanish Dominions on the river Mississippi and the Floridas; the countries of the Creek Nations, and many uninhabited parts. 104 p. Richmond, printed by John Dixon for the author, 1792. Reprinted, New York, Woodward, 1888.

Price, R. N. Holston Methodism; from its origin to the present time. Publishing House of the Methodist Episcopal Church South. 4 vols. Smith & Lamar, Agents, Nashville, Tenn., 1904.

Ramsay, David. History of South Carolina from its First Settlement in 1670 to the year 1808. 2 vols. Charleston, David Longworth, 1809.

Ramsey, James G. M. Annals of Tennessee to the End of the Eighteenth Century. 744 p. Charleston, Russell, 1853.

Ranck, George W. Boonesborough, Its Founding, Pioneer Struggles, Indian Experiences, Transylvania days, and Revolutionary Annals. 286 p. (Filson Club Publication No. 16.) Louisville, John P. Morton & Co., 1901.

Redd, John. Reminiscences of Western Virginia, 1770–1790. Edited by Lyman C. Draper. In the Virginia *Magazine of History and Biography*, VI: 337; VII: 1, 113, 242, 401.

Robertson, James Rood. Petitions of the Early Inhabitants of Kentucky to the General Assembly of Virginia, 1769–1792. 246 p. (Filson Club Publication No. 27.) Louisville, Ky., John P. Morton & Co., 1914.

Roosevelt, Theodore. The Winning of the West. 6 vols. New York, G. Putnam's Sons, 1900.

Ross, Peter. The Scot in America. 446 p. New York, Raeburn Book Co., 1896.

Rule, William, and Gen. F. Mellen and John Woolridge, collaborators. History of Knoxville, Tennessee; with full outline of the natural advantages, early settlement, territorial government, etc. 590 p. Chicago, Lewis Publishing Co., 1900.

Rupp, I. Daniel. A Collection of Upwards of Thirty Thousand Names of German, Swiss, Dutch, French, and other Immigrants in Pennsylvania, from 1727 to 1776. 495 p. Philadelphia, Kohler, 1876.

Salley, Alexander S. History of Orangeburg County, South Carolina; from its first settlement to the close of the Revolutionary War. 572 p. Orangeburg. S. C., Berry, 1898.

Savage, William. Observations on Emigration to the United States, illustrated by original facts. 66 p. London, Sherwood, Neely and Jones, 1819.

Schenk, David. North Carolina, 1780–81; being a history of the invasion of the Carolinas by the British Army under Lord Cornwallis in 1780–81. 498 p. Raleigh, Edwards & Broughton, 1889.

Schuricht, Hermann. History of the German Element in Virginia. 2 vols. Baltimore, Kroh, 1898, 1900.

Scotch-Irish Society of America. The Scotch-Irish in America. Proceedings of the 1st–8th Congress. 1889–96. 8 vols. Cincinnati, R. Clarke & Co.

Searight, Thomas B. The Old Pike; a history of the national road, with incidents, accidents, and anecdotes thereon. 384 p. Uniontown, Pa., the Author, 1894.

Semple, Robert B. History of the Rise and Progress of the Baptists in Virginia. 446 p. Richmond, the Author, 1810.

Shaler, Nathaniel S. Kentucky, a Pioneer Commonwealth. 433 p. Boston, Houghton, Mifflin and Co., 1895.

Smith, George G. The Story of Georgia and the Georgia People, 1732 to 1860. 664 p. Macon, Ga., Smith, 1900.

Smyth-Stuart, John F. D. A Tour in the United States of America. 2 vols. London, Robinson, 1784.

Speed, Thomas. The Wilderness Road; a description of the routes of travel by which the pioneers and early settlers first came to Kentucky. 75 p. (Filson Club Publication No. 2.) Louisville, Ky. John P. Morton & Co., 1886.

Summers, Lewis P. History of Southwestern Virginia, 1746–1786. 921 p. Richmond, Va., J. L. Hill Printing Co., 1903.

Thom, William Taylor. The Struggle for Religious Freedom in Virginia: The Baptists. 96 p. Johns Hopkins University Studies in Historical and Political Science. Series 18, nos. 10–12. Baltimore, 1900.

Thwaites, Reuben Gold. The Colonies, 1492–1750. 301 p. New York, Longmans, Green & Co., 1891.

Daniel Boone. 257 p. New York, D. Appleton and Co., 1902.

Trent, William. Journal of Captain William Trent from Logstown to Pickawillany, A.D. 1752. 117 p. Cincinnati, R. Clarke, 1871.

Turner, Francis M. Life of General John Sevier. 226 p. New York, Neale Publishing Co., 1910.

Turner, Frederick Jackson. The Old West. In proceedings of the State Historical Society of Wisconsin at its 56th Annual Meeting, October 15, 1908. Madison, Wis., 1909.

The Rise of the New West, 1819–1829. 366 p. In The American Nation: A History, Vol. XIV. New York, Harper Bros., 1906.

The Significance of the Frontier in American History. In American Historical Association, Annual Report, 1893. p. 199–227.

Western State Making in the Revolutionary Era. In the *American Historical Review*, I: 70–87, 251–269.

United States. Senate Papers, 23rd Congress. Pension Lists of 1834.

Bureau of Ethnology: Fifth Annual Report to the Secretary of the Smithsonian Institution, 1883–84, J. W. Powell, Director. Washington, Government, 1887.

Verhoeff, Mary. The Kentucky Mountains, Transportation and Commerce, 1750–1911; a study in the Economic History of a Coal Field. (Filson Club Publication No. 26.) Louisville, Ky., John P. Morton & Co., 1911.

The Kentucky River Navigation. 257 p. (Filson Club Publication No. 28.) Louisville, Ky., John P. Morton & Co., 1917.

Waddell, Joseph A. Annals of Augusta County, Virginia; with reminiscences illustrative of the vicissitudes of its pioneer settlers; biographical sketches of citizens locally prominent, and of those who have founded families in the south and western states, a Diary of the War, 1861–5, and a Chapter on Reconstruction. 374 p. Richmond, Va., Jones, 1886.

Walker, Thomas. Journal of an Exploration in the spring of 1750. 69 p. Boston, Little, Brown & Co., 1888.

Warfield, Ethelbert D. The Constitutional Aspect of Kentucky's Struggle for

Autonomy, 1784–1792. In American Historical Association Papers, Vol. IV, p. 347–365. October, 1890.

Wayland, John Walter. The Germans of the Valley. In Virginia *Magazine of History and Biography*, IX: 337; X: 33, 113.

Weeks, Stephen B. Church and State in North Carolina. In Johns Hopkins University Studies in Historical and Political Science. Series II, Nos. 5, 6. May, June, 1893.

Weeks, Stephen Beauregard. General Joseph Martin and the War of the Revolution in the West. In American Historical Association, Annual Report for 1893. p. 401–477. Washington, 1894.

Weiss, Charles. History of the French Protestant Refugees from the Revocation of the Edict of Nantes to Our Own Days. 2 vols. New York, Stringer & Townsend, 1854.

Wheeler, John H. Historical Sketches of North Carolina from 1584–1851. 2 vols. in one. Philadelphia, Lippincott, Grambo & Co., 1851

Williamson, Hugh. History of North Carolina. 2 vols. Philadelphia, Thomas Dobson, 1812.

Winsor, Justin. The Westward Movement. 595p. Boston, Houghton, Mifflin and Co., 1897.

Wise, John Sargent. The End of an Era. 474 p. Boston, Houghton, Mifflin and Co., 1899.

Withers, Alexander Scott. Chronicles of Border Warfare, or History of Settlement by the Whites of Northwestern Virginia, and of the Indian Wars and Massacres. 447 p. Edited by R. G. Thwaites. Cincinnati, R. Clarke, 1895.

STATISTICS

Reports of the State Boards of Health for the Year 1916, for Kentucky, Maryland, North Carolina, South Carolina, Tennessee, and Virginia.

United States Census Bureau. A Century of Population Growth; from the First Census of the United States to the Twelfth, 1790 to 1900. Washington, Government, 1909.

Heads of Families at the First Census of the United States; taken in the year 1790: North Carolina, South Carolina, Virginia (record of state enumerations, 1782–85), Pennsylvania. Washington, Government, 1908.

Mortality in 1916. Washington, Government, 1918.

Religious Bodies. 1906. Part II, Separate Denominations, History, Description, and Statistics. Washington, Government, 1910.

Thirteenth Census of the United States; taken in the year 1910. Washington, Government, 1912–14.

Twelfth Census of the United States; taken in the year 1900. Washington, Government, 1901–02.

HEALTH

Bradley, Frances S., and Williamson, M. A. Rural Children in Selected Counties of North Carolina. United States Children's Bureau, Publication No. 33, 1918.

Child Welfare in North Carolina; an inquiry by the National Child Labor Committee for the North Carolina Conference for Social Service. New York, National Child Labor Committee, 1918.

Goldberger, Joseph, and Wheeler, G. A. Experimental Pellagra in the Human Subject Brought About by a Restricted Diet. Reprint No. 311 from the Public Health Reports, U. S. Public Health Service, Washington, Government, 1915.

Hills, J. L., Wait, C. E., and White, H. C. Dietary Studies in Rural Regions, in Vermont, Tennessee, and Georgia. U. S. Department of Agriculture, Office of Experiment Stations, Bulletin No. 221, 1909.

McMullen, John. Trachoma; a disease of equal importance to the ophthalmologist and public health officer and what the government is doing to eradicate and prevent its further spread. Reprint from *Southern Medical Journal:* X: 130-135. February, 1917.

    Trachoma; a survey of its prevalence in the mountain section of eastern Kentucky. U. S. Public Health Service Reports, Reprint No. 263, 1915.

Rockefeller Sanitary Commission for the Eradication of Hookworm Disease. Annual Reports, 1910-14.

Scientific Memoirs by Officers of the Medical and Sanitary Departments of the Government of India. (1908.) Calcutta, India.

Wait, Charles E. Dietary Studies at the University of Tennessee in 1895. U. S. Department of Agriculture, Bulletin No. 29, 1896.

    Nutrition Investigations at the University of Tennessee in 1896 and 1897. U. S. Department of Agriculture, Bulletin No. 53, 1898.

TOPOGRAPHY AND RESOURCES

Arnold, J. H. Ways of Making Southern Mountain Farms More Productive. U. S. Department of Agriculture, Farmers' Bulletin No. 905, 1918.

Ayres, H. B., and Ashe, W. W. The Southern Appalachian Forests. Department of the Interior, U. S. Geological Survey, Series H, Forestry 12, Professional Paper No. 37. 291 p. Washington, 1905.

Branson, E. C. Farm Life Conditions in the South. State Normal School, Athens, Georgia.

Brigham, Albert Perry. Geographic Influences in American History. 366 p. Boston, Ginn & Co., 1903.

Gannett, Henry. Physiographic Types. Washington, Geological Survey, 1898. (U. S. Geological Survey, Topographic Atlas, Folio 1.)

Glenn, Leonidas Chalmers. Denudation and Erosion in the Southern Appalachian Region and the Monongahela Basin. U. S. Geological Survey, Professional Paper No. 72, 1911.

Hall, William L. The Waning Hardwood Supply and the Appalachian Forests. U. S. Department of Agriculture, Forest Service, Circular 116, September 24, 1907.

Holmes, J. S. Forest Fires in North Carolina during 1912. North Carolina Geologic and Economic Survey, Economic Paper, 1913, No. 33.

Kentucky Geological Survey. The Eastern Coal Field; comprising eight reports on the resources of some of the counties located in the eastern coal field. 304 p. Frankfort, 1884.

Leighton, M. O., and Horton, A. H. Relation of the Southern Appalachian Mountains to Inland Water Navigation. U. S. Department of Agriculture, Forest Service, Circular No. 143, 1908.

and Hall, M. R., and Bolster, R. H. Relation of the Southern Appalachian Mountains to the Development of Water Power. U. S. Department of Agriculture, Forest Service, Circular No. 144, 1908.

McCalley, Henry. Report on the Coal Measures of the Plateau Region of Alabama. 238 p. Montgomery, A. Smith & Co., 1891.

Report on the Valley Regions of Alabama (Paleozoic Strata). 2 vols. Montgomery, Armstrong, 1896–97.

Report on the Warrior Coal Basin. 327 p. Jacksonville, Fla., Vance Printing Co., 1900.

Message from the President of the United States transmitting a Report of the Secretary of Agriculture in Relation to the Forests, Rivers, and Mountains of the Southern Appalachian Region. Washington, Government, 1902.

Miller, E. E. Some Problems of the Southern Hill Country; a land of wonderful possibilities for the stockman, fruit grower, and general farmer, some of the special needs of this section and some of the problems it has to solve. In *Progressive Farmer*, XXV: 726, 736–737. September, 1910.

National Conservation Commission, Report of February, 1909. 3 vols. Washington, Government, 1909.

National Forest Commission. Annual Report for fiscal year ending June 30, 1919. Washington, Government, 1920.

Physiography of the United States, Ten Monographs, 345 p. New York, American Book Co., 1896.

Safford, J. M., and Killebrew, J. B. Elements of the Geology of Tennessee. 264 p. Nashville, Foster and Webb, 1900.

Smith, J. Russell. Farming Appalachia. American *Review of Reviews*, LIII: 329–336. March, 1916.

Spencer, J. W. The Paleozoic Group: The Geology of the ten counties of northwestern Georgia, and resources. 406 p. Atlanta, G. W. Harrison, Printer, 1893. (Georgia Geological Survey.)

Tate, W. K. The Enrichment of Rural Life in South Carolina. University of South Carolina, Founder's Day Bulletin, 1911.

United States, Department of Agriculture. Report of the Secretary of Agriculture on the Southern Appalachian and White Mountain Watersheds; commercial importance, area, condition, advisability of their purchase for national forests, and probable cost. Washington, Government, 1908.

United States, Bureau of Soils. Soils of the United States, Edition 1913, by Curtis F. Marbut, Hugh H. Bennett, J. E. Lapham, and M. H. Lapham. Bulletin No. 96, 1913.

Field Operations in the Southern States.

United States, Geological Survey. Geographical Atlas of the United States. Folios and Quadrangles for the Southern Highland States.
Mineral Resources of the United States, 1914. Washington, Government.
Mineral Resources of the United States, 1917. Washington, Government.
Mineral Resources of the United States, 1918, Preliminary Report. Washington, Government.
United States, House of Representatives. Survey of the Big Sandy, West Virginia, and Kentucky, including Levisa and Tug Forks; Preliminary Report. 56th Congress, Document No. 326. First Session.
United States Senate. Water Power Development in the United States, 1912. Senate Document No. 316, 64th Congress.
Yeates, W. S., McCallie, S. W., and King, F. P. A Preliminary Report on a part of the Gold Deposits of Georgia. 542 p. Atlanta, Ga., Franklin Printing and Publishing Co., 1896. (Georgia Geological Survey.)
Reports of State Departments (nine Southern Highland States).
Agriculture (including soil surveys).
Forestry.
Geological Survey.

EDUCATION

Anderson, David C. The School System of Norway. 232 p. Boston, R. D. Badger, 1913.
Coates, T. J. Demonstration Schools in Kentucky. In Proceedings of the 15th Conference for Education in the South. Nashville, Tenn., 1912.
Education in Sweden, with special reference to hygienic conditions. Royal Swedish Committee for the second International Congress on School Hygiene, London, August, 1907. P. A. Norstedt and Soner. Stockholm, 1907.
Frost, Norman. A Statistical Study of the Public Schools of the Southern Appalachian Mountains. U. S. Bureau of Education, Bulletin, 1915, No. 11.
North Carolina Club Year Book, 1916–17; 1917–18. University of North Carolina Record, Extension Series No. 23, 30. Chapel Hill, N. C.
United States, Bureau of Education. State Laws Relating to Education enacted in 1915, 1916, 1917. Compiled by W. R. Hood. Bulletin, 1918, No. 23.
Digest of State Laws relating to public education in force January 1, 1915, compiled by William R. Hood, with the assistance of Stephen B. Weeks and A. Sidney Ford. 987 p. Washington, Government, 1916.

DANISH FOLK SCHOOLS

Appel, Jacob. The Danish High Schools. Darlington, England, North of England Newspaper Co., Ltd., 1904.
Bay, J. Christian. The "Peasant Universities" of Denmark. In *Education* XXII: 15–22, 1901.
Bruun, Christopher. Folkelige Grundtanker. 208 p. Christiania, Norway, Albert Cammermeyer, 1898.

Butlin, F. M. Among the Danes. 278 p. New York, J. Pott & Co., London, Methuen & Co., 1909.

Foght, Harold W. Danish Elementary Rural Schools; with some reference to seminaries for the training of rural teachers. U. S. Bureau of Education, Bulletin, 1914, No. 24.

The Educational System of Rural Denmark. U. S. Bureau of Education, Bulletin, 1913, No. 58.

Rural Denmark and its Schools. 355 p. New York, The Macmillan Company, 1915.

Friend, L. L. The Folk High Schools of Denmark. U. S. Bureau of Education, Bulletin, 1914, No. 5.

Hegland, Martin. The Danish People's High School; including a General Account of the Educational System of Denmark. U. S. Bureau of Education, Bulletin, 1915, No. 45.

Jonsson, J. V. The "People's High-Schools." In Sweden, a short summary of their origin, development, and aims. Printed by Orebro Dagblad's Office, Orebro, 1904.

Povlsen, Alfred. The Danish Popular High School. Reprint of the Oxford University Extension Gazette, September, 1894. Odense, Andelsbogtrykkeriet i Odense, 1907.

Swenson, John Robert. Grundtvig and the Common-people's High School; Denmark's contribution to the history of education. (Course Thesis in Education 5, University of Texas, February 29, 1904. MSS.)

Thornton, Joseph S. The People's High Schools in Denmark. In Continuation Schools in England and Elsewhere. p. 483–512. Edited by M. E. Sadler, Manchester, University Press, 1907.

Recent Educational Progress in Denmark, p. 587–614. In Great Britain, Educational Department, Special Reports on Educational Subjects, Vol. I. London, Eyre and Spottiswoods, 1897-98.

CO-OPERATIVE MOVEMENT

Doane, Charles F., and Reed, A. J. Cheesemaking Brings Prosperity to Farmers of Southern Mountains. p. 147–152. U. S. Department of Agriculture, Yearbook, 1917.

Faber, Harald. Co-operation in Danish Agriculture. 176 p. London, Longmans, Green and Co., 1918.

Ireland, Commission of Agriculture. Report on Co-operative Agriculture and Rural Conditions in Denmark. Dublin, Alexander Thom & Co., 1903.

Knapp, S. A. Demonstration Work in Co-operation with Southern Farmers. U. S. Department of Agriculture. Farmer's Bulletin, 1908, No. 319.

Morris, Lloyd. The Celtic Dawn. (Ch. VI.) 251 p. New York, The Macmillan Company, 1917.

Plunkett, Sir Horace. Ireland in the New Century. 300 p. New York, E. P. Dutton and Co., 1904.

Plunkett, Sir Horace, Pilkington, Ellice, and Russell, George W. United Irish-women, Their Place, Work, and Ideals. Dublin, Maunsel and Co., Ltd., 1911.

Russell, George W. The Rural Community. In *Rural Manhood*, March and April, 1914.

Smith-Gordon, Lionel, and Staples, Laurence G. Rural Reconstruction in Ireland. 280 p. London, P. S. King and Son, 1917.

GENERAL

Billups, Edward W. The Sweet Songster. A collection of the most popular and approved songs, hymns, and ballads. Catlettsburg, Ky., C. L. McConnell, 1854.

Campbell, Olive D., and Sharp, Cecil J. English Folk Songs from the Southern Appalachians. 341 p. New York, G. Putnam's Sons, 1917.

Campbell, Olive D. Old Songs and Ballads of the Southern Mountains. In *Survey*, January 2, 1915.

Campbell, Robert F. Classification of Mountain Whites. Hampton Institute Press, 1901.

Child, Francis J. English and Scottish Popular Ballads. 730 p. Boston, Houghton, Mifflin and Co., 1904.

Combs, Josiah H. The Kentucky Highlanders from a Native Mountaineer's Viewpoint. Lexington, Ky., J. L. Richardson and Co., 1913.

Kephart, Horace. Our Southern Highlanders. 395 p. New York, Outing Co., 1913.

Miles, Emma B. The Spirit of the Mountains. 201 p. New York, James Pott and Co., 1905.

Murdoch, Louise S. Almetta of Gabriel's Run. New York, Meridian Press, 1917.

Mutzenburg, Charles G. Kentucky's Famous Feuds and Tragedies. 333 p. New York, R. F. Fenno, 1917.

Semple, Ellen C. The Anglo-Saxons of the Kentucky Mountains, a Study in Anthropogeography. Reprint from *Bulletin* of the American Geographic Society, Vol. XLII, August, 1910.

Sharp, Cecil J. The Country Dance Book, Part V. London, Novello. New York, H. W. Gray.

Thomas, E. D. A New and Choice Selection of Hymns and Spiritual Songs for the use of the Regular Baptist Church and all Lovers of Song. Catlettsburg, Ky., C. L. McConnell, 1871.

Whitaker, Fess. History of Corporal Fess Whitaker, Life in the Kentucky Mountains, Mexico, and Texas. 152 p. Louisville, Ky., Standard Printing Co., 1918.

Wilson, Samuel Tyndale. The Southern Mountaineers. 202 p. Literature Department, Presbyterian Home Missions, 156 Fifth Avenue. New York, 1914.

INDEX

INDEX

(Italics denote publications)

27   395